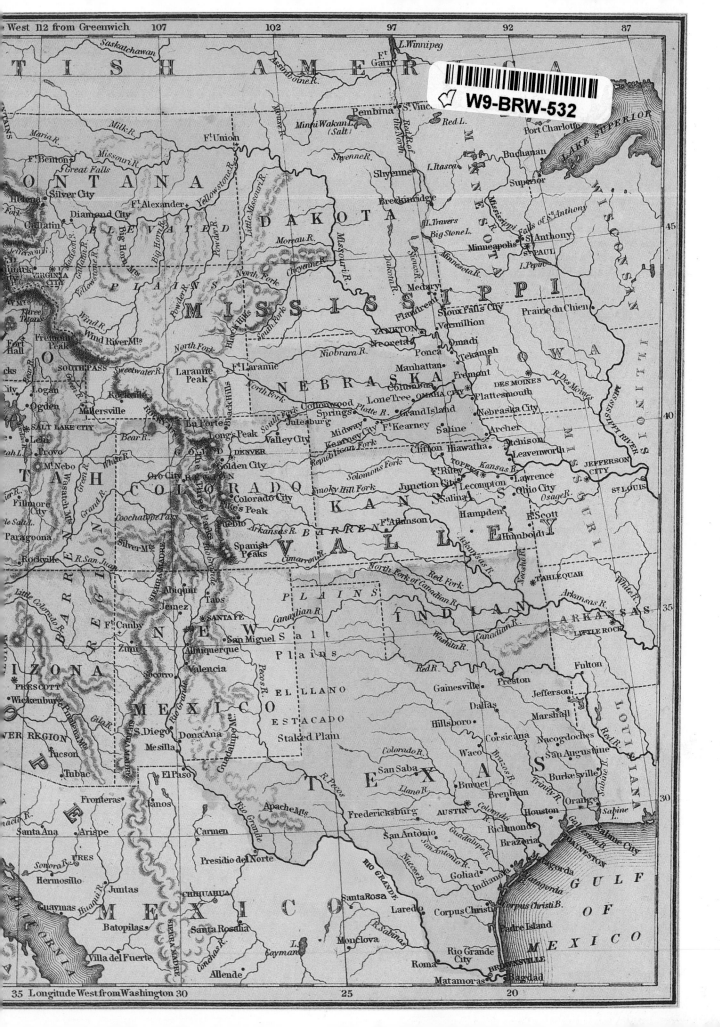

Time-Life Books
THE OLD WEST

TIME-LIFE BOOKS

THE OLD WEST

By the Editors of Time-Life Books

PRENTICE
HALL
PRESS

New York • London • Toronto • Sydney • Tokyo • Singapore

Time-Life Books The Old West
was produced by
ST. REMY PRESS

PUBLISHER	Kenneth Winchester
PRESIDENT	Pierre Léveillé
Editor	Dianne Stine Thomas
Art Directors	Normand Boudreault, Solange Pelland
Associate Editor	Pierre Home-Douglas
Editorial Assistant	Megan Durnford
Senior Art Director	Diane Denoncourt
Designer	Shirley Grynspan
Index	Shirley J. Manley
Administrator	Denise Rainville
Accounting Manager	Natalie Watanabe
Production Manager	Michelle Turbide
Coordinator	Dominique Gagné
Proofreaders	Joseph Marchetti, Judy Yelon

Time-Life Books Inc. is a wholly owned subsidiary of
THE TIME INC. BOOK COMPANY

President and Chief Executive Officer	Kelso F. Sutton
President, Time Inc. Books Direct	Christopher T. Linen

TIME-LIFE BOOKS INC.

EDITOR	George Constable
Director of Design	Louis Klein
Director of Editorial Resources	Phyllis K. Wise
Director of Photography and Research	John Conrad Weiser
PRESIDENT	John M. Fahey Jr.
Senior Vice Presidents	Robert M. DeSena, Paul R. Stewart, Curtis G. Viebranz, Joseph J. Ward
Vice Presidents	Stephen L. Bair, Bonita L. Boezeman, Mary P. Donohoe, Stephen L. Goldstein, Juanita T. James, Andrew P. Kaplan, Susan J. Maruyama, Robert H. Smith
New Product Development	Trevor Lunn, Donia Ann Steele
Supervisor of Quality Control	James King
Editorial Resources	Blaine Marshall
Production Manager	Prudence G. Harris
PUBLISHER	Joseph J. Ward

CONSULTANT

George Daniels, Consulting Editor, is a writer, editor and editorial consultant who has served as senior editor of *Time* Magazine and executive editor of Time-Life Books.

WRITERS

Ronald H. Bailey, a former senior editor of *Life* Magazine, is the author of 14 books non-fiction and contributor to more than than 40 other volumes. He has written extensively about American history.

Champ Clark teaches newsmagazine writing at the University of Virginia, and is a former Senior Editor of *Time* Magazine.

Jill Corner, educated at Cambridge University, is a writer, editor and translator who specializes in art and history.

William K. Goolrick, a former editor at Time-Life Books and senior editor of *The Saturday Evening Post*, is presently a freelance writer.

Pierre Home-Douglas, is a former college English professor who now works as a book editor and freelance writer in Montreal.

Bryce S. Walker, a former editor at Time-Life Books, is author of *The Great Divide*, a non-fiction book about wilderness adventures in the Rocky Mountains. He is presently a freelance writer.

Ian Walker, a graduate of McGill University and a former Senior Editor at Reader's Digest (Canada) Books, is the author of five non-fiction books.

Prentice Hall Press
15 Columbus Circle
New York, New York 10023

LC No. 90-53249

ISBN 0-13-631151-2

Manufactured in the United States of America

10 9 8 7 6 5 4 3 2 1

First Edition

CONTENTS

FOREWORD by Robert M. Utley   **6**

I.   **THE EARLY FRONTIERS**   **16**
1. Across the Appalachians   18
2. The trailblazers   32
3. A world of beaver   56
4. The desperate struggle for Texas   74

II.   **THE LURE OF THE WEST**   **96**
5. Wagon trains across the plains   104
6. The rush to El Dorado   128

III.   **JOINING THE COASTS**   **152**
7. Expressmen: an assault on distance and time   160
8. Rivermen and railroaders   180

IV.   **ASSERTING A MANIFEST DESTINY**   **202**
9. The last stand of the plains tribes   212
10. Battered cavaliers of the Indian wars   248

V.   **PUTTING THE OPEN SPACES TO WORK**   **272**
11. An empire of longhorns and woollybacks   274
12. The hard-working hombres who rode the range   302

VI.   **A ROUGH-HEWN SOCIETY**   **322**
13. The sprouting of cities and towns   330
14. Gamblers and gunfighters   356

VII.   **THE FINAL FLOURISHES**   **382**
15. Kingdom of the loggers   390
16. The last great frontier   408

PICTURE ESSAYS
The lure of the wild country   8
The great fur rush upriver   50
"The best land in all these Indias"   68
Hopeful novices on a perilous journey   98
A rough way to get rich quick   122
A continent's lengthening lifelines   154
A 3,000-mile waterway west   174
The faces of a proud people   204
Sudden fury in a long, slow war   242
A sweaty little man, tall in the saddle   296
Making nowhere somewhere   324
The deadly brotherhood of the gun   350
A treasure richer than gold   384
The most American part of America   416

INDEX   **422**

PICTURE CREDITS AND ACKNOWLEDGMENTS   **430**

FOREWORD

The American West never shook to the tread of elephants, yet generations of Americans went west "to see the elephant." In that vast and varied landscape with its climatic excesses; the giant herds of buffalo and other strange beasts; the Indians in all their exotic and menacing splendor; and the eccentric adventurers drawn to the frontier's unbridled environment, those who braved the wilderness saw the elephant. Capturing the awe and delight with which Americans beheld the wonders beyond the frontier, the metaphor embedded itself in contemporary usage. "To see the elephant" became synonymous with the Western experience.

Vicariously, Americans have seen the elephant ever since. The West, and the westward movement, have always loomed large in the national memory and the national imagination. Indeed, the lure has leaped oceans. English, French, Germans, Italians, Japanese—all have been captivated by the spell of the Old West.

For more than a century, the media of popular culture have fed this public fascination. Indians, mountain men, traders, soldiers, miners, cowboys, outlaws, sodbusters, merchants—all in countless mutations of verity, distortion, exaggeration, parody and fakery have peopled the world of our fancy. They crowd the dime novels and penny dreadfuls of the Gilded Age; the fiction of Zane Grey, Louis L'Amour and their clones whose paperbacks line the racks of drug stores, supermarkets and airline terminals; movies from William S. Hart to John Wayne to Emilio Estevez; television from "Gunsmoke" and "Bonanza" to "Lonesome Dove"; art from George Catlin and Alfred Jacob Miller to Frederic Remington and Charlie Russell to today's practitioners of "cowboy art", so numerous they band together in professional societies.

Not only in popular culture has the West flourished. Hardly had the census statisticians of 1890 failed to trace a distinct western line of settlement on the map than the frontier experience attracted scholarly attention. At the American Historical Association annual convention in 1893, Professor Frederick Jackson Turner of the University of Wisconsin propounded his celebrated "frontier hypothesis."

At the edge of settlement, Turner argued, the ways of life pioneers brought from their Eastern homes collapsed under the harsh conditions of the wilderness. New institutions took shape, similar to the old but reflecting the realities of the new environment. In this process, constantly operating as the frontier moved westward, Turner believed that he had discovered the ingredient that set Americans apart from their European forebears and made the United States unique among the nations of the world. "The existence of an area of free land," he declared, "its continuous recession and the advance of American settlement westward explain American development."

For all his learned discourse, Turner was not immune to spectacle. He saw the pioneers as writing a stirring chapter in the history of the United States, a saga of heroic proportions. His mind's eye pictured the westward movement in graphic images rare among professors. "Stand at Cumberland Gap," he invited, "and watch the procession of civilization, marching single file—the buffalo following the trail to the salt springs, the Indian, the fur trader and hunter, the cattle raiser, the pioneer farmer—and the frontier has passed by. Stand at South Pass in the Rockies a century later and see the same procession with wider intervals between."

Although Turner and his disciples shaped the interpretation of American history for a generation, the notion that the frontier explained American character did not reign unchallenged. Beginning in the 1920s, historians assailed it as far too sweeping and simplistic. Many other forces also guided American development, they argued. Political scientist and historian Charles A. Beard, for example, contended that industrialization and the class struggle overshadowed the frontier as historical determinants. Besides, other critics charged, Turner's frontier was peopled almost entirely by white Anglo-Saxons. He ignored the rich Hispanic role of the "Spanish Borderlands" from Florida to California, and he looked on Indians simply as another impersonal wilderness obstacle to be overcome, like forests and wild animals. The great academic debate left Turner's theory badly shaken, but still intact in many of its essentials.

Further disputing Turner and advancing still another view of the West is a new crop of scholars, young historians who join with earlier critics in two ways. They reject Turner's grand portrayal of sturdy frontiersmen freeing America from European models and laying the groundwork for a flourishing democracy destined to climax in national greatness. They also ridicule the colorful myths and stereotypes of the Old

Historian and author Robert Utley has written twelve books on Western subjects including the Sioux Nation, the Indian wars and the biography of George Armstrong Custer. He has served the U.S. Government in a variety of capacities, including as Chief Historian and Assistant Director of the U.S. National Park Service.

West of popular imagination. Their West, in fact, is a somber West, devoid of light, marked by hardship, suffering and failure. It is populated less by hardy Anglo-Saxon yeomen than by victims of the institutionalized brutality and avarice. These victims were Indians, Hispanics, blacks, Chinese, women and impoverished drudge laborers who toiled in unsafe environments for the enrichment of corporate America. The victims also, more impersonally but no less devastatingly, were the wild game and the land itself, with its abundance of natural resources.

These new dimensions of the Western experience are hardly new. They have always been credited as part of the complicated mix that trailed the frontier across the continent. The West was indeed racist, sexist and exploitive. Failure did indeed dog cattlemen, miners, farmers, merchants, traders, trappers, military commanders and even outlaws. The West was indeed full of victims—and those who made them victims. The West was indeed ravaged, of its minerals, its soil, its timber, its grass, its water, its native human and faunal populations.

All these dark strains have long been recognized as part of the Western heritage. Alone, however, they do not yield a faithful representation of the Old West. It was not a picture of unrelieved bleakness. Sharply constricted, Turner's concepts retain validity. Beneath the gaudy splashes of myth that have always encrusted frontier history lie some brightly colored patches of reality. In short, the elephant cannot be slain because he is real, but now we can see perhaps more clearly than our forebears that, not surprisingly, he wallowed in the mudhole of reality.

The splatters of mud do not diminish the drama of the westward movement or its contribution to traits that set Americans apart from other peoples, as Turner postulated. The adventures and achievements of Daniel Boone and the intrepid "Corps of Discovery" headed by Lewis and Clark are undimmed by the searchlight of reality. Conquistadors, voyagers, mountain men, cowboys, hardrock miners and troopers of the frontier army bestowed no less on the American character for the flaws today's generation identifies in their behavior. Champions of "Manifest Destiny" expounded an arrogant, self-serving, chauvinistic concept that left tragic casualties in its wake—Indians and

Mexicans, most conspicuously. But it also helped fling the Western borders to the Pacific and transform the United States into a continental nation. The builders of roads, waterways, telegraph lines and railroads forged a unified polity from a sprawling continent even though they floated on rivers of fraud and corruption.

The story of the American West is one of triumph and tragedy, of majesty and wretchedness, of innocence and guile, of benevolence and greed, of spectacle and tedium. It is a thrilling story, central to understanding America and Americans. It deserves retelling, for each generation should be afforded the opportunity to see the elephant.

Robert Utley

7

A thunderstorm sweeps through the Grand Canyon in Thomas Moran's *The Chasm of the Colorado*.

8

The lure of the wild country

As the 19th Century began, the vast area west of the Mississippi was a mysterious void to most Americans. But then in 1803 President Thomas Jefferson completed the Louisiana Purchase — and opened the West to anyone with the curiosity and courage to probe it. Over the next 75 years more than two million square miles revealed their secrets to an army of hunters, soldiers, naturalists and other adventurers.

Not until mid-century, however, did most citizens get their first look at this wild land, and then it was through the eyes — and canvases — of a few bold painters, some of them Europeans. The landscapes they painted, shown here and on the following pages, fired their imaginations, prompting them at times to add all sorts of embellishments.

Yet such was the dramatic variety of the West that as each region opened, explorers found actual scenes surpassing the artists' wildest imaginings.

On an exploration of what is now Montana and the Dakotas, German artist Charles Wimar painted this eerie impression of a buffalo herd plunging across a river to escape a prairie fire. Wimar's imagination re-created the riverbank in the form of a southwestern pueblo lit by the fire's glow.

For his romanticized landscape of the Wind River country in Wyoming, German-born Albert Bierstadt made a series of sketches of this spectacular region of the Rocky Mountains during a trip to the area in 1859. Returning to the East, he created a dramatic vision from the sketches, adding a waterfall and a different perspective to the actual scene.

13

Karl Bodmer painted Montana's Citadel Rock (since re-named Cathedral Rock) with the look of a castle on the Rhine. Bodmer's Swiss hand gave the Rockies the darker, more forbidding aspect of mountains in his native Europe.

In this lithograph based on an actual event, mountain man S. E. Hollister battles with a she-bear whose cubs he had tried to capture. Though horribly bitten, Hollister nevertheless managed to kill the huge bear with his hunting knife.

I. THE EARLY FRONTIERS

1. Across the Appalachians

The Scotch-Irish farmers of Draper's Meadows, Virginia, had become accustomed to the sight of passing tribal bands during seven peaceful years at their remote settlement in a hollow of the Appalachians. Their cabins and cornfields lay in the great north-south trench west of the Blue Ridge Mountains—a natural highway from Pennsylvania to Georgia for Indians as well as settlers moving ever deeper into virgin forestland. The New River, which bordered their homesteads, flowed north and west into what today is West Virginia. It perforated the wall of the Appalachians through deep gorges, and in so doing opened a route from Ohio for Shawnees and other tribes of Algonquins bent on raids against Catawbas of the South.

But on the morning of July 8, 1755, the Shawnees did not pass tranquilly by. This time they came through the mountains as newly committed allies of France bent on ravaging the English frontier. The settlers of Draper's Meadows had not the slightest inkling of danger. William Ingles and John Draper, its husky young founders, were in distant corners of their fields as the painted braves materialized among the log dwellings. Colonel James Patton, a 63-year-old militia officer who was sitting inside one of the cabins, managed the settlement's only moments of resistance. His broadsword was lying on a table before him as two Indians burst into the room. He seized it and hacked them to death before he was killed by a third marauder who fired a shot through the open door.

Others of the war party raced among the remaining cabins and jerked open the doors. They trapped and shot two more men, killed Draper's mother and stopped his wife, Bettie, in her tracks with a bullet, which broke one of her arms after she picked up her infant son and tried to escape. An Indian seized the baby by his ankles and smashed his head against a log house. The whooping intruders rifled the cabins and set them on fire, and then having rounded up the settlers' horses, hoisted the wounded woman onto the back of one of them. William

Ingles' wife, Mary, was nine months pregnant; she was hoisted up on a horse, too, with her four-year-old son, Thomas, and his two-year-old brother, George. All were carried away as the Shawnees left the blazing cabins behind, heading northwest through the New River gorges into the wilderness of western Virginia.

This savage and tragic incident initiated a far more important chapter in American history than any of the participants could have suspected. Early frontier families like the Ingleses and Drapers were flanked, north and south, by foreign enemies as they pushed into the West—by the French and later the British in Canada, and by the Spanish and French in Florida and Louisiana. All three enemies used Indians as auxiliaries in their schemes of empire, and backwoods settlements were subject to raids so constantly for 50 years after the incident at Draper's Meadows that the threat of forest war became as much a part of border life as hunting and planting corn.

The Indians gave the settlers cruel instruction in survival and war, torturing frontiersmen and slitting the bellies of their pregnant wives. In return, the frontiersmen ambushed, murdered and scalped the Indians and their women. Simultaneously, since they were largely ignored by the Americans in power, pioneers on the Western frontier developed a stubborn resentment of Eastern politics, Eastern taxes and the elitist attitudes of those who ruled in towns and plantations on the coastal shelf. They became a breed unto themselves: stern, violent and clannish, but brave, upright and wildly independent. Danger made them stoic, suspicious and realistic, and attuned them to concepts of righteous revenge straight from the Old Testament. These qualities played an integral part in shaping the United States, in pushing the frontier across the Eastern mountains to the far West, and in altering politics forever by sending Andrew Jackson to Washington later on.

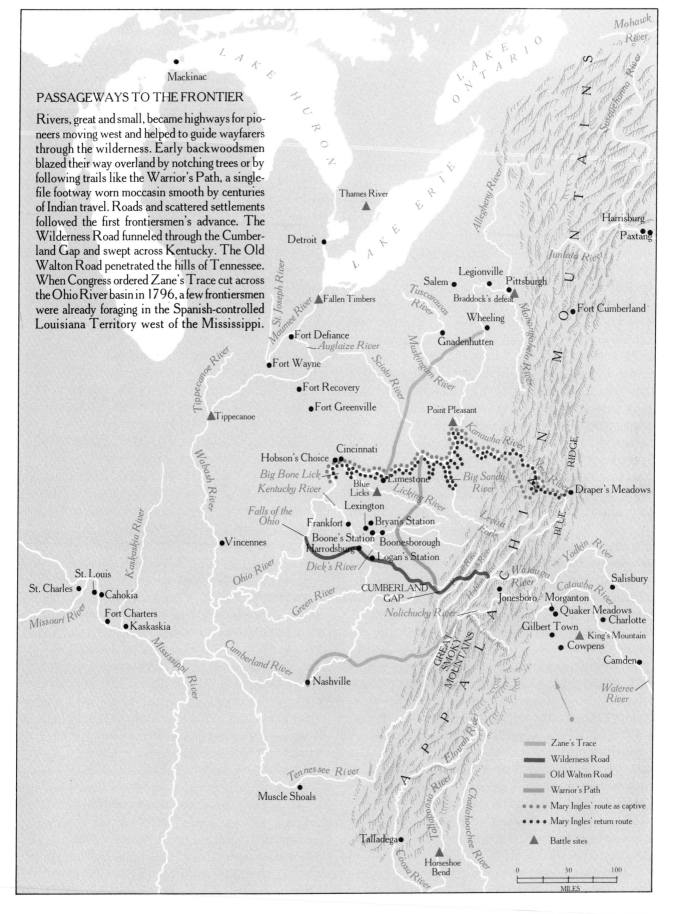

PASSAGEWAYS TO THE FRONTIER

Rivers, great and small, became highways for pioneers moving west and helped to guide wayfarers through the wilderness. Early backwoodsmen blazed their way overland by notching trees or by following trails like the Warrior's Path, a single-file footway worn moccasin smooth by centuries of Indian travel. Roads and scattered settlements followed the first frontiersmen's advance. The Wilderness Road funneled through the Cumberland Gap and swept across Kentucky. The Old Walton Road penetrated the hills of Tennessee. When Congress ordered Zane's Trace cut across the Ohio River basin in 1796, a few frontiersmen were already foraging in the Spanish-controlled Louisiana Territory west of the Mississippi.

Mackinac

LAKE HURON

LAKE ONTARIO

Mohawk River

APPALACHIAN MOUNTAINS

Susquehanna River

Thames River

LAKE ERIE

Harrisburg
Paxtang

Detroit

Allegheny River

Juniata River

Salem
Legionville
Pittsburgh
Braddock's defeat

Fort Cumberland

St. Joseph River

Maumee River

Fallen Timbers

Tuscarawas River

Wheeling

Monongahela River

Fort Defiance
Auglaize River

Gnadenhutten

Muskingum River

Tippecanoe River

Fort Wayne

Scioto River

Fort Recovery

Fort Greenville

Point Pleasant

Kanawha River

Tippecanoe

Wabash River

Cincinnati
Hobson's Choice
Big Bone Lick
Kentucky River

Limestone

Blue
Licks

Licking River

Big Sandy River

New River

BLUE RIDGE

Draper's Meadows

Lexington

Levisa Fork

Kaskaskia River

Falls of the Ohio

Frankfort
Boone's Station
Harrodsburg

Bryan's Station
Boonesborough
Logan's Station

Vincennes

Ohio River

Dick's River

CUMBERLAND
GAP

Clinch River

Holston River

Yadkin River

Salisbury

St. Louis
St. Charles
Cahokia

Missouri River

Fort Charters
Kaskaskia

Green River

Watauga River

Nolichucky River

Jonesboro
Morganton
Quaker Meadows
Charlotte

Catawba River

Gilbert Town
Cowpens

King's Mountain

Camden

Mississippi River

Cumberland River

GREAT SMOKY MOUNTAINS

Nashville

Wateree River

Tennessee River

Etowah River

Chattahoochee River

Muscle Shoals

Coosa River

Tallapoosa River

Zane's Trace

Wilderness Road

Old Walton Road

Warrior's Path

Mary Ingles' route as captive

Mary Ingles' return route

Battle sites

0   50   100

MILES

Talladega

Horseshoe
Bend

19

Backwoods life was a hard, often agonizing experience for even the strongest of men and women. The settlers of Draper's Meadows learned this earlier than most. Yet the travail they endured at the hands of the Shawnees was only typical of a thousand episodes of death and abduction that were to break up families and instill an implacable hatred of Indians in early pioneers. William Ingles and John Draper were forced to choose between suicide and a wretched prudence when they heard the distant sounds of whooping and gunfire at the Meadows settlement. With a kind of bitter realism that was condoned in the backwoods country, each concealed himself helplessly until his wife and children were taken away. Harboring a profound need for revenge, both men became well-known wilderness militiamen in the years that followed.

Mary Ingles gave birth to her baby during the third night of the Shawnee party's retreat, but rode on with her captors the next day, the infant clutched to her. John Draper's wife, Bettie, suffered the pain of her shattered arm with equal courage. But the captives preserved themselves only to be parceled out to various Shawnees as prizes of war. Bettie Draper was forced into slavery and concubinage; the little boys were carried off by different bands—George to Detroit, Thomas to a village in Ohio. Mary Ingles saw an opportunity for escape. But she knew she must leave her baby behind to be killed if she was ever to rejoin her husband, which she perceived as her overriding duty. An athletic 23-year-old woman, she did in fact escape, and journeyed more than 700 miles, battling bitter cold, hunger and hostile terrain before finally making her way back to civilization.

Mary Ingles never again heard of her baby or the younger of the captured boys. The older, Thomas, was traded back from the Indians at 16—a wild, furtive creature who regarded his parents as strangers. John Draper did not see his wife, Bettie, for six years and found, on buying her freedom, that she was no longer the woman with whom he had lived before the Shawnees took her away.

Such were the realities of the early American frontier, a life of hardship, brutality, death and valor. Though confronted by foe in the form of Indian warriors, bear, wildcats, panthers, venomous snakes and wolves, the early settlers rose with unflinching heroism to the challenges of carving out a new life from the uncharted wilderness.

In the decades before the American Revolution, Scotch-Irish, English and German immigrants ventured across the Atlantic by the thousands every year, seeking betterment in the New World. More than 400,000 had arrived in America by 1770. The tide spread to Pennsylvania and moved into the immense forests when open land was gone. The flow then turned north into New England and south down the Appalachian trench before finally spreading beyond the Eastern mountains into the heart of the woodland Indians' homeland.

Armed with a long-barreled flintlock rifle and that other basic tool of the frontier—the ax—the frontiersmen hacked a living out of the forest, provided their own food and clothing, and built rude log cabins in one or two days with the help of neighbors and relatives. Furniture—a rough table, a plank bed or so, some three-legged stools and a few wall pegs for clothing—was knocked together on the spot. Hunting knives, hoes, iron skillets, cooking pots and other utensils were largely obtained by barter in deer hides. This practice gave rise to the term "a buck," since a buckskin bought a dollar's worth of goods for many years.

Safety was an ever-present concern on the frontier.

Although there never was an accurate count of the Indians who existed east of the Mississippi in the early 18th Century, whites reckoned their numbers in the scores upon scores of thousands. There were almost certainly far fewer: perhaps 10,000 Iroquois, possibly 20,000 to 30,000 Southern Indians and a like number in the Algonquin tribes. Between the Appalachians and the Mississippi, the forest-dwelling Indians were grouped in three distinct regions. The Six Nations of the Iroquois (Mohawks, Oneidas, Onondagas, Cayugas, Senecas and Tuscaroras) occupied the area below Lakes Ontario and Erie in northern New York and Pennsylvania. The Algonquins, meanwhile, were spread from Virginia and Tennessee in the South to Canada in the North.

To keep the Indians—and their white allies—at bay, every settlement raised its own local militia. Officers were elected or "hit upon," since backwoodsmen would follow only men they knew and trusted. They would not accept discipline for the sake of discipline nor, often, orders with which they disagreed. But when sufficiently stirred and properly led, the frontiersmen were fearsome fighters, with their disregard of hardship, their tradition of violence, their long rifles and their skills in the forest. They took greater losses than the Indians because they fought for land and their families. The Indians, by contrast, fought for glory as well as to preserve tribal hunting grounds, and thought it madness to die when outnumbered.

The backwoods riflemen proved their mettle on numerous occasions over a period of years. At Point Pleasant on October 10, 1774, a thousand Virginia militiamen achieved a bloody standoff against a like number of Shawnee warriors under conditions in which Regulars probably would have faced certain massacre.

Another momentous battle occurred six years later against a white-skinned foe. The Revolution had triggered bitter civil war in the Southern colonies, and in October 1780 Loyalist American Tories and rebel American Whigs engaged in a bitter battle at King's Mountain. Although the British-led Tories and the Whig frontiersmen were almost evenly matched in numbers, their battle skills were not. The Tory commander believed in cold steel bayonet charges with swords flashing. The frontiersmen had been instructed to scatter, then rally and strike back. "Give them Indian play," was the order, and the men were exhorted to "each be his own officer." When the angry backwoodsmen lay down their arms only an hour later, 150 Tories had been killed and 800 taken prisoner, as compared to a total of 96 Whig casualties.

The victory at King's Mountain shook the British hold on the South. Perhaps more important, it was a revelation of things to come. The triumph bespoke the fervent refusal of restraint that would soon send those new Westerners flowing in increasing numbers over the mountain barrier—and made plain, above all, their fitness to enter the vast, empty spaces that lay beyond.

Of all the early frontiersmen, the most celebrated was Daniel Boone, who endured every tribulation and survived every test to emerge, as a friend said, "a noble and generous soul, despising everything mean." Boone was a man of affairs and the possessor of an active and judicious mind. He had a shrewd eye for opportunity, becoming variously, a publican, a surveyor, officer of the militia, land speculator, blacksmith and tavern keeper. But these undertakings were always secondary to his life in the forest.

Boone had been drawn to the wilderness even as a boy in the woods of Pennsylvania, where he studied animals and learned from the peaceful Pennsylvania Indians how to hunt with a spear. There was something of genius in his sensitivity to variations of light and shade, sound and flow of air, and to the wild men and animals who moved so softly in the wilderness. In a world of remarkable adventurers and remarkable achievements, Daniel Boone would become the king of the forest—the ultimate woodsman.

He was born into a Quaker family that was disowned by its congregation after his sister and brother married "worldlings," or outsiders. The Boone family moved in May 1750 to the Yadkin River on North Carolina's western frontier. This was wild country, where a hunter like 15-year-old Daniel could shoot a dozen deer before noon and a youth with his innate instinct for profit could carry hides east by pack horse for sale in the little market town of Salisbury; thus he embarked upon his life's most enduring vocation. He encountered a hostile Indian for the first time two years later, when a Catawba named Saucy Jack, enraged at Boone's superior marksmanship, threatened to tomahawk him. He crossed paths with many more hostiles in 1755 while in the service of Major General Edward Braddock, whose big British expedition was ambushed and defeated by 800 French and Indians at Turtle Creek.

The following year, Boone married a tall, dark-haired girl named Rebecca Bryan, bought 640 acres from his father on the Yadkin, built a cabin and put in a crop of corn. Rebecca proved to be a tough and resourceful match for her trailblazing husband. She hoed their garden, chopped wood, bore 10 children and tended the homestead while Boone ranged the raw frontiers.

Boone was one of the earliest of the "long hunters" who crossed the Appalachians in the 1760s to roam for months—or, in his case, for two years on one expedition—through the game-rich wilds of Kentucky. He was fascinated by the new country—Indians and all—and always ached to see more of it. With a burning conviction that the Bluegrass country would make him his fortune, he left the Yadkin River in 1773 with Rebecca, his eight sons and daughters and five other families to make a home in Kentucky. The trip was abandoned after Boone's eldest son and a companion were ambushed, tortured and killed by the Indians. (Nine years hence, he would lose another son to Indian attack at the Battle of Blue Licks, the last considerable combat of the Revolution.)

Boone went on believing that Kentucky was to be his Utopia. He was a captain of the permanent settlers who labored westward over the mountains with families, cattle and goods to occupy the Bluegrass country in 1775. And it was Boone who, thanks to the financing of a flamboyant North Carolina promoter, Judge Richard Henderson, hacked the first crude road over the Cumberland Gap in the Appalachians to found the settlement of Boonesborough.

With the intrusion of the white frontiersman, tribe after tribe of Indians grew alarmed. Their restiveness was encouraged by the settlers' arch-enemy, England's commander and lieutenant governor at Detroit, Henry Hamilton. In addition to providing the Indians with arms and supplies, Hamilton rewarded those who returned from Kentucky with scalps by giving the triumphant warrior as great a weight of goods as could be held in his arms. Thus, his chilling nickname: "the Hair Buyer."

Hamilton hoped to destroy Boonesborough and the other Kentucky settlements as a first step in taking Fort Pitt—key to all the frontier because of its position at the fork of the Ohio River. This would enable him to push American influence east of the Appalachians for good, and to restore the upper Mississippi and all its drainage to England's tribal allies and to the embrace of British trade. His plans, however, were eventually thwarted by the courage and stamina of the Western settlers, in particular Daniel Boone.

In September 1778, the Shawnee chief Blackfish and 444 warriors attacked the stockade at Boonesborough, using

Only the white mane suggests his age as Daniel Boone peers with piercing blue eyes from a portrait based on one painted in 1818, two years before he died at 86.

ammunition and supplies provided by Hamilton. The Battle of Boonesborough, as it was called, developed into a nine-day-long siege, with wild exchanges of fire, and the settlers' desperately striving to knock away the burning arrows launched at their roofs. At the same time, scores of Indians were toiling, day after day, to build a tunnel from the riverbank to the nearest wall of the stockade.

By the second week of siege, Boonesborough was nearly lost: food was running short inside the fort, and the hoarded water was all but gone. The two acres inside the settlement's palisade made cramped quarters for the scores of settlers and their cattle, horses, pigs and poultry; wounds, sleeplessness, strain and personal animosities were fast eroding the little garrison's responsiveness to danger. The defenders contemplated a hideous fate. Blackfish had powder to burn, and his warriors had begun yelling "Digging hole! Blow you to hell tonight."

But night brought thunder, lightning and torrential rain and a morning sight the settlers could hardly believe: a silent and empty landscape. The Indians, seldom prepared temperamentally to besiege a frontier fortress, had discovered their tunnel collapsed in the downpour. Drenched and disgruntled, they had vanished. Boonesborough, a key American outpost in the Revolution, had been saved.

Boone by now was 43 years old and renowned throughout the frontier. With fame came the opportunity of acquiring enormous areas of virgin countryside. Easterners called upon Boone to locate, survey and stake out suitable tracts as their proxy. In turn, he asked that half the land be deeded to him to pay for his services. By 1788, he owned 50,000 acres, but he had a lamentable tendency—after locating and surveying land—to put off establishing clear, legal title to it while he went hunting. Stung by some of Boone's careless transactions, Kentuckians began to regard him as a fraud. He was deluged by lawsuits and heard rumors that he was to be assassinated.

But the outcry died when it became obvious that the ever-noble and generous Boone was determined to settle his debts with honor. The state named a county for him in 1798—the same year sheriffs sold off 10,000 acres of his holdings to pay taxes. He turned his affairs over to a nephew, and ordered payment of every honest claim. Then he went west again, settled above St. Charles on the lower Missouri River, hunting and roaming the forest almost until the day of his death.

When he died in 1820, at the age of 86, all of his debts had been duly paid. He was buried on a knoll overlooking the Missouri, and remained there for 25 years. Then the people of Kentucky, having driven him out, came for him at last. They dug up his bones, took them back and buried him beside Rebecca in the earth he had come over the Cumberland Gap to find so many years before.

The Indian warriors whom Boone and the other frontiersmen encountered in the forests were far more sophisticated and resourceful than most backwoodsmen acknowledged. They hunted men as skillfully as they hunted animals, were disciplined, well equipped and expert in the use of arms. They retreated swiftly and artfully when a contest was lost—and tomahawked captives who were unable to keep a proper pace. If captured, a white or enemy warrior had to expect torture when pursuit faded, and to be put on display as an entertaining exhibit after the party's triumphal return to its home village.

Antoine de la Mothe Cadillac, a French lieutenant who was commandant of a post near Lake Huron, described one of these grisly ceremonies. The captive was fastened to a stake, after which his nails were torn out, and his teeth were pulled. The victim's fingers were then put in the bowl of a pipe and the ten fingers smoked. Burning firebrands were applied to the ankles, wrists and temples. A necklace of glowing, red hot hatchets was placed over the neck. The genitals were burned. "Last of all," wrote Cadillac, "they take off his scalp and throw hot ashes and sand upon the raw and bleeding flesh, and cut off his head, while all the village resounds with shouts of joy and delight, as if they had won a great victory."

In the service of the British during the Revolution, the Indians presented a formidable barrier to frontiersmen hungry for land, especially in the Northwest. Even after the British conceded defeat in 1783, the Algonquins continued conducting raids from their forest fastness and—supported by their white ally—ravaging American settlements in the West.

In response, dozens of pioneer border captains rose in the final decades of the 18th Century to secure the advancing frontier. None were as crucial as George Rogers Clark, the hero of Vincennes, and Anthony ("Mad Anthony") Wayne, the victor at the Battle of Fallen Timbers. The two men operated in strikingly different but remarkably effective ways, in circumstances that imperiled the very existence of the young nation. Together, they helped shape the future of the American West.

Clark's invasion of Illinois in 1778 stands as one of the most audacious and improbable military adventures in American history. Clark was no stranger to peril; he had made his way to the frontier as a surveyor when hardly out of his teens and had evolved into a hard-bitten roughneck who knew the wilderness as well as any backwoodsman. The elder brother of William Clark, who was to explore the far West with Meriwether Lewis, the redheaded Virginian had helped sustain the Kentucky settlements in 1776 by getting them 20 kegs of gunpowder and delivering it down the Ohio River himself. He now offered to save the West from England and the Indian tribes. He was determined to seize Detroit, the linchpin of British influence in the Northwest. However, he sensed that "it was a general oppinion that it would take several thousand to approach that Place." So he planned a preliminary campaign, arduous enough in itself: he would capture the Mississippi River towns of Kaskaskia, Cahokia and Vincennes, which Britain used as bases for Indian raids south into Kentucky.

Delaware tribesmen burn a captured Revolutionary officer—Colonel William Crawford—in Ohio in 1782. A second captive, Dr. John Knight *(lower right corner)*, was also marked for death—with charcoal-blackened face—but escaped to recount the awful tale.

When Clark set out into the wilds of Illinois, he was accompanied by only 175 men—half the number he had expected to join him. But, even though his recruiters had failed to supply more men in the beginning, the gods of war would bless his clever manipulation of the enemy thereafter.

Clark's little band reached the Kaskaskia River a few miles above its juncture with the Mississippi at sundown on July 4. They were half starved, having jettisoned baggage "except as much as would equip us in an Indian mode," but they had come 120 miles, much of it across open prairie, without having encountered a soul. As they approached the peaked roofs of the town, the dogs of Kaskaskia set up a frantic chorus, but miraculously no sentries materialized to challenge the intruders. The gate of the stockade swung open, and backwoodsmen were loosed into the streets to tell the populace—at the top of their lungs—that the town was taken by the Long Knives, and to order all, "on pane of Death" to stay indoors until morning. The entire settlement was Clark's within 15 minutes. "Nothing," he wrote, "could excell the Confusion these People seemed to be in." They had been taught, it seemed, "to expect nothing but Savage treatment from Americans."

"It was my Interest to Attach them to me," Clark reasoned. But his strategy was to let them tremble "as if they were led to Execution." Finally, Clark appeared ominously before a committee of the settlement's elders. He asked if they "mistake us for savages," and went on to explain "that our Principal was to make those we Reduced free instead of enslaving them, and that if I could have surety of their Zeal and Attachment for the American Cause, they should enjoy all the previleges of our Government." He had word, he added, that had not reached their distant prairies: France had joined the 13 states in their war with England. In that moment, as things turned out, Clark won all of Illinois.

The Kaskaskians trooped into their market square to swear allegiance to Virginia, and emissaries were dispatched to Cahokia and Vincennes, where the inhabitants were similarly persuaded to support the American cause. In Detroit, Henry "the Hair Buyer" Hamilton was appalled upon hearing the news, and lost no time in responding. On October 7, he left Detroit with a force of more than 200 men, and after marching 600 miles in 71 days retook Vincennes.

Meanwhile, at Kaskaskia and Cahokia, Clark was continuing his bluff and bombast, with remarkable results.

Large numbers of Indians—chiefs, sub-chiefs and warriors from almost every Algonquin tribe between the Great Lakes and the Mississippi—had arrived in the area, and as autumn approached they began to advance menacingly on Cahokia to test his mettle for themselves. Though greatly outnumbered, Clark managed to appear unconcerned.

He dealt with the Indians as he had with the Kaskaskians: as a conqueror who expected submission. Addressing the chieftains of all the tribes, he said that the Long Knives and the "Red People" were very much alike; both had been victimized by the English. But the Long Knives had finally sharpened the hatchet, and the English, having become frightened "like deer in the woods," had hired Red People to do their fighting for them. Did the Indians wish to go on with war against him? He warned them to think of their women and children if they opposed him. The speech, Clark noted later, "did more good than a Regiment of Men." Every tribe entreated him for peace, and the Indians melted back into the woods. Clark now held sway over a domain larger than France.

No sooner was the Indian threat eliminated than Mother Nature presented another. Cold rain and melting snow had turned the prairie route to Vincennes into a bog, and had raised every river above its banks. Still, Clark saw no other recourse but "to attack the enemy in his stronghold." On February 5, with only 200 men, he "set out on a Forlorn hope, indeed." Through 240 miles of hard fortune—incessant rain, quagmire, hunger and stream after frigid, flooding stream—Clark's confidence became the sole sustenance of the expedition.

As his force approached Vincennes—remarkably without having lost a man—Clark was determined "to be as daring as possible." His scouts waylaid a duck hunter who had come out from town, and Clark sent him back with a message for the French inhabitants: "Being now within two miles of your village I request such of you as are true citizens, and willing to enjoy the liberty I bring you, to remain still in your houses. Those that are true friends to Liberty may depend on being well treated. But every one I find in arms on my arrival, I shall treat as enemy."

As on numerous occasions before, this rashness proved to have been the course of wisdom when the little army marched into the town after dark. Vincennes' citizens had kept the secret of his presence so well that Hamilton, locked serenely in his fort, believed drunken Indians were celebrating in the streets when Clark's riflemen first

LITTLE TURTLE

In 1790 and 1791, the great Miami chief Little Turtle inflicted a pair of bloody defeats on American frontier forces. But after the rout of the Indians in 1794, Little Turtle reconciled himself to the newcomers and counseled peace to his tribesmen.

Outside his fort at Greenville, Anthony Wayne, flanked by his officers, dictates treaty terms to the chiefs routed at the Battle of Fallen Timbers. In exchange for $9,500 in annuities to be distributed among the tribes, Wayne exacted two thirds of Ohio, a sliver of Indiana and strategic outposts in Illinois and Michigan.

began sniping at glimmers of light behind the fort's gun ports. The fort eventually erupted with answering fire. But Hamilton's French volunteers "hung their heads" and murmured that their own countrymen had gone over to the Americans. By mid-morning, "the Hair Buyer" accepted defeat and marched out of the fort and into the hands of the Americans.

Clark had dashed British hopes of dominating the American West, and his victory at Vincennes—for all his failure to take the ultimate prize, Detroit—vastly encouraged the flow of migration over the Appalachians. During the year, 5,000 people settled in Kentucky, and 30,000 by the end of the Revolution. Clark was at the apogee of his career. In the years that followed, he led raids against the Indians, but he was severely reprimanded by Virginia's bookkeepers for failing to provide an accounting of the notes he had drawn on the state of Virginia while campaigning. Relieved of his commission in 1783 at the age of 30, he took to drink and began a long twilight existence. He lingered on, a lonely and embittered victim of his alcoholism until 1818, when he died of a stroke at the age of 65. But meanwhile, another star had risen—that of Anthony Wayne.

The area north of the Ohio River had become a hotbed of problems which seemed to grow increasingly more insoluble. Raids and counterraids kept the territory seething with unrest, culminating in a massacre of 630 militiamen by Algonquin Indians under Miami chief Little Turtle. The Algonquins were now prepared to fight for the Ohio boundary if it was not granted to them by treaty.

In their euphoria, however, they failed to consider President George Washington's capacity for indignation. He resolved to find a commander capable of reorganizing the ragtag American Army and of using it—if the Indians would not have peace—to end forest warfare forever. Washington appointed Anthony Wayne commander in chief of a new army, called the Legion of the United States.

A rugged, dark-eyed and animated Pennsylvanian, Wayne had a reputation for impetuosity. He believed that there were few exigencies in war that could not be overcome by headlong attack, preferably with the bayonet. This recklessness had earned him the nickname of "Mad Anthony." It had exposed him to entrapment on some occasions, and taken a high toll in men on others. But soldiers trusted him, and time, it turned out, had tempered his belligerency with patience and judiciousness.

He went about his job methodically, making it plain from the beginning that he did not propose to take the field before creating an army capable of fighting any troops in the world. It was a formidable task. The nucleus of the army he found waiting for him was composed of the hapless survivors of the Algonquin attack, and the newcomers were even worse. Such men as recruiters could scrape up were often the same ne'er-do-wells, felons, drifters and barflies who had joined the army for food and shelter in the years since the Revolution. "The offscourings of large towns and cities; enervated by Idleness, Debaucheries and every Species of Vice," snorted one disgusted officer.

Wayne dealt with malingerers with a heavy hand. He offered rewards for deserters and had them shot when returned, or subject to 100 lashes on the naked back. He marched his troops 22 miles west along the Ohio and put them to work with saws and axes at raising a new encampment he called Legionville. All through the winter, spring and summer, the army drilled incessantly, practicing at targets, mastering the bayonet and participating in endless and exhausting mock skirmishes in which the enemy was always presumed to be firing from the cover of stumps and trees.

Meanwhile the government attempted to arrange a last-ditch meeting with the Algonquins. The suspense ended in August: the Indians notified three United States land commissioners (in a note written by functionaries of the British Indian Service) that there would be no conference and that the Ohio must "remain the boundary line between us."

"We now," scribbled an excited young lieutenant, "have but one alternative left and this is we must meet the savage foe; the Emortal Washington at the Head of our Government, and the Old Hero, Gen'l Wayne and his well disciplined legion. We have little to fear accept our god, and fear him in love." The Legion set out in August 1794, moving ponderously as it halted to set up a fortified camp at the end of each day's march. On August 17, Wayne ordered his army up the Maumee River, stopping 10 miles short of a tangle of fallen trees left by some ancient cyclone, where 1,300 Algonquin warriors had positioned themselves in the hope of luring the Americans into an ambush.

Wayne was now 49 years old and corpulent. His left leg ached unbearably from an old wound, but he rose early on the morning of the 20th, powdered his hair and had the offending limb wrapped in flannel from ankle to thigh. He

Corn likker: the drink that "every boddy" took

"It smells like gangrene starting in a mildewed silo, it tastes like the wrath to come, and when you absorb a deep swig of it you have all the sensations of having swallowed a lighted kerosene lamp." So lamented one imbiber after sampling a jug of Kentucky-made corn whiskey. But for every critic of the frontier brew, there were thousands of Western Americans who enjoyed its unique sour-mash flavor and hundreds who distilled it to pay for the goods they had to import from the cities back East.

Converting surplus corn into whiskey was the most practical way for homesteaders in the remote hills of Kentucky and Tennessee to get their grain to market. Shipping corn overland was difficult and expensive: a pack horse could carry only four bushels across the mountains. But the same horse was able to carry the equivalent of 24 bushels of corn when it was condensed into two kegs of distilled whiskey.

To make whiskey from corn the settlers first concocted a mashy liquid called still beer. They scalded ground cornmeal in homemade wooden tubs, then added barley malt, bran and yeast, and poured in a measure of pure spring water. After letting the mash ferment, they obtained a brew—

about 7 per cent alcohol—that was ready for distillation.

A typical frontier still consisted of a pear-shaped copper kettle topped by a detachable head with a tapered neck that ended in a spiral of tubing called a worm. When the still was fired, alcoholic spirits vaporized upward into the head and through the worm. The worm was immersed in a barrel of cold water, which caused the heated vapor to condense into whiskey. Drawn off through the end of the worm, the "corn likker" was distilled a second time, or "doubled," to increase its alcoholic content. The spent "stillage" of corn mash was saved for hog feed.

A fanciful portrayal of distilling—from corn mash to corked jugs—was Douglass Hewitt & Co.'s trademark for Old '76 whiskey.

mounted his horse, and the legion moved up the Maumee.

A furious fusillade greeted his troops as they approached the Indian stronghold. Wayne sent masses of rifle-carrying mounted Kentuckians to contain the Indians' right flank and sword-swinging dragoons off on the left flank. Then he positioned his infantry in two ranks before the Indian defenses. The men were told to endure the enemy's first fire and attack with the bayonet while the Indians struggled to reload. The battle was over almost before the smoke of the defenders' first volley had drifted away in the hot summer air. The Indians in the center scrambled for the rear and those on the flanks were penned in by plunging, leaping horses and the sabers of their American riders.

Organized Indian resistance in Ohio ended with that engagement, thereafter called the Battle of Fallen Timbers. Wayne had confronted the Indians with a display of preparation and force beyond their experience. Survivors of the debacle learned the bitter truth about their supposed allies as they burst out of the woods and crossed an open prairie toward the nearby English fort. Its cannon remained silent, its loopholes empty, its gate locked fast as the Indians ran up to its stockade crying for rescue from their pursuers. Wayne spent nearly two months laying waste to Indian towns and gardens that stretched for 50 miles along the Maumee, and building a log fortress—which its commandant immediately named Fort Wayne. In February, a procession of chastened and impoverished chieftains called upon him and sued for peace, resulting in the signing of the Treaty of Greenville, by which great areas of Ohio were formally deeded to the United States. After 40 years of bloody resistance by the tribes, the Northwest was now opened for peaceful settlement and British influence there was permanently weakened.

As Indian raiding subsided, new settlers flooded west. By 1800 Kentucky boasted almost a quarter of a million people; there were nearly half that many in Tennessee; and Ohio attracted 200,000 new settlers in the next decade. Slowly, inexorably, the West was looking less like a frontier and more like a civilization—a transformation not always welcomed by the implacably independent frontiersmen.

The first adventurers who had crossed the Appalachian wall had been able to turn their backs on the constriction of civilization. But now the new Westerners felt threatened on all sides. Eastern legislatures taxed them, speculators jostled for control of enormous areas of Western land, and Spain blocked their hopes of commerce on the Mississippi and the Gulf Coast. The frontiersmen yearned to wrench free in order to control their own destiny.

The United States' declaration of war against England on June 17, 1812, elated the growing bloc of Westerners in Congress. These avid "warhawks" burned to punish the British for inciting Indian violence on the frontier; more important, they regarded Britain as the main obstacle to American growth. It was on this stage that Andrew Jackson would join the West's pantheon of heroes.

Andrew Jackson was a lawyer, planter, speculator and politician, border captain and Indian fighter, Tennessee's first Congressman and one of its early Senators, and eventually the seventh President of the United States. The founder of the modern Democratic Party, "Old Hickory" ushered in the era of the common man in America.

Jackson was a product of the frontier. But he did not fit the mold of frontiersman; he strove to shape rather than reflect the attitudes of the border country, and he reached heights of leadership when he rushed to rescue the Mississippi and the West from the designs of England at the Battle of New Orleans. Born in a hill district of South Carolina, he was orphaned at the age of 14. That same year, he fought with a local militia company, and was captured by British dragoons, then imprisoned, and hacked at with a sword. That incident left Jackson with a scar on his forehead and an abiding hatred of England and Englishmen.

If war shaped his character, a little money ($400 left him when he was 16 by a relative in Ireland) shaped the manners and attitudes by which he was to reveal it to the world. He traveled to Charleston where he used his inheritance to make himself into a gentleman, and next he persuaded an attorney in Salisbury, North Carolina, to let him join the young bloods who were reading law in his office. He was admitted to the bar at 20 and was appointed public prosecutor of North Carolina's western district (Tennessee) where his zealous pursuit of malefactors soon made him a man who counted with the people "Up West." The self-made gentleman now speculated in land, acquired title to almost 80,000 acres and raised a large house, called the Hermitage, on a tract near Nashville. The house would become his lifetime home.

At 35, with scarcely any military background, Jackson was elected a general of the Tennessee militia. In 1814, during the War of 1812 with Britain, he defeated the Creeks at Horseshoe Bend on Alabama's Tallapoosa River, killing 900 Indians and forcing the Creek nation into an eclipse from which it would never recover.

The hard eyes that faced down many a foe gaze from this portrait of a remarkably youthful Andrew Jackson, made after the Battle of New Orleans, when he was 48.

At once, Jackson found himself being celebrated as the first genuine hero of the war, "standing," as his friend John Overton put it, "as high as any man in America." The War Department in Washington made him a major-general in the U.S. Army and commander of the 7th Military District (Tennessee, Louisiana and Mississippi).

In 1814, the British dispatched a fleet toward the Gulf Coast, calculated to take New Orleans, seize control of the lower Mississippi, and open up the subcontinent beyond to agents of the British Crown. Jackson responded with feverish exertions and a sense of strategy rare in civilians turned soldier during middle life. He ordered the mobilization of militia in Mississippi, Tennessee and Kentucky, marched down to Mobile and reinforced the garrison there, and sent troops to Baton Rouge. Then, with 4,000 troops, he swept boldly into Spanish Florida and stormed Pensacola at sunrise on November 7. The town and its Forts St. Rose and St. Michael were his by afternoon; the English garrison withdrew to ships offshore after blowing up a third fort, Barrancas.

By December 1, Jackson was in New Orleans to await the main British thrust. There followed a month of indecisive fighting, and then, on the morning of January 8, Old Hickory delivered the fatal blow.

Jackson's frontiersmen were waiting along a rampart they had constructed behind a canal that ran at a right angle from the Mississippi. A little breeze moved the mist; 650 yards away, a great body of British soldiers appeared—crossbelts bone-white against their scarlet tunics, bayonets gleaming in rows. Jackson was ready: 13 U.S. cannon began to fire, tearing great gapes in the advancing lines.

"Aim above the crossbelts," Jackson ordered his sharpshooters when the redcoats were 300 yards away, and coming on the dead run. The riflemen from Tennessee and Kentucky aimed, fired a volley at the command, and then stepped down. The second rank leaped to the firing step while the first pushed to the back of the line and swiftly reloaded.

"Fire!" A third line was up and aiming. And so they continued, with stunning effect. Red-jacketed soldiers began tumbling by the hundreds; the troops panicked and broke ranks. The British commander, Major General Sir Edward Pakenham, tried to rally his men, but a rifle ball shattered his knee; another broke his right arm and a third slammed into his spine. "Never before," said a lieutenant who survived, "had British veterans quailed, but it would be silly to deny that they did so now."

All halted, however, once out of range of the rifles. They threw off their knapsacks, shuffled into ranks and moved stolidly forward once more, only to be slaughtered by Jackson's riflemen. The attack was smashed, but Jackson did not pursue the enemy. The British, with 2,000 dead or dying, were left to find the bivouacs they had vacated the night before.

Ten days passed before the English army was transported to the waiting fleet. It took with it a somber memento of the ordeal: Pakenham's body, preserved in a barrel of rum. Finally, 18 days later, the fleet vanished over the horizon. With Jackson's triumph at the Battle of New Orleans—for a price of only 13 casualties—the last serious foreign threat to American soil had been stifled. The Mississippi was an American stream forever after. The way was now open into the vast plains and awesome mountains beyond the river's western bank, following in the footsteps of a pair of intrepid explorers named Lewis and Clark.

2. The trailblazers

"The object of your mission is to explore the Missouri River, & such principal stream of it, as, by it's course & communication with the waters of the Pacific Ocean may offer the most direct & practicable water communication across this continent for the purposes of commerce." Thus, in 1804, began an extended list of instructions that would launch one of the most carefully conceived, brilliantly led and enormously profitable pieces of trailblazing in all of history up to that time.

The mission was designed by President Thomas Jefferson, who was both a scientist and a shrewd geopolitician, and had long promoted American exploration of the West. With only one transcontinental journey previously recorded—that of Scottish fur trader Alexander Mackenzie *(page 34)*—Jefferson had entered the White House in 1801 with westering ambitions and firm resolve to act upon them.

The opportunity presented itself only two years later, in the form of the Louisiana Purchase Treaty with France. Under that historic document, the United States acquired the western Mississippi drainage, extending north to the British possessions in Canada and southwest to lands claimed by the Spanish—800,000 square miles in all. In one stroke, the size of the young nation was doubled. Now the President had a legitimate duty to examine the new lands, where he was convinced American destiny lay.

For years, Jefferson had been grooming his own private secretary, Captain Meriwether Lewis, as leader of the first great epic of exploration. Lewis' family had been neighbors of Jefferson's in Albemarle County, Virginia. After Lewis' father died, his mother remarried and the family moved to the frontier in Georgia. Lewis spent his boyhood on the very fringes of the American wilderness. By the time he returned to Virginia in his teens to manage his father's land, he had acquired an essential qualification of exploration—the ability to live in wild country.

The statesman and the young man became friends; whenever Jefferson felt like talking, he would summon Lewis with a mirror blinking in the sun.

In Lewis, Jefferson had a superb leader with strength of body, woods-wisdom, an inquiring turn of mind, determination and coolness under stress. But in addition, Jefferson felt, the ideal man for this journey should possess a knowledge of "botany, natural history, mineralogy & astronomy." Accordingly, in the spring of 1803, Jefferson sent Lewis to Philadelphia for intensive tutoring from experts in these fields. While he was undergoing this educational marathon, Lewis settled upon the man who would accompany him as co-commander. He chose a Kentucky frontiersman and old Army comrade, William Clark, younger brother of the famous frontier fighter of the Revolution, General George Rogers Clark.

The expedition—formally designated as the Corps of Discovery—left St. Louis on May 14, 1804 after a year of preparation. Its principal transport, a specially commissioned 60-foot keelboat, or barge, started up the Missouri carrying a party of 30, each man carefully selected to ensure a wide range of skills. The party included 17 regular soldiers, 11 enlistees, a half-breed Indian to serve as an interpreter, Clark's giant black servant, York, and Lewis' dauntless Newfoundland dog, Scannon.

The expedition was armed with swivel cannons and with a rifle Lewis himself had adapted from the Kentucky long rifle; so effective was Lewis' redesign that it became the first mass-produced infantry weapon for the U.S. Army. The explorers also carried a lavish stock of gifts for the Indians they would meet, including colored beads, calico shirts and peace medals.

As they wound their way along the serpentine Missouri River with its caved-in banks and treacherous sand bars, the Corps soon tasted life in the wild, coming upon herds of more than 10,000 buffalo and experiencing mosquitoes so painfully pestiferous that they made

Lewis' dog howl. The Indians they encountered proved occasionally more benign. The amiable Oto tribesmen were suitably impressed by Lewis' speech offering "parental regard for his newly adopted children" from the "Great Father" in Washington. At the mouth of the Teton River in the future South Dakota, however, the explorers ran into a party of warlike Teton Sioux. At one point, Clark faced them down standing alone on shore—albeit with the swivel cannons and all the rifles on the keelboat aimed at the pugnacious Indians—until Lewis sent reinforcements. Thereafter, the Teton Sioux never again mounted a serious threat against the Corps.

After wintering among the Mandan tribe in North Dakota in temperatures cold enough to freeze solid some of the expedition's hard liquor in just 15 minutes, Lewis and Clark resumed their journey on April 7, 1805. The following month, in Montana, they glimpsed the snow-covered peaks of the Rocky Mountains and, presently, came to a confusing fork in the Missouri. The silt-laden northerly branch was the obvious choice because it looked like the muddy Missouri, but the clarity of the south fork suggested an origin in the high barren Rockies. Lewis and Clark explored both for a little while and then correctly selected the south fork. The wrong choice would have sent them wandering futilely into the endless plains of Canada.

Following a protracted portage around the Great Falls of the Missouri, a roaring torrent 300 yards wide and at least 80 feet high, they ascended the Continental Divide,

33

The first white man to span the trackless wilderness

A dozen years before Lewis and Clark made their historic expedition across the North American continent, a Scottish fur trader had quietly beaten them to it. In 1793, Alexander Mackenzie pierced the western Canadian wilderness and became the first white man to surmount the Rockies and reach the West Coast overland. An employee of the Canadian-owned North West Company, Mackenzie set out to discover the Northwest Passage, a mythical water route to the western ocean. Through it, he planned to open the lush fur country of the coast for his company — and at the same time claim all promising territories for Britain.

He had first conceived the idea during a tour of duty at a remote fur-trading outpost on Lake Athabasca, in what is now northern Alberta. Excited by Indian tales that the Pacific was not far to the west, Mackenzie determined to make a probe in that direction. In the summer of 1789, the 25-year-old trader set off with eight men (plus four Indian wives) in three birchbark canoes. They paddled up the Slave River to Great Slave Lake, then onto another broad river (later named for Mackenzie himself) that swung north at the Rockies. As they floated onward, the landscape became bleak and forbidding. For 40 days they continued until the river spilled into the tidal edges of a vast icebound body of salt water. Mackenzie had reached an ocean, but it was the Arctic Ocean. Bitterly disappointed, he turned around and, in a race with the waning sun, managed to get back to the post before winter.

The directors of the North West Company were not at all pleased. But in May 1793, the company gave him one more chance. This time, taking nine men in a 25-foot birchbark canoe, he headed upstream from Fort

Alexander Mackenzie reached the Pacific — and the Arctic Ocean as well.

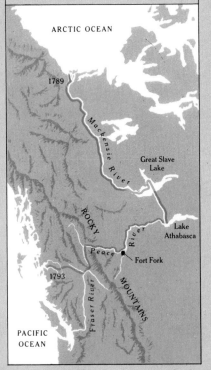

Fork, situated on the more southerly trending Peace River. As the party headed into the Rockies, the stream grew narrow and roilsome; the canoe had to be hauled through the tumbling white water and portaged around

falls. For a week the men struggled up the slopes, then wandered for more than another week from stream to stream in a series of alpine canyons. At one point (and without suspecting it) Mackenzie crossed the Continental Divide. Up to this time he had been plagued by difficulties; but now his luck ran out entirely. In the furious rapids of the Bad River (later called the Fraser), the party's canoe capsized, and only a lucky current swept the men into shallow water and saved them from drowning.

Defeated by the river, Mackenzie and his men trekked westward over the Coast Mountains. On July 20, 73 days after embarking on the Peace River, the exhausted party, having begged a last ride in the canoes of some Bella Coola Indians, floated into an arm of the Pacific just north of Vancouver Island. Mackenzie had finally found his Northwest Passage — but an unnavigable, useless one.

After a quick return trip (he was back at Fort Fork in a month), he tried to convince the directors of the North West Company that just one more try would find the easy route they wanted. They turned him down. Eventually, Mackenzie left the company and went to England to drum up government support for his plans. To that end he published a book in 1801 called *Voyages from Montreal*, which included the diaries of his two journeys and an epilogue urging Great Britain "to secure the trade of [Western Canada] to its subjects."

The Crown was as uninterested as the North West Company had been. However, Thomas Jefferson was fascinated by Mackenzie's tale, of which he pored over every word. Three years later, when he sent Lewis and Clark to seek out a transcontinental route for the United States, a copy of Mackenzie's book went with them.

crossed it and began to descend the Pacific slope. Their guide in this perilous high country was the extraordinary teenage Indian princess known as Sacajawea. She and her French-Canadian husband, Toussaint Charbonneau, had joined the expedition the previous winter during the encampment with the Mandans.

Sacajawea—Lewis and Clark wrote of her as "the Indian Woman" because they could not spell her name—was a Shoshoni who had been captured by the Minnetarees when she was 11 years old and later sold to Charbonneau. Lewis had hired Charbonneau as an interpreter, but it was his young wife, scarcely 16 years old and the mother of an infant son born in winter camp, who turned out to be a priceless asset. When her inept husband nearly capsized one of the smaller boats in a squall and then sat panic-stricken at the tiller "crying to his god for mercy," as Lewis put it, his wife showed courage and presence of mind by alertly retrieving the gear that had spilled overboard.

Sacajawea's worth became even more apparent in the high country when the Corps met up with her old tribe, the Shoshoni. Lewis and Clark had been forced to abandon the boats as the headwaters of the Missouri narrowed in the mountains. They needed horses to continue the journey and hoped to get them from the Shoshoni. The tribesmen seemed uneasy and skittish, however, until a woman who had been a childhood friend of Sacajawea rushed to embrace her. Then, as the Indians relaxed somewhat and a formal powwow began, Sacajawea suddenly ran forward and threw her arms around the chief, Cameahwait; she had recognized him as her brother.

When Lewis and Clark set off again in late August, they had Shoshoni horses and their Shoshoni princess, who chose to forge on to the Pacific with husband and baby. The climactic moment came on November 7, 1805, after

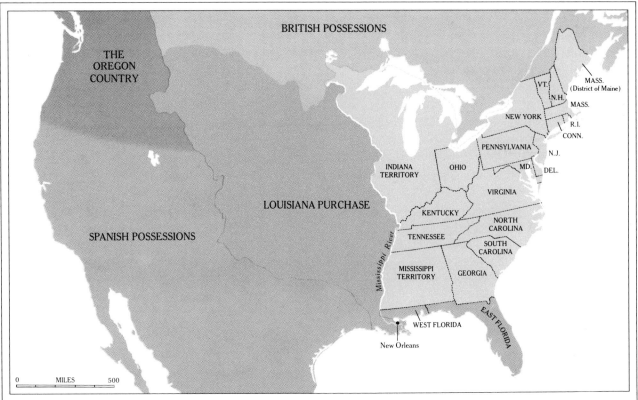

The Louisiana Purchase Treaty of 1803 gave the United States the western Mississippi drainage, extending north to the British possessions and southwest to lands claimed by the Spanish. Although later exploration defined the watershed as shown above, in 1803 the western limits were unknown. However, it was assumed, correctly, that the northwest boundary of Louisiana adjoined the unexplored Columbia River Basin or Oregon country, to which the U.S. held vague claim since the discovery of the river mouth in 1792 by an American fur ship. Together they would provide a broad land corridor to the Pacific.

the Corps had spent weeks descending the precipitous western face of the Rockies along the course of the Columbia River. Far off the men heard for the first time the rumble of Pacific breakers. They hewed a stockade and spent the winter on the south bank of the Columbia—so near the Pacific that Clark, listening to its "repeeted roling thunder," grew sick of the roar they had come so far to hear. "I cant say Pasific," he wrote with his deplorable spelling, "as since I have seen it, it has been the reverse."

President Jefferson, who seemed to think of everything, had even made provisions for getting the Corps home. He had furnished Lewis with a letter of credit drawn upon the U.S. Treasury to pay the expedition's passage back east by ship—if they could intercept some trader's vessel. No ship came into view, however, and in any event Lewis wanted to conduct further investigations. The expedition began the homeward trek via their newly established Lewis and Clark Trail on March 23, 1806. Their arduous journey was completed six months later when they paddled down the lower Missouri and arrived in St. Louis on September 23, 1806.

Lewis and Clark and their men had more than vindicated the President's faith and vision. They brought back notebooks crammed with their observations, hundreds of plant and animal specimens—many of them new to science—and topographical sketches that would form the basis for the first official map of the West.

Differing fates awaited the two leaders whose discipline and common sense had opened the way to half a continent. Only three years later, Lewis would die at age 35 under mysterious circumstances—of gunshot wounds inflicted either by a robber or by his own hand in a fit of depression. Clark would die peacefully in 1838 at the age of 68, having served as U.S. Superintendent of Indian Affairs, a respected friend of the red brothers he had first embraced on the trail westward.

Even before Lewis and Clark had completed their expedition, they had helped launch a second surge of exploration. This new wave was led by a remarkable assortment of explorers and fur trappers who came to be known as mountain men. One of the very first was a member of Lewis and Clark's own Corps, John Colter. A tall, lean Virginian, Colter in 1807 undertook what may be the most extraordinary solo exploration by any American in the history of the West. Searching for beaver

water, he set off on a mighty trek through land that was neither accurately charted nor even named. He skirted the eastern flank of what would later be called the Absaroka Range, ascended the Wind River valley, crossed the Continental Divide at Union Pass, descended the Pacific slope, then crossed and recrossed the Snake River and the Tetons.

In his circuit through what is now Wyoming, Montana and Idaho, he was almost continuously in virgin wilderness. He was the first explorer to come upon such wonders as the hot springs, boiling mudholes and geysers near what is now Yellowstone Park. But Colter received scant credit for these discoveries; he created no charts and kept no journal. Indeed, many people thought his stories of underground infernos preposterous and referred scornfully to the region as "Colter's Hell" *(map, page 66)*.

But few doubted Colter's endurance and courage. In the fall of 1808, on the upper Missouri, he and a companion were attacked by 500 Blackfeet, who killed his partner and captured, stripped and tortured Colter. The chief then challenged him to some grisly sport: Colter was to run for his life; the warriors would follow in about 30 seconds with every intention of making mincemeat of him. Colter sprinted barefoot through the prickly-pear thorns and rocky scree of the canyon rim, heading for the Jefferson Fork of the river, six miles away.

Halfway there he had outrun all of his pursuers but one. When this swift warrior pulled close, Colter turned and tripped him and dispatched him with his own lance. Colter reached the river, hiding under driftwood while the Blackfeet scoured the shore. Then he swam downstream five miles or so, scrambled ashore and resumed running. Seven days and 200 miles later, naked, blistered, dehydrated and all but starved—his feet flayed and his body festering with thorns—he arrived safely at a trapper's fort on the Bighorn River.

Colter soon went back to the wild, blazing new trails and cheerfully bushwhacking Blackfeet. But in 1810, after one more hairbreadth escape from those marauders, who shot down five men around him, he made his way back to the fort on the Bighorn River. There, he threw his hat to the ground and solemnly announced to the assembled company: "If God will only forgive me this time and let me off I will leave the country day after tomorrow—and be damned if I ever come into it again!"

He then got into a canoe and in a month paddled 2,000 miles downriver to St. Louis and the comforts of the old frontier.

Unlike Colter, the mountain men who came after him in search of beaver seldom thought of themselves as explorers. Trappers like the storied Jedediah Smith typically found new ways west as much by accident as by design—a sort of brave, muddling through approach. A native of New York State, Smith turned up in St. Louis at age 23, answered an advertisement for enterprising young men to serve as fur trappers and soon sported a receding hairline—the legacy of grappling with a grizzly bear that ripped open his scalp above his left eye.

In August 1826, Smith led a party of 15 men to the southwest in search of new trapping country. The group passed the Salt Lake and wandered southward through the Wasatch Mountains on the eastern rim of the Great Basin, with its vast badlands, then into sagebrush and reddish sand that Smith called "a Country of starvation." Soon, the trappers were in the Black Mountains of northwestern Arizona, short of water and food and traveling on foot because so many of their horses had died.

Worse was yet to come. The last leg of Smith's trip took them through the lethal heart of the Mojave Desert. For 15 grueling days of constant thirst and hunger, his men trudged across a flat, salt-crusted plain blazing in the autumn sun, trying to follow the Mojave River, which kept disappearing underground for miles at a time. It was an exhausted and soul-weary group of men who, in mid-November, arrived in the vicinity of Los Angeles.

In 1830, he returned to St. Louis, intending to make maps of the wild country through which he had traveled. Instead, he set off on a trading expedition to Santa Fe. Leading a party of 83 men, he traveled into a section of Cimarron River country known to be almost waterless. Apparently confident that their mountain-man instincts would lead them to a spring or stream, no one had taken the precaution of stocking up on water. The thirsty group soon had to break up and scatter across the desert in search of a water source. A hunting party of Comanches came upon Jed Smith, alone and weakened, and shot him

Joseph Walker

to death. He was only 32, and his maps went unmade.

No such end was likely to befall Smith's contemporary, Joseph Reddeford Walker, a trailblazer and trapper with too much foresight to go unprepared into the wilderness. Walker was arguably the greatest of the mountain men and certainly the beau ideal. He measured six feet tall, weighed more than 200 pounds and was blue-eyed and handsome in a craggy, hawk-beaked way. He wore his hair long in the Indian style, had a full beard and attired himself in leggings, hunting shirt and plumed slouch hat elegantly worked by the Indian girls who idolized him. For all that, he was a careful planner and superb leader with a remarkable intuitive sense for the shape, texture and topographical details of the Western wilderness. Walker "didn't follow trails," it was said, "but rather made them."

Joe Walker had been born into an extraordinary frontier clan in the Tennessee mountains. His father had pushed across the Piedmont to join the first settlers in the Appalachians. One of his brothers was to die at the Alamo with Davy Crockett; another would lead wagon trains across the continent. Joe went west to Missouri in 1818, helped make illegal runs of trade goods to Spanish territory in New Mexico, then joined the surveying team that marked the way soon to become famous as the Santa Fe Trail *(page 43)*. Back again in Missouri, he served as sheriff of Jackson County before organizing an expedition of 40 trappers for a trek that would take them as far as the California coast if necessary to find new beaver water.

To prepare for the odyssey, Walker and his party met in the summer of 1833 in the Rockies—at the Green River rendezvous, one of the annual affairs where mountain men reoutfitted for the next trapping season. When Walker's group left on August 20, each man had not only his own mount but also led three heavily laden pack horses. In addition, four days later, Walker halted the group and set them to hunting until each man had added 60 pounds of meat to his pack. When he reached the Salt Lake vicinity after a three-week journey, he again showed his pru-

Hardscrabble heroes who forged the trails

In the first three decades of the 19th Century, a new breed of explorers pressed up the Missouri River to the northern Rockies. Farther south, they fanned out across the plains and deserts into California. Known as mountain men, they were a tough, ragtag assortment of adventurers, explorers, trappers and back-country entrepreneurs. With disparate backgrounds and varied reasons for choosing the rugged life, they all had one quality in common—a taste and talent for the wilderness.

For an entire winter's work, the typical mountain man wore only one outfit of buckskins with an extra set of leggings. He carried several knives, a pipe, tobacco and perhaps some reading matter for idle moments (the Bible, Shakespeare and books of poetry occasional-ly turned up in trappers' camps). Spare locks and flints, some 25 pounds of powder, a hundred pounds of lead and a gun made up the rest of his baggage. More often than not, the gun was a heavy .40- to .60-caliber rifle, preferably hand-made by the Hawken brothers of St. Louis—an accurate weapon powerful enough to knock down a buffalo, a grizzly bear or a Blackfoot.

Except for a little flour, coffee, tea and salt, mountain men carried no food. Bread was an unattainable luxury and, according to one trapper, "Vegetables were out of the question in the Rocky Mountains except for a few kinds of roots of spontaneous growth." And so they consumed prodigious amounts of meat, from buffalo, deer and antelope to bobcat, hawk or even a stray dog. In true "starvin' times," however, moccasins, leather lariats—or worse—became candidates for the pot. Once when a tenderfoot was repelled by watching an Indian suck down a raw buffalo intestine, trailblazer Jim Bridger commented quietly, "I've eaten that kind of stuff myself when I had to."

All in all, it was a life that produced casualties in countless ways, from falling off mountains to maulings by grizzly bears. Still, a number of mountain men survived into distinguished old age. Many, in fact, went on to become scouts, Indian fighters and army commanders. Within their lifetimes, the West was discovered and mapped to its farthest corners. All was found and laid ready for the generations ahead.

Jim Beckwourth *(left)*, son of a Southern planter and a Virginia slave, discovered a High Sierra pass that became part of a major emigrant route to California. Kit Carson *(right)* blazed a few trails of his own and helped pathfind for John Frémont during three expeditions west.

A mountain man at 18, Joe Meek later became U.S. Marshal for Oregon Territory.

Jim Bridger posed for this *carte de visite* in the 1860s. He was still guiding in the Rockies at the time.

dence by seeking out the local Bannock Indians, and questioning them closely on the character of the country and the best routes west.

The route Walker finally selected passed north of the Salt Lake and headed west across the parched plains of northern Nevada. It was hard going, but far better than an alternative southern route through the salt desert. He then followed the Humboldt River downstream to the swampy Humboldt Sink, tracing a passage that would be taken years later by the first transcontinental railroad.

Early in September, the mountain men began to encounter Digger Indians, a poor, scrawny lot who lived by grubbing up roots, beetles and lizards, and hunting small game. The Diggers were amazed by the white man's metal tools and buzzed around the mountain men like mosquitoes, stealing whatever they could. Much to the consternation of the prudent Walker, who hated to see the Indians provoked needlessly, a group of his men killed several Diggers who had stolen their traps.

Bent on revenge, eight or nine hundred Indians surrounded the 40 mountain men, who quickly built a breastwork. The Diggers marched straight at it, feigning friendship by "dancing and singing in the greatest glee," according to one of the mountain men, Zenas Leonard, who often chronicled his experiences. Walker tried without success to warn them by demonstrating the power of the white man's rifles. But the next morning, about a hundred of the boldest Diggers persisted in their threatening gestures, and Walker ordered his men to charge. Only after 39 of their tribe lay dead did the Indians understand what guns could do—and stop threatening the Walker party.

Walker now confronted the most forbidding barrier to westward travel in the whole continent. Before them lay the unbroken mass of the Sierra Nevada, stretching nearly 400 miles from north to south and with peaks more than 14,000 feet high. The men began to work their way up the range in snow so deep that they had to break a path so the horses could get through. The crossing of the Sierra took almost three weeks, and both man and beast suffered intensely from cold and hunger.

A few men wanted to turn back. Walker considered denying them horses or ammunition for their retreat, but fearing an outright mutiny, he found a happier solution. The men were permitted to butcher two horses that were on their last legs. Everyone ate his fill that night, morale lifted and the disciplinary crisis was over.

After reaching the crest, the party inched westward along the divide between the Tuolumne and Merced rivers and came upon one of the great moments of all Western exploration. Below them lay the Yosemite Valley, more than seven miles long, studded with great granite monoliths and lined with feathery cataracts as high as 1,500 feet. By fastening ropes around their horses and lowering them down the precipitous incline one at a time, they descended onto the spectacular valley floor.

Many of the men later counted their brief sojourn amid the splendors of Yosemite as the supreme experience of their long journey—or, possibly, of their lives. Walker himself would go on to new adventures and successes in his more than half century in the West—as Indian fighter, Army scout, wagon-train guide, gold seeker and cattleman—but when he died 43 years later at age 77, the epitaph on his headstone included the words: "Camped at Yosemite, November 13, 1833."

Walker and his party came down the western slope of the Sierra and into the heart of California. They savored its flowering warmth, found easy forage for the tired horses and plentiful game for the pot, and became the first Americans to gaze upon the giant redwood trees—"some of which," noted one expedition member, "would measure from sixteen to eighteen fathom round the trunk." Late in November, they skirted the eastern shore of San Francisco and San Pablo bays and crossed the low coastal range. Then, Leonard wrote, "the broad Pacific burst forth to view"; they camped that night "quite close to the beach near a spring of delightful water."

The Spanish settlers and the sunny climate proved so hospitable that six of Walker's men elected to remain there. According to Leonard, Walker himself was offered a 50-square-mile tract of land if he would stay on and bring in "fifty families, composed of different kinds of mechanics." But the restless Walker declined; on February 14, 1834, he headed back toward the mountains with his party, driving 340 horses, 47 head of cattle and 30 dogs (bought, like the cattle, as a food supply).

This time he found a less taxing passage across the Sierra—a notch at the easy elevation of 5,200 feet. Later to be named Walker Pass, it would serve as the point of entry for emigrants bound for California. But the Nevada badlands proved as bad as ever: To survive, the men drank the blood of stock that had died of thirst.

Zebulon Pike and the road to Santa Fe

Lieutenant Zebulon M. Pike

Long before the mountain men charted ways to California, American explorers and traders were forging a solid southerly link with Spanish domains. In 1806 a young Army lieutenant named Zebulon Montgomery Pike left St. Louis to explore the vaguely defined southern border of the Louisiana Territory. Traveling along the Arkansas River with a party of 15 men, Pike decided to climb the towering peak that bears his name *(below)*, thinking it was only a few miles away. Several days later and 40 miles farther on, Pike was still far from his goal. He gave up and in an outburst of defeatism declared "no human being could have ascended to its pinical." Pike may have had shortcomings as trailblaz-er and speller, but he proved to be an excellent propagandist. His published account of the rich Spanish towns in the Southwest sent traders scurrying there. The Spanish responded to their initiative by throwing them in jail.

The traders had better luck after Mexico took over the area in 1821. In 1824 expansionist-minded frontiersmen demanded that a federal suveying team provide a well-marked road from Missouri to New Mexico. Although the wind erased the mounds of earth the surveying crew (including a young Joe Walker) threw up as waymarks, thousands of wagon tracks soon incised into the prairie the famous Santa Fe Trail.

Pikes Peak looms straight up from the level plains. It was scaled by three other explorers 14 years after Pike said it could not be done.

John Charles Frémont may not have lived up to his nickname—Pathfinder—but nevertheless as a promoter he wielded immense influence in the development of the West.

On July 12, Walker arrived at the Bear River—150 miles southwest of the expedition's departure point—where trappers were gathering for the 1834 season. During the full year in which he and his mountain men had been gone, the expedition had suffered not a single fatality; they had found a better route to California, and were now boosters of its virtues and pleasures.

Before leaving California, Zenas Leonard had written prophetically: "Yes, here, even in this remote part of the great West before many years, will these hills and valleys be greeted with the enlivening sound of the workman's hammer, and the merry whistle of the ploughboy. Our government should be vigilant. She should assert her claim by taking possession of the whole territory as soon as possible—for we have good reason to suppose that the territory *west* of the mountain will some day be equally as important to a nation as that on the *east*."

Over the next decade, the expansionist sentiments expressed by Leonard circulated widely and came to be embodied in the loose creed known as Manifest Destiny. At the heart of this movement was the notion that the North American continent, from one shining sea to the other, should belong to the citizens of the United States, and that securing these lands was in keeping with the purpose of some higher power—Nature, History or God.

Perhaps the most inspired of all the steps taken to fulfill this swelling ambition was the creation in 1838 of the U.S. Army's Corps of Topographical Engineers. Ostensibly a group of surveyors and mapmakers at the service of the infantry and cavalry, the Corps soon developed into an elite body of military explorers dedicated to Manifest Destiny. These officers, men of exceptional vigor and intelligence, would systematically map the West and lead both the Army and the people as a whole to the shores of the Pacific.

By all the odds, the best known of the Topographical Engineers was John Charles Frémont. Between 1842 and 1854 Frémont made five expeditions in the West, a record that earned him the popular nickname of the "Pathfinder." The designation galled many of his contemporaries, for Frémont in fact found few new paths himself and sometimes needed help to stay on paths that other men had

already established. Yet, while he was sometimes a slipshod explorer, he was such a glamorous, persuasive and appealing figure that he aroused the westering impulse of the American people like no other man before or after.

Quite likely because of a wandering boyhood and his illegitimate birth—in 1813 to the daughter of a prominent Virginian and her French refugee lover—Frémont developed early a knack for attaching himself to people of means and power. While still in his teens he found his first important patron, Joel Poinsett, whom he met while studying in Charleston College, South Carolina.

A distinguished diplomat, world traveler and patron of natural history (the poinsettia was named for him), Poinsett became Secretary of War under President Martin Van Buren and helped organize the Topographical Engineers. He secured for young Frémont a second lieutenant's commission and assignment to the Corps' first major project in the West, an expedition into the country between the upper Mississippi and Missouri rivers. Frémont found another patron in the expedition's commander, Joseph Nicollet, an outstanding topographer and, like Frémont's father, a French émigré. Nicollet taught him the essentials of his trade: how to take astronomical and barometric readings; the technique of making systematic botanical, mineralogical and meteorological observations; and the art of sketching an accurate field map.

Frémont's most important attachments of all resulted from his romance with a 15-year-old Washington beauty named Jessie Benton. Extraordinary in her own right—bright, brave and a gifted writer—she was the daughter of one of the most powerful men in the nation's capital: Thomas Hart Benton was the senior U.S. Senator from Missouri and the leading expansionist of the day. Known for his ill temper and bombast, Benton violently opposed the romance. After Jessie and Frémont were secretly married in October 1841, he melodramatically ordered his new son-in-law out of the house. When Jessie responded in equally melodramatic fashion—grasping her husband's arm, she echoed the Biblical Ruth, "Whither thou goest, I will go"—the Senator was silenced, and shortly Frémont came to live with his in-laws.

Benton and Frémont now took mutual advantage of their new familial relationship. The Senator saw in his charismatic and energetic young son-in-law an ideal instrument to advance his expansionist policies. He helped push through Congress an appropriation of $30,000 for a survey of the Oregon Trail and then won for Frémont the assignment of heading it. In addition to mapping and describing the area leading through the central Rockies to Oregon, which was jointly held by Britain and the U.S., Frémont's mission was promotional. He would present the Far West to Americans in such an attractive way as to lure American settlers of all kinds—including farmers, ranchers, miners, storekeepers and their families.

When Frémont left Fort Leavenworth on the Missouri in mid-June 1842, he was guided by a remarkable mountain man he had recently met: Christopher (Kit) Carson. Quiet, competent and schooled by such trailblazers as Joe Walker, Carson was happy to serve as a deputy rather than boss. Perhaps as a result, he and the fiercely ambitious Frémont took an immediate liking to each other. Carson would help guide Frémont to fame; Frémont in turn would publicize Carson furiously as a Hawkeye of the West.

By July 5, Frémont's party had reached the gateway to Oregon—the South Pass—and he was disappointed. This wide, gently sloping crossing of the Rockies was only 7,550 feet high and too tame for Frémont, who looked around for something more dramatic to climb. A few days later, in the Wind River range in Wyoming, he selected the peak that now bears his name. Though its height of 13,785 feet was exceeded by scores of other peaks, he arbitrarily decided that it was the highest mountain in the Rockies. By the droll account of one participant, German-born topographer Charles Preuss, the climb was more comic than heroic, with the leader interrupting its progress once because of a headache and on another occasion because he "was again feeling peckish and had retired to camp."

But Frémont's own account described an audacious ascent through ice and snow, and he made it the climax of the 207-page report prepared on his return to Washington in late October. He began dictating the manuscript to his wife Jessie, only a few days after she presented him with their first child. "The horseback life, the sleep in the open air," Jessie explained later, "had unfitted Mr. Frémont for the indoor work of writing. After a series of hemorrhages from the nose and head had convinced him that he must give up trying to write his report, I was let to try and thus slid into my most happy life-work."

In the end, the report consisted of large helpings of useful factual information—descriptions of the landscape, Indians, animals and where to find the supplies that the emigrant would need—all served up in a sauce of rich, evocative prose. After relating Frémont's herculean conquest of Fremont Peak, Jessie concluded with a truly inspired passage destined to capture the imagination of those who had never even dreamed of leaving their homes in the East:

"Here, on the summit, where the stillness was absolute, unbroken by any sound, and thus the solitude complete, we thought ourselves beyond the region of animated life; but while we were sitting on the rock, a solitary bee (*bromus, the bumble bee*) came winging his flight from the eastern valley, and lit on the knee of one of the men. It was a strange place, the icy rock and the highest peak of the Rocky Mountains, for a lover of warm sunshine and flowers; and we pleased ourselves with the idea that he was the first of his species to cross the mountain barrier, a solitary pioneer to foretell the advance of civilization."

The report was presented to Congress in March 1843, and so dazzled the legislators that they ordered the printing and distribution of 10,000 copies. It was an immediate sensation among the press and public, spreading the notion into the far corners of the republic that going west was both an exciting and an easy thing to do. Years later, poet Joaquin Miller remembered that, when his father read it aloud to him at their Indiana farm, he suddenly felt "inflamed with a love for action, adventure, glory, and great deeds away out yonder under the path of the setting sun."

Frémont's second expedition, in 1844, took him beyond Wyoming's South Pass to map the Oregon Territory. Increasingly vainglorious, he insisted on dragging along a carriage-mounted brass howitzer that fired 12-pound cannonballs. This disgusted the men who had to do the dragging across 3,000 miles of prairie, desert and mountain, and alarmed his superiors in Washington who feared that the reckless Frémont might create an international incident with Mexico or Britain. He argued later that the purpose was to frighten potentially hostile Indians, though it is likely that he simply enjoyed the image of himself leading his horsemen across the continent with a cannon trundling in his wake.

An artistic tribute to a vanishing people

In 1832, after witnessing a gruesome rite of self-torture conducted by the Mandan tribe, George Catlin wrote, "Thank God, it is over, that I have seen it, and am able to tell it to the world." Telling the world about Western Indians was the mission and the obsession of artist Catlin's life. After some casual painting of Indians on reservations in the East while earning his living as a society portraitist, Catlin left his family to spend 10 years studying the alien ways of the Plains tribes. His observations were published in a two-volume work, *Illustrations of the Manners, Customs, and Condition of the North American Indians*. Despite its ponderous title, Catlin's book was highly readable, combining evocative prose with vivid, richly detailed engravings, two of which are reproduced at right.

Although Catlin was not the first artist to visit the Western tribes, he had a unique respect and affection for Indian culture that allowed him to interpret it on its own terms. In return, the Indians warmed to this free spirit who roamed across their land working with furious intensity. (During one 86-day trip on the upper Missouri, Catlin produced 135 paintings while traveling an average of 18 miles a day.) His efforts to win the Indians' trust gained him access to many of their secret rites and sanctuaries, including a sacred quarry in Minnesota where tribes obtained stone for pipe bowls. No white man had ever been permitted to visit the site before.

This engraving of Mah-to-toh-pa includes battle scenes and symbols of valor on his robe.

Scalping was not always fatal, as Catlin showed in a droll sketch of a scalped man removing his derby (below, right). Once scalps had been stretched on hoops, they were hung from weapons, horses and tipis.

Reaching his objective in the heart of Oregon Territory, Frémont in late November decided to further burnish his romantic image. Instead of returning eastward on the Oregon Trail as ordered, he led the party south toward California. He followed the Sierra Nevada in the dead of winter, and conditions grew so bleak that he was forced to abandon his cannon in a deep snowdrift. Farther along, more or less backtracking ill-fated Jed Smith's old California trail, the party ran into difficulties with Indians in Utah. Frémont and his men were extricated from these troubles only by the timely appearance of the great mountain man Joe Walker, who guided them eastward across the Rockies.

The second installment of Frémont's adventures was no less compelling and no less popular than the first, though marred by several serious errors of fact. Unaccountably, he reported that the freshwater Utah Lake and the Great Salt Lake were the same body of water. Worse, he touted north-central Utah as a "bucolic region," fertile and well-watered—a judgment that contributed to the subsequent migration of the Mormons to the area and was largely responsible for the low opinion that Brigham Young, struggling with sagebrush and drought, formed of Frémont's veracity and intelligence.

For his third expedition, in the summer of 1845, Frémont had the benefit of 60 men plus two extraordinary guides: Walker and Carson. After exploring the Great Basin and then the passes through the Sierra, the expedition arrived in California that winter at a tense time. The Mexican authorities, fearing a repetition of the rebellion that had cost Mexico her Texas territory, looked at this well-armed party of 60 Americans and ordered them to leave the province. Frémont put on a brief show of defiance, but then thought better of it when the Mexicans began gathering their forces and slipped away northward, leaving California in late April 1846. He left without Joe Walker, who had little regard for Mexican fighting abilities, severed his connection with Frémont and later called him "morally and physically the most complete coward I ever knew."

In a few weeks, however, Frémont returned to California with his men in time to take part in the so-called Bear Flag revolt. This uprising of American settlers was part of the war that had just broken out between the U.S. and Mexico. Frémont organized his own men and the Bear Flag rebels into a motley organization known as the California Battalion and, after the weak Mexican resistance ceased, wound up being appointed the civil governor.

But then Frémont came into conflict with General Stephen Kearny, the hot-tempered commander of the official U.S. invasion force that had marched overland from Fort Leavenworth. After Frémont refused orders to disband his irregulars, Kearny had him arrested and sent back to Washington for a court martial on charges that included mutiny. Found guilty, Frémont resigned his commission despite an offer from President Polk to let him remain in the Army.

The Pathfinder bounced back—into another imbroglio. In 1848, he went west on the first of two surveys to explore a potential route for the transcontinental railroad, a mission obtained for him by one of the prominent promoters of the railroad, his father-in-law. Heading west on a path that led roughly along the 38th parallel, Frémont insisted on forcing a way across the worst of the mountains in the worst of weather. A December blizzard caught his party high in Colorado's San Juan mountains, and 10 members died of cold and hunger. "The result was entirely satisfactory," Frémont said later with evident indifference. "It convinced me that neither snow of winter nor mountains were obstacles in the way of a road."

Just in time perhaps, Frémont now embarked on a new career that promised to be as glorious as the best moments of his past. In California, he struck it rich beyond dreams when gold was discovered on a 70-square-mile tract of wilderness he had purchased in the Sierra foothills. With his wealth and connections, he won a seat in the U.S. Senate after California became a state in 1850. Six years later he became the first Presidential candidate of the newly founded Republican Party and made a surprisingly good run in a losing cause.

But fate was turning against John Charles Frémont. Thereafter, while a growing flood of Americans followed their manifest destiny along the routes west, disaster after disaster befell the erstwhile Pathfinder. During the Civil War, he served as an impolitic and bungling general, whom Lincoln eventually stripped of command. The great riches were frittered away on a money-losing California ranch and a failed scheme to connect Memphis and San Diego by rail. In the later years, Jessie alone supported the family by turning out a stream of well-received books and articles. Frémont died in 1890, lying in a dreary Manhattan boardinghouse, pathetically separated in distance, time

and spirit from the young hero who had ridden across the West with Kit Carson at his side, "caught up in the true Greek joy of existence—in the gladness of living."

Yet all along, the dogged Army engineers and a handful of determined civilians had been carrying on the vital work, uncovering the West's final secret places and codifying its assets and liabilities. In 1860, the Army consolidated all the gleanings on a single, monumental map drawn to a scale of 1:3,000,000 which encompassed the entire trans-Mississippi region to the Pacific and gave the nation its first dependable geographic portrait of the West.

After the Civil War, the task of filling in the small gaps fell largely upon the shoulders of four exceptional men: Ferdinand Vandiveer Hayden, Clarence King, John Wesley Powell and Army Lieutenant George Montague Wheeler. The next 15 years were known for the "Great Surveys," as these last of the trailblazers prowled most of the territory that would one day comprise eight Western states—Nebraska, Colorado, Wyoming, Utah, New Mexico, California, Nevada and Arizona—and penetrated into Montana, Idaho and Oregon as well.

The surveyors analyzed the region's geologic underpinnings, measured its awesome mountains (55 "fourteeners"—peaks above 14,000 feet—in Colorado alone), shot the boiling rapids of its rivers, located and assayed most of its astounding minerals, catalogued its flora and fauna, staked out its arable sections, delineated its deserts, and studied how best to make use of the land while preserving it from despoliation.

All in all, by the time they completed their work in 1879, they had cost the American taxpayer something more than a million and a half dollars. It was a bargain. Precious little about the face of the Great West remained to any man's imagination.

The great fur rush upriver

In 1806, when pathfinders Meriwether Lewis and William Clark returned to St. Louis after their epic exploration of the Missouri and points west, they reported exultantly: "We view this passage across the continent as affording immence advantages to the fir trade."

Their glowing tales of the beaver supply on the upper Missouri and in the Rockies instantly set off a frenzied fur rush up the Big Muddy. Entrepreneurs and adventurers of every description attempted the river in keelboats or in dugouts made from giant cottonwood logs. Rowing, sailing and—more often than not—hauling their clumsy craft against the current, they generally expended an entire summer in attaining the upper reaches of the stream. But once a trapper arrived in beaver country he could expect to harvest about 120 pelts per year—worth the then-tidy sum of $1,000 or so back East.

There was no artist on hand to record the beauties and hazards of their first journeys. But in 1833, a peripatetic German naturalist, Prince Maximilian, boarded the keelboat *Flora* to explore the upper river, unchanged since the early days of the fur trade. With him was a Swiss artist, Karl Bodmer, who faithfully recreated life on the Missouri as it was before the age of steam.

The keelboat *Flora*, anchored near a Gros Ventre camp on the Missouri, is besieged by Indians eager to barter beaver pelts for brandy.

A cavalcade of Mandan Indians crosses the frozen Missouri after a midwinter visit to Fort Clark, a major trading post sited on a bluff near present-day Bismarck. The ice could easily support them: it formed early in November, reached a thickness of four feet, and did not break up until April.

53

In artist Bodmer's dramatic masterpiece, trappers receive an unpleasant — but not uncommon — surprise: a pair of ravenous grizzlies has discovered the meat cache left by an advance contingent of hunters, leaving little but bones for the landing party to take back with them to their keelboat.

3. A world of beaver

"I have been 24 years a canoeman and 41 years in service; no portage was ever too long for me. Fifty songs could I sing. I have saved the lives of ten *voyageurs*. Have had 12 wives and six running dogs. I spent all my money in pleasure. Were I young again, I should spend my life the same way over. There is no life so happy as a *voyageur*'s life."

For an old man looking back on his pursuit of pelts in Canada's fur trade, memory was highly selective and tended to blur reality. In fact, the French *voyageurs*, a breed of tireless men who pushed their birchbark canoes thousands of miles into the Canadian West, endured dangers and discomforts that placed them on the raw edge of human existence.

"They shivered on the sunless trails deep in the woods, fought colds and insects and dysentery," wrote one observer. Rheumatism was an occupational hazard for men who waded into icy water to set their traps. A broken ankle could mean lonely starvation. Wild animals—grizzly bears in particular—posed a danger, and there was the ever-present peril of Indians.

But despite the unending pain of knotted muscles and lamed backs they forged onward. In the process, they explored and mapped the labyrinthine waterways, the rugged mountains and the bleak tundra of a trackless land that teemed with beaver and otter, fox and lynx, marten and mink.

The westward quest in Canada had long ago been nurtured by, of all things, a fashion in hats for European dandies. In 1535, the French explorer Jacques Cartier had sailed 550 miles up the St. Lawrence River, only to find his route blocked by formidable rapids just beyond the present site of Montreal. Undaunted, Cartier began trading with local Indians, who, in their eagerness for French knives and kettles, offered him everything they possessed—including the beaver pelts off their backs.

Those skins stirred a sensation among European hat-makers, who found them ideal for making felt. The demand was soon so great that French traders in the New World recruited whole tribes of Indians as commercial hunters. The Indians were such excellent providers that within a few decades the supply of beaver was waning in Eastern Canada, and by the early 17th Century, the future of the fur trade had already shifted to the West.

Another fur-trading Frenchman, Samuel de Champlain, who arrived in New France in 1603, decided to seek out merchandise instead of waiting for Indian hunters to deliver it. Under his leadership, a group of strong-armed young men from Montreal climbed into Indian canoes and paddled lustily west on the Indians' traditional thoroughfares, the Ottawa and French rivers. Calling themselves *voyageurs*, they set up trading posts along their routes, and by 1650 they were exploring the Great Lakes.

Meanwhile, hundreds of miles to the north, the English navigator Henry Hudson had already discovered an immense body of water—a bay that would bear his name, extending even farther west than the Great Lakes. To exploit the region's priceless bounty of furs, the British Crown in 1670 issued a charter to "the Governor and Company of Adventurers of England Tradeing into Hudsons Bay." Thus was born the Hudson's Bay Company, soon to become a trading and shipping colossus with title to an area of nearly 1.5 million square miles.

The French, however, were not prepared to go quietly and simply cede control of the lucrative Canadian fur trade to their English rivals. Damning each other as invaders, the two forces fought a long and bitter struggle for command of the Indian trade. Several British posts on Hudson Bay changed hands repeatedly; some were destroyed, rebuilt and destroyed again.

In 1713, the French finally abandoned their efforts to oust the English from Hudson Bay. Still, they continued to control the interior of Canada and preempted the main source of furs. It took far greater wars—fought out

A party of *voyageurs* from the Hudson's Bay Company portages trade goods at a supply post along the route to the fur country.

by England and France on two continents over five more decades—to decide the fate of Canada and its fur trade. In 1763, after British armies had won smashing victories at Montreal and Quebec, the Treaty of Paris put a formal end to the French and Indian Wars, with France handing over all of its territory in the New World to Britain.

The managers of the Hudson's Bay Company assumed that they would now have an easy time taking over the whole Canadian fur trade. They were woefully wrong. Instead, they faced stiff competition from a group of Scots who, decades before, had emigrated to Canada's eastern maritime region to escape despotic overlords in their homeland. Hardly had the French colonial government fallen in Canada than the Scots began moving to Montreal and setting up fur-trading companies.

The animals were unimaginable in their multitudes, the treasure inexhaustible, or so everyone thought. In 1760 alone, the Hudson's Bay Company had sent back to England enough beaver pelts to make 576,000 hats, and other, more ornamental furs increasingly adorned the collars, sleeves, hems, gloves and boots of ladies and gentlemen on both sides of the Atlantic. The canny, energetic Scots proved to be ardent purveyors and worthy competitors in the rush to satisfy fashion's craze. Adopting the French system wholesale, they hired canoemen and—to the astonishment of the sedentary English governors on Hudson Bay—led their crews in person, along the old *voyageur* routes westward to the Great Lakes and north to the edge of the fur frontier. The Scots quickly earned a reputation for daring and determination and for supplying rum to the Indians.

In 1775, several of the Scottish merchants merged to form the nucleus of the North West Company, whose members called themselves Nor'Westers. Thirteen years later they outflanked their powerful rival by penetrating far into what is now northern Alberta. There, they established a trading post at Fort Chipewyan near Lake Athabasca, only a few days' journey from the divide that separated the Hudson Bay and Arctic watersheds.

For the next four decades the Hudson's Bay and North West companies struggled for supremacy along the canoe routes and dogsled trails of a vast and virgin land. By 1818, both companies were suffering unacceptably heavy losses in their fierce rivalry, with bloody clashes in the wilderness and costly lawsuits in London. To save the fur trade from ruin, the British Crown stepped in and

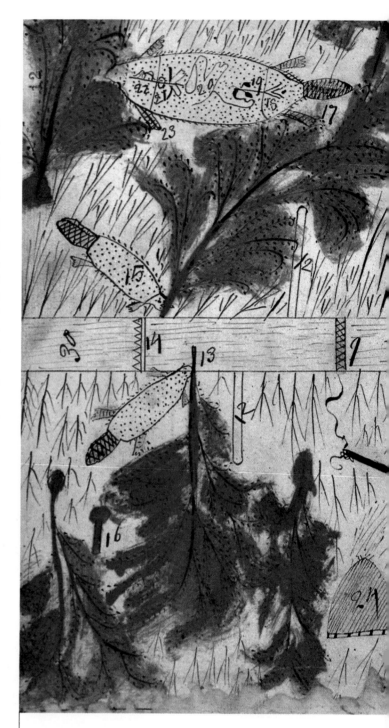

EVERYTHING ANYONE WANTED TO KNOW ABOUT BEAVER
In 1743 James Isham, a Hudson's Bay trader, made this attempt to satisfy European curiosity about beaver. Besides sketching all possible details of beaver and beaver hunting in his composition, Isham wrote the following interpretation, keyed to the images.

(1) A Beaver house; (2) the thickness made of stone, mudd, & wood & c.; (3) where the Beaver Lyes within the house; (4) when the Beaver are Disturb'd, or hear a noise they make into the water, from 3 and 6; (5) where their food Lyes; (6) the half Beaver or small Beaver Lyes; (7) a Indian breaking the house

op'n with a Chissel, tied to a Long stick; (8) the Beaver making out of the house hearing a noise and makes to the Vaults; (9) netts sett in the Creek with a string and a stick at the End to catch the Beaver as they come out of the house; (10) a Indian sitting by a fire watching a Nett, with a stick by him to Kill them as he hauls them out; (11) Dam's made by the Beaver, that the water show'd not Run too fast upon them; (12) Vaults the Beaver makes into when Disturb'd. out of the house, they Run abt. 12 or 14 foot in Land (i.e.) and abt. 2 foot under the Ground; (13) a Beaver hawling a tree by the teeth into the water; (14) a stop'age made by Inds. with stakes to Keep the Beaver from going into the River; (15) a Beaver cutting a tree Downe with his teeth; (16) the stump where cutt Down; (17) the tail of a beaver; (18) the Castor under wch. Lyes the oyly stones or 2 bladder's; (19) the penis and stones; (20) the Gutts or Interials; (21) the heart & Liver; (22) the Lights; (23) the fore feet; (24) Inds. tent in the woods; (25) a Indian going a hunting; (26) willows on the Edge of the creek; (27) a flock of partridges; (28) thick woods; (29) a stick Lying by the Indn. to Kill Beaver & c.; (30) the Creek which Runs into the Large Rivers & c.

pressed for a merger. When the rivals finally made peace in 1821, it was under the name and control of the Hudson's Bay Company.

Yet the merger produced no great change for anyone but the partners of the North West Company. Most of the Scottish traders and clerks went on with their work as Hudson's Bay employees. The *voyageurs* continued their annual rounds; new bosses could hardly alter the rhythm of the seasons. If anything changed for the canoemen, it was that expanding fur trade provided them with more jobs and sometimes with better pay.

The men who brought back the furs and helped establish an empire were well suited to the hardships of their sinew-straining work. Mostly of French or mixed French and Indian blood, the *voyageurs* tended to be short, wiry men with deep chests and big muscular shoulders built for—and by—the brutal work of loading, paddling and carrying their canoes.

In currentless lakes or smooth stretches of river, the *voyageurs* paddled tirelessly, keeping up a steady pace of about 40 strokes a minute, covering four or more miles an hour. In the long northern twilights, many a day started at 3 o'clock in the morning and lasted until 9 o'clock at night, with only two brief breaks for breakfast and lunch. On one such day, a visitor watched in amazement as his hosts paddled for 16 hours and still refused to stop for the night. When they finally pulled ashore two and one half hours later, the *voyageurs* had covered an astonishing 79 miles since their paddles had first touched water early that morning.

Setting forth in search of beaver, the Canadians traveled a route that swept west to Lake Superior, then north and west to Lake Athabasca, following a 3,000-mile network of waterways linked by occasional portages. The arrival of the canoe brigades at one of the many isolated fur-trading posts attracted Indians from far and wide. The overtures to trade were always elaborate. "At a few yards distance from the gate they salute us with several discharges of

their guns," one witness described. "On entering the house they are disarmed, treated with a few drams and a bit of tobacco, and after the pipe has been plyed about for some time they relate the news with great deliberation and ceremony relaxing from their usual taciturnity in proportion to the quantity of Rum they have swallowed, till at length their voices are drowned in a general clamour. When their lodges are erected by the women they receive a present of Rum, and the whole Band drink during 24 hours and sometimes much longer. When the drinking match has subsided they begin to trade."

Trading was done on credit; an Indian hunter was given a gun, powder, shot and other necessities, which he swore to pay for with the returns from his winter traplines. The debt was reckoned in terms of beaver skins, or *plus* (pronounced and often spelled "plews"). A gun had to be repaid with 14 *plus* and a blanket with six, while two *plus* would settle for such small items as a beaver trap, a kettle or a length of cloth.

The most valuable item of barter was distilled spirits, which the traders watered down to suit the tastes—and the alcoholic tolerance—of the various tribes. For the veteran tipplers of the Saulteaux tribe near Lake Superior, for example, eight or nine quarts of 180-proof spirits were mixed with enough water to fill a nine-gallon keg. For the less-experienced Western tribes, four or five quarts of spirits were usually sufficient to make a keg of "Blackfoot rum."

Whatever the mixture, the concoction drove the Indians to debauchery, fighting, occasional murders and a few sizable raids. Recorded a trader on a Red River post south of Lake Winnipeg: "Indians having asked for liquor, and promised to decamp and hunt well, I gave them some. Grand Gueule stabbed Capot Rouge, Le Boeuf stabbed his young wife in the arm, Little Shell almost beat his old mother's brains out with a club, and there was terrible fighting among them. I sowed garden seeds."

Though the rum trade was at best irresponsible, it detracted but little from the constructive relations between the red

men and the traders. Besides commercial pelts, the Indians contributed corn, pemmican, wild rice, moccasins and the indispensable canoe. Indians guided the traders through the maze of waterways, showed them how to fish through holes in the ice, and taught them the ways of winter travel in the frigid north country.

An even greater Indian contribution to the trader was the woman who became his wife and the mother of his children. For a few blankets, an Indian father would gladly sell his daughter, who might be no more than 12 years old. Few *voyageurs* had any qualms about making a buy, or reselling the chattel. A departing *voyageur* who could not find a buyer for his woman might simply abandon her. Still, after several years and a couple of children, many a *voyageur* discovered that his Indian alliance had become permanent and deeply felt. Large numbers of *voyageurs* returned to their Indian mates for 20 or 30 winters, and as the fur trade spread, their descendants—known as half-breeds, mixed-bloods and Métis—became the backbone of numerous frontier settlements throughout Canada.

In their amicable relations with the Indians and in myriad other ways, Canada's fur men were far different from their American counterparts. The Americans had been galvanized into action in 1806, when Lewis and Clark returned from their pathfinding exploration with glowing reports of the new opportunities presented by the fur trade. Among those taking an avid interest in that prospect was one Manuel Lisa, a black-browed bravo of Spanish blood who would become the most prominent and one of the most controversial of the entrepreneurs seeking wealth in the kingdom of the beaver.

Although old records show that he was born in New Orleans, little else is known of Lisa until 1798 when he arrived in St. Louis at the age of 26. There he seems to have dabbled in government contracts and bribes, dealt in slaves, trafficked in contraband, and engaged in his lifelong habit of making enemies. "Rascality," wrote one of his employees, "set on every feature of his dark-complexioned Mexican face."

Whatever his faults, Lisa was both farsighted and courageous. In the spring of 1807, after assaying the Lewis and Clark report, he bought two keelboats and hired 50 men to accompany him to the upper reaches of the Missouri River, or Big Muddy as it was called. Once there, according to Lisa's plan, the men would become trappers. This was

a radical departure from the fur business of Canada and the Lower Missouri, where Indians harvested the pelts. But Lisa had little choice; Lewis and Clark had made it clear that the Indians of the upper regions of the Missouri were warriors with a considerably keener interest in taking human scalps than the skin of such an odd little beast as the beaver.

And so, off went Lisa and his men to make their fortunes in the vast emptiness that spread out from the banks of the Big Muddy. In running the gauntlet of Indian tribes that lived along the river, Lisa used guile whenever possible. At one point, he went ashore himself and walked through 20 miles of scattered Mandan villages, handing out gifts to distract the chiefs while his tiny flotilla slipped safely by.

On other occasions, a show of force was prudent. Once, a great mob of war-painted Assiniboins—apprised of Lisa's approach by scouts—painted themselves for war and gathered along the shore. "The prairie," he later told people in St. Louis, "was red with them." Lisa coolly loaded a swivel gun and headed directly for the gesticulating warriors, sending them "tumbling over each other" by loosing a blast over their heads.

This West Coast trapper dressed himself up in a gaudy but warm Cossack costume.

THE
TRAPPER'S GUIDE;
A MANUAL OF INSTRUCTIONS

For Capturing all kinds of Fur-Bearing Animals, and Curing their Skins; with Observations on the Fur-Trade, Hints on Life in the Woods, and Narratives of Trapping and Hunting Excursions.

To aspiring 19th Century trappers, the title page above introduced the imaginative works of Sewell Newhouse, an Oneida, New York, businessman who tried to cash in on the fur boom by his own unique methods.

Newhouse's manual, *The Trapper's Guide,* was dedicated to "poor men who are looking out for pleasant work and ways of making money." Not only was trapping profitable, he told readers, but it would transform anyone into "a stouter and healthier man." The author admitted that he had a vested interest in boosting fur trapping since he manufactured a widely sold steel trap *(below).* But he also itemized equipment such as snowshoes, tents and even canoes that could be bought from other sources.

While Newhouse's idealized trapper at right bore little resemblance to rugged mountain men — even to those who had developed into backwoods dudes *(left)* — nevertheless *The Trapper's Guide* was genuinely useful. Newhouse advised would-be trappers to work in pairs, each packing 50 pounds of equipment including traps, fishing tackle and plenty of food. Such a team, he said, could "make five hundred dollars in a trapping season."

The Newhouse beaver trap was a major improvement over previous snares. When an animal stepped on the disk, the steel jaws snapped shut and the leaf springs on either side flew up to lock them as shown.

"Snowshoes are indispensable to the trapper wherever deep snows prevail," Newhouse advised. To put on a snowshoe, the trapper wound the strap around his boot, then knotted the ends behind his ankle.

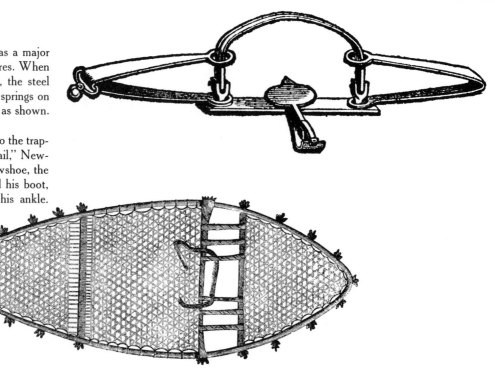

This illustration from *The Trapper's Guide* showed a highly romanticized view of a grubby, uncomfortable profession. Not only was this dandified trapper absurdly clad for the wilderness, but real trappers did not shoot their prey, because bullets tore up the fur.

Newhouse praised the dugout canoe as "strong, serviceable, durable," though many trappers found it heavy to carry.

The birchbark canoe, "preferred on streams where portaging is necessary," was sewn together and sealed with pine pitch.

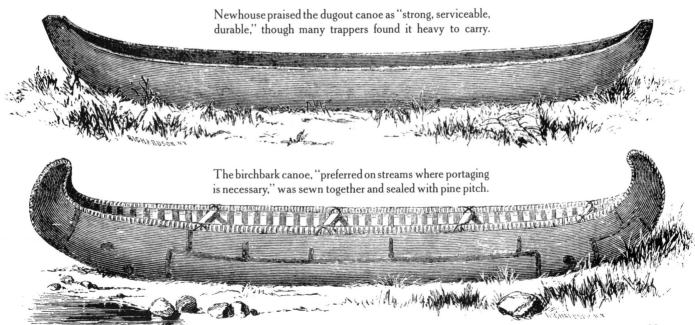

An Indian guide converses with two trappers in this 1830s painting by Alfred Jacob Miller. The ambivalent relationship between red men and white men veered from butchery to brotherhood.

Even more troublesome was the great river itself, and Lisa's men fought it yard by hard-won yard, pushing with their poles from running boards or hauling from the bank on the long cable, or *cordelle*, that was attached to the keelboats' masts. Miseries and hazards abounded; submerged, waterlogged trees threatened the vessels, and both crafts and crew were imperiled by drifting trees and caving banks.

Yet on they went, eventually turning up at the Yellowstone River and, in November, setting up camp at the entrance of the Bighorn River. There, Lisa's prescience and perseverance paid off: The Yellowstone country was alive with beaver, and his new system of using white trappers proved more productive than he had dared to imagine. Back in St. Louis by August 1808 with a small

fortune in pelts, Lisa set up the Missouri Fur Company, and the very next year sent no fewer than 350 men upstream in a fleet of 13 keelboats and barges. In the decade that followed, Lisa traveled an astonishing 26,000 miles on the Missouri, ascending and descending the great river a dozen times, while building an empire of furs and establishing the Big Muddy as an enduring artery of western commerce. In 1820, he returned to St. Louis in failing health, and on August 12 the venturesome life of Manuel Lisa, 47, finally came to an end in a comfortable bed in a health spa.

There was no lack of candidates to replace Lisa as king of the fur country. On February 13, 1822, a memorable ad was placed in the help-wanted section of the *Missouri Gazette* by Missouri's Lieutenant Governor William Ashley, soliciting "enterprising young men" who were willing to go into the wilderness. Ashley attracted an astounding group of youthful nomads whose names in later years would read like a roll call of the West's great mountain men: Jedediah Smith, Jim Bridger, William and Milton Sublette, Tom Fitzpatrick, James Clyman, Antoine Leroux and Edward Rose.

They were a ragtag bunch. Young Jim Clyman was working as a surveyor, and Jim Bridger had been an apprentice blacksmith. William Sublette was serving as the underpaid constable in St. Charles, Missouri (he sold his most valuable possession, a bedstead, for one dollar upon joining Ashley); his brother Milton, only 21, had not done much of anything. Tom Fitzpatrick (who would become known to Indians as "Broken Hand" after his wrist was shattered in an accident with a gun) was born to gentlefolk in Ireland's County Cavan, while Antoine Leroux was of French and Spanish blood, with a dab of Indian mixed in.

In all, Ashley recruited about 70 men, and in the spring of 1823 he led them out of St. Louis, planning to follow the Missouri north to the Yellowstone region, where the party would disperse and set about trapping beaver. But on June 2, near the present border of North and South Dakota, the fledgling mountain men were attacked by a howling horde of some 600 Arikara warriors, who killed 12 of Ashley's men and put the others to flight.

Retreating downstream, Ashley sent off an urgent plea for help to the U.S. Army. In response, Colonel Henry Leavenworth assembled about 200 men of the U.S. Sixth Infantry and started upriver. Along the way, the relief force—which came to be called, rather grandly, the Missouri Legion—was joined by about 700 Sioux allies, along with various trappers and other white men, bringing the total to at least 1,100. But Leavenworth, for all his overwhelming superiority, was at best a timid commander, and after some skirmishing the Arikaras slipped out of their villages at night, leaving the Missouri Legionnaires as conquerers of no more than some empty huts.

Having been outfought and outfoxed, the whites suffered a loss of prestige among all the river tribes, who now closed down the traditional routes to the mountains. But the setback turned out to be a blessing in disguise: If Ashley still meant to enter the fur business, his only option was to head directly west, overland. He did precisely that—and in the doing his men rode a new wave of exploration that pushed deep into the vastness of the Rockies and beyond.

Relations between the white men and red men were not always confrontational, however. Often the Indians proved helpful, teaching the mountain men much about the mysteries of the wilderness. They found the trappers apt students in the use of sign language, the system used by Indians to overcome differences in tribal dialects. The white man also became adept at reading the language of the trail—"sign," it was called—what a broken twig, a dislodged stone, the dew missing from a leaf, a scuff mark in the dust might indicate, both in the recent past and for the immediate future. The trappers came to know, among many things, that furrows in among the hoof prints of the Indian ponies were made by lodgepoles and signified Indians on the move with their women and belongings, and not a party of young braves on the warpath. Such information was crucial for survival in a merciless land that swiftly punished the inexpert and the unwary.

Like their Canadian brethren, many mountain men also found mates among the Indians. Although one of them claimed to have paid $2,000 in beaver skins for a chief's daughter, the usual rate was much lower. Among the Mandans, the value of even the most beautiful girl was, according to one observer, "only equal perhaps to two horses, a gun with powder and ball for a year, five or six pounds of beads, or a couple of gallons of whiskey." Availing himself of some such bargain, Edward Rose, one of Ashley's original crew, enjoyed a harem of four wives as well as the rank of chief.

But for most trappers, mistrust and misunderstanding of the Indians never lay far from the surface. Expressing his opinion of Longfellow's heroic Hiawatha, Jim Bridger sourly remarked that "no such Injun" ever lived. During one painful period, Bridger went about his business for three years with a Blackfoot arrowhead embedded in the muscles of his back. When he finally found a frontier doctor to remove the three-inch iron barb, the physician marveled that the wound had not putrified. "In the mountains, Doctor," Bridger said, "meat don't spoil." On another occasion, Bridger went into the brush to scout an Indian war party that had taken cover there. He returned to his white companions a few minutes later with what one of them recalled as a "warm, bloody scalp."

Of all the Indian tribes, the Blackfeet and the Arikaras were the most implacably hostile, and toward them the mountain men responded in kind. On one occasion, while trapping alone in the Yellowstone country, a veteran called "Old Bill" Williams was set upon by three Blackfoot braves who stole his rifle, his mule and his

By the early 1830s, fur trappers were both pleasurably and violently acquainted with a vast area of the West. The map below locates their far-flung world, including sites of Indian brawls and annual rendezvous.

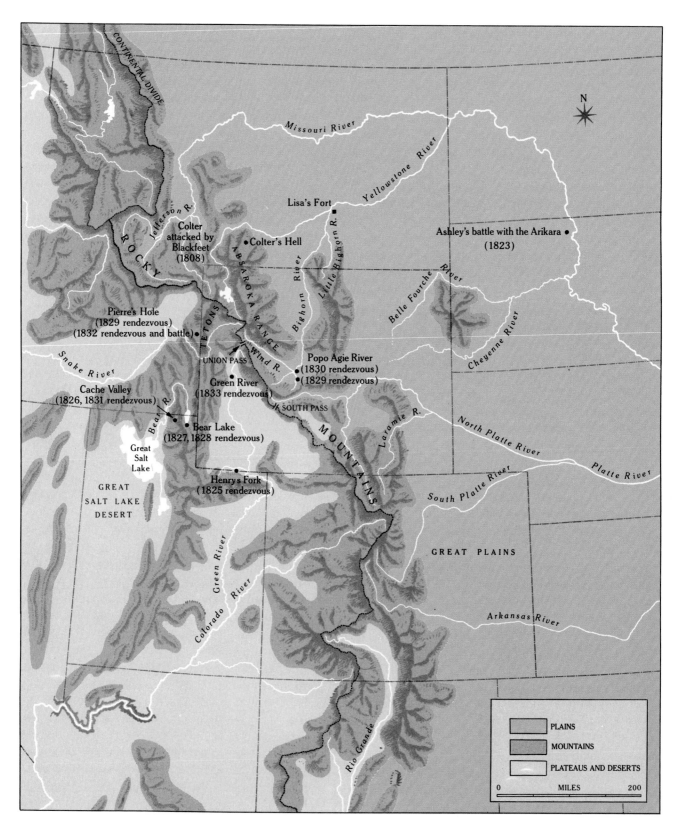

beaver pelts. With arrow wounds in his shoulder and thigh, Williams escaped into a thicket.

He still had his knife, however, and after pursuing the thieves for four days he sneaked into their camp by night and scalped two of them without waking the third. Then, after stirring the fire to make a little light, he roused the remaining Blackfoot, who opened his eyes to see the bloody scalps of his comrades dangling before his face. The terrified Indian took off like an antelope. Later, asked by his nephew why he had let the last Indian escape, Old Bill replied: "Ef I'd a kilt that Injun, thyar wouldn't a been nobody left ter tell them Blackfeet how them bucks had gone under nor who'd a rubbed 'em out."

For all the dangers faced by the trappers in the form of Indians and bears, far more fell victim to the rigors of their calling. Men died of drowning or tetanus; they fell off cliffs or were bitten by rattlesnakes. Even their diet of meat posed a mortal threat: *le mal de vache*—literally, cow sickness—a form of dysentery caused by a steady intake of fat meat, was sometimes fatal. Toting up the casualties from all causes, James Ohio Pattie, a trapper in the southern mountains in 1826, claimed that of the 116 men who left Santa Fe that year, only 16 survived until the next. In later years, trapper Antoine Robidoux, then 62, was able to count only three men living out of 300 he knew to have roamed the Rockies.

Why did mountain men go out again and again? Adventure, in many cases. Escape, in others—a yearning to be alone in the wilderness when it was still truly wild. Some men simply liked the life, while a few cherished the company of Indians, or relished the notion of living the Indian life themselves for a while. Most commonly, however, the motivation was much the same as it has always been with so many men everywhere: money. A good trapper might return from the wilds with three or four hundred pelts. After unloading his furs he might have between a thousand and two thousand dollars in his pocket. This was at a time when a skilled worker, such as a carpenter or a mason, could hope to earn little more than $1.50 a day.

In effect, the trappers worked 11 months of the year for the sake of blowing their earnings in one grand debauch. As early as July 1825, William Ashley's far-flung fur men had assembled on the Green River in present-day Wyoming to be paid off for their pelts and re-outfit themselves for the next season. They lounged around for a few weeks, swapping tall tales, drinking whiskey and pleasuring themselves with Indian girls. Thus it was that the rendezvous came into existence and continued at various sites long after Bill Sublette and others bought out Ashley in 1826.

Although the rendezvous was the most famous social and business institution of the mountain men, the economics of the affair worked strongly against the trappers, who received two to four dollars a pound for fur that would later bring six to eight dollars in St. Louis, the hub of fur-trading activity in the United States.

The trapper could do nothing to raise the price because the rendezvous was his only market. Furthermore, he had to buy all his goods for the next season from the agents of St. Louis suppliers, who operated a back-country version of the company store, complete with sky-high prices. The average St. Louis price for tobacco, coffee or sugar was ten cents a pound; lead cost six cents and gunpowder seven cents. At the rendezvous, each of those items cost two dollars. Worse yet, that essential commodity—whiskey—was originally purchased in St. Louis for 30 cents a gallon, cut with water and sold to the mountain men at three dollars a pint.

But many of the trappers still thought it was all worthwhile. During the rendezvous they found what they had yearned for all year: company, conversation, new clothes, dry shoes, a variety of women, tobacco and booze. For one glorious month they talked, bragged, fought, gambled, fornicated and drank in a mighty exhibit of manliness before, broke and drained, they turned back into the mountains for another perilous year.

In celebrating the rendezvous with such unfettered abandon, mountain men seemed to be offering their own raucous protest against the impending death of their way of life. Sizable numbers of them did not start probing the wilderness until the 1820s; two decades later, with the fur-bearing animals largely trapped out, their day was over. Now it was time to move on to other pursuits, from guiding soldiers to building railroads to fighting Indians with the U.S. Army. They would turn the West over to its next generation of pioneers—Americans who had already begun to view it as a potential home, a place where they could carve out farms, start businesses and raise their families.

Mounted Franciscan friars bearing crosses lead a procession forth from the California mission of San Carlos Borromeo in the early 1800s.

68

"The best land in all these Indias"

When Cabeza de Vaca, a lost Spanish explorer, emerged from the wilderness in 1536 after eight years of wandering through parts of the vast country that was to become the American West, he reported, "It is, no doubt, the best land in all these Indias. Indeed, the land needs no circumstance to make it blessed." Later generations of Westerners could consider it twice-blessed—by the fruits of Spanish culture and labor as well as by natural endowment.

For 300 years the territory north of Mexico was part of a vast Spanish empire that, at one point, covered half the known world. The first adventurers to penetrate the region went there in search of gold and silver. Although these riches turned out to be only a glittering mirage, missionaries, ranchers and farmers later made their way into the wilderness, bringing with them their customs and laws, art and architecture, animals and agriculture. And when their Anglo-Saxon counterparts eventually arrived on the scene, they frequently found, as one observer put it, that "the backbreaking work of pioneering was already done for them. They came into an established community."

Cattle, poultry and goods heaped on two-wheeled ox-drawn *carretas* await sale or barter in San Antonio's Market Plaza, as traders from outlying ranchos pause for an alfresco repast. Town plazas continued to be centers of commerce in the Southwest long after Spanish rule had come to an end.

At seaside festivities near Santa Barbara, California, aristocratic rancheros and their families watch as a dauntless *vaquero* riding at full gallop swoops down to pull a partially buried rooster from the sand. Other popular horseback sports included throwing bulls by the tail and roping grizzly bears.

4. The desperate struggle for Texas

On July 15, 1821, a 27-year-old law student named Stephen F. Austin bade a last farewell to the United States, and guided his horse across the Sabine River into the vast open wilderness of Spanish Texas. Slight of build, modest in manner, Austin scarcely seemed cut out for the brawny labor of empire-building. But he was driven by a deep sense of duty. Scarcely five weeks earlier Moses Austin, Stephen's father, had expired of pneumonia, his fondest dream unfulfilled. In his death-bed delirium the old man had talked of it again—a visionary scheme to found an American colony on Texas soil.

The potential was almost beyond imagining. An expanse of land swept westward from Louisiana, across the Red and Sabine rivers, rolling away in gentle woods and prairie to the Rio Grande River and the Rocky Mountain foothills. The canebrakes along the Gulf Coast reached 25 feet overhead, attesting to the richness of the deep black soil. The air in the high country was crisp and bracing, the streams ran clear and sweet. Herds of deer and buffalo, wild turkey and other game roamed freely. What is more, the entire region was virtually uninhabited.

There were difficulties, to be sure. Texas at the time was a frontier territory of Mexico, thus an imperial possession of the Spanish crown. And the Spanish did not look kindly on American settlement. Already the Americans were flooding into the Louisiana Territory, once Spanish land, and spreading out, as a Spanish statesman put it, "like oil on cloth." Just two years earlier, Spain had been forced to give up Florida to the aggressive Yankees.

Still, as Stephen Austin rode west he carried in his pocket a charter, obtained by Moses from the Spaniards just weeks before his death, which offered title to 200,000 acres in Texas. For his part of the bargain, the elder Austin had agreed to become a citizen of Mexico and pledge allegiance to the Spanish king. His colonists would also live under Mexican law and pay Mexican taxes.

Traveling on an old traders' route, Stephen Austin forded the Brazos and Colorado rivers, and noted the lush stands of cottonwood and pecan trees that lined their banks. Some 400 miles into the heart of Texas he rode past the deserted mission of San Antonio de Valero, soon to be known as the Alamo. Just beyond lay his goal, San Antonio, a sleepy territorial capital of 800 souls. Austin presented his papers to the Spanish governor, Antonio de Martinez.

Governor Martinez received him cordially, impressed by young Austin's sober mien and obvious filial devotion. He quickly confirmed the grant. In return, Austin pledged his undying loyalty to the Spanish crown. Together, the two men worked out a plan for distributing land in the colony. Each settler would get 640 acres, plus additional acreage for his wife and children. Then Austin headed southeast, toward the coast, to pick out the site for his enterprise.

He found what he wanted in the fertile lower reaches of the Brazos River—"the most favored region I had ever seen," as he described it. On a timbered bluff 15 miles inland from the Gulf Coast swamps, he staked out his future capital, San Felipe de Austin. Then he began the hard work of bringing his colony to life: raising capital, attracting settlers, shipping in tools and provisions, and seeing to the welfare of all concerned.

By the spring of 1822, more than 150 pioneering farmers had begun clearing land in the colony. All had

Stephen Austin reaches for a rifle as a scout bursts in with word of an Indian raid on San Felipe, Austin's first colony. The men, gathered in 1824 to map boundaries before issuing title to a parcel of land, included Austin's land commissioner, Baron de Bastrop (left edge of painting).

been carefully screened by Stephen himself, who spared no effort to keep out the ordinary run of uncouth, lawless frontiersmen. "No drunkard, no gambler, no profane swearer, no idler" would be tolerated, he declared. He felt personally responsible to the Mexican government for the conduct of his people.

The early settlers needed all the dedication they could muster. Trees had to be felled, log cabins built, crops planted. Raids by the local Karankawa Indians were a constant threat, and a number of settlers died that first year defending their homesteads. Nor did it help that a vital shipment of tools, grain and other provisions foundered on Galveston Island, with a loss of all cargo. Then there was the political turmoil within Mexico itself.

On a visit to San Antonio, Austin learned that the citizens of Mexico had revolted against their arrogant overseas masters. They had overthrown the Spanish government in Mexico City, and had set up an independent state. As a result, the original grant for Austin's colony was nullified. This meant a 1,200-mile journey to Mexico City to negotiate a new grant.

Austin remained in the Mexican capital nearly a year, while the new congress debated the larger issues of government policy. He polished his Spanish, courted key politicians, and took a lively interest in local affairs. The Mexicans were impressed. This sober Yankee confounded every stereotype of the brash American land *empresario*. When the new grant was issued, its terms were more favorable than Austin could have anticipated.

The original colony had already been expanded, by earlier agreement, so that it now encompassed 18,000 square miles. Of this, most settlers would now receive 4,605 acres, instead of the 640 acres originally allotted, and they would pay no taxes for the next six years. Austin himself would get 100,000 acres for his own use. He was also named the region's Civil Commandant, or chief government administrator.

Over the next decade the colony flourished. By 1830 it had attracted 4,000 settlers, most of them cattle ranchers and corn farmers. Another crop, cotton, was fast becoming important. Cotton yields in the rich bottomlands along the rivers were soon running as high as 2,000 pounds per acre, and one grower was said to have realized $10,000 on a single year's harvest.

With the scent of high profits wafting across the border, other *empresarios* from America began moving in, obtaining grants and setting up colonies. Some 16,000 Americans were living in Texas by 1830—about four times the Mexican population. And though many of the newcomers were as temperate and industrious as Austin could have wished, many were not. All manner of buckskin-clad adventurers started drifting in—"leatherstockings," Austin called them. Some merely sought opportunities that had eluded them back home, others were escaping the sheriff; few had much patience with the niceties of Mexican law. In the face of this influx, control began slipping from Austin's hands.

The man who would seize the banner of American leadership rode into Texas on December 2, 1832, splashing across the Red River from Indian Territory to the north. Sam Houston was a tall, powerfully muscled buccaneer of a man, exactly Austin's age, and also a lawyer; in character, the two men were as different as fire from frost. Houston rode alone, astride a high-stepping broom-tailed mare, his bedroll lashed behind him. In his pocket he carried a commission from his friend Andrew Jackson, President of the United States. The President wanted Houston to confer with certain Comanche chieftains, and persuade them to quit raiding across the border.

Houston's personal purpose was to start a new life. Like many of the new breed of Texans, Houston was a man with a past—in his case, an illustrious one. He had been a general of militia, a U.S. Congressman and the Governor of Tennessee. Keen of mind, brave beyond measure, possessed of profound notions of patriotism and honor, he wore the scars of his military campaigns like so many battlefield decorations. He also had a volcanic temper, and a huge thirst for whiskey. This, plus a scandal in his married life, had combined to bring about his eclipse.

Houston was no stranger to adversity. His father had frittered away a family fortune, leaving Houston's mother and nine children nothing more than a satchelful of debts when he expired in 1806. The family then moved across the Alleghenies into Tennessee, where they cleared land for a farm at the edge of the wilderness.

Sam was 14 at the time—even then a proud, restless spirit who chafed at family chores and schoolwork.

(The one exception was studying the classics, which he adored.) At 17 he slipped away from home to explore the nearby countryside. He stumbled into a camp of Cherokee Indians, who adopted him as their own. The clan's chief, known to white men as John Jolly, conferred on Sam the Indian name Co-lon-neh, the Raven—a bird honored for its sagacity and boldness.

Weeks passed. Sam's mother was distraught; family and neighbors scoured the woods. Eventually Sam's two older brothers found him at the Indian camp, sitting under a tree reading Homer's *Iliad*. Marking his place, he coolly informed them that he "liked the wild liberty of the Red men better than the tyranny of my own brothers"—and added that he preferred to read in peace.

For the better part of three years Houston lived with the Cherokees—"wandering," as he later wrote, "along the banks of streams, side by side with some Indian maiden, sheltered by the deep woods." Then in 1813 this sylvan idyll came to an abrupt end. A bloodthirsty faction of Creek Indians was rampaging through what is now Alabama, and the U.S. Army was preparing to march in. For a young man with Houston's zest for action, it was a call to arms; at age 20, he enlisted.

His moment of glory came the following March 27, at the Battle of Horseshoe Bend on the Tallapoosa River. Only a third lieutenant, Houston led a charge against a thousand heavily armed Creek, taking an arrow in his thigh and two rifle balls in his shoulder while helping to subdue the foe. His courage and leadership caught the notice of the commanding general, fellow Tennessean Andrew Jackson. Promoted to second lieutenant, Houston decided to make a career as a soldier.

Because of his friendship with the Cherokees, Houston was assigned the post of army subagent for Cherokee affairs. Again he called attention to himself. The War Department had been slow in granting the Cherokees some promised annuities, and to speed matters Houston led a delegation of tribal chiefs to Washington. For the occasion he dressed, like them, in breechcloth and blanket. His superiors were not amused.

Then a more serious matter arose—a charge that Houston was smuggling slaves through Indian lands. An investigation proved the allegation to be totally false; in fact, Houston was trying to stop the smuggling. But having been cleared of all charges, Houston wanted more: an apology from the Secretary of War. When none came, he resigned his commission.

Houston settled in Nashville, read 18 months of law in half a year, passed the Tennessee bar and set up his own law practice. From there he moved into politics. With his magnetic personality and quick grasp of local issues, he rose with astonishing rapidity: Attorney General of Tennessee in 1819, a commander of Tennessee militia in 1821 and, two years later, United States Congressman.

His mentor in this ascent was none other than his old army chief, Andrew Jackson. Already a national hero, Jackson pulled the strings of power in Tennessee, was himself a U.S. Senator, and would soon run for President. Riding in part on Jackson's coattails, Houston in 1827 was elected governor of Tennessee.

To make it all complete, Houston took a bride—the shy and sheltered Eliza Allen. The result was catastrophe; within three months the marriage was broken. Eliza returned to her parents, and Houston, drinking heavily, retired into seclusion. As to the cause of their separation, no explanation was given. "This is a painful, but it is a private affair," he declared. The public did not agree. Had Houston's drinking proved

"Greater than Caesar, nearly equal to Thor!"

Even as a youth Jim Bowie was the sort to inspire awe. Born to a rugged frontier family in 1796, he grew up on the Louisiana bayous, and by the time he was 18—raw-boned big and rawhide tough—he was already riding alligators and stalking deer with a lasso. Over the next two decades Bowie made a fortune in slave-smuggling and land speculation, courted society ladies and fought Indians with equal flourish—before he went to a hero's death in the defense of the Alamo. But it was as a knife fighter that Bowie became a legend in his time.

In the early 1800s the knife was the preeminent sidearm—more efficient by far than the muzzle-loading pistols of the day. Men carried everything from pocketknives to butcher knives. But the favorite combat knife was the blade designed in 1830 by Jim Bowie to stab like a dagger, slice like a razor and chop like a cleaver.

The foundation for Bowie's fame as a fighter rests on two battles. The first took place on a Mississippi River sand bar near Natchez in 1827 when two pistol duelists faced off to settle a grudge. After the duelists fired at each other twice, missing both times, fighting broke out among the

Jim Bowie, about 35 years old

10 opposing seconds. One was Bowie, armed with a butcher knife (he had yet to design the Bowie knife).

In the melee, Bowie was shot in the hip and shoulder, stabbed in the chest and beaten on the head. But before he collapsed he disemboweled one assailant, slashed another to ribbons and helped his comrades put the opposing seconds to rout.

The second battle—in which Bowie first tested the weapon that bore his name—took place in Texas in

1830. Bowie was ambushed by three knife-wielding assassins hired by a saloon-keeper he had once wounded in a fight. The first antagonist to reach Bowie was nearly beheaded by one stroke of Bowie's heavy blade. The next inflicted a slight wound on Bowie's leg before Bowie ripped open his belly. The third tried to flee, but Bowie, according to one overenthusiastic account, "split his skull to the shoulders" with a single blow.

Not all of Bowie's storied confrontations were bloody. Henry Clay was witness to one incident and enjoyed recounting it ever after. Clay was on a stagecoach ride in 1832, during which an obnoxious fellow ignored a lady's request to extinguish his pipe—and suddenly found another passenger, by the name of Bowie, holding a monstrous knife to his throat. He reconsidered.

Clay later celebrated Bowie as "the greatest fighter in the Southwest." But Clay's appraisal was pale compared to that of British historian Thomas Carlyle, who, hearing about Bowie, exclaimed: "By Hercules! The man was greater than Caesar—nay, nearly equal to Odin or Thor! The Texans ought to build him an altar."

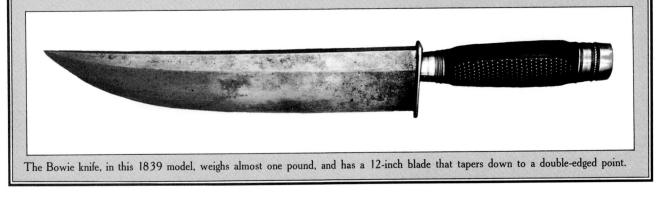

The Bowie knife, in this 1839 model, weighs almost one pound, and has a 12-inch blade that tapers down to a double-edged point.

intolerable? Did he beat his wife in a jealous rage? Placard-bearing crowds picketed the state house, demanding answers. Stunned and humiliated, Houston tendered his resignation.

It was time to go home to the Cherokees. By now the tribe had been moved to a reservation in Arkansas Territory, so Houston boarded a river steamer to join them. He drank his way up the Arkansas River, brooding on his sorrows and boasting of the glorious future that awaited him in the West. One of the passengers was the famed knife fighter Jim Bowie, who had settled in Texas and was extolling its riches. "I will conquer Mexico or Texas," Houston is said to have shouted, in a boozy moment.

Instead, he moved in with the Cherokees, and rapidly went to seed. He earned a new Indian name: Oo-tse-tee Ar-dee-tah-skee, or Big Drunk. Twice he sobered up enough to journey to Washington to complain about the dishonesty of Indian agents. And on his second trip, his life took another sharp turn.

New charges of corruption had surfaced in Congress, and Houston's name was mentioned. Outraged at this accusation—which was false—Houston sought out the man who had made it, and thrashed him with a hickory cane. Assaulting a Congressman was a breach both of law and of Congressional decorum, and Houston was ordered to stand trial in the House. He was found guilty, of course; but so eloquent was his defense that the entire body rose to its feet, cheering wildly. The ovation sent a thrill of triumph to the very core of his being.

Burning with enthusiasm, Houston now turned his attention to Texas, his mind awhirl with schemes and possibilities. The townsmen of Nacogdoches named him their representative to a Texas state convention, soon to be held at San Felipe. Life was looking up. "Texas is the finest portion of the globe that has ever blessed my vision," Houston wrote in a letter to his cousin.

But Texas was in trouble, brought on by continuing turmoil in Mexican national affairs. In the years since the revolt from Spain, the reins of government had passed to and fro as factions rose and fell. Monarchists and republicans, liberals and conservatives, Centralists and Federalists all battled for supremacy, aided by a succession of military strongmen with their own private armies. By the early 1830s, the government had been taken over by a dictator, Anastacio Bustamante, who was intent on bringing all Mexico under rigid control.

Already Bustamante had decreed the military occupation of Texas by government troops. In 1831 he sent a small force of soldiers to take over the garrison at Anahuac, a small American community on Galveston Bay. The colonists, outraged at this affront to their liberty, marched on the garrison while another group of Americans clashed with a Mexican garrison at Velasco, 80 miles to the southwest. There, in a short, sharp fight, five soldiers and 10 colonists were killed before the Mexicans threw down their arms and fled. Thus flowed the first blood in what would soon become the Texas Revolution. The date was June 26, 1832.

One of the generals who had helped bring Bustamante to power was a tall, theatrically handsome soldier named Antonio López de Santa Anna, a self-styled "Napoleon of the West." With his regal air, bemedaled uniforms and gaudy cocked hats, he seemed the very image of heroic destiny. He had trounced the Spanish at Tampico Bay, set up and then unseated several Mexican heads of state. Now he turned on Bustamante. In January 1833 Santa Anna marched into Mexico City, sent the dictator fleeing, and had himself elected president.

The Texans were jubilant. Mexico's new ruler had billed himself as a champion of democracy and self-government. So when the Texas delegates convened at San Felipe, on April 1, 1833, they expressed their support. Then, relying on Santa Anna's liberal stance, they drew up a state constitution based on American democratic principles. Sam Houston helped draft it, and Stephen Austin then carried it to Mexico City, along with some other resolutions, to submit to Santa Anna.

This time Austin's reception was anything but friendly. Santa Anna, once in office, lost no time in showing his true colors. No liberal at all, he was turning out to be a rank opportunist, greedy for wealth and fame. Stories began to circulate—of his womanizing, of his taste for opium and, most tellingly, of his unbridled lust for power. "Were I made God," the new president once said, "I should wish to be something more." A man of this temper was hardly prepared to look with favor upon the noisy, obstreperous Americans.

Austin spent a frustrating 11 weeks in Mexico City, shunted from office to office, without ever getting to see

Santa Anna. Finally, when an audience was arranged, the president granted a few grudging concessions, and reversed an earlier decree that had prohibited further American immigration into Texas. But to the Texans' plea for self-government, he refused to listen.

There then occurred one of those odd twists of fate that change the course of history. While cooling his heels in the outer chambers of Mexican officialdom, Austin had addressed an ill-conceived letter to some officials in San Antonio. In it, he blasted Santa Anna's administration, and declared that Texas should make its own laws whether Mexico City liked it or not. "This country is lost if its inhabitants do not take its affairs into their own hands," he wrote. By a roundabout route the letter ended up on Santa Anna's desk. The president angrily decided that it was a call to rebellion; Austin was arrested, and clapped into prison in Mexico City.

A dangerous quiet settled over Texas. One American faction had in fact been urging that Texas secede from Mexico, and become her own republic, but cooler heads had always prevailed. Still, the impulse to revolution bubbled and seethed. It came to a head in mid-1835, as Santa Anna began tightening his control over the Mexican states. Texas at the time came under the official jurisdiction of a neighboring state, Coahuila, whose governor opposed the Santa Anna regime. So the president sent his brother-in-law, General Martín Perfecto de Cós, to take over Coahuila. Then he himself made plans to march north, on a punitive sweep across Texas to discipline the upstart Americans.

As news of these arrangements filtered north, the Texans began loading their rifles. A flamboyant young lawyer named William Barret Travis rallied a force of 25 volunteers and headed for Anahuac. He arrived on June 29, 1835, and fired a single cannon shot at the Mexican garrison there. Next morning the garrison's commander surrendered his 44 men and promised to leave Texas. Travis returned to San Felipe in triumph—only to be condemned for his rashness. An uneasy caution had set in, and the Texans sent an apologetic letter to the commander at Anahuac disclaiming responsibility for the "outrage against the supreme government." Travis was pressured to offer his own apology, but General Cós would not be mollified. He demanded William Travis' arrest—almost surely to face a firing squad. And this the Texans would not submit to.

Events began to outrun plans. Word came that Cós was entering Texas with a force of trained regulars to make good his demands. Then came news that the Mexican commander at San Antonio had sent a detachment of 200 dragoons 70 miles east, to the town of Gonzales, to take from the settlers a small brass cannon given them in 1831 for defense against Indians. Although the cannon was virtually useless, it was important symbolically to keep it from the Mexicans, and the Texans at Gonzales intended to do just that.

As the dragoons neared the town, on October 2, they met a volley of rifle fire from 160 angry Texans, who were lined up at a ford on the Guadalupe River. One Mexican fell dead, and the rest retreated in haste.

The Texas Revolution had begun, and it seemed so easy. By now, Cós was in San Antonio reinforcing the garrison with his 1,400 men. But he had left a small detachment at Goliad, 95 miles to the southeast, to guard ammunition and to keep his supply lines open to the sea. The Texas volunteers pouring into Gonzales attacked Goliad, and they put the Mexicans to rout after a brief skirmish. Aflame with success, the rebels now turned for San Antonio. A ragtag army, scarcely 300-strong, began its march on October 13.

"Buckskin breeches were the nearest approach to uniform there was wide diversity even there," recorded volunteer Noah Smithwick, "some being new and soft and yellow, while others, from long familiarity with rain and grease and dirt, had become hard, black and shiny. Boots being an unknown quantity, some wore shoes and some moccasins . . . . Here a big American horse loomed up above the nimble Spanish pony, there a half-broke mustang pranced beside a sober, methodical mule. A fantastic military array to a casual observer, but the one great purpose animating every heart clothed us in a uniform more perfect to our eyes than was ever donned by regulars on dress parade."

Their leader, by popular election, was none other than Stephen Austin, who by a quirk of Mexican politics had been released from prison under a general amnesty. Austin had returned a changed man. "War is our only recourse. No halfway measures, but war in full," he announced.

Austin was no soldier, but he did know enough to organize his men into companies, and to appoint experienced field commanders. His meager force ap-

proached San Antonio on October 27. The lead company, 90 men under Jim Bowie, scouted ahead, and next day it was attacked by 400 Mexican cavalry. Bowie managed to capture some Mexican field guns, then turned them on his attackers. Sixty Mexicans were killed; the survivors fled; only one Texan was lost.

But not even the most impassioned revolutionary was prepared to risk a direct assault on the 1,400 Mexicans entrenched within the city itself. The Texans settled down to a siege. October slipped into November, and then it was winter. With supplies running short, Austin left for the United States to appeal for war funds and volunteers. Some of the men began drifting back to the warmth of their homes and families, and there was talk of withdrawing. Then Colonel Benjamin Milam, a plucky Welshman from Kentucky, stepped forward.

Milam had sniffed more than his share of gunsmoke, and in all his 47 years he had yet to walk away from a fight. He drew a line in the dust and shouted: "Who will go with old Ben Milam into San Antonio?" Hundreds of voices roared in response.

On the morning of December 5, 1835, the Texans pushed into the city, Milam in the lead. They fought their way from alley to alley, from rooftop to plaza, against heavy artillery fire. On the third day Milam took a bullet in the head, and died instantly, but still the Texans drove on.

Cós began to panic. He was not used to this American style of street fighting, nor to such blazing determination. To make matters worse, the Texans' American-made rifles were proving more accurate than the Mexican muskets. He entrenched his troops in the Alamo mission but their nerve was gone. Casualties were heavy, and the Texans brought up cannon and mercilessly battered the walls.

By the fifth day of fighting, Cós had had enough. He ran up a white flag, and the jubilant Texans accepted his surrender of 1,100 officers and men. Then, in a gesture of overwhelming leniency, the Texans let them go. The Mexican general, promising never again to make war against the settlers, led his army south toward the Rio Grande, after accepting a gift of arms and powder for defense against Indians.

Texas was free to go her own way—or so it now seemed. During the siege of San Antonio, her political leaders had again convened at San Felipe, arguing the issue of statehood versus separatism. The result was a compromise: Texas would continue to oppose the Santa Anna regime, but would remain a loyal state of Mexico, under the Constitution of 1824. Meanwhile, the small Texan army disbanded; the volunteers went home to their businesses and the chores of spring planting.

A few wise heads, however, saw more trouble ahead; among them was Sam Houston. With Cós' humiliating defeat, Houston reasoned, Santa Anna would surely arrive in force to exact retribution; Texas must prepare herself. What she needed was a real army, highly disciplined and trained in the art of war. In the first days of fighting, Houston had issued a stirring call to arms: "The morning of glory is dawning upon us. The work of Liberty has begun." Now, elected at San Felipe to be the state's supreme military commander, he repeated the cry. But hardly anyone listened.

Santa Anna's intentions soon became apparent. By late January he had assembled a massive army at Saltillo, south of the Rio Grande—6,000 highly trained professionals who knew their business and were not likely to run at the first sting of musket shot. On February 16 the first major target was San Antonio, and the Alamo.

To Sam Houston, the Mexican strategy was obvious: a sweep across Texas along El Camino Real. And Houston had his own ideas about meeting his foe. The Texans should feint, skirmish, withdraw, leading the enemy ever

An improvised fortress too large to defend

The fortifications drawn to scale in this view of the Alamo as it appeared on the eve of the siege were the inspiration of Green Jameson, a 29-year-old Texas lawyer turned military engineer.

The most critical structures were the wood and earth platforms that partially protected sharpshooters and artillerymen along the 12-foot-high walls. On the southeast side, Jameson built a palisade of heavy logs to seal off a 75-foot gap between the church and the Low Barracks; he also constructed a semicircular gun position, or "lunette," to guard the south gate. In the southwest corner, he put an 18-pound cannon to command the approach from San Antonio, and spotted remaining guns, ranging from four- to 12-pounders, at other strategic sites. A pair of eight-pounders in the plaza were last-ditch weapons in case the Mexicans broke through.

Makeshift as it was, the Alamo proved a mighty bastion. But its very size contributed to its doom; it sprawled across nearly three acres, giving 183 men a perimeter of about a quarter-mile to defend. It was a task, as one Alamo scholar commented, for which "a thousand men would have barely sufficed."

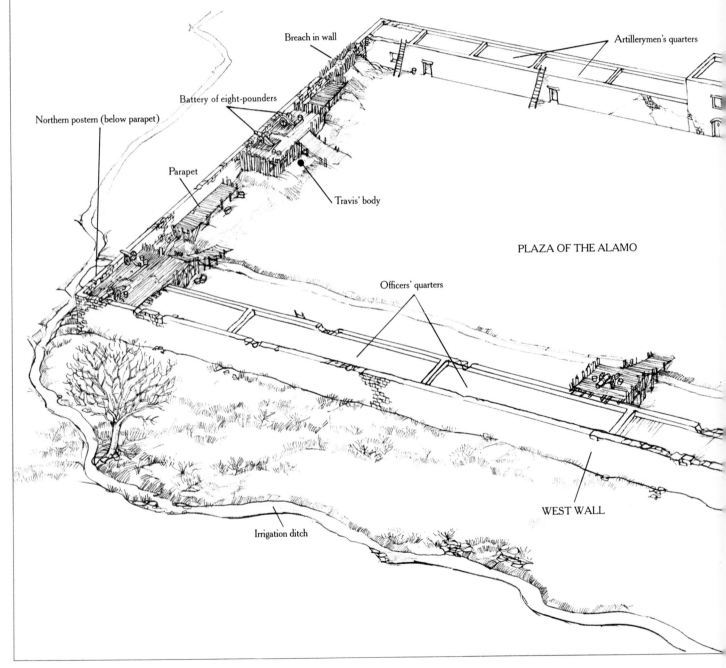

Breach in wall

Artillerymen's quarters

Battery of eight-pounders

Northern postern (below parapet)

Parapet

Travis' body

PLAZA OF THE ALAMO

Officers' quarters

WEST WALL

Irrigation ditch

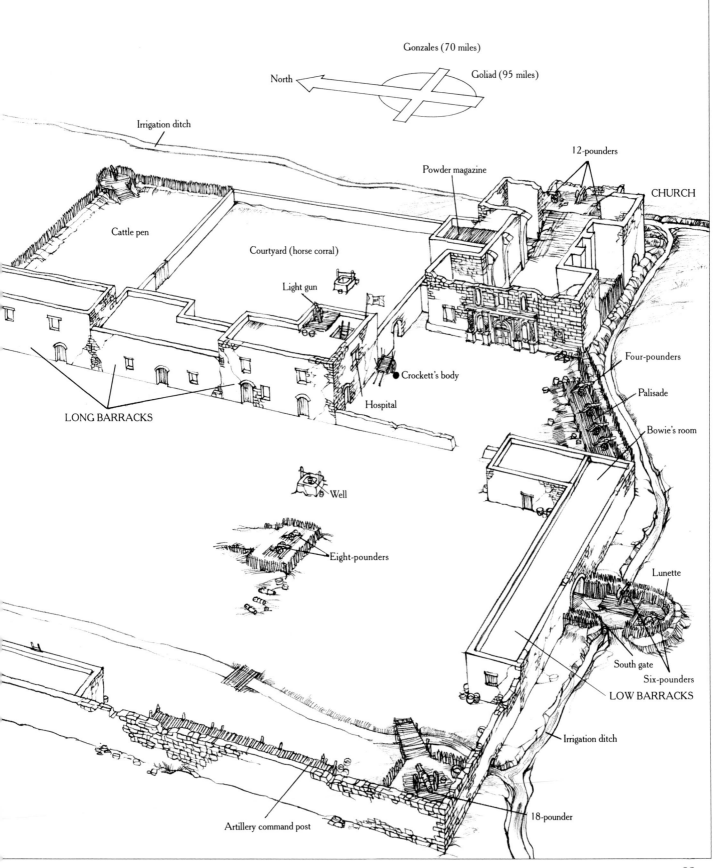

Gonzales (70 miles)

Goliad (95 miles)

North

Irrigation ditch

12-pounders

Powder magazine

CHURCH

Cattle pen

Courtyard (horse corral)

Light gun

Four-pounders

Palisade

Crockett's body

Bowie's room

Hospital

LONG BARRACKS

Well

Eight-pounders

Lunette

South gate

Six-pounders

LOW BARRACKS

Irrigation ditch

Artillery command post

18-pounder

deeper into alien territory, and wait for an opportunity to strike. In no case should they stand in direct confrontation; no lives should be squandered defending San Antonio. To that end, Houston sent his friend Jim Bowie and a 30-man detachment with orders to evacuate the city, and blow up the Alamo.

A token force of 104 volunteers had stayed in San Antonio, and when Bowie arrived these men were busily attempting to build up the Alamo's defenses. The old mission was hardly an ideal fortress, and it had suffered badly in the recent bombardment. Still, with more than 20 cannon left by the Mexicans, it was the best stronghold available. As the volunteers repaired walls, dug trenches, erected gun platforms and parapets for riflemen, Bowie and his men pitched in to help. Perhaps the old knife fighter's judgment was impaired by ill health; he was plagued by bouts of fever from what may have been tuberculosis. Or perhaps he simply could not bring himself to sound a retreat. "We will rather die in these ditches than give it up to the enemy," he wrote. In either case, Houston's orders were quietly forgotten.

Other volunteers began to ride in. William Travis, who had routed the Mexican garrison at Anahuac, arrived with 25 men. A tall, sinewy, red-headed Alabaman of 26 years, Travis had kindled his heroic impulses on the romantic novels of Sir Walter Scott. "We consider death preferable to disgrace, which would be the result of giving up a Post which has been so dearly won," he wrote the Texas governor, Henry Smith. A lieutenant colonel of cavalry, he took joint command of the Alamo with Jim Bowie.

Then came the most notable of all the Alamo's defenders, Davy Crockett. He rode up unexpectedly on February 8 at the head of a dozen sharpshooters he called his "Tennessee Mounted Volunteers." When Travis offered him command, Crockett declined. "All the honor that I desire is that of defending as a high private the liberties of our common country," he declared.

In late afternoon of February 22, the advance units of Santa Anna's army reached the low hills south of San Antonio. A lookout caught the flash of sunlight on their cavalry lances as they broke camp the next morning. A panicky exodus began, as the city's Texas families packed up their belongings and fled. A number headed for the Alamo. When Travis finally barred the gates, the fort held 150 fighting men, along with 25 refugees, mostly women, children and servants.

Santa Anna marched into San Antonio that afternoon, and raised a flag from the church belfry—not the familiar Mexican tricolor, but a blood-red banner that flapped and coiled in the breeze. Every Texan recognized the ancient signal: Santa Anna would take no prisoners. Travis replied with a shot from his 18-pound cannon.

The Texans took up positions along the Alamo's battlements. Crockett and his men would defend a newly built palisade that filled a 75-foot gap between the Low Barracks and the ruins of the mission church. The refugees took shelter in the church itself. The next morning at daybreak, Mexican artillery began lobbing in shells. The guns were dug in along a stream at a range of 400 yards.

During a lull in the bombardment, Travis dashed off an urgent plea for reinforcements. He sent it to Gonzales, the nearest large settlement, but it soon would circulate across the continent. "To the People of Texas & all Americans in the world," he wrote in his fluid, impatient hand, and the phrases swept across the page: "I am besieged, by a thousand or more . . . have sustained a continual Bombardment . . . have not lost a man . . . our flag still waves proudly from the walls . . . *I shall never surrender or retreat* . . . I call on you in the name of Liberty, of patriotism & of everything dear to the American character, to come to our aid, with all dispatch . . . *Victory or Death.*" The last words he underlined three times.

At Gonzales, a small militia company of 25 men, under the command of George Kimbell, responded to Travis' plea. This tiny force gathered its weapons and set out for the Alamo. They were the last Americans to reach the fort.

Over the next week the bombardment intensified, as Santa Anna brought up more troops and more heavy guns. By Friday, March 4, the Mexican forces encircled the Alamo, and their cannon were pounding its walls from a distance of 250 yards. Stone chips flew like hail across the main plaza. All day long the volleys continued, and when they resumed on the morning of the 5th, the Mexican gunners had advanced to 200 yards. The Alamo's walls were beginning to crumble faster than the weary defenders could shore them up. In the distance Mexican soldiers could be seen making scaling ladders.

Davy Crockett's adventures in life and legend

By far the most famous defender of the Alamo, better known even than Jim Bowie, was a graying, 49-year-old folk hero from Tennessee: Davy Crockett. In a wilderness where men survived by their marksmanship, Crockett was renowned for his ability to shoot the wick off a candle at 300 feet. He was a great hunter who once bagged 47 bears in a single month, and a fearsome fighter who was tested in frontier battles throughout the War of 1812.

No less was Crockett a spell-binding backwoods orator and humorist, who loved spinning such tall tales as the one about the time he idly pointed his rifle at a tree and a raccoon yelled out, "Don't shoot, Davy, I'll come down." So popular did Crockett become in Tennessee that he was elected to Congress in 1827, 1829 and 1833. At one point, there was even talk of Crockett for Vice President on the Whig ticket. But his political career ended bitterly in 1835 when he was defeated for re-election by a Democratic candidate supported by President Jackson. Crockett reportedly told his erstwhile constituents that he was going to Texas and they could go to hell.

Yet if Crockett was gone, he was hardly forgotten. That same year an enterprising Nashville publisher printed the first issue of what was called "Davy Crockett's Almanack." Along with the usual almanac information, it featured a number of illustrated fantasies, ostensibly by Davy, that expanded wildly on his many exploits.

The periodical was a huge success, in no small part due to Crockett's martyrdom at the Alamo. Over the next 20 years, five different publishers put out 55 issues of the almanac, filled with wonderfully impossible accounts of Davy scrapping with panthers and bears, sinking pirate ships, and outwitting everyone from Indians to redcoats.

In this almanac cartoon, a knife-slashing, rifle-shooting Davy Crockett rides his pet bear, Death Hug, down a 90-foot waterfall to escape from an army of Spaniards.

Defending New Orleans against the besieging British, Crockett charges into battle on an appropriate land-and-sea mount: an alligator carrying a cannon and ammunition.

A doomed Davy Crockett swings an empty rifle at on-rushing enemy soldiers in Robert Onderdonk's *Fall of the Alamo*. Though Onderdonk has Crockett defending the south wall gate *(right)*, Alamo survivor Susannah Dickerson saw his body nearer the chapel *(left)* after the battle.

A relic of the Alamo, this powerful muzzle-loader was picked up after the battle by a Mexican peasant who had been ordered to remove the bodies of the defenders. He later gave the weapon to a Texas colonel.

A sense of doom began to penetrate the beleaguered fort. By now Travis was in sole command; Bowie, overcome by fever, lay delirious on a cot in the Low Barracks. Travis called the defenders together, and offered them a choice. They could stay with him and fight, or they could try fleeing. Only one man decided to leave, a soldier of fortune named Louis Rose, who slipped out under darkness and made his way to safety through the Mexican lines.

Across the river in San Antonio, Santa Anna now reviewed his plans for the attack. Four columns of infantry would strike together: one each at the Alamo's northwest and northeast corners, one at the east wall, and one at the newly built south wall palisade. A troop of cavalry would guard the roads, and 400 men would wait in reserve. In all, Santa Anna would use 4,000 men.

In the pre-dawn darkness of March 6, just after 5 a.m., the assault began. Someone cried "Viva Santa Anna," a bugle sounded, and the cool air shivered with the thud and rumble of thousands of advancing Mexicans. Travis, asleep fully clad, jumped to his feet. Seizing his loaded, doubled-barreled shotgun, he sprinted to the north wall.

The attack did not begin well for Santa Anna's forces. The column striking from the east was pinned by the murderous shot from the cannon on the church, and Crockett's sharpshooters blew back the column charging at the south palisade. Travis, striding the north wall, fired both barrels into the mass of men below. Then a musket ball struck him in the forehead. He reeled back, tumbling down the embankment to the bottom, where he sat up stunned and staring. He was dying.

Again the Mexicans charged; again the withering sheets of grapeshot and rifle fire turned them back. In the confusion, the northern and eastern columns drifted together. On the next thrust all three columns—a single mass of men, the front rows falling like grass before the scythe—came surging toward the Alamo.

There was no way of stopping them. Trampling over the bodies of dead and wounded comrades, the attackers clawed their way up a barricade in the northeast corner. Then they tumbled inside. Moments later, other units scaled the northwest corner. Someone opened the northern postern, and thousands of Mexicans began pouring into the Alamo plaza.

The defenders retreated to the Long Barracks. Every Texas rifle, every cannon, poured its lethal charge into the plaza, until the Mexican dead lay like stacks of cordwood. But still the Mexicans came on. As Crockett and his men fought their way toward the barracks, the south-wall attackers swarmed over the palisade and rushed at them from behind. Crockett, encircled, aimed his rifle coolly, never missing a shot. He killed at least eight Mexicans, then dropped as a sword thrust caught him above the right eye. No less than 20 enemy bayonets jabbed at his body.

The Mexicans fought their way into the Long Barracks and massacred everyone inside. In the nearby Low Barracks, Jim Bowie lay on a cot. Mexican soldiers burst through the door and, in the words of an observer, "tossed Bowie's body on their bayonets until his blood covered their clothes and dyed them red."

Then, just 90 minutes after the Mexican bugler signaled the attack, the guns fell silent. All of the Texans were dead save a handful of women and children, a slave and a San Antonian who claimed to have been a prisoner in the Alamo. Santa Anna sent one woman—18-year-old Susannah Dickerson—to Gonzales to deliver his message: This would be the fate of all those who opposed him. Then he built a pyre of branches. On it he piled 183 corpses, the remains of every last Texan who had stayed to defend the Alamo. His own losses were huge—possibly 1,500 men, more than a third of the attacking force. No one knew just how many, because he quickly had the Mexican bodies buried.

Neither tactical necessity nor plain common sense could justify the sacrifice of Texan lives at the Alamo. But the brave stand of those 183 men had left an indelible legacy. Jolted into stark awareness of Mexico's capacity for tyranny, the settlers now had a rallying cry. There were no longer any alternatives. They must win their freedom, or die in the attempt.

Even as Santa Anna was laying siege to the mission, delegates from the Texas colonies and townships were meeting to decide their future course. There were 59 of them, gathered in the muddy, wind-swept frontier hamlet of Washington-on-the-Brazos, in a dwelling so new that it still lacked doors and window glass. George C. Childress, a lawyer from Tennessee, composed a brief document, and on March 3 he read it out. It was a Declaration of Independence, and it closely resembled a similar Declaration signed at Philadelphia in 1776. The delegates approved it unanimously. They then wrote a constitution, also based on the American original, elected officers, and formed a provisional government. The Republic of Texas was born.

More than any other delegate, Sam Houston impressed his personality upon the proceedings. Just 43 years old, his tall frame worn by travel, crisis and occasional bouts of malaria, he nonetheless cut an imposing figure. In sonorous, compelling tones, he stressed the vital importance of establishing a sound government. Meanwhile, as commander-in-chief, his own responsibilities lay elsewhere. Midway through the session, he rose from his chair and strode from the hall, the three-inch rowels jingling on his spurs. He would ride to Gonzales and rally an army.

Houston quickly recruited what men he could, 375 in all. Surveying Gonzales' pitifully weak defenses, he evacuated every last soul. Never again, he resolved, would Texans attempt to defend an untenable position for the sake of honor alone.

There now began a long and dismal retreat before the advancing might of Santa Anna's armies. Moving as swiftly as he could along the mud-clogged roads, gathering reinforcements along the way, Houston led his men eastward through the colonies, across the Colorado River, across the Brazos, gambling for time.

The spring rains poured down in unrelenting torrents. Houston slept in his saddle blankets and he often wore moccasins, since his only pair of boots was giving out. Cursing and complaining, the men trudged on. When would their leader stand and fight? Why this humiliating retreat? Calls for Houston's ouster reached the government at Washington-on-the-Brazos. The delegates grew increasingly edgy. As the Mexicans drew closer, they packed up and moved east to Harrisburg.

Fanning the discontent was news of a second Mexican outrage. At Goliad, far to the southwest, a swashbuckling colonel named James Fannin had gathered 400 volunteers to defend the town. When Houston ordered him to evacuate, he had simply dug in tighter. The result was predictable: 1,400 Mexicans arrived, led by General José Francisco Urrea, and after two days of savage fighting they forced Fannin's surrender. The Texans, now prisoners of war, were led to a field outside the town, and there gunned down in cold blood.

Houston was not going to fall into the same trap. With every mile his men moved east, supplies became more plentiful, the populace friendlier, the land more familiar. New recruits rallied to Houston's banner until, by the time he reached the huge Groce plantation on the Brazos, his command included 800 men. At Groce's, he paused to drill his fledgling army in the disciplines of battle. The bedraggled Texans came to resemble something like a fighting force. And all the while Houston studied his maps, waiting for some tactical slip by Santa Anna that would allow him to confront the enemy on near equal terms. His chance came during the third week of April, in the bayou country at the head of Galveston Bay.

Santa Anna ordered his forces, which were advancing in three widely separated columns, to converge at Fort Bend, a river crossing of the Brazos. His plan was to lead them from there to Harrisburg, on Buffalo Bayou, thus capturing the Texas government. Then he would turn north to destroy Houston.

Santa Anna arrived first at Fort Bend, with 750 troops and a cavalry detachment. Impatient for victory, he pressed on without waiting for the others. On April 14 he stormed into Harrisburg, only to find the town abandoned. The delegates had fled downriver to New Washington, where they again eluded capture. Santa Anna turned his attention to Houston's army. He decided to concentrate his forces at Lynch's Ferry, a strategic spot near the head of Galveston Bay where the Harrisburg road crosses the San Jacinto River.

Here was the moment Houston had been waiting for. Despite its strategic location, the ferry landing was a death trap hemmed in by marsh and bayou. If Santa Anna headed into it, with his vanguard force of only 750 men, Houston's 800 Texans would be there first, ready to pounce. Over the past several days the Texans had been speeding east from Groce's, bound initially for Harrisburg, covering 60 miles in just two and a half days. They were now within striking distance of Lynch's Ferry.

Houston ordered his men into parade formation. Mounting his big white stallion, Saracen, he addressed his troops. "Victory is certain!" he cried, his deep voice ringing out across the field. "Trust in God and fear not! The victims of the Alamo and the names of those who were murdered at Goliad cry out for vengeance. Remember the Alamo! Remember Goliad!" The ragged, tired men roared back, "Remember the Alamo! Remember Goliad!"

The Texans crossed Buffalo Bayou on rafts. On the bayou's south bank they marched on through the night, and just after dawn on April 20 they took control of the ferry landing. They then camped in some woods at the edge of the bayou.

Early that same morning Santa Anna set fire to New Washington, and headed up the road toward Lynch's Ferry. He had sent for his generals, back at Fort Bend, with orders to bring reinforcements. General Cós was already on the way with 500 men; the rest were expected to arrive well before the Texans. So it was with some measure of surprise that Santa Anna's scouts spotted Houston's pickets in the tall grass of the San Jacinto prairie.

The Mexicans hurriedly took positions on the far side of the field. Dragging up a light cannon, they began firing in the direction of the Texan lines. An assault by the Texans might come at any moment, Santa Anna reasoned, and to meet it he started building barricades of pack saddles and supply boxes.

Houston's own men were itching to attack. But they had been moving for days with little sleep, and had scarcely had time to catch their breath. So Houston held them back. That night they rested, and all through the following morning. The Mexicans, meanwhile, labored through the night to complete their defenses. Cós pulled in about 9 a.m., raising the Mexican strength to around 1,250 troops. Confident he could handle whatever the Texans might fling at him, Santa Anna began to relax.

It now appeared that Houston would not attack this day, either. A deep lethargy came over the Mex-

ican camp. Santa Anna's troops, exhausted by their all-night labors, began to doze off. His sentries lay down and slept.

In the hush of the afternoon siesta, Houston began moving his men through the high grass of the San Jacinto prairie. The Texans crept forward in a double line 900 yards long, their left flank hugging the woods, their right flank guarded by a cavalry detachment under Mirabeau Lamar. To cut off any further Mexican reinforcements, Houston sent a scout to destroy Vince's Bridge on the Harrisburg road. There was now no exit from the battlefield. It was victory—or death.

General Houston rode in front, on Saracen. At 4:30 p.m., on April 21, he gave the signal to attack. As the Texans charged at the enemy lines, some 200 yards ahead,

all the pent up fury of the previous weeks burst out in a single echoing roar: "Remember the Alamo! Remember Goliad!" Pausing only to fire and reload, they swarmed over the barricades. The startled Mexicans, groggy with sleep, barely had time to pick up their weapons.

Houston, leading the charge, made an easy target. Five musket balls slammed into Saracen, and as the horse fell under him Houston leapt off. He mounted another. A moment later, a copper ball struck him just above the ankle, shattering both bones in his right leg. The second horse collapsed, and someone helped him onto a third. On he rode, into the Mexican camp, slashing with his saber, his boot filling with blood.

Utterly overwhelmed, the Mexicans turned to flee. But where to? With all roads blocked, some headed for the marshes, where the Texans gunned them down until the bodies lay in soggy windrows in the reddening water. Some tried to escape to the south, across the prairie, but were cut down by Lamar's cavalrymen.

The assault lasted a bare 18 minutes, by Houston's estimate, from the moment the first shot was fired, until the Texans held control of the Mexican camp. But if the fighting was over, the killing continued. The Texans charged about like madmen, blood-crazy, shooting and stabbing at any enemy who moved. Their officers were helpless to control them. Snarled one soldier, "If Jesus Christ were to come down from heaven and order me to quit shooting Santanistas, I wouldn't do it, sir!"

By twilight the guns were silent and the carnage ended. Houston, weak from loss of blood, lay on a

Mud-spattered and downcast, Santa Anna is brought before the wounded Sam Houston after San Jacinto. As Deaf Smith and other Texans look on, in this 1886 recreation by William Huddle, Houston offers the defeated general a seat on an ammunition box before accepting his surrender.

blanket, sipping water from a gourd. His officers delivered their reports. Incredibly, the Texans had lost only two dead and 23 wounded. Mexican casualties were about 600 dead and 650 taken prisoner.

One of the few who escaped was Santa Anna. Early in the battle he had fled into the woods, leaving his men to their fate. The next day a search party found him wandering alone along the bayou, dressed in a farmer's discarded jacket. He was brought to Houston.

Their discussion was brief and to the point. Houston impressed upon the Mexican dictator that, if he wanted to live, he must remove his army forthwith, and never again bring troops onto Texas soil. An order to this effect, signed by Santa Anna, was delivered to his commanders at Fort Bend. To make sure the Mexicans actually left, and stayed away, Houston held the dictator captive another six months before releasing him.

With the Republic of Texas at last a reality, its spirited citizens hurried back to their farms and businesses, eager to tackle the chores of building a new nation. The tasks were staggering. Most institutions of orderly life had yet to be set in place. There were no courts, no public schools, and minimal law enforcement. Roads were few, postal service non-existent. Raids by Comanche Indians plagued the western sectors. Devastation of crops in the recent fighting meant that food was scarce and prices astronomically high. Cash was so short that most transactions were conducted by barter. The state was bereft of funds.

The only visible asset was land—242,594,560 acres, as the borders then stood, and much of it fertile beyond dreams. A typical East Texas farm could be expected to yield up to 2,000 pounds of cotton per acre or 80 bushels of corn, on soil so rich, people said, that "if you put ten-penny nails in the ground you will have a crop of iron bolts." To the west and south, in grasslands that seemed to have no end, an enterprising rancher could make his fortune in a few short years of vigorous labor.

Land became the currency of the new Republic. The government, in its search for funds, sold off vast tracts of public domain, enticing settlers with an initial offer

of two square miles per family, free of charge. As a result, 5,000 newcomers swarmed into Texas in its first year of independence, and over the next decade the population increased fourfold, from 35,000 to 140,000. New towns took shape: the cotton port of Galveston in 1836, Houston a year later as the Republic's new capital, then the present capital of Austin in 1839.

Presiding over this upsurge of growth in the Republic's early years was Sam Houston. Elected president by an overwhelming margin, the hero of San Jacinto turned his energies to promoting the national prosperity. The first step was to secure recognition from the United States, with an eye to eventual Union. To this end, he

Flown during Sam Houston's second term as President, this handmade wool Lone Star flag exemplified the only known official design used by the Republic of Texas from 1839 to 1846.

appointed the nation's most adroit and painstaking diplomat, Stephen Austin, as his Secretary of State.

The war had left Austin in abject poverty, his plantations destroyed, his town of San Felipe burned to the ground by the Mexicans. Never physically strong, he suffered from ill health brought on by long years of heroic toil. Nonetheless, he plunged into the delicate negotiations with Washington. Then on Christmas Eve of 1836, he took a severe chill. Two days later he was dead.

Houston summed up Austin's accomplishments in a brief public statement: "The father of Texas is no more. The first pioneer of the wilderness has departed. General Stephen F. Austin, Secretary of State, expired this day."

Less than three months later, Washington extended recognition and, on December 29, 1845, Texas was admitted to the Union as the 28th state.

Hardly had Texas joined the Union when the tide of secession began to sweep the Southern states, Texas among them. The issue was not only the abolition of expansion of slavery, but also the right of state governments to determine their own course rather than allow the national government to mandate it. From the beginning, Sam Houston argued spiritedly against secession. "I wish if this Union must be dissolved, that its ruins may be the monument of my grave," he declared impassionately. But many of his fellow Texans disagreed. The idea of bending to pressure from the national government and the powerful Northern states struck at their pride. They had managed to sustain themselves as an independent republic; they had no doubt that they could do so once again.

Support for secession ebbed and flowed, losing ground when Houston was elected governor in 1859, then gaining momentum with a surging reactionary swing in the country's political temper. On February 1, 1861, at a convention endorsed by the Texas state legislature, an ordinance of secession passed by a vote of 166 to 8. The following month the convention declared Texas independent of the Union and voted to join the newly formed Confederate States of America. When Houston was asked to take an oath of allegiance to his new political masters he refused. Withdrawing from office, he moved into an uneasy retirement, watching helplessly as the Union he had worked so hard to preserve was torn apart in a bloody civil war.

In mid-July 1863, Sam Houston came home to his wife, Margaret, with a cold that developed into pneumonia. On July 25, 1863, he slept through the night and stirred briefly the next day. Margaret reached for his hand. "Texas—Texas!—Margaret!" he cried out, and fell back into sleep. He died that day at sunset.

When Emanuel Leutze evoked the pioneer spirit in a canvas commissioned by Congress in 1860, he titled it with a clarion call for Manifest

II. THE LURE OF THE WEST

Destiny: *Westward the Course of Empire Takes Its Way.* The line is from a poem by the 18th Century British philosopher George Berkeley.

An 1860 wagon train pulls into Manhattan, Kansas, for a last purchase of supplies before crossing the plains.

Hopeful novices on a perilous journey

"In prosecuting this journey," warned an 1849 guidebook to the West, "the emigrant should never forget that it is one in which time is every thing." Thus, while pioneers had a sense of making history, they could rarely afford to halt for the hour or so needed to assemble and sit for portraits in front of the cumbersome cameras of the day.

History had to be content, in the main, with the often blurred visual record made by itinerant photographers who snatched glimpses of wagons in transit.

But there were other observers to help round this record out. In 1846 a veteran mountain man wrote of seeing a train on the Oregon Trail in which 30 wagons were "all busily engaged in crossing a river which was found not to be fordable." To him the pioneers were the greenest of greenhorns — farmers who had no idea how to live off wild country. Many oldtimers shared his belief, but they failed to take into account the pioneers' iron determination to press on. And in the end, most of the greenhorns got through to their goal.

Floating their wagons on improvised ferries and swimming their horses alongside, emigrants cross a river. Chaos often attended the maneuver; at a Kansas river in 1850, a traveler noted, "the fiendish swearing shouted in all languages by furious madmen would becraze Christendom's greatest stoic."

Reflecting the strain of their journey, westbound pioneers pause in the foothills of the Rockies. In the heat of the day, after a morning of five hard hours on the trail, emigrants often unhitched their wagons, watered their stock, ate the noonday meal, rested — and sometimes posed for the camera.

5. Wagon trains across the plains

It was the latter part of June, a Wednesday afternoon in the year 1845. Two groups sat facing each other in a green meadow near the eastern edge of what would one day be the state of Wyoming. Nearby stood the fur trading post of Fort Laramie, surrounded by an adobe wall 15 feet high, and a North American wilderness 600 miles wide. The only other link with civilization in that barren world of plains and sky was a pair of parallel wagon wheel ruts stretching eastward to Independence, Missouri—and westward all the way to Oregon.

Ten weeks before, at the tenuous track's eastern terminus, a high-browed, raw-boned man named Joel Palmer had ventured forth, along with 150 men, women and children, and a train of 41 canvas-covered wagons piled high with provisions. Now, Palmer and his fellow pioneers were meeting with a hundred or so Oglala Sioux Indians who frequented the region around Fort Laramie. With 600 miles of the Oregon Trail behind them and 1,400 rough-and-ready miles still to go, Palmer's party wanted to insure that the next leg of their journey, which crossed Indian country, would pass unhindered.

As captain of the expedition, Palmer offered the Indians a ceremonial feast of meat, cakes, rice mush, bread and coffee—and promises of peace. The Indians, however, were more interested in purchasing guns and powder. "This country belongs to the red man," said the Sioux chief, "but his white brethren travels through, shooting the game and scaring it away. The children of the red man cry out for food." Only with the white man's weapons, said the chief, could the Indian kill the wild animals that were now too skittish to be taken by bow and arrow.

Unfortunately, Palmer had little to offer. The suspendered men and bonneted women seated beside him were not traders; they were farmers on their way "to plough and plant the land." Such powder and ball as they possessed were barely sufficient for their own needs and they had none to trade or give away.

Palmer then urged the assembled Indians to help themselves to the food. Dipping their fingers in, the Indians ate, understanding all too clearly that nothing would be gained by further talk. The unstoppable American white man was on the move once more and the resistant American Indian was again being told that he would have to settle for apologies and a few handouts of food. When they got up to leave, the Oglala Sioux glumly collected the leftovers and took them home.

As Joel Palmer watched the Indians depart, unrequited, for their tipis that afternoon at Fort Laramie, he was standing witness to a small but significant scene in the drama of American expansion. In more than 200 years, since the first white settlers came ashore at Plymouth, the frontier had expanded from the Atlantic seaboard with a kind of pulsing, move-and-hesitate rhythm. The Indians, and the wilderness itself, were being forced to give way to a new kind of people, who would settle, and eventually dominate, the great empty spaces of America.

When those 41 wagons started from Independence, the westernmost edge of the formally constituted United States ended at the Missouri River. California appeared on the map as a northern province of Mexico, and already there was a small but prosperous community of Spanish-speaking cattle ranchers. The Oregon country was a huge tract of wilderness that extended north from California all the way up the Pacific Coast to Alaska, and from the Pacific Ocean in the west to an eastern boundary running along the Continental Divide in the Rocky Mountains—thus encompassing today's states of Oregon, Washington and parts of Canada, Montana, Idaho and Wyoming. No one knew for certain to whom this land really belonged; it was claimed by both the United States and Great Britain, which in 1818 had signed an unusual treaty allowing for "joint occupation."

Thus the overland pioneers were, in a very real sense, emigrants. They went out from their own country into what was basically a foreign land, and an uncivilized one

With tomahawk in hand and lance athwart the trail, an Indian hunter orders the leader of an advancing wagon train to retreat. Such confrontations were usually resolved peaceably by an exchange of gifts.

With tomahawk in hand and lance athwart the trail, an Indian hunter orders the leader of an advancing wagon train to retreat. Such confrontations were usually resolved peaceably by an exchange of gifts.

at that, to commence their farming and homemaking. Here, there were almost no trees for houses or fences, and scarcely any water for farm crops. This forbidding countryside broiled in the summer, froze rock-hard in the winter, and was tormented by a wind that never seemed to blow itself out. Children's geography books labeled the area the Great American Desert, and the United States government had designated it as Indian land, fit only for aborigines and a few fur traders and hardy missionaries.

But no mere tract of prairie, however bleak, could block the 19th Century American's westering urge, his quest for a better chance and for more room. Somehow the West always seemed to promise something extra: blacker soil, bluer skies, a rosier future. In large part it was an emotional urge, this inclination to move west, an itch in the brain, a restlessness in the feet, a rising to the challenge of new land that no one else had settled. A popular saying had arisen about it: "If hell lay to the west, Americans would cross heaven to get there."

From Maine to Missouri, men and women heard amazing claims about the beneficent land beyond the Rockies. Oregon was a "pioneer's paradise," one of the region's advocates told a party of emigrants as they were about to start out in 1843. In the Willamette valley, "the pigs are running about under the great acorn trees, round and fat, and already cooked, with knives and forks sticking in them so that you can cut off a slice whenever you are hungry."

The truth was close enough for Joel Palmer when he and his party arrived in Oregon City on November 1, 1845, after 200 arduous days on the trail. The town had been established a few years before by missionaries and retired fur trappers from the Hudson's Bay Company, and now it was thriving. After the winter had passed, Palmer returned east to collect his wife and children in Laurel, Indiana.

The following spring—it was 1847—all of them were traveling the Oregon Trail. And riding at the head of the wagon train, elected by a vote among the adults in the

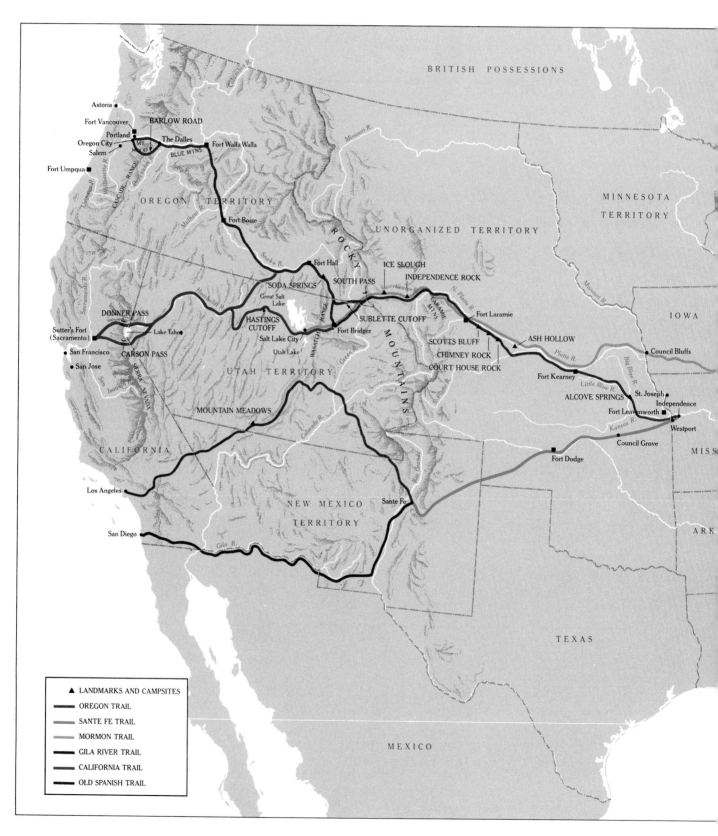

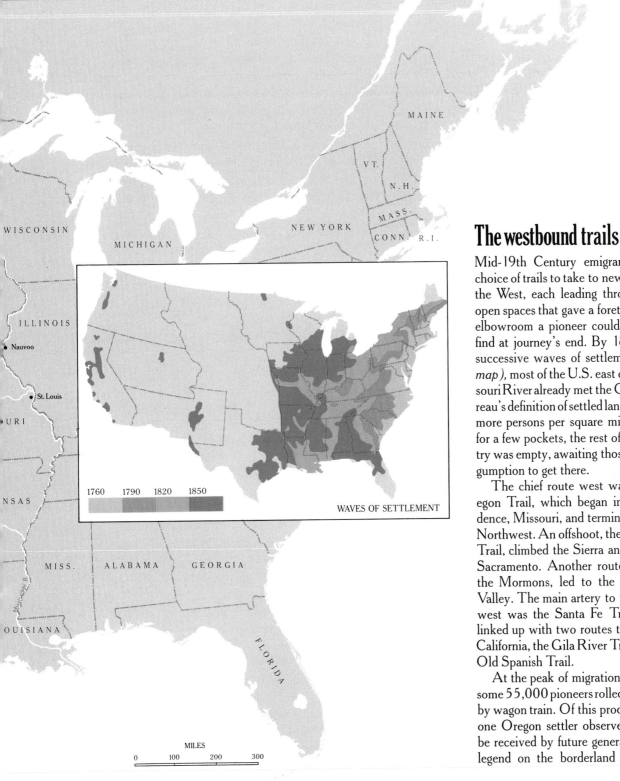

WISCONSIN

MICHIGAN

ILLINOIS

Nauvoo

St. Louis

URI

NSAS

MISS.   ALABAMA   GEORGIA

OUISIANA

FLORIDA

MAINE

V.T.

N.H.

MASS.

NEW YORK   CONN. R.I.

1760   1790   1820   1850

WAVES OF SETTLEMENT

MILES

0   100   200   300

The westbound trails

Mid-19th Century emigrants had a choice of trails to take to new homes in the West, each leading through great open spaces that gave a foretaste of the elbowroom a pioneer could expect to find at journey's end. By 1850, after successive waves of settlement *(inset map)*, most of the U.S. east of the Missouri River already met the Census Bureau's definition of settled land — two or more persons per square mile. Except for a few pockets, the rest of the country was empty, awaiting those with the gumption to get there.

The chief route west was the Oregon Trail, which began in Independence, Missouri, and terminated in the Northwest. An offshoot, the California Trail, climbed the Sierra and ended in Sacramento. Another route, used by the Mormons, led to the Salt Lake Valley. The main artery to the Southwest was the Santa Fe Trail, which linked up with two routes to southern California, the Gila River Trail and the Old Spanish Trail.

At the peak of migration, in 1850, some 55,000 pioneers rolled westward by wagon train. Of this prodigious tide one Oregon settler observed: "It will be received by future generations as a legend on the borderland of myth."

company, was Captain Joel Palmer, following the American Manifest Destiny to populate and exploit the promised land of the West.

No less was a passionate Manifest Destiny evident among the churches of mid-19th Century America. From the very start, evangelistic missionaries had pioneered the way west, determined to bring salvation to the lost souls of the Oregon tribesmen. In setting up their wilderness missions, they helped found the first American towns in the Pacific Northwest, and provided the oases of American civilization—places like Oregon City—toward which the emigrants would wend their hopeful way.

Among the first of the devout to heed the call was a small-town New York physician named Marcus Whitman, who would accomplish more for Oregon settlement than anyone else. The 34-year-old doctor had always felt a strong missionary urge and had dreamed of becoming a Protestant minister, but family finances could not support the seven years of required training. So he became a doctor instead, since medical schools demanded considerably less time and far less money. In 1832, Whitman began his medical practice; in his spare time he gave evening temperance lectures and taught Sunday school.

Two years later, dreaming of establishing a mission in the West, Whitman made a preliminary journey of reconnaissance to Oregon, in company with a missionary, Reverend Samuel Parker, and a group of rowdy fur traders. Besides exploring the feasibility of an Oregon mission, Whitman had a personal quest: he wanted to know if a woman could endure the hazardous overland journey. Shortly before leaving, he had met the buoyant, blond Narcissa Prentiss.

Whitman found Narcissa pretty, engaging and full of delightful good humor—though in ecclesiastical circles humor was considered next to ungodliness. But Narcissa was also deeply devout. She, too, informed the church fathers of her hope "to be employed in their service among the heathen, if counted worthy." If Whitman and Parker's reconnaissance should show that women could travel the Oregon Trail, why, said Miss Prentiss to Dr. Whitman, they would certainly travel it together as man and wife.

During the journey, Parker busily sized up the Indians' conversion potential and Whitman gauged the success the fur men were having at moving their wagons full of trade goods. Wagons, the doctor concluded, were the key to founding a mission, and to all other settlement in Oregon. If wagons could be taken, so could families and everything needed for setting up a household in the wilderness. He returned home in December, reported to his missionary board and immediately started laying plans for his second trip the following spring. In February he married Narcissa.

In preparation for the journey, Narcissa stitched up a conical tent of striped bed ticking, oiled to make it water-resistant. The tent appeared to be uncommonly roomy for a couple on their honeymoon, and indeed it was. Narcissa had designed it not only as a bridal bower but as a shelter for a number of people who signed up for Whitman's second expedition: a carpenter and mechanic named William Gray, and Eliza and Henry Spalding, another missionary couple.

Never before had women attempted the overland journey to Oregon. Even more significant, perhaps, was the fact that the missionaries were traveling with wagons. They brought two: a heavy farm wagon and a light Dearborn belonging to the Spaldings. Marcus Whitman was determined to prove that these utilitarian vehicles could be cajoled along the full length of the Oregon Trail.

In addition to the multiple sense of mission, Whitman's humble party, like so many of those to follow, was propelled westward by a sense of adventure and discovery. From Independence, Missouri, which in 1835 consisted of a mere dozen log-huts, grogshops and stores, the wagon party started west at the tail end of a fur caravan headed by a rough and rangy trail veteran named Broken Hand Fitzpatrick. Narcissa's letters home and her diary describe the bizarre domesticity of trail life. "Our table is the ground, our table cloth is an India rubber cloth, used when it rains as a cloak." "Husband," as Narcissa was wont to refer to Marcus, "always provides my seat, and in a way that you would laugh to see us. We take a blanket and lay down by the table."

At Fort Laramie, to Marcus' intense disappointment, Fitzpatrick insisted that the missionaries abandon their heavy wagon, which he was certain would never negotiate the mountains ahead. However, the party was able to keep the Dearborn, which—if it could get through—would still provide some proof of Whitman's wagon theory.

As they descended into the rocky sagelands to the west, food became scarcer. "I thought of Mother's bread and but-

ter many times, as any hungry child would," wrote Narcissa. "I fancy pork and potatoes would relish extremely well." By now she had become pregnant, and Husband Marcus was having trouble coaxing their one remaining wagon over the jagged terrain. "Husband had a tedious time with the waggon today," she wrote in her diary. "Waggon was upset twice. Did not wonder at all this. It was a greater wonder that it was not turning a somerset continually."

Narcissa did not share her husband's obsession with bringing wagons to Oregon, and she devoutly hoped he would give up the whole idea. She even confessed to being "a little rejoiced" the day an axle broke at Soda Springs in Idaho; surely he would leave it now. Instead, he rigged up a cart with the two rear wheels and kept going.

Narcissa's mood reached its nadir at Salmon Falls on the Snake River, where Husband lightened the load on his precious vehicle by unloading her clothes trunk. But when the missionaries reached Fort Boise, a Hudson's Bay trading post at the junction of the Snake and Boise rivers, Narcissa recovered her customary good cheer. With Eliza, she was able to do the laundry for only the third time since they had left their homes six months before. The men spruced up. Better yet Marcus, after 1,500 miles of tribu-

lation, reluctantly gave up on the confounded cart. "Perhaps you will wonder why," Narcissa told her parents. "Our animals were failing & the route in crossing the Blue Mountains is said to be impassable for it."

At long last, it seemed that the end of the trail was at hand. Past Fort Boise the route carried through woodland slopes of the Blue Mountains, which reminded Narcissa joyfully of her New York Catskills. The tempo of the journey increased with the party's spirits.

On September 1, 1836, they sighted their final landmark—the wooden palisade of Fort Walla Walla, the Hudson's Bay trading post in the southeast corner of what was to become the state of Washington. After nearly 4,000 miles and six and a half months of travel the Whitmans had reached the place where they would build their own home, plant their own garden—and by springtime celebrate the birth of their daughter, Alice Clarissa. A resident cock at Fort Walla Walla crowed, heralding the start of a new era of American growth.

Thereafter, Henry and Eliza Spalding built a mission at Lapwai, at the junction of the Snake and Salmon rivers, and proceeded to spread God's word among the intelligent and receptive Nez Percé Indians. Marcus and Narcissa

The miseries of westering travelers included prairie blizzards, which could devastate a wagon train overnight. As temperatures plummeted to 40 degrees below zero, cattle would inhale particles of sleet and snow and die of suffocation.

Whitman established the Waiilatpu mission near the Walla Walla River's junction with the Columbia. But for them, the Promised Land turned into a curse. At age two, their daughter fell into the Walla Walla River and drowned. Eight years later, Marcus and Narcissa's own lives were at stake.

In 1847, an outbreak of measles struck the Cayuse Indian tribe at the Waiilatpu mission. Marcus struggled desperately to relieve the suffering, but the Indians lacked natural immunity; more than half of the 350 Cayuse died.

Cayuse custom decreed that any medicine man unable to balk death might be required to pay with his own life. By tribal rumor, Dr. Whitman was not only a powerless medicine man but one who was causing sickness on purpose, poisoning the Indian children even as he pretended to treat them. He had to be stopped. On November 28 the Indians went on a rampage of killing, raping and beating. By the time they were finished, 14 men, women and chil-

dren were dead—among them Marcus Whitman and his wife, Narcissa, who had left their Eastern home with so many dreams 11 years before.

Marcus Whitman may have been mistaken in his belief that the Western Indians could be Christianized, but his conviction that wagon trains could bring emigrant families west was prescient. On May 19, 1841, the first train of wagon-borne pioneers left the Missouri frontier for the Pacific Coast. The party consisted of some 70 people, including five women and at least seven children, with all their movable goods crammed into a dozen covered wagons.

At the head of the caravan rode Broken Hand Fitzpatrick, this time on his way to Oregon with a delegation of Catholic missionary Jesuit priests. The emigrants themselves were bound mostly for California. The company agreed to travel together along the Oregon Trail to the California fork on the far side of the Rockies, where it would split. In all, it was a grand scheme, bold, hopeful, naive and historic.

Some of the travelers gave up halfway and went home. Thirty-two decided to go to Oregon. The rest, 34 in all, turned off at Soda Springs, heading for California; they barely survived the journey. Water and grass in the Utah and Nevada deserts were far scarcer than anticipated. The draught animals weakened from thirst and hunger, and it became necessary to abandon the heaviest wagons amid the sand and sagebrush. By the time the emigrants reached the Sierra Nevada, they were forced to eat the oxen to keep from starving. But the pioneers kept plodding forward, and by sheer fortitude they made it; by early November they had reached the game-rich and fertile San Joaquin Valley. The settlement of California by American overland emigrants was successfully established, fragile for the moment, but nonetheless assured.

Each year thereafter, new emigrants took the Oregon Trail, some headed for California and others for Oregon, where the Willamette valley's rich topsoil and gentle rainy climate beckoned with promises of glorious harvests. In all, more than 1,000 pioneers crossed the continent to various destinations in the Far West during 1843. The following year the number rose to 4,000, then to 5,000 in 1845—the same year Joel Palmer and his fellow emigrants finally reached Oregon City after their 200-day trip.

By now, the call of the West had been heard across the Atlantic, and English, Irish, Scandinavian and German emigrants were joining the wagon trains. The discovery of gold in California in 1848 brought 30,000 pioneers along the Oregon Trail in 1849. By 1850, the peak year of travel along the trail, the number had risen to 55,000. The wheels of their wagons cut gashes in the continent that would still be evident a century and a quarter later.

Few who embarked on their western quest were adequately prepared for the ordeals that awaited them. Back in Illinois—or Tennessee or Pennsylvania or wherever the travelers came from—they had pictured themselves building new homes and creating bright futures in the West. But the strain of getting there proved far worse than any guidebook had hinted. The reality of life on the trail was an ever-more-difficult roadway, with failing supplies of food and water, bone-wrenching weariness and accumulating miseries of every sort. As the pioneers pushed overland, per-

haps 15 miles a day, many lost sight of the vision that had set them going. Instead, they saw only the tragic signs of families that had preceded them: the wolf-pawed graves of the dead, the putrefying carcasses of mules and oxen, the splintered wrecks of abandoned wagons.

Yet they kept going: After a few weeks on the trail, most of them had come too far to return. One plains farmer who did leave penned this wry note: "250 miles to the nearest post office; 100 miles to wood; 20 miles to water; 6 inches to hell. Gone to live with wife's folks."

Separated from civilization by an ocean of wilderness, the trail-weary travelers had little choice but to trudge on, setting one foot doggedly ahead of the other. "The trail west," said one emigrant, "is a treadmill." Pioneers were forced to endure everything from heat prostration to a mule kick in the shins.

Keeping pace on that treadmill demanded a stoicism painfully captured in the diary of Amelia Knight, who with her husband, Joel, and their seven children set out for Oregon in 1853. "Made our beds down in the tent in the wet and mud," Amelia wrote. "Have to eat cold supper. We are creeping along slowly, one waggon after another, the same old gait; and the same thing over, out of one mud hole and into another all day. Them that eat the most breakfast eat the most sand."

As the journey went on, Amelia's litany of tribulations increased. "Chatfield quite sick with scarlet fever. A calf took sick and died before breakfast. Lost one of our oxen; he dropped dead in the yoke. I could hardly help shedding tears. Yesterday my eighth child was born."

Trouble with Indians was relatively rare, contrary to legend, and almost never in the history of Western migration did an Indian war party descend upon a circle of corralled wagons. However, a single wagon traveling alone or straggling at the end of a long train would sometimes be attacked and robbed, and those who resisted might get themselves killed.

Far more deadly were the everyday trail hazards of accident and illness. Fatalities on the trail were so numerous that the emigrants averaged one grave dug every 80 yards between the Missouri River and the Willamette valley. Most of the 20,000 buried beside the trail succumbed to the very illness that many pioneers went west to escape. "Died: Of Cholera" was the most frequent epitaph.

No wonder that some chose to bypass the overland trails altogether. An emigrant bound for the coast had

The shape of a day on the Oregon Trail

In the early morning bustle of eating, loading up the wagons and yoking the teams, a trumpeter on horseback sounds a call to assemble the caravan.

One of the best firsthand accounts of emigrant life en route west was provided by Jesse Applegate, captain of a contingent of several hundred pioneers whose horde of cattle and horses made the trek an especially ponderous undertaking. This extract from Applegate's memoir, "A Day with the Cow Column in 1843," describes an 18-hour period that advanced his party some 20 miles nearer Oregon despite logistical—as well as human—complications.

It is four A.M.; the sentinels on duty have discharged their rifles—the signal that the hours of sleep are over; every wagon and tent is pouring forth its night tenants, and slow-kindling smokes begin to rise. Sixty men start from the corral and by five o'clock they have begun to move the herd of 5,000 cattle and horses toward camp.

From six to seven o'clock is a busy time; breakfast is eaten, tents struck, wagons loaded, and teams yoked. There are 60 wagons in 15 divisions or platoons of four wagons each.

The women and children have taken their places in the wagons. The pilot stands ready to mount and lead the way. Ten or 15 young men set off on a buffalo hunt. As the unfriendly Sioux have driven the buffalo out of the Platte, the hunters must ride 15 or 20 miles to reach them.

It is on the stroke of seven that the clear notes of the trumpet sound in the front; the leading division of wagons moves out of the encampment and the rest fall into their places with the precision of clockwork until the spot so lately full of life sinks back into that solitude that seems to reign over the broad plain and the rushing river.

The hunters are a full six miles from the line of march; though everything is dwarfed by distance, it is seen distinctly. The caravan has been about two hours in motion. First, near the bank of the shining river, is a company of horsemen. A member of the party has raised a flag, no doubt a signal for the wagons to steer their course to where he stands. The wagons form a line three quarters of a mile in length; some of the teamsters ride upon the front of their wagons, some walk beside their teams; scattered along the line companies of women and children are taking exercise on foot; they gather bouquets of rare and beautiful flowers that line the way.

Next comes a band of horses, the docile and sagacious animals scarce need attention, for they have learned to follow the wagons. Not so with the large herd of horned beasts that bring up the rear; lazy, selfish and unsocial. They move only in fear of the whip; there is never a moment of relaxation of the tedious and vexatious labors of their drivers.

At the nooning place, the teams are not unyoked, but simply turned loose from the wagons. Today an extra session of the Council is being held to settle a dispute between a proprietor and a young man who has undertaken to do a man's service on the journey for bed and board. The high court, from which there is no appeal, will define the rights of each party.

The evening is far less animated than the morning march; a drowsiness has fallen apparently on man and beast; teamsters fall asleep on their perches and even when walking by their teams. A little incident breaks the monotony of the march. An emigrant's wife whose state of health has caused Dr. Whitman to travel near the wagon is now taken with violent illness. The doctor has had the wagon driven out of the line, a tent pitched and a fire kindled.

We must leave it behind for the sun is now getting low in the west, and at length the painstaking pilot is standing ready to conduct the train in the circle 100 yards deep which he has marked out. So accurate the measurement and perfect the practice, that the hindmost wagon always precisely closes the gateway. Within ten minutes from the time the leading wagon is halted, the barricade is formed.

Everyone is busy preparing fires of buffalo chips to cook the evening meal, pitching tents and otherwise preparing for the night. There are anxious watchers for the absent wagon. But as the sun goes down it rolls into camp, the bright, speaking face of the doctor declares without words that both mother and child are well.

It is not yet eight o'clock when the first watch is to be set; the evening meal is just over. Near the river a violin makes lively music, and some youths improvise a dance; in another quarter a flute whispers its lament to the deepening night. It has been a prosperous day; more than 20 miles have been accomplished.

All is hushed and repose from the fatigue of the day, save the vigilant guard, and the wakeful leader who still has cares upon his mind that forbid sleep. The night deepens. At length a sentinel hurries to him with the welcome report that a party is approaching. He is at no loss to determine that they are our missing hunters who have met with success. He does not even await their arrival, but the last care of the day being removed, he too seeks the rest that will enable him to go through the same routine tomorrow.

As the first wagons get underway, an outrider gallops off to hunt, a teamster cracks his whip and three women indulge in a last-minute chat.

another dramatic alternative—passage on a sailing ship from New York or Boston for the six-month, 13,000-mile sea voyage around Cape Horn. (Pressed for time, the voyager could save three months—but risk yellow fever—by shortcutting across the Isthmus of Panama.)

No one knows how many strong-stomached men, women and children braved the sea voyage; perhaps 100,000. Of those, probably more than a few shared the feelings of one ship's passenger who was caught in a storm shortly after sailing. Writing in his diary, the reluctant traveler wistfully confessed, "Commenced reading today a work entitled *What I Saw in California* by Edwin Bryant. Mr. Bryant traveled the overland route to California, and I regret very much that I did not take the same."

But for every adventurer who tried to circumvent the hardships of trail travel by sailing around it, there were three who endured the overland route. Although most reached their destination free from catastrophe, one ill-fortuned pioneer group did not.

In 1846, George Donner was a prosperous 62-year-old farmer from Illinois, traveling west with his wife and five young children, and an assemblage of 12 yoke of oxen, three wagons, saddle horses and cattle, all managed by several hired hands. His older brother, Jacob, had a similarly affluent train, as did their neighbor, 46-year-old James Reed with his wife, mother-in-law and four children.

The Donners and the Reeds made every mistake that neophyte travelers could make. Not only did they overload their wagons, but they started late in the year. Upon reaching Fort Bridger in the Utah Territory, they decided to take a shortcut to California, across the Wasatch Mountains, on the sole advice of a guidebook whose author had not tested his own shortcut before publishing.

In the Wasatch, the party was joined by 13 other pioneers and three wagons, bringing their number to 87. Almost immediately the caravan got into trouble. They lost four days trying to penetrate the Weber River gorge, decided that it was impassable and turned back to find an alternate path over the mountains. It took them 28 days to reach Great Salt Lake, a distance of about 50 miles. They pushed on.

The desert exacted a terrible toll. It ate up six precious days of traveling time, killed off almost 100 oxen and forced some of the emigrants to abandon their wagons and supplies. By the time the caravan reached the Humboldt River on September 30, the pioneers were tired, hungry and quarrelsome. In a short, vicious fight, James Reed killed a young teamster, and the company expelled Reed from the train; some people wanted to hang him on the spot. Forced to leave his wife and children with the group, Reed rode off for California, caught up with another company and finally reached the Sacramento Valley, where he began organizing an expedition to fetch his family and to bring food to the rest of the Donner company.

By this time, the Donner party was close to starvation; threats of murder for food and water were becoming more frequent. The vanguard reached Truckee Lake, beyond which the trail climbed precipitously to Truckee Pass—the last major barrier before the Sacramento Valley. It was vital to cross this pass before further snowfalls made travel impossible. The families that were camped at the lake made several attempts at the pass, but high snowdrifts and then a storm forced them to turn back.

Five miles back, the tail end of the wagon train was also hit by the storm where they were encamped at Alder Creek. The snow continued falling, off and on for two weeks, and an ominous truth began to dawn on everyone: eighty-one people were now mired in at the two camps— 41 of them were children—and they would probably have to stay there all winter. It was snowing, too, on the west face of the mountains, where James Reed's rescue party was obliged to turn back after all the horses foundered and died.

By December the outlook in the two camps was grim. The remaining meat would not last through Christmas. A few cupfuls of flour were hoarded to make a thin gruel for infants; hides were boiled and the resultant glue eaten. In one cabin, children cut up a fur rug, toasted it and ate it. Death began to stalk the marooned travelers. On December 16, the campers at Truckee Lake, including Charles Stanton, William Eddy, "Uncle Billy" Graves and 14 others, set out on snowshoes to try and cross the pass. After two turned back, the others succeeded, but were struck by snow blindness on the far side.

On the morning of the sixth day, Stanton sat by the campfire as the party prepared to move out. Asked whether he was ready, he replied, "Yes, I am coming soon." In fact, he could not go on, and did not want to delay his companions. He died by the fire's embers. The others kept going, Eddy subsisting on some buffalo meat he found hidden in his pack, with a note from "Your own dear Eleanor." Eddy's wife had deprived herself and their children to provide this extra food for him.

Wagons forsaken, members of the Donner party struggle upslope in a vain attempt to surmount a snow-clogged Sierra pass. Two men reached the top, but they turned back rather than leave the others.

This prairie schooner—with a plow and hoe tied to its side—carried three men and a boy from Missouri to Oregon in 1845.

The sturdy wagon that crossed a continent

Nothing affected the outcome of the pioneers' gamble more directly than the wagons that had to carry them across 2,000 jolting miles of wilderness. There was no standard solution to the problem of conveyance. Some emigrants rolled westward in farm wagons that had been modified by craftsmen in jumping-off towns; others bought rigs specifically built for the one-way journey. But most wagons incorporated certain features (shown at right) that increased the likelihood of a successful passage.

A wagon had to be light enough not to place undue strain on the oxen or mules that pulled it, yet strong enough not to break down under loads of as much as 2,500 pounds. To meet these requirements, most wag-

ons were constructed of hardwoods such as maple, hickory and oak. Because of its weight, iron was used only to reinforce parts that took the greatest pounding. These included the tires, axles and hounds—bars that served to connect and provide rigidity to the undercarriage.

The wagon's sole concession to passenger comfort was the cloth covering, which shielded travelers—imperfectly, to be sure—from rain and dust. When the interior became stifling in midsummer heat, the cover could be rolled back and bunched, permitting freer circulation of air. Passengers could also count on plenty of exercise. Since the wagon lacked springs, everybody who could walk had to take to the footpaths when the wagon trail hit a rocky

stretch. Yet these evictions could be an enjoyable escape: there was hardly any place to sit inside the wagon; most space was taken up by the diverse cargo necessary to sustain emigrants during the long trip and to set up homes at its conclusion.

As oxen wearied and weakened, the load had to be lightened, and many a family heirloom suffered the fate of the "massive bureaus of carved oak" that one emigrant sadly reported seeing abandoned along the Oregon Trail in 1846. But apart from such losses and other contingencies, a pioneer who exercised "all due and proper diligence in traveling," as one guidebook said, could "cherish a reasonable hope that he will arrive at his journey's end safely and in season."

The three main parts of a prairie schooner were the wagon bed, the undercarriage and the cover. The wagon bed was a rectangular wooden box, usually about four feet wide and 10 to 12 feet long. At its front end was a jockey box to hold tools.

The undercarriage was composed of the wheels; the axle assemblies; the reach, which connected the two axle assemblies; the hounds, which fastened the rear axle to the reach and the front axle to the wagon tongue; and the bolsters, which supported the wagon bed. Dangling from the rear axle was a bucket for grease or a mixture of tar and tallow to lubricate the wheels.

The cover, made of canvas or cotton, was supported by a frame of hickory bows and tied to the sides of the bed. It extended beyond the bows at either end of the wagon and could be closed by drawstrings.

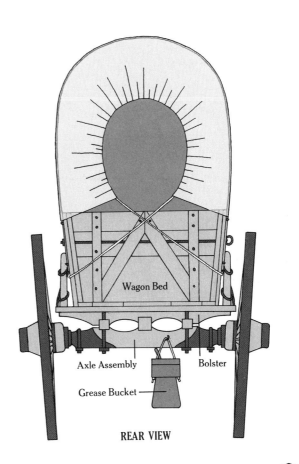

REAR VIEW

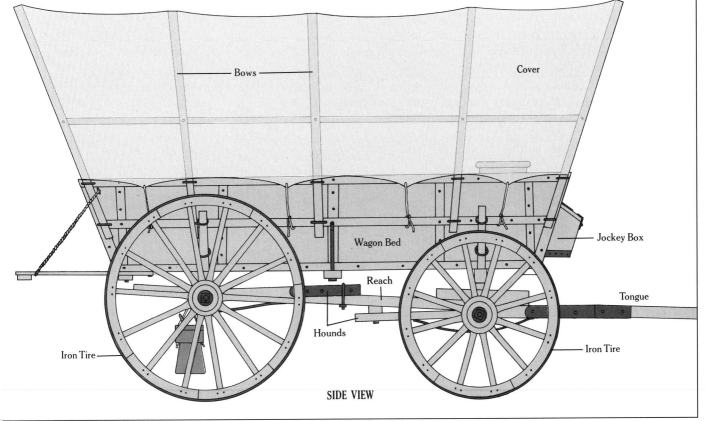

SIDE VIEW

Back at the lake, where the last of the livestock had been slaughtered and eaten, the huddled families gnawed boiled hides and bones seasoned with pepper. Margaret Reed killed the family dog, Cash, to feed her four children. As 13-year-old Virginia recalled, "We lived on little Cash for a week." And now began a gruesome series of events that stood in bleak contrast to Stanton's quiet act of heroism on the trail, and Mrs. Eddy's sacrifice of food to help her husband. Through these events the Donner expedition would earn a unique place in the annals of emigrant travel.

As the snowshoe party, now totally without food, groped down the west face of the mountains through a succession of blizzards, two members died of cold and starvation. With his last words, one of them, Uncle Billy Graves, urged his daughters to eat his body. The horrified survivors held back a day before taking this step, but finally yielded, roasting and eating strips of flesh. The group struggled on, and when two more died, they too were consumed. Of the 17 who had left the lake camp a month earlier, Eddy, Foster and five women lived to reach the Sacramento Valley.

Four rescue parties were sent out from California to save those still encamped at Alder Creek and Truckee Lake. On reaching the camps, they found a hideous situation. Thirteen people had died, including Eddy's wife and daughter. Jake Donner was dead, and George dying of gangrene. Many of the living seemed to be teetering on the verge of lunacy. At the lake camp the idea of cannibalism had become so commonplace that one emigrant remarked casually in his diary, "Mrs. Murphy said here yesterday that thought she would commence on Milt and eat him, it is distressing Sat 27th beautiful morning."

One band of rescuers led by James Reed found his wife and children safe, but when Eddy and William Foster arrived in another rescue team they found that their two young sons had been consumed. They collected George Donner's sons and left. Donner, unable to walk, stayed behind to die, his wife still with him.

Of the 81 travelers who had camped east of the pass on October 31, a total of 47 survived. One of these was young Virginia Reed, who wrote to a cousin back home with a poignant warning to future travelers: "Never take no cut ofs and hury along as fast as you can."

The Donner tragedy dissuaded practically no one. That same year, the U.S. had struck a treaty with Great Britain by which it gained sole possession of all Oregon territories south of the 49th parallel. (In 1848, after the Mexican War, the U.S. would own California as well.) The wagon trains multiplied year after year; by 1869, when the first transcontinental railroad was completed, no fewer than 350,000 emigrants had rolled and plodded along the trail.

Most emigrants were bound for the pastures of the Pacific Coast. As settlers arrived by the thousands, the stillness of the forests gave way to the ring of axes, the rasp of saws, the lowing of cattle and the creak of plows. The pioneers covered the landscape with wheat fields and dairy farms, built sawmills, laid out towns, organized governments and transformed the Northwest into one of the richest and most bountiful of American provinces.

Nowhere did the wilderness seem so raw or remote as in Oregon. And nowhere else was the act of pioneering so fundamental or so dramatic. Most newcomers headed for "the best poor man's country on the globe"—the Willamette valley, a broad tract of prairie and timberland south of the Columbia River, cupped between the lofty spine of the Cascade Range to the east and the coastal mountains on the west.

The earliest settlers simply cleared a likely spot in the wilderness and started farming. No boundaries were laid out, no deed was filed, no limitations were placed on the amount of land a man could claim. But as early as 1843, the pioneers enacted their own extremely generous land law. Each man was allotted a square mile—640 acres—provided he staked out his land, filed a claim and built a cabin within six months.

With only the most basic tools, coupled with an infinite willingness to expend huge quantities of sweat, most settlers first tackled the elemental task of building a house. "Weeks of hard labor were required to fell the trees, clear away the brush, and prepare the site," rem-

The odyssey of the Saints

Of all the forces that drove families west, none was stronger than the urge to escape religious persecution—the heart-felt motive of the Mormons.

Their sect—the Church of Jesus Christ of Latter-day Saints—was founded in 1830 by Joseph Smith, who claimed direct contact with the Almighty. Although rapidly attracting followers, it also drew the hostility of nonbelievers to whom the Mormons' theocratic government, communal economics and practice of plural marriage seemed threats to American values. Beginning in 1832, the Mormons suffered violent persecution and were forced to flee from Ohio, Missouri, then Illinois.

After Smith was murdered in 1844, the Saints resolved to move westward into the unknown. Three years later, they reached their ultimate sanctuary in Utah's Salt Lake Valley.

Their 1,400-mile journey was the most superbly planned pioneer migration of the 19th Century. Brigham Young, Smith's dynamic successor and a brilliant organizer, arranged that the refugees make their way in small, manageable groups. The first of these plowed fields and planted crops. Later groups harvested the food and left behind new plantings for those in the rear.

According to tradition, while Young was still in the mountains overlooking their final destination in July 1847, he experienced a vision of the future city of God. "This is the right place!" he declared confidently. What the Mormons had anticipated as an earthly Eden was, in fact, one of the most inhospitable environments ever to confront American pioneers.

During their first days in Utah, the Mormons' struggle was simply to stay alive. The fate of the entire church hung on their efforts. Following the advance party, 1,800 more of the faithful plodded in bands of 10, 50 or 100 people each. In addition, 13,000 well-disciplined Mormon refugees waited patiently in the Iowa and Nebraska prairies for the word to join their brothers and sisters. By the mid-1850s, Mormon missionaries had recruited thousands of converts from Europe, who began their Mormon life by walking 1,300 miles from Iowa to the Salt Lake Valley hauling their possessions in two-wheeled handcarts.

By the time another decade had passed, the Saints had constructed 1,043 miles of canals, which irrigated 154,000 acres of formerly arid terrain. Salt Lake City hummed with industry. In later years, this Mormon nation-within-a-nation would become a major Western metropolis.

Mormon converts from Europe, trekking to Salt Lake City, haul their handcarts across a prairie stream and prepare to make camp.

inisced Charlotte Cartwright, who arrived in 1845. "Trees were cut the proper length, one side of the log hewed smooth with a broadax, and fitted so they would join at the corners and lie compact. Logs for the floors were split and smoothed with an adze."

Rough-hewn timbers set on log rafters provided the roof. Then came the finishing work on the structure. "The fireplace and chimney was built with sticks and plastered inside and out with a thick coating of clay," recorded Cartwright. "Windows were a sort of sliding door in the wall, without glass." The door consisted of hewn planks pegged together and hung on wooden or leather hinges; sometimes a buffalo hide was draped over the door to help keep out the winter cold.

With the same kind of ready ingenuity, the pioneers built rudimentary furnishings. An Ohio rocking chair might have survived the overland trip, but the oak dining table had probably been abandoned on some uphill stretch. For dishes, most settlers used the same tin plates that they had used on the way west.

One frustrating problem, the settlers soon discovered, was clothing. No cotton grew in Oregon, and there were as yet no sheep to be sheared for wool. Cloth for making garments was scarce and costly. So settlers cut up tents and wagon covers into overcoats, lining them with skins or rags. Or else they turned to the old standby of the mountain men—buckskin. When their trail-tattered footwear proved beyond repair, children, and many adults, went barefoot.

The pioneer woman quickly learned to improvise. She manufactured soap from animal fat and lye. She extracted dye from tree bark, brewed tea from sage leaves, and boiled carrots with sugar syrup to make jam. When children caught cold or fever, a pioneer mother rubbed their skin with goose grease and turpentine, which seemed to be a standard salve for almost any disorder. "It was all you could smell in a schoolroom," one settler remembered.

Beyond the material needs, there was something else that settlers in the lonely Oregon forests craved: the society of other people. A pioneer family might hike miles through the woods on Sunday to attend church at one of the missions—an occasion that combined piety with a chance to talk crops and exchange gossip.

In time, the log cabins of the early settlers gave way to neat frame houses with glass windows, painted woodwork and papered walls. Oregonians exchanged their moss-filled mattresses and buffalo robes for feather beds,

and they bought dressers and easy chairs from local cabinetmakers. A small steam-powered riverboat puffed up and down the Willamette River, hauling goods and people. Mail arrived regularly by ship around Cape Horn and was distributed to the territory's 40 post offices.

From the beginning of Oregon settlement, there had been a dearth of women. In some parts of the territory, the male population outnumbered the female by a dreary ratio of nine to one. Desperate bachelors in the back-

woods sometimes married Indian girls, paying dowries in blankets to their fathers. And after 1850, the demand for brides grew greater still when Congress cut the permissible size of a land claim from 640 acres to 320 acres—but allowed a pioneer to claim another 320 acres for his wife, if he had one.

Meanwhile, in the northeastern U.S., there was an estimated surplus of at least 30,000 unattached women. One solution was to rearrange the population some-what, and there were numerous enterprising schemes to bring Eastern women west. It took a little time; there was no immediate rush to Western altars among the ladies. But by the 1860s, a steady stream of women from the East were helping shape the fabric of a new society. They were teaching Western youngsters, marrying western men and giving birth to a new generation of Americans who would know the Pacific Northwest as their native land.

A rough way to get rich quick

"What a clover-field is to a steer, the sky to a lark, a mudhole to a hog, such are new diggings to a miner." So, in 1862, wrote *The Oregonian* about the men who roamed the West in a tireless search for precious metal. Once the great California gold strike of 1848 had shown what riches the Western earth could hold, hordes of Americans hurried to every other promising corner of the wilderness.

The grip of gold or silver fever was more than just a yearning for wealth and luxury. To many the game was the thing: a man never knew when he might spy a glint of bright metal on a remote hillside or in a virgin stream—and he never ceased expecting it to happen. A Montana gold rusher described his vice as "falling victim to *ignis fatuus,* the will-o'-the-wisp of Coeur d'Alene, Peace River, Stinkene, Cassiar, White Pine, Pioche or Yellowstone, and last but not least the Black Hills."

Through winter and summer the prospectors kept at the search; no gorge was too precarious to descend, no river too treacherous to navigate, no peak too difficult to explore. Writing from Colorado in 1860, Samuel Mallory, a gold-struck former mayor of Danbury, Connecticut, told the folks back home: "You can form no idea of the mountain we climbed (unless you can think of one ten-hundred thousand million feet high). One company of miners ran their boiler wagon off a bank 50 ft. high, and killed two pair of oxen. We feel very thankful for our safe deliverance."

A miner surveys the scene from an aerie fit for falcons at the Dolly Varden silver mine, in the Rockies near Georgetown, Colorado.

Deadwood, the capital of Black Hills gold, teems with traffic in what a resident called "mud of adhesive properties rare, its depth unfathomable." Here the banks handled $100,000 a day, a bunk cost $1 a night and "Coal Oil Johnny" monopolized kerosene sales at $3.75 a gallon.

Cripple Creek miners of the 1890s assemble around a pair of compressed-air drills mounted on an iron column by universal joints. The speedy pneumatic drills put an end to laborious hand-jacking—and in the process they drastically reduced the number of jobs available to men in the mines.

127

6. The rush to El Dorado

James Wilson Marshall was making his regular daily inspection along the south fork of the American River in central California. A 36-year-old carpenter and jack-of-all-trades, Marshall was the working partner in the sawmill called Sutter's Mill. Every morning he went there to check for a buildup of sediment in the millrace that carried water from the river to the wheel that powered the mill.

On this fateful Monday morning, January 24, 1848, a few tiny chunks of metallic rock beckoned to him from the delta of mud, sand and gravel at the lower end of the race. Marshall picked up a piece and banged it between two rocks; it flattened out (iron pyrites, or fool's gold, would have shattered). He took a piece to the cook, who boiled it in her soap kettle with lye and baking soda; the metal was unchanged. He treated it with nitric acid; the acid had no effect. The substance passed all the tests. As Marshall had suspected from the moment he first spotted the glittering metal, this was gold.

The discovery at Sutter's Mill triggered one of the great mass adventures of all times, perhaps even the greatest since the Crusades. From all parts of the globe—North and South America, Europe, Asia, Australia—a polyglot horde of gold seekers descended upon the streams and mountains of California, eager for wealth. These men—doctors, lawyers, preachers, farmers, mechanics, scholars, illiterates, merchants, ne'er-do-wells—helped create the new Golden State. And when the fever had subsided there, new epidemics raged farther inland, transforming Colorado, Nevada and other frontier territories as men rushed to the newest spot where precious metals had been uncovered.

El Dorado was the way they described such a place, borrowing the name of the legendary city of treasure sought by early Spanish explorers in South America. The Spanish had never found it, but for a few turbulent decades El Dorado would actually exist in scores of locations scattered across the American West.

At first, John Sutter, Marshall's partner in Sutter's Mill, tried to hush up the discovery, to prevent a rush of adventurers from trampling the fields of his 50,000-acre ranch and destroying his stock. He feared that gold fever would prove such an irresistible lure that he would lose the many workers he needed to man his vast empire. "Of course I knew nothing of the extent of the discovery," Sutter later recalled, "but I was satisfied, whether it amounted to much or little, that it would greatly interfere with my plans."

But gold was such a mesmerizing force that it was impossible to prevent reports of its presence. Within six weeks, all of Sutter's workers had deserted his stores, farms and ranches to look for gold. On March 15, 1848, the first printed report appeared in a San Francisco newspaper, the *Californian*, under the headline "Gold Mine Found."

The epidemic remained largely local until California's military governor, Colonel R.B. Mason, toured the gold fields and sent a report to Washington in August, buttressed with $3,900 in gold samples. This report provided welcome substance for the opening message to Congress by President James K. Polk, who was looking for a way to justify the recent war with Mexico. The accounts of gold in California, he said, "would scarcely command belief were they not corroborated by authentic reports."

The Presidential message galvanized the nation as no official utterance had since the Declaration of Independence. By early 1849 gold fever was raging all along the Atlantic seaboard, through the South and across the broad Mississippi valley—the areas that contained most of the nation's 22 million people. Men sold their businesses and quit their jobs. They borrowed money, pawned their belongings, studied maps and took off by sea and

Gold fever fills a Long Island, New York, post office in William Mount's 1850 painting *California News*. Amid ship-sailing notices, the artist *(right foreground)* and friends read reports from the gold fields.

A clipper ship traveling to San Francisco guaranteed fast, clear sailing, according to an East Coast line advertising card. There is no hint of the gales and doldrums that plagued the long sea voyage.

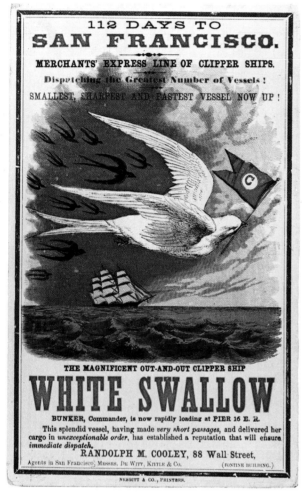

112 DAYS TO **SAN FRANCISCO.**

MERCHANTS' EXPRESS LINE OF CLIPPER SHIPS.

Dispatching the Greatest Number of Vessels!

SMALLEST, SHARPEST AND FASTEST VESSEL NOW UP!

THE MAGNIFICENT OUT-AND-OUT CLIPPER SHIP

WHITE SWALLOW

BUNKER, Commander, is now rapidly loading at PIER 16 E. R.

This splendid vessel, having made *very short passages*, and delivered her cargo in *unexceptionable order*, has established a reputation that will ensure *immediate dispatch.*

RANDOLPH M. COOLEY, 88 Wall Street,

Agents in San Francisco; Messrs. De Witt, Kittle & Co.   (TONTINE BUILDING.)

NESBITT & CO., PRINTERS.

by land, filled with optimism. Because of the year, they became known as the forty-niners—a label that applied even to those who went a year or two later. They also took the name Argonauts, after the band in Greek mythology who sailed in search of the Golden Fleece.

Forty-niners or Argonauts—the prospect of gold engulfed them. One man in Rochester, New York, hired a personal clairvoyant to aid his search. Others hopefully stocked up on evening clothes in which they might celebrate. They bought guidebooks that told of riverbeds "paved with gold to the thickness of a hand" and sang suddenly popular tunes such as "The Gold Diggers Waltz."

Everyone was impatient to reach the gold fields before the lustrous metal played out. But how to go? Overland was the most direct but also the most demanding of the three principal routes. Forty-niners could travel about half the way by train and riverboat.

Then, however, they faced an arduous journey by wagon train through scarcely charted terrain of hostile Indians, terrible deserts and difficult mountain passes. "There is surely no Royal road to California," wrote young Ohioan Peter Decker, "& traveling it is labor indeed."

The most favored route was by ship around Cape Horn at the tip of South America. The 13,000-nautical-mile trip took an average of six months—nearly twice as long as the overland journey—and offered its share of hazards: monstrous seas, bitter cold, seasickness and food so verminous, one passenger complained, that "there were two bugs for every bean." Even so, more than 50 California-bound ships—sleek clippers, reconditioned hulks, even coastal freighters—left New York harbor in February 1849 alone.

Many Argonauts compromised by taking the combination route: by ship to Central America, overland to the Pacific and then by sea again. This was usually the fastest but most expensive way to go. The favored crossing was at the narrow Isthmus of Panama. Forty-niners made the bulk of this 75-mile journey in long dugout canoes called bungos, passing the time by drinking brandy and trying out their new firearms on alligators, iguanas and other wildlife along the Chagres River. In Panama City, on the Pacific Coast, they booked passage to California, but sometimes waited for weeks for their ship to arrive.

No matter what route they took, the forty-niners could only breathe a sigh of relief once they reached port in San Francisco or one of the staging stops like Sacramento or Tuleburg, later named Stockton. The odyssey was not complete until they journeyed into the mountains, fanning out along the American River and the Yuba and the Feather and the Tuolumne and the smaller streams that would enter history and legend.

Over the ages, these swift waters had abraded and broken off the gold-bearing granite and quartz of the High Sierra. Along with the usual load of sand, dirt and other sediment, they carried the gold down into the valleys in the form of powdery dust, flakes, seedlike chunks, even heavy nuggets. There, as the current slowed, the stream relinquished its precious burden to gravel banks, sand bars and the stream bed. The resulting deposit was known to miners as a placer, which was taken from the Spanish for an underwater plain and pronounced to rhyme with "passer."

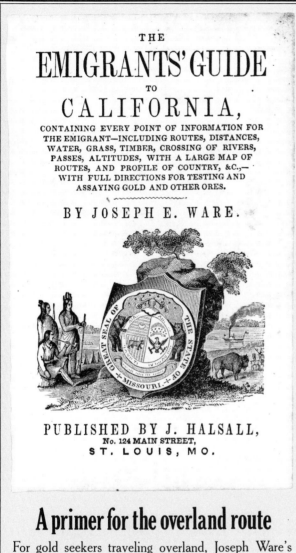

A primer for the overland route

For gold seekers traveling overland, Joseph Ware's 1849 guide served as an invaluable source book. Its title page *(above)* indicates the range of its contents; examples of its pithy, practical advice appear below.

Start at 4 — travel till the sun gets high — camp till the heat is over. Then start again and travel till dark.

After the upper Platte Ford, for over fifty miles, the water is impregnated with poisonous matter. If you would avoid sickness, abandon its use.

TRUCKIE'S PASS, You will be tried to the utmost. Pack everything over the summit, then haul your wagons up with ropes. You will certainly save time, and perhaps hundreds of dollars.

Stories of the best gold strikes typically featured a great deal of wondrous good fortune and not a whole lot of hard work. One tale told how a Southerner brought his slave with him to the diggings near Coloma. The slave had a recurrent dream about finding gold under a certain cabin in the settlement. When the master had a similar dream, he bought the cabin, and together the two men dug up the dirt floor and panned out $20,000 in gold. Another man in town took $2,000 from under his own doorstep. Three Frenchmen uprooted a tree stump in the middle of the Coloma road and dug $5,000 from the hole. A man who had been sitting on a rock, moping in discouragement and homesickness, arose and kicked the rock in anger; the rock rolled aside, disclosing a nugget of shining gold. A little girl found a strangely discolored rock and took it to her mother. The mother washed it off and saw that it was a seven-pound nugget. A prospector's mule was staked out for the night. When the stake was pulled up in the morning, there in the hole was the welcome glint of gold. And way up north above the Feather River, a fellow claimed that he had found a lake whose shores were littered with big clumps of gold—only he could not remember exactly where it was.

A favorite story related how, down on the Tuolumne River, a hunter shot a bear and the bear tumbled over the edge of a canyon, landing on a ledge at a lower level. When the hunter climbed down after the bear, what should he find? The ledge was quartz, of course, richly laced with gold. Another tale explained how a twice-lucky fellow found gold after a gunfight in which the bullet missed him, but dug a furrow in some quartz near his shoulder; there was gold in the quartz. Near Carson Creek, a miner died and his fellow diggers decided to send him off in decent style instead of the usual quick burial. After drinks all around, the miners marched solemnly to the grave site. One of them, who had been a powerful preacher back home, preached and prayed while the miners knelt at the graveside. As the praying and preaching went on and on, the mourners grew restless, and began idly gathering loose dirt from the grave and letting it run through their fingers, as miners will. Suddenly, one of them yelled "Color!" The dirt from the grave had encouraging traces of gold. "Congregation dismissed!" bellowed the preacher. The body was hastily removed from the hole and set aside.

In Nebraska one of the six groups into which former West Pointer Bruff divided his uniformed, quasi-military company cooks a meal.

Vivid record from the journey of a brave and lonely man

Ugly descent & crossing, of Salt — (Stinking) Creek

Bruff tersely describes his passage over a Nebraska creek that stank of marsh grass.

One of the most vivid records of the overland journey to California was compiled by a traveler named Joseph Goldsborough Bruff. Bruff began his career as a West Point cadet. He later served as a sailor, then became a U.S. government draftsman in Washington, D.C. But in 1849, when he was 44, gold fever inspired Bruff to give up drawing official maps and designing buttons for officers' tunics. He organized the Washington City and California Mining Association and led 63 men in 13 wagons across the Plains. On the way, he filled his notebooks with a narrative of the journey, including observations of topography, plants, animals and weather. Bruff embellished his text with quick sketches bearing his own laconic captions, and later elaborated some drawings in haunting watercolors.

The mules has got through, but the owner aint,— by a long ways.

The Desert

When a mule gave out on the trail, as Bruff's sketch shows, its owner shouldered the load.

In 120 days Bruff's party trekked from the Missouri River to the Sierra Nevada, losing only two men to illness and none to Indians, accidents or harsh deserts shown here. Then his luck failed. In the Sierra he stayed with his snowbound wagons and sent his men ahead; despite their promises, none hiked back from the gold fields to help him. Ill and alone, he staggered 30 miles to the nearest settlement carrying his notebooks, which he hoped to publish as a gold-seekers' guide. He found no gold himself and went home via Panama. Then, in New York, thieves took all of his possessions except his journals. But Bruff was able to find no market for them; almost a century passed before his great adventure story became the book that he had planned.

In an especially effective watercolor, Bruff painted a hot, dry Wyoming defile and the "rugged, bare and harsh-looking Rattle-Snake Mts."

All—preacher and mourners alike—began digging. Profitably, too.

Some of the tales were most likely apocryphal—the kind of folklore that flourishes wherever wandering, lonely men get together. But no one could be sure. Many of the stories bore the names of real people, and all sustained the giddy gold fever. Miners loved to tell about a fellow named George McKnight, who went chasing after a runaway cow at Grass Valley and stubbed his toe on an outcrop of quartz—that was, sure enough, rich with the precious metal. And then there was a chap named Bennager Raspberry—nobody could invent that name—who worked as a storekeeper at Angels Camp. He was locally famous because of the time when he had in his stock a keg of brandied peaches that had spoiled on the long trip around Cape Horn and up to San Francisco. He threw out the peaches, and all the pigs in Angels Camp ran around squealing drunk for four days and nights. Bennager went hunting one day and got the ramrod stuck in his musket. He could not pull it out, so he fired it at a hillside and the ramrod went through the exposed roots of a manzanita shrub. To get his ramrod back, old Raspberry had to pull up the manzanita, roots and all, and there in the ground was lots of gold. Things had been quiet at Angels Camp for a while; now a big rush was on.

But the prosaic reality was backbreaking work with shovel and pan. The miner dug the dirt and sorted out the most promising material to fill the pan. He then swirled it around under water to separate out the lighter sand and gravel from what he hoped would be the heavy gold-carrying residue remaining in the bottom. Working 50 pans of dirt in a 10-hour day was regarded as a reasonable goal. To speed up the process, many miners teamed up and put together devices such as the cradle and long tom that used the same principle as the panning method *(pages 138-139)*.

A few miners enjoyed the rare and exhilarating experience of washing $1,000 or more in gold from a single panful. Most were lucky, however, if they could pan a couple of teaspoons—the half ounce a day, worth $8, that was generally recognized as the bare minimum necessary to keep them at work. This would allow them to pay the inflated prices for food and supplies and put a little aside to get them home some day.

If a miner found gold or the promise of it, he staked out his claim to the patch of ground. This legally entitled him and no one else to mine the parcel. Each mining camp improvised its own claim laws. The size of the claim was usually determined by the richness of the diggings in the area; in very rich camps it might be as little as a hundred square feet. A miner proved possession of a claim by the presence of his tools and his continued work on the site.

Disputes were settled by juries of fellow miners—or by more primitive means. At a particularly lucrative field known as Rich Bar, where single pans frequently yielded as much as $2,000, and miners took away a total of more than $14 million, contending groups of Americans and Frenchmen decided to adjudicate their claim dispute with a fist fight. The two chosen gladiators slugged it out for three hours, and the American eventually won. The Frenchmen moved out and found another prospect, a ravine that turned out to be French Gulch, the richest of the diggings in the area around Rich Bar.

Few miners stayed put in their claims. Every few days, a new rumor raced through the camps and set off a fresh outbreak of "lump fever"—the chronic itch to abandon one claim and move on in search of a more lucrative one. Lump fever raged, it seemed, irrespective of the rumor's source or evident reliability: "It had confidingly come to our ears," wrote D.R. Leeper of his life as an Argonaut near a place known as Old Dry Diggings, "that someone had affirmed that he had seen a man who had heard another man say that he knew a fellow who was dead sure that he knew another fellow who, he was certain, belonged to a party that was shoveling up the big chunks."

By preventing a thorough working of their claims, the itch to move on probably ensured that most miners would never strike it rich. But it sometimes brought stunning success. William Downie, who had knocked around the world as seaman, trader and lumber dealer since leaving his boyhood home in Scotland, noticed that one group of miners consistently paid for their provisions at the camp store with large lumps of gold. When he learned that they came from farther up the Yuba River, he mounted a nine-man expedition to go upriver. En route, his party stopped at the junction of the Yuba and its north fork to catch their dinner. They

A deserter heads for the diggings in an engraving from *Three Years in California,* an 1850 book by Walter Colton, a magistrate of Monterey.

A lopsided struggle between duty and the lure of the diggings

In the early days of the gold rush, soldiers in towns like Monterey and San Francisco felt doubly aggrieved. Victors in the Mexican War (though few actually had seen combat), they were pulling garrison duty while civilians got rich overnight in nearby diggings. Worse yet, by mid-1848 a rocketing local inflation had made a private's pay, six dollars a month, worth about three pounds of flour.

"No time in the history of our country has presented such temptations to desert," wrote California's acting governor, Colonel R. B. Mason, to the War Department. His soldiers agreed. "The struggle between *right* and six dollars a month," said one, "and *wrong* and $75 a day is rather a severe one."

A soldier who lost the struggle wrote: "A frenzy seized my soul; piles of gold rose up before me at every step; thousands of slaves bowed to my beck and call; myriads of fair virgins contended for my love. In short I had a violent attack of gold fever."

Whole platoons deserted with their arms and horses. In the 18 months beginning July 1, 1848, the Army in northern California lost 716 men of a total 1,290. So many sailors jumped ship that the Pacific Squadron's commander, Thomas ap Catesby Jones, advised the Secretary of the Navy: "for the present and I fear for years to come, it will be impossible for the United States to maintain any naval establishment in California."

Army Lieutenant William Tecumseh Sherman complained: "None remain behind but we poor devils of officers who are restrained by honor." He worked as a surveyor to make ends meet. He also zealously pursued deserters, once capturing 27 of a band of 28—18 of them at one swoop when he stormed alone into a cabin with a cocked musket.

But most got away. "Others were sent to force them back to duty," wrote historian Zoeth Skinner Eldredge, "and all, pursuers and pursued, went to the mines together."

snagged a 14-pound salmon and, after boiling it, found specks of gold in the bottom of the cookpot.

The party began searching and quickly found gold in the seams of the rock. Downie himself seldom took out less than a pound of gold a day—at least $250. He was an amiable man, "one of the best fellows in the world," wrote a storekeeper who embezzled from him, "ready to do all in his power to assist a stranger." Downie spent the gold just as fast as he could pan it. "We have seen the Major go through two or three pounds of dust on one Sunday," said an acquaintance, "and after emptying the company sack, the party would sober up, disperse and dig more."

The place where Downie found gold and expended it so freely became an embryonic settlement known simply as the Forks. Soon it blossomed into a full-fledged town of several thousand population, and the citizens changed its name to Downieville, in honor of the easy-going founder.

Settlement here and in scores of other gold camps tended to follow a pattern. An enterprising merchant would establish a camp store, often a tent erected in the middle of the diggings. He sold clothing, tools and whiskey and sometimes even rented space on the floor where a newcomer could unroll his blankets for the night. His store served as a social center, and he often acted as the local repository of information and occasionally even as adjudicator of disputes. The miners built canvas-covered shacks and log cabins nearby. A blacksmith and pharmacist opened shop, a banker showed up and rudimentary civilization set in. All the same, most such shantytowns survived only as long as there was gold to be panned. When the gold gave out, all the bustle subsided quickly as the inhabitants simply packed their mules and headed for another camp.

Mining settlements were born and died so quickly that no one could keep track of them. For a fleeting period, there flourished a bewildering profusion of towns with picturesque names—frequently the same. No fewer than four camps were named for the lost Biblical region of Ophir, the source of King Solomon's wealth. In addition, there were four Poverty Bars, four Missouri Bars, three Long Bars. The Bar referred to the source of the gold—a gravel or sand bar.

No recorded census of saloons existed for the settlement called Whiskytown. But the name was apt. Min-

ers celebrated their success or drowned their disappointments in everything from genuine New England rum, at $20 a bottle, to home-brewed spirits with names like Tarantual juice and a pricetag at whatever the market would bear. The saloon was so central to the miner's life in fact that the barman's measures frequently dictated the value of gold dust. A wineglass filled with gold dust was worth $100 and a tumbler $1,000. The basic measure was a pinch of gold between thumb and forefinger, the worth of which was reckoned at one dollar and which was usually good for at least one drink.

On Sunday, some forty-niners sought solace or inspiration in improvised church services conducted by visiting preachers or by one of their own. The services were often held in saloons while liquor sales were temporarily suspended and the nude paintings turned to the wall. A miner named Charles B. Gillespie later recalled a typical Sunday in the town of Coloma, California, near where the gold rush had begun. A crowd was gathered in and around an unfinished house, he wrote, and inside was a miner-preacher, "as ragged and hairy as myself, holding forth to an attentive audience. He spoke well and to the purpose and warmed every one with his fine and impassioned delivery. He closed with a benediction, but prefaced it by saying 'There will be divine service in this house next Sabbath—if, in the meantime, I hear of no new diggin's!'"

Occasionally, the shantytowns featured organized public entertainments. Itinerant performers and minstrels made the rounds of the mining camps. Some towns staged bull-and-bear fights, a variation on the bullfight tradition brought to California by its Spanish pioneers. Instead of men, these cruel encounters pitted a 1,000- to 1,500-pound grizzly bear against a fierce bull. Most of the time, however, the miners had to seek amusement in more mundane entertainments. "If a terrier catches a rat," wrote Hinton Helper about one of the gold towns, "or if a big turnip is brought to market, the people cluster together and scramble for a sight with eagerness and impetuosity."

Ever certain to draw a crowd was the sight of a woman. In 1850 less than 8 per cent of California's population was female, and in the gold fields the percentage was usually much lower. Everyone knew and talked about the few women in a town. The first woman to arrive in Rich Bar quickly became a legend. Known as

The Indiana Girl because her father ran a hotel called the Indiana, she was large and brawny, with a voice to match, and wore miner's boots. Once, when the snow was five feet deep, she trudged into camp carrying a 50-pound sack of flour on her back.

Back East, recruiters with varying purposes in mind strove diligently to increase the California female population. Several employment agencies signed up both professional prostitutes and unwary working girls to be shipped west, ostensibly to work as domestics. A temperance lecturer named Sarah Pellet had less luck in her recruiting campaign. She conceived a plan to remedy the rowdiness of the male mining camps by importing "5,000 virtuous New England women," but found few takers.

No wonder. Miss Pellet had experienced the lawlessness of Downieville firsthand when she appeared there to deliver a temperance talk. The saloons emptied for the occasion, and the audience was so impatient for her to begin that pistol shots were fired in the air to hurry along the introductory speaker. In the ensuing confusion that speaker was killed by a shotgun blast. Miss Pellet fled in great haste and alarm, and the cause of temperance received a setback as business at the saloons immediately resumed.

In the saloons and elsewhere during the early days of the gold rush, a friendly male bonding, a fraternal camaraderie, tended to prevail. But as gold became harder to find and more and more men tried to find it, good feelings gave way to suspicion, envy and hostility. To begin with, enmity sprang up between men from different parts of the country. But Americans reserved their strongest dislike for those marked as different by language, culture or skin color. The mining towns were the most cosmopolitan places on the North American continent: of the approximately 85,000 men who swarmed to California in 1849, about 23,000 were not U.S. citizens. Few Americans relished sharing gold with these foreigners and, the following year, the infant state legislature imposed a special tax on aliens.

Simple tools for separating out the gold

Of all the contraptions designed to help the Argonaut separate his gold from the earth around it, the most popular was the lowly pan. The pan was simple to use and versatile: you could wash a shirt, feed a mule or fry bacon with it.

But panning meant hours of squatting in ice-cold water, rotating the pan until a man's arms were numb. To alleviate the struggle, the miners whacked together all sorts of ingenious gold separators. Though none proved less laborious than the pan, the three types shown here—the cradle, long tom and sluice box—did make the job move faster. Yet they were all simply extensions of the pan-washing method. And in the final cleanup, it was the pan that kept the last particles of gold from escaping.

THE WASH PAN

Usually made of tin or iron, the pan was flat-bottomed with gently slanting sides. The miner first filled it with dirt and then began swirling it around under water *(left, above)*. Next he raised it up from the water, continuing the circular motion and punctuating it with small jerks in and out of the water that washed out lighter sand *(right)*, and left only gold-carrying residue.

THE CRADLE

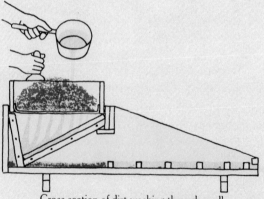

Cross section of dirt washing through cradle

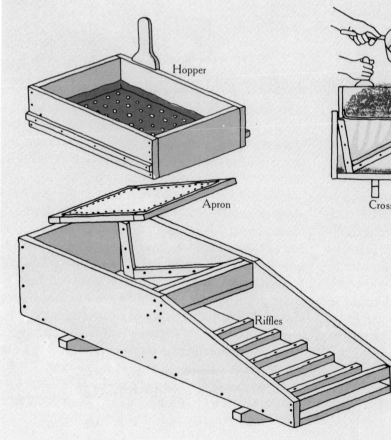

Hopper

Apron

Riffles

The cradle was an oblong wooden box about three feet in length and mounted on rockers. Bars called riffles were nailed along the bottom of its open lower end; and an apron made of canvas stretched over a frame was placed at a slant inside its upper end. A hopper with a perforated base and a side handle fitted over this end. Rocking the cradle with the handle, the miner poured water over gravel in the hopper *(above, right)*. Strained through the hopper and deflected by the apron, the water ran out of the rocker's lower end, leaving gold-bearing sediment behind each riffle.

THE LONG TOM

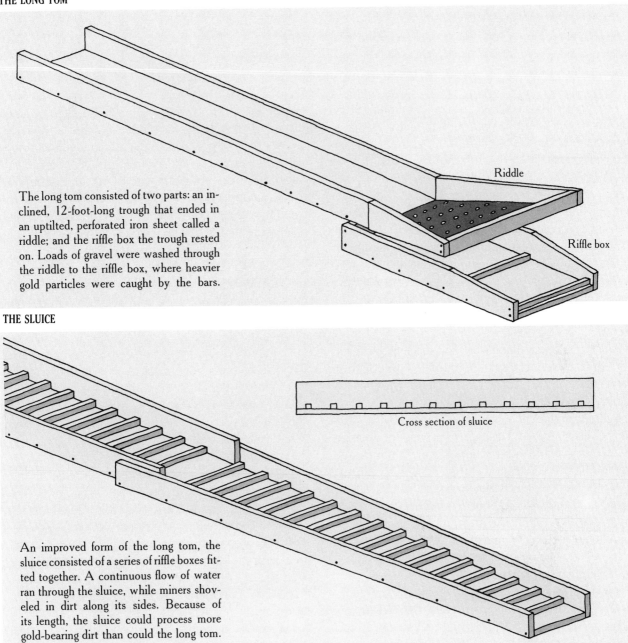

The long tom consisted of two parts: an inclined, 12-foot-long trough that ended in an uptilted, perforated iron sheet called a riddle; and the riffle box the trough rested on. Loads of gravel were washed through the riddle to the riffle box, where heavier gold particles were caught by the bars.

Riddle

Riffle box

THE SLUICE

Cross section of sluice

An improved form of the long tom, the sluice consisted of a series of riffle boxes fitted together. A continuous flow of water ran through the sluice, while miners shoveled in dirt along its sides. Because of its length, the sluice could process more gold-bearing dirt than could the long tom.

THE THREE BASIC TYPES OF RAW GOLD

Nuggets

Dust

Flakes

Once it had been separated from all surrounding material, gold appeared in one of the three forms shown here. Though the relative purity of the different samples causes the piles to vary in size, each weighs about one ounce—worth $16 to a miner in San Francisco in 1849.

The Americans disdained Mexicans and other Spanish Americans as "greasers," though many Mexicans were members of the families that had originally settled California. They made fun of the frugality and industry of the Chinese, who were willing to work abandoned claims and tailings for specks of gold white men considered unworthy of the effort. But they saved the worst indignities for people who were not foreigners at all—the California Indians. It was not a crime to kill Indians nor to press them into service in the gold fields at starvation wages. Indian labor was the key to many mining fortunes, including that of the Murphy boys—John and Daniel—who harvested $1.5 million in gold in less than a year.

Foreigners and Indians were also more likely to run afoul of the primitive system of justice practiced in many mining towns. At Old Dry Diggings, lynch law frequently prevailed. A group of five men, including two Frenchmen and a Chilean, were sentenced by an informally chosen jury to 39 lashes with a whip for attempted robbery. Additional charges were then raised against the three foreigners for an alleged attempt at robbery and murder elsewhere in California the previous year. A crowd of about 200 miners constituted itself as a jury, found the men guilty and sentenced them to hang, all in the space of a half hour. The defendants, who spoke no English, went to their deaths trying to get an interpreter.

The town of Old Dry Diggings thereby acquired its notorious nickname, Hangtown. Later, happy with neither name, the town fathers sought a new one out of civic pride. They mulled over the name Ravine City and finally settled for the more euphonious Placerville.

One of the fastest-growing settlements was Sacramento. This bustling town sprang up on John Sutter's land at the confluence of the American and Sacramento rivers, about 50 miles southwest of the sawmill that started it all. Sacramento, which was selected as the capital when California became a state in March 1848, served as the staging area for the northern mines. By the end of 1849, it had a population of 12,000 and more people were camped temporarily outside town in a sea of tents and wagons.

But for meteoric growth and sheer excitement, none of the mining settlements could begin to compete with the fabled boomtown on the bay, San Francisco. In 1847, a few months before the cry "Gold! Gold!" echoed through the streets, this hamlet on the sandy windswept tip of the peninsula that commanded the Golden Gate had called itself Yerba Buena and counted a population of 459—only one of whom considered himself a miner. In the subsequent two years, the town had taken the name of San Francisco—from a Spanish settlement that once had existed nearby—and transformed itself into a city of 25,000.

For nearly a decade, San Francisco was the most exciting city on earth. Every ship that crowded into the harbor brought not only gold seekers—all needing food, lodging, supplies, services and agreeable diversions—but the merchants, traders, speculators, money men, gamblers and prostitutes who could provide it. "I have seen purer liquors, better segars, finer tobacco, truer guns and pistols, larger dirks and bowie knives and prettier courtesans than in any other place I have ever visited," a new arrival wrote of San Francisco. "California can and does furnish the best bad things that are available in America."

Gold from the diggings to the east was the very foundation of San Francisco. From the original strike in 1848 until the mid-1850s, when the initial boom subsided, $345 million in pay dirt arrived there. Most of it whirled away on the winds of celebration and wild chance. Some successful miners considered it bad luck to head back to the mines after visiting San Francisco if they had not spent every ounce they had brought with them.

One such celebrant, remembered only as Flaxhead, came to town with 20 pounds of gold dust, worth about $5,000. Even after paying exorbitant prices for food, lodging and drink, even after losses at the gaming tables and generous tips to bar girls and female dealers in the gambling halls, Flaxhead still had some gold dust left when it was time to return to the mines. He poured it into a boot, slung the boot over his shoulder and made his way to the bar of the city's foremost hotel, the Parker House on Portsmouth Square. Here, Flaxhead drank and bought rounds for everybody until the boot was empty. To an onlooker who chided him about his spendthrift ways, Flaxhead replied: "There's plenty more at the mines."

In this flush of inexhaustible plenty, the entrepreneurial spirit—and inflation—flourished. Housing was in such enormous demand that the cost of lumber

San Francisco burgeoned into a major seaport within one year of the discovery of gold in the Sierra. This 1850 photograph — the earliest live visual record of the city — shows the bay thick with vessels behind a waterfront of multistory brick buildings where, as recently as 1847, cows had grazed and farmers and a modest handful of sea traders had dozed.

UCTION SALES ROOM.

RY R. A. LITTE & CO.
CTIONEERS. 279

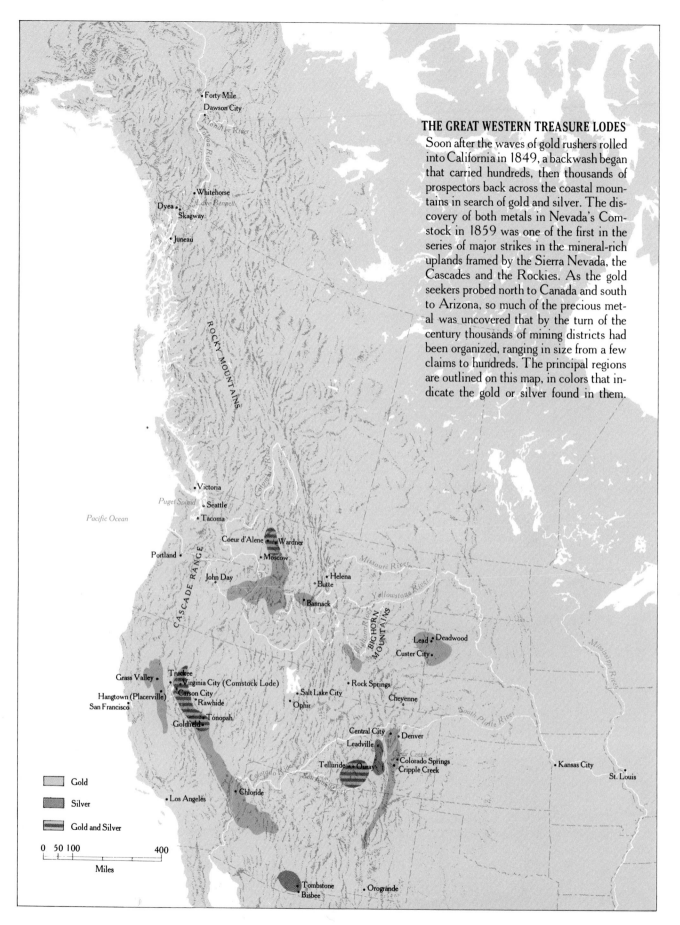

THE GREAT WESTERN TREASURE LODES

Soon after the waves of gold rushers rolled into California in 1849, a backwash began that carried hundreds, then thousands of prospectors back across the coastal mountains in search of gold and silver. The discovery of both metals in Nevada's Comstock in 1859 was one of the first in the series of major strikes in the mineral-rich uplands framed by the Sierra Nevada, the Cascades and the Rockies. As the gold seekers probed north to Canada and south to Arizona, so much of the precious metal was uncovered that by the turn of the century thousands of mining districts had been organized, ranging in size from a few claims to hundreds. The principal regions are outlined on this map, in colors that indicate the gold or silver found in them.

Gold

Silver

Gold and Silver

0 50 100   400

Miles

soared from four cents a board foot to a dollar or more. The supply of labor was so depleted by the rush to the mines that wages jumped from one dollar a day to as high as $30 a day.

Practically everyone dabbled in business. A ship captain, noticing the abundance of rats in the city, brought in a load of stray cats and sold them for $10 apiece. A merchant bought 1,500 dozen eggs off a coastal schooner and quickly sold them at 37 1/2 cents a dozen. Minutes later, he saw the same eggs offered for resale at four dollars a dozen. He bought every egg back, took them to Sacramento on the river steamer and sold the lot for six dollars a dozen.

The real business of San Francisco, however, was pleasure. A survey in 1853 showed 537 places where liquor was sold, 46 gambling houses and 48 places "kept by bawds." The hub of all this was Portsmouth Square, a onetime potato patch now offering the best hotels and finest diversions. A miner could gorge on wild game, oysters and other delicacies prepared in the French, German, American, Mexican or Chinese style. He could gamble in elegant salons like the Parker House, wagering up to $20,000 on the Mexican card game, monte. He could pay up as much as $600 to spend the night at one of the high-class bordellos known as parlor houses, where exotic foreign women—French, Mexican, Chilean, Chinese—exercised a special attraction for the forty-niners.

If the pleasures these places offered proved ephemeral, so also were the cities themselves. Towns burned so often during the gold rush that the conflagrations became a kind of grim joke. "You have heard of our fires," wrote a lawyer named Joseph Glover Baldwin. "They throw light on our character. We burn down a city in a night and build it in a day. Contracts for new buildings are signed by the light of the fire that is consuming the old."

The first major fire broke out on Christmas Eve, 1849, in Dennison's Exchange, a popular saloon and gambling hall. By the most probable account of events that holiday eve, racism touched off the blaze: it was the practice of Dennison's and other bars to discourage black patrons by serving them one drink on the house and no more at any price. When a black tried to buy a second drink at Dennison's, the bartender stabbed him. As he fell, the victim knocked over a lantern. The resulting fire destroyed more than one million dollars' worth of property around Portsmouth Square, including Mrs. Irene McCready's high-class parlor house.

Mrs. McCready's and many of the other affected establishments rebuilt almost immediately, only to be leveled again by an even bigger fire four months later. Over the next 13 months or so, four more disastrous fires swept the city. The worst of them occurred on May 4, 1851, the anniversary of the second blaze to level Mrs. McCready's, and destroyed 18 blocks with 2,000 buildings—many of them new and supposedly fireproof structures of brick.

The scourge of fire helped contribute to the formation of one of San Francisco's most auspicious institutions—self-appointed citizen law-enforcement groups. San Francisco's first "Committee of Vigilance for the protection of lives and property of the citizens" was formed in 1851. The committee's aim was to combat criminal elements—including those suspected of setting several of the fires—with whom the graft-infested police force and corrupt courts refused to deal.

Its 103 charter members had scarcely signed up when they were summoned to duty by the emergency signal—a series of double strokes on the fire bell in the tower of City Hall. Some boatmen had seized an Australian named Simpton who had stolen an iron cashbox from the office of a shipping agent and was trying to escape in a rowboat. They turned him over to the newly formed committee of vigilantes who, in little more than five hours, found Simpton guilty at a kangaroo trial and hanged him. Soon thereafter, the committee executed three additional men, including a pair of the so-called Sydney Ducks, a notorious gang of emigrants from Australia who, among other depredations, were said to have deliberately set fires so they could loot stores during the resulting confusion.

San Francisco was not the first place where citizens took law into their own hands, of course. But this boomtown's fear of arsonists and other rampant criminals produced on a grand scale the model for the vigilantes who would practice lynch-mob justice on the Western frontier for decades to come.

The California rush reached its peak in 1852 when 100,000 miners swarmed through the valleys of central

California, extracting $81 million worth of gold. After that, output gradually decreased, and mining it increasingly required large outlays of capital—to drive deep shafts into mountains and to hose away entire hillsides with hydraulic jets to lay bare the gold.

In the decade after the discovery at Sutter's Mill in 1848, nearly 400,000 had people flocked to California. Only a few had struck it rich, and fewer still succeeded in multiplying that into something larger. One of the Murphy brothers, Daniel, parlayed the gold dust Indian labor helped him harvest into holdings of three million acres of cattle land in California and neighboring territories. John Bidwell, building upon his own lucrative pannings, carved out of the upper Sacramento Valley a lush empire of ranches, farms and orchards so vast that it required 60 miles of board fence to enclose it all.

Their success rendered all the more ironic the fate of the two men who had figured most directly in the original discovery at Sutter's Mill. For James Marshall, who had found the first little nuggets, life become one disappointment after another. The sawmill went broke, and claim-jumpers took over the area he had staked out around the mill.

He prospected elsewhere without success, hounded all the while by uninvited followers who thought he possessed psychic powers for finding gold. Down at the heels, he toured as a lecturer, retelling over and over again the story of his discovery. The state legislature eventually granted him a pension of $200 "in recognition of his considerable service to the state"—but cut it in half when he showed up drunk in Sacramento to lobby for more. Marshall died in abject poverty in 1885 and was buried on a hill overlooking the mill where it all began.

The downfall of his partner at Sutter's Mill was even more dramatic in light of John Sutter's grandiose vision of a great agricultural empire in California. His land holdings, together with the livestock and crops he began to develop on them, had quickly made him one of the most important men in all of the American West. After the discovery of the first nuggets, Sutter's name became synonymous around the world with California gold. Sutter himself recognized that, with all this, he should have become one of the world's richest men.

As it was, Sutter showed himself to be appallingly careless about his debts and his business generally. He had pronounced weaknesses for Indian girls and for the potent brandy called *aguardiente* that he distilled from his own grapes. As the gold rush swept over him, washing away first his dreams and then his fortune, he spent more and more of his waking hours befuddled by alcohol. He lost most of his vast land grants to creditors and squatters. Friends won him a $15,000 grant from the state legislature, but that was practically nothing to a man of Sutter's tastes. In 1880, he died in Washington, D.C., at age 77, while waiting for Congressional approval of a relief bill—legislation which would have awarded him $125,000 in partial compensation for the losses he had suffered because of the discovery of gold at his own Sutter's Mill.

The consequences of the gold rush far transcended individual winners and losers. Most important, it expanded the physical scope of the United States to embrace the entire width of the continent. Though many forty-niners returned home afterward, having engaged in a great adventure they would not have missed for the world, far more were added to the West. They settled down in California, which was no longer a distant, alien territory but the Golden State, and took their places in its new and workaday world of stores, factories and farms.

Even as the vision of easy riches gave way to more practical concerns after a decade of frenzy in California, a new gold rush galvanized Argonauts farther inland. During the spring of 1859, an estimated 100,000 prospectors headed for the new El Dorado in Colorado. Responding to greatly exaggerated reports of strikes the previous year in the South Platte River, they came in wagons painted with the slogan "Pikes Peak or Bust" in honor of the region's best-known terrain feature. Most of these so-called fifty-niners found not a whit of gold and eventually made their weary way home with the wagon slogans changed to read "Busted, by God." Many of them, waylaid by hostile Indians or beset by thirst, hunger and disease, did not return home at all.

But there was gold out there, and a lanky young prospector named George Jackson already had found it. On January 7, 1859, the veteran gold seeker stopped at a promising gravel bar in a frozen stream called Clear Creek, 30 miles west of a new miners' shantytown called Denver. He built a big bonfire to thaw out the

surface of the gravel bar, hacked out some slushy sand with his knife and panned a few heavy yellow flakes.

Jackson's was the first in a series of major strikes in the continent's mountain-bound interior, a vast region framed by the Sierra Nevada, the Rockies and the Cascades. These strikes would bring new torrents of tenderfoot prospectors streaming westward—and seasoned miners eastward from California—and yield riches far beyond the harvest produced by the old forty-niners. In a decade, Colorado would supplant California as the biggest gold producer in the U.S., and the mining-induced influx of settlers would lead to statehood in 1876.

In Colorado, as elsewhere, the dream of every prospector was to unearth the mother lode from which the placer deposits, the so-called river gold, had come. Sometimes the clue to the mother lode was not flakes in a placer but a piece of gold-flecked rock called float—a chunk broken off the lode itself and nudged downslope by rainstorms, earthquakes and landslides. In 1878, a drifter with a weakness for booze found such a piece of float while working on a ranch 100 miles south of Denver at Cripple Creek—so-called because stray cattle were sometimes lamed on its boulders. For 12 years, Bob Womack had worked his way painstakingly uphill, digging holes, panning samples of the dirt and earning the nickname Crazy Bob. In 1890, at a place called Poverty Gulch, Womack's search ended successfully not far from where he had started.

The mother lode lay atop an ancient volcano whose throat and radiating vents were choked with high-grade ore and veins of nearly pure gold. Womack started digging a shaft, but he lacked the money to develop the mine, which he called the El Paso. He sold the El Paso for $300 during a drinking spree; it eventually earned three million dollars. Meanwhile, thousands of

miners and prospectors swarmed into the district. The surface placer deposits soon played out, and companies were formed to burrow hundreds and even thousands of feet into the earth to extract the gold-laden ore. Here, over the next quarter century, 475 mines in an area six miles square produced gold worth $340 million—nearly as much as had been taken from all of California during the decade of the gold rush.

Though the early prospectors focused on gold, it soon became apparent that the Western mountains were also prodigiously gifted in other precious metals, in particular silver. Silver presented special problems. It seldom occurred in easy-to-find and mine, placer deposits. Nor would it reveal itself to simple tests under field conditions. And since silver combined so readily with other minerals and took on their coloration, it appeared in a bewildering variety of guises. An ounce of refined silver, moreover, was worth only about $1.60, one tenth the value of an ounce of gold. On the other hand, an exceptional vein of silver-bearing ore might fetch $7,000 a ton—considerably more than the average gold-bearing ore.

Nowhere did the two precious metals come together more spectacularly than in Nevada's fabled Comstock Lode. This lode, more than a mile up the slopes of Mount Davidson, was named after its first claimant, a Canadian-born former fur trapper named Henry Comstock. Together with three companions, Comstock discovered gold there in June 1859.

Other prospectors arrived and became curious about the heavy blue sand in which the gold flakes were embedded. It kept getting in the way of their pan-

COMPLEX INNARDS OF A COMSTOCK MINE

The unique engineering required by the lode is detailed in this 1876 lithograph. The large, unstable ore bodies called for a support system known as the square set—short timber joined into a boxlike frame—within which men could work safely. Ore was sent down chutes or hauled up in buckets for loading into cars in the main lateral tunnel, or drift *(lowest full level shown)*. From there, it went to a shaft *(lower right)*, for reloading into a giraffe, a car designed to travel at an angle *(inset, showing tools)*. The giraffe was then drawn up to the main vertical shaft *(far right)*, where the ore was then hoisted to the surface. Because of the heat, men had to cool off with ice in a special chamber *(inset, center right)*. For ventilation and communication the miners sank winzes *(bottom left)* along the vein from one level to another.

147

The social ascent of an unsinkable lady

By and large, the consorts of the gold and silver kings were remarkable mainly for their conspicuous consumption. But there was one lady who came to a good bit more. She was Mrs. James J. Brown, whose husband made his fortune in Colorado gold.

Born Maggie Tobin, in 1867 in Hannibal, Missouri, she started life as a ditch-digger's daughter. Pretty and vivacious, she married Jim Brown at 19; he was a mine manager in Leadville, and soon was able to give her all she had ever hoped for: clapboard house, steady income and two children.

Life grew complicated—and wonderful—in 1894 when Jim struck a vein of gold and swept her off to an 18-room mansion in Denver. Carved Nubian slaves decorated the foyer, while the parlor exhibited ornately framed paintings and a rare pianoforte. With such a showplace, Maggie felt ready to take her place in society. She posted invitations and made preparations for gala soirees. But Denver's upper crust wanted no part of the nouveau riche and obviously lower-class Browns. Maggie had to call in neighborhood kids to eat the feasts her chefs had prepared.

However, she was nothing if not determined. To correct her lack of education and polish, she hired tutors, read all the best books and toured Europe several times. In time, she became fluent in several languages, was a witty raconteur and grew to be friends with the Astors, Whitneys and Vanderbilts she had met on her travels.

Maggie—who by now had adopted the more voguish diminutive Molly—did not conquer Denver until 1912. At that time she won the entire nation's admiration for her heroism on the sinking liner *Titanic*. Taking command of a lifeboat, she organized the rowers and nursed the injured. When reporters later asked Molly how she had survived, she lightly replied, "I'm unsinkable." And thus the Unsinkable Molly Brown became a part of American lore.

Foliage bedecks the foyer of Molly Brown's mansion. She is shown in the inset with husband and children.

Onetime innkeeper Thomas Walsh had made millions in gold when this photograph was taken in 1904. The earnings allowed Walsh and his wife, Carrie, to build a 60-room palace in Washington, D.C.

ning operations. Finally, someone sent away a sample for assaying. The word came back that the ore was worth $876 a ton in gold but $3,000 in silver. Over the next three decades, the precious metals extracted from the Comstock Lode—55 per cent silver, 45 per cent gold—brought nearly $400 million. Henry Comstock and the others who first worked the lode received only the tiniest fraction of this. Comstock himself sold his share for $11,000, became increasingly demented and, 11 years after finding the lode, shot himself to death.

Almost from the beginning, the Comstock necessitated enormous investments of money. The veins of gold and silver ore were among the largest—some of them several hundred feet thick—but getting at the stuff required sinking shafts as deep as 3,000 feet. From these vertical shafts branched horizontal tunnels in a complex honeycomb that eventually comprised scores

of mines covering an eight-mile span. Mount Davidson's remoteness, bounded on the west by the snow-capped Sierra and on the other three sides by desert, also inflated the financial overhead. To get the supplies and new mining machinery in and the ore out, a railroad line had to be blasted out of solid rock.

At the Comstock and throughout the West, mining was now big business. It was a far cry from the storied romance of adventurous prospectors panning gold by a sun-streaked mountain stream. Miners were company employees, who worked in dark and dank tunnels far below the surface. They formed unions and, at the Comstock in 1867, won an eight-hour shift at a minimum wage of four dollars a day—perhaps the best wage in American industry at the time. But they paid dearly. By 1880, a census showed 2,770 men working below ground at the Comstock. They suffered in underground temperatures of up to 130 degrees, breathed noxious fumes, incurred fatal diseases of the lung, died when dynamite misfired and were buried alive in cave-ins. For a time, in fact, so many accidents befell the Comstock that a worker died every week. Overall, as many as 7,500 men died digging out silver and gold on the Western mining frontier, and perhaps 20,000 were maimed.

Even as the big corporations took over the new El Dorados and mining evolved into an industry, there was still room sometimes for the little man with luck and initiative. Warren Woods and his sons Frank and Harry went west to Colorado during the 1890s, intending to build a modest hotel. They settled in Victor, a suburb of the Cripple Creek boomtown, and started digging a foundation. An usually heavy material made it difficult to dig. After they recognized its nature, they gave up on the hotel and earned $30,000 a month excavating the gold-rich ore. And then there was their patient contemporary, Thomas Francis Walsh of County Tipperary, Ireland, who methodically explored a played-out Colorado silver mine and extracted more than $7 million in gold—enough to vault himself and his wife to the pinnacle of society and enable their daughter to purchase a number of pretty baubles, including the Hope Diamond.

But mainly it was a world of corporate titans. One of the greatest empire-builders was George Hearst, who earned his first major stake in the early days of the Comstock Lode. Hearst went to Nevada in 1859 from

150

California, where he tried his hand unsuccessfully as a placer miner. He bought a one-sixth share in Henry Comstock's old mine and, working with friends, took out 38 tons of high-grade silver ore in two months. The group managed to get the ore across the snow-laden Sierra passes on mules to a smelter in San Francisco, realizing a profit of more than $90,000.

This was only the beginning for Hearst. During the late 1870s, he put together a partnership with two other San Francisco businessmen and headed eastward for the Black Hills of the Dakota Territory. There, three miles south of Deadwood, Moses Manuel and his brother Fred had established the promising Homestake mine on a large vein of gold-flecked quartz. Hearst bought and bullied his way into control of a score of nearby claims and then purchased the Homestake itself and a neighboring mine for $105,000. In the process, he stirred up so much litigation and hostility that he professed fears for his own life. As it turned out, his life was never in danger and his ruthless campaign paid off fantastically. The Homestake would turn out to be perhaps the richest single mine in the world. Its output eventually reached one billion dollars.

To achieve that mind-boggling yield, Hearst had to create an enormous industrial colossus that over the years would spend $650 million to dig and refine the ore. Most costly were the new systems for breaking down the ore. A machine known as the Blake Jaw-Crusher pounded large chunks of ore into pellet-sized pieces. The pellets were then pulverized by stamping machines that emulated the action of a simple mortar and pestle. These machines, powered by water or steam, were as large as a house. Hearst installed hundreds of them, and their rhythmical thudding resounded miles downwind as they reduced huge mountains of ore.

Even so, at least 10 per cent of the gold could not be recovered by milling. Hearst remedied this by importing from Scotland a new chemical refining method. The residue of gold or silver embedded in the ore could be dissolved in a weak solution of sodium cyanide and recovered by running the solution through fine zinc shavings. The precious metals adhered to the zinc, and the two could then be separated by heating. Hearst's metallurgists adapted this new process of cyanidation on so vast a scale in his South Dakota mines that by 1902 they were recovering one million dollars a year in gold from what was supposed to be waste.

At the Comstock, Leadville, Coeur d'Alene, Cripple Creek, Telluride, Tombstone, Chloride, Orogrande and thousands of other mining areas, cyanidation recovered at least one billion dollars in gold or silver that had been thought lost forever. Everywhere small steam shovels could be seen tossing sands into cyanidation plants with their vats of clear, light-green liquid. It was a great day for free-lance operators, too. All it took was a shovel, a few old barrels, some cyanide and some shredded zinc. For a little while at least, moribund mining towns felt a new breath of life as thousands of men hurried in to work over the wastes in the old abandoned dumps.

Ironically, this was the richest of all the gold rushes, yielding a value nearly three times what the forty-niners had taken from the valleys and foothills of California nearly a half century before. But the spirit of adventure was gone. This time the rush to El Dorado was so quiet and undramatic that the promoters and the headline writers gave it scarcely any attention at all.

A Denver & Rio Grande train, with two engines pulling, inches up the side of a granite gorge in the heart of the Rockies. Carving the right of way through country like this was heartbreakingly slow, requiring tons of blasting powder and often measuring no more than a few feet per day.

III. JOINING THE COASTS

A continent's lengthening lifelines

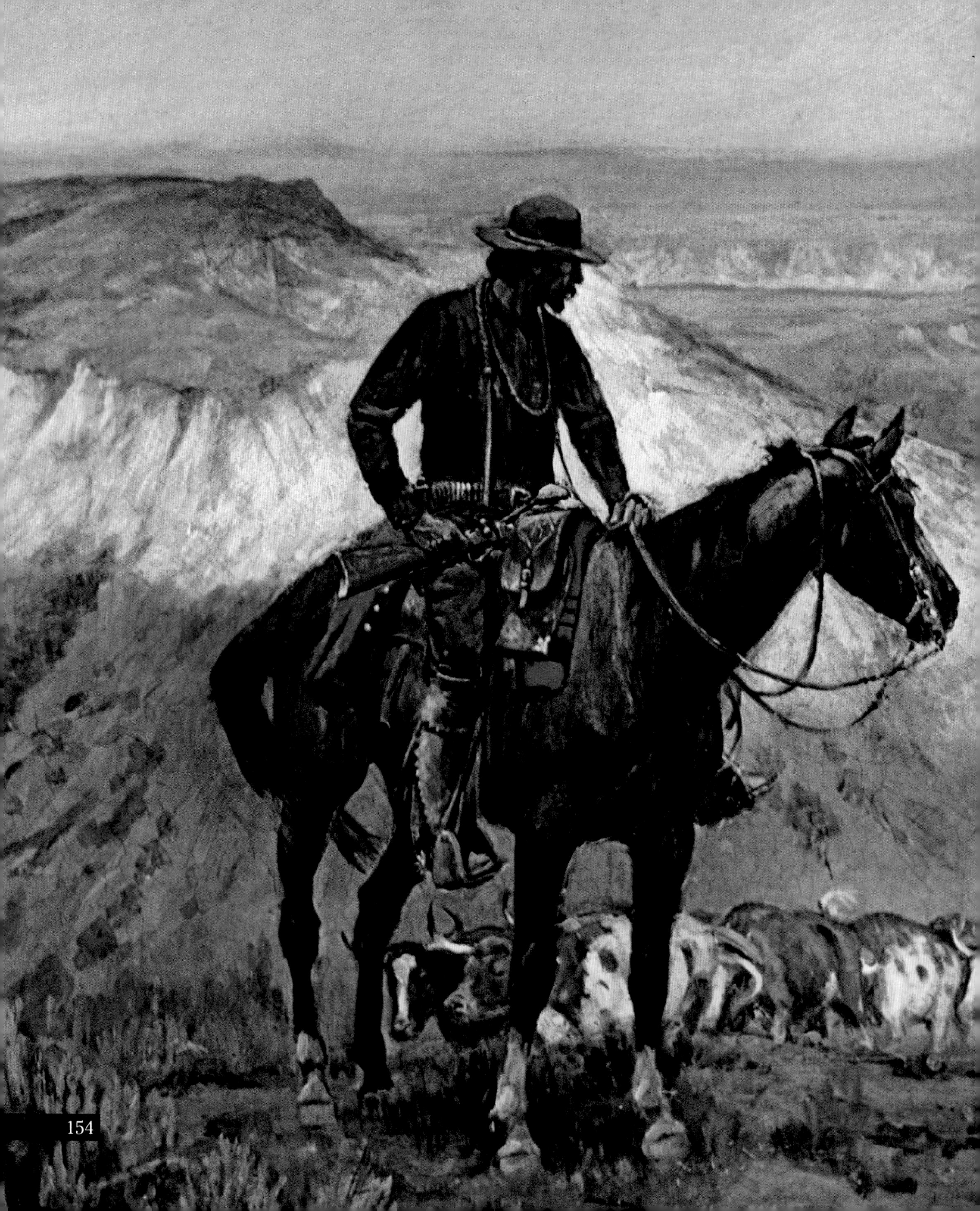

When President James Buchanan predicted in 1858 that the country would someday be bound east and west "by a chain of Americans which can never be broken," the links were already being forged by an army of entrepreneurs known as the expressmen. Their freight and stagecoach services moved Eastern goods westward, Western ores eastward, and shuttled people, money and mail both ways. By 1860, Pony Express riders were relaying mail across more than half the country in the amazingly brief time of 10 days. Such labors, celebrated here and on the following pages in paintings by Western artists, were eventually to be supplanted by the railroads and the telegraph. But until then, the expressmen persisted as though the fate of a fledgling civilization rested in their hands—and it did.

A wagonmaster watches his ox-drawn freight caravan roll out of Fort Benton on the Missouri in this scene by Charles Russell.

Through Hostile Country was the title artist Oscar Berninghaus gave this painting of a stagecoach speeding across a desolate landscape — probably western Wyoming or Montana. An escort of cavalry with an Indian scout in buckskin helped deter attacks by local tribes resentful of intrusion.

Mounted on a fresh horse, a Pony Express rider, as painted by Frederic Remington, charges out of a station on the mail route from Missouri to California. Couriers changed horses every dozen miles or so, often tiring out as many as six mounts before passing on the mail to the next relay rider.

7. Expressmen: an assault on distance and time

In the summer of 1849, what the California argonauts cherished above all else—next to a gleaming nugget of gold, or possibly a shot of whiskey—was news from home and their loved ones back East. But while mail was pouring into the San Francisco post office, the letters were effectively out of reach. Since there was no system for deliveries to the mining country, the only way a miner could obtain his mail was to make the laborious trek into town to pick it up himself—a trip that not only cost weeks of precious working time but also left his digs at the mercy of claim jumpers.

Into this bleak situation stepped a young man named Alexander Todd. A desk-bound bookkeeper back East, Todd had arrived in San Francisco after a horrendous 170-day sea voyage around South America. Now, having suffered through a few lusterless weeks wading around icy streams, Todd glumly realized that he lacked the stamina for prospecting.

What to do? What indeed. Perceiving a dual opportunity to render humane service while turning a tidy profit, Alexander Todd declared himself a mail carrier.

At that time, the Post Office Department charged five cents for a half-ounce letter going a distance of less than 300 miles, and 10 cents for more than 300 miles. While the government held a monopoly over the flow of mail, Todd rightly suspected that in this instance the postal service would not object to a bit of help.

Recognizing that the law of supply and demand augured well for generous profits, Todd devised a system of three fees. For carrying a letter from the gold fields to the San Francisco post office, he stipulated a charge of $2.50. But incoming mail was naturally more prized. Merely for inquiring after a miner's mail at the post office, Todd set a fee of one dollar, and placed the man's name on a subscription list. If he found a letter for the subscriber, the price for bringing it back would be one ounce of gold dust, then worth about $16.

Hundreds of prospectors, hardly blinking at these rates, paid the requisite sums. Todd invested in two horses—one for himself and the other to carry a sack of outbound mail—and rode out of the Sierra foothills to the town of Stockton, a sprawl of tents beside the San Joaquin River. He planned to board a boat there and travel down to San Francisco. In Stockton, however, some merchants had heard of his trip and asked him—a total stranger—to deliver $150,000 in gold dust to a certain company in San Francisco. Todd was willing to run the errand: for 5 per cent of the value of the dust, or $7,500. The merchants assented.

Reaching San Francisco without misadventure, Todd delivered the gold dust. He then made his way to the post office, where people stood in lines up to half a mile long waiting to get to a window in the building. The lines barely moved, since each query about a letter required a postal clerk to sift through tons of unsorted envelopes. When Todd finally came face to face with the harried postmaster, unburdened himself of his sack of outgoing mail and then explained the nature of his subscription list, the postmaster quickly displayed an entrepreneurial instinct of his own. In return for swearing in Todd as a postal clerk and allowing him to search through the mountains of mail from the East, he levied a kickback of 25 cents for each letter that Todd turned up for a client.

The ex-bookkeeper quickly repaired this small dent in his profits by investing in a load of weeks-old New York newspapers for a dollar or two a copy, convinced he could sell them at a healthy markup in the gold camps. To convey his newspapers and mail, he bought a big rowboat for $300 and looked around for passengers who might be willing to help him bend the oars. Sixteen signed on and plunked down $16 apiece for the privilege of rowing Todd and his cargo to Stockton. There he sold the boat at a $200 profit and made his

Delivering letters at up to $16 apiece, an expressman rides the mining trails in this drawing from prospector Alonzo Delano's *Pen Knife Sketches*. "There's scarcely a gulch he doesn't visit," Delano wrote.

in conveyance—of objects animate and inanimate; all were expressmen.

For two tumultuous decades, from the giddy gold rush year of 1849 to the completion of the first transcontinental railroad in 1869, the expressmen would transport the essentials that nurtured the development of the West: people and food and clothing, household utensils, merchants' wares, farm supplies and mining equipment, bank and government documents, gold and currency, letters and newspapers. Even after the railroads usurped their primacy, Alexander Todd would carry on in a long, valiant diminuendo, supplying the needs of the more remote settlements until steam and wheels of steel finally caught up with them.

By 1850, the East was tied together by an expansive network of railroads, steamboats and stagecoaches. And the West, thanks to the ingenious efforts of some of its newest citizens, was starting to be well knit. The trouble lay in the lack of adequate linkage between the coasts, which frustrated the increasing dreams of continent-wide unity. There were two main routes, both starting in western Missouri, from which a wagon traveler could choose. The more northerly route was the 2,000-mile Oregon Trail, essentially a trunk line of old Indian paths that had been widened by the wagon wheels and grazing oxen of pioneers heading for the Pacific Northwest to settle. The second major route was the Santa Fe Trail, which traversed 800 miles in its southwesterly course to the 17th Century Spanish city for which it was named; two extensions, the Gila River Trail and the Old Spanish Trail, led to California from the south.

One familiar sight along these passageways west was the freight caravan—a seemingly endless stream of lumbering ox- and mule-drawn freight wagons. With their curved bodies, sharp prows and clouds of canvas, they reminded people of boats and "prairie schooners" was, in fact, their fond nickname. To one tall veteran of the trail with a touch of poet in him, they looked like nothing so much as "a fleet sailing with canvas all spread over a seeming sea."

The grand era of the freight wagon had begun in 1848, at the end of the war with Mexico. Not only were hordes of settlers pouring into the new lands but the Army itself was in dire need of supply. For the next two

way back to the Mother Lode in the Sierra. The miners not only fell upon their mail but also gobbled up the old newspapers—at eight dollars per copy. Todd soon had 2,000 names on his subscription list. He was also earning $1,000 a day, regularly, for delivering and safeguarding gold dust.

Although his enterprise was the first of its kind in California or anywhere in the West, Todd would soon be emulated by a whole army of freight entrepreneurs and stagecoach owners who operated not only in California but throughout the frontier. All of them waged a ceaseless battle against distance and time to link the near and the far. All were specialists

decades, the long hauls of civilian-owned freight caravans were of vital moment to people on the frontier, serving quite literally as lifelines. Until rails spanned the continent, both the survival and the economic growth of the West depended on the durability of wagon axles, the hardihood of oxen and mules, the tenacity of wagon drivers—and perhaps most important—the vision and daring of the freight entrepreneurs.

Principal among them was a trio whose names became so synonymous with freighting that it sometimes seemed as if they had invented the idea. Three months after they joined forces in December 1854, William Hepburn Russell, William Bradford Waddell and Alexander Majors signed a two-year contract giving the new partners a monopoly on military freighting west of the Missouri. To fulfill the agreement, Majors organized a caravan system that was eventually copied all over the West.

A wagon train of 26 wagons—25 for freight and one a kitchen wagon—carried at least 150,000 pounds of cargo. Six pairs of oxen pulled each wagon, and there were about 30 extra head driven in a herd behind the train; it was important to have replacement animals, but not so many as to exhaust the forage en route. Only about 35 men managed this considerable undertaking. Each wagon had a driver—the bullwhacker—and each train had a wagonmaster, an assistant wagonmaster, two day herders and a night herder to handle cattle going to or from pasture. In addition there were three or four extra hands to guard the cattle and also to replace men who fell sick, were killed by Indians or simply deserted because the job was too much for them. There were saddle mules for the wagonmaster and his assistant as well as for the herders and messengers.

For Russell, Majors & Waddell, the freighting season began in spring, when the ice broke at the port of St. Louis, permitting the passage of cargo-laden river boats. By the time the first of them poked upstream, freight wagons had been repaired and taken out of their winter storage in wagon yards, hordes of draught animals had been mustered, and teamsters had poured in from all over the East.

The journey ahead, whether it led southwest, northwest or directly west, held perils both known and unknown. Since a wagon train could cover an average of only 15 to 20 miles a day, distance itself posed prob-

With much of their cargo already off-loaded at previous settlements along the trail, wagons inch along a path cleared between steep snowbanks near the summit of the Sierra Nevada. Mountain passes were snowbound half of the year, restricting wagon freighting to spring and summer.

lems. Wagons and animals and men alike had to be made of sturdy stuff to endure hundreds of miles on the open trail. Most of the time, the weather was too dry or too wet, too cold or too hot. When the sun burned down, the teamsters walked for miles in clouds of their own dust; even with kerchiefs wrapped around their faces, many suffered lasting damage to their eyes and noses and throats—to say nothing of their lungs. Alkali dust burned even more than regular dust. Buffalo gnats almost too small to see worked their way into men's ears. Rattlesnakes lurked to bite both man and beast. Ticks infected oxen with Texas fever; disease and exhaustion reduced the life expectancy of an ox to a single freighting season.

The hazards notwithstanding, most wagon trains eventually reached their destinations. The terminus of a trip might be Santa Fe, or Denver, or Salt Lake City, or Helena, or a lonely town with only one street, or a fort, or an Indian agency. Wherever it was, the squeak of the wagon wheels heralded the train's coming, and assured the local residents that they would be provisioned for the year to come.

After washing their faces, combing their hair and drawing their wages, the drivers hit the town for a little excitement. Some might be heading back East with the caravan; for most, it was the end of a one-way trip. They had done their part to help forge the way West, and would now start a new life as a farmer, a prospector or a trooper in the Army.

With the opening up of the West, a central problem that faced Congress was the establishment of an overland coast-to-coast mail service. Thus far, mail had been dispatched by sea, a journey of intolerable slowness. The first person to establish an overland system of mail delivery was Samuel H. Woodson, who was awarded funding of $19,500 by Congress. Though Woodson's route did not run all the way to the Pacific, it did appear to provide a promising start—from Independence, Missouri, to Salt Lake City, Utah, embracing 1,200 miles of the Oregon Trail.

Woodson gamely launched his venture on July 1, 1850, and almost immediately realized that the schedule—30 days each way, employing pack animals—was impossible. Among other things, he could exchange his exhausted animals for fresh ones at

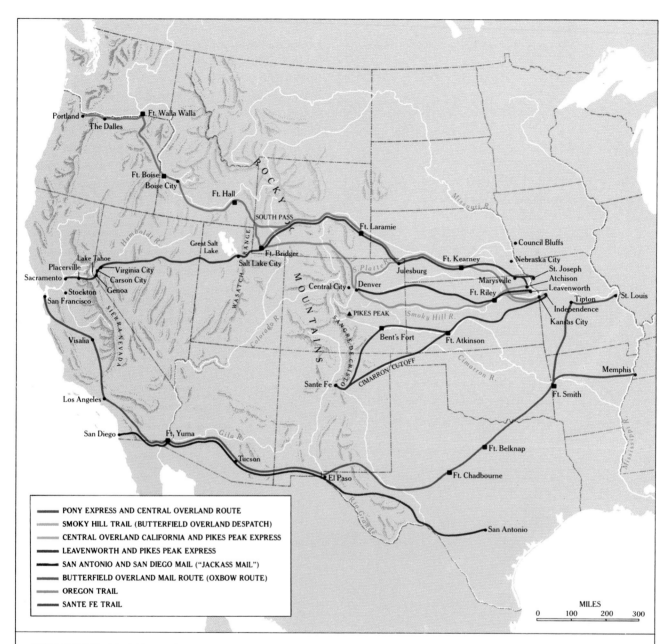

PONY EXPRESS AND CENTRAL OVERLAND ROUTE
SMOKY HILL TRAIL (BUTTERFIELD OVERLAND DESPATCH)
CENTRAL OVERLAND CALIFORNIA AND PIKES PEAK EXPRESS
LEAVENWORTH AND PIKES PEAK EXPRESS
SAN ANTONIO AND SAN DIEGO MAIL ("JACKASS MAIL")
BUTTERFIELD OVERLAND MAIL ROUTE (OXBOW ROUTE)
OREGON TRAIL
SANTE FE TRAIL

RIVAL ROUTES ACROSS THE WEST

As a rule, the routes that served as major express conduits to the West for mail, freight and passenger traffic grew naturally from paths blazed through the wilderness by the mules and wagons of pioneers and traders. The earliest, the Santa Fe Trail, came into use in 1821. But the great bulk of Western traffic converged on the Oregon Trail, opened by fur traders' wagons in 1830, and on its branches to the Great Salt Lake Valley and California. This central route was used by freight trains from the 1840s on, by the riders of the Pony Express in 1860

and 1861, and by stagecoaches both before and after that time.

The central route's chief rival, and the only one not dictated by the path of population or commerce, was the Oxbow Route, so-called because of the circuitous direction it took to satisfy the regional interests of Southerners in Congress. This route, opened in 1858, was followed part of the way by the "Jackass Mail" (the name suggested what critics thought of it) and by John Butterfield's stagecoach line over its entire length, until the great arc was interdicted on the eve of the Civil War.

only three stops en route. As a result, deliveries were slow that summer and almost nonexistent during the following winter.

The situation did not improve with time. Deliveries proved so unreliable that Mormon leader Brigham Young wrote in a letter to a Utah Territory delegate in Washington: "So little confidence we have in the present mail arrangement that we feel considerable dubiety of your receiving this or any other communication from us." After four years of discouraging travail, Woodson chose to step aside and let fresher hands compete for the job.

In the end it became clear that the idea of combining the transport of passengers and mail via stagecoach service was perhaps the best way of forging a link with the West Coast. Bids were submitted to Congress for the contract. The man who won—29-year-old James Birch—had pioneered stagecoach travel in California at the dawn of the gold rush. A former stable hand in Rhode Island, the enterprising Birch promised semimonthly service commencing July 1, 1857.

The route Birch would follow was hotly contested, reflecting growing dissent in both American politics and society. Southern Congressmen were loath to establish a communication link to California along a route through Northern territory; antislavery legislators were equally determined to keep this vital link safely distant from Southern control. Moreover, both factions believed that the first transcontinental railroad—a project already in the wind—would follow the course of the first overland stage line; hence the stakes were high indeed.

Congress sidestepped the issue by authorizing a circuit that, as one wag later said, went "from no place through nothing to nowhere." This assessment was not far off the mark; the route was to run between Texas and California with the terminal points at San Antonio, which was reachable from the East via New Orleans, and San Diego. To travel between the two cities the stages would be compelled to cross 1,475 miles of desert-and-mountain wilderness.

The life of the first stage line to span the continent was brief and none-too-glorious. In his own short time with the enterprise, Birch used mules instead of horses to draw the stages—earning for the venture the tag of the "Jackass Line." The nickname turned from a mild jest to an epithet after Birch's premature death in the summer of 1857: While returning home to his wife and son, the man whose whole life had been bound up with overland transport went down with the steamer *Central America* in a savage storm off Florida.

Under Birch's successor, George Giddings, service went from bad to worse. At times, coaches were dispensed with, and mail and passengers alike had to cross the mountains on muleback. During the ill-fated line's four-year history the number of passengers who availed themselves of the service probably totaled only a few score. As a result, according to one estimate, every letter delivered between San Antonio and San Diego cost the government approximately $65.

Aware early on of the line's shortcomings, Congress fostered the development of an alternative system. This route, chosen by Postmaster General Aaron Brown, had not one but two starting points—St. Louis and Memphis, Brown's hometown. These roads joined at Fort Smith, Arkansas. The route then described an enormous southward arc, to El Paso and Fort Yuma on the Mexican border, and thence to Los Angeles and San Francisco—a total distance of 2,795 miles. The Northern press howled. New York newspapers dubbed it "the oxbow route" and "the side line." The *Chicago Tribune* referred to it as a gigantic swindle.

Yet the man to whom Brown awarded the contract, a New Yorker named John Butterfield, made the route work—and work beautifully. A stage driver in his youth, he had gone on to win control of all the principal stage lines in central New York State. For his newest enterprise, Butterfield came up with one million dollars, built 139 relay stations and way stops, cut new roads, bridged streams and graded hilly stretches. Then he bought 1,800 head of stock and 250 of the best coaches, and hired 800 men to keep the stages rolling along.

On September 15, 1858, the Butterfield Overland Mail Company was ready for its maiden run. For the first time in history, a traveler could buy—for $200—a ticket to ride overland by coach all the way from the banks of the Mississippi to the far edge of the American domain. Shortly after start-up, the stages were able to traverse the great arc twice a week in as little as 21 days each way.

One passenger's view of the nature of Butterfield's accomplishment was published in the *New York Post*.

Referring to the bugle that was used by stage drivers to announce their approach, he wrote: "The blast of the stage horn as it rolls through the valleys and over the prairies of the West, cheers and gladdens the heart of the pioneer. As it sounds through the valleys of Santa Clara and San Jose, it sends a thrill of delight to the Californian. He knows that it brings tidings from the hearts and homes he left behind him; it binds him stronger and firmer to his beloved country."

On April 3, 1860, less than two years after the Butterfield Overland Mail Company had completed its first run, an operation hailed as "The Greatest Enterprise of Modern Times" made its debut. In its aims alone it certainly deserved superlatives, for the newly formed Pony Express intended to carry mail across the West in less than half the fastest time ever before recorded.

The scheme verged on the incredible. Before the inaugural day was over, a mail-bearing daredevil in St. Joseph, Missouri, and another in San Francisco—nearly 2,000 miles away—would begin hurtling toward each other, galloping full tilt for 35 to 75 miles, then passing the mail to the next relay rider. Speeding through daylight and darkness, the mails would reach their respective destinations in just 10 days. At least that is what the Pony's astonishing schedule claimed.

No allowance had been made for the caprices of weather, failures of muscle or nerves, or unpredictable Indian attacks. The runs were slated to start from each terminus once a week, and to continue the year round without interruption. At issue was the desire of Russell, Majors & Waddell, the giant freighting firm that had foaled the Pony, to prove that the overland route across

NEWS!!

PONY EXPRESS AT CARSON CITY.

[SPECIAL DISPATCH TO THE ALTA CALIFORNIA.]

TEN DAYS LATER.

St. Louis Dates to 12th April.

Eight Days and Nineteen Hours on the Way......... Rhode Island Democratic.........Row in Congress ....American Vessel Stopped by a Spanish Steamer......Siege of Vera Cruz Abandoned...... Eight Days Later from Europe.........Liverpool Dates to March 29th......The Two Annexations Finished......Excommunication of Victor Emanuel......An Occasion of National Rejoicing...... End of the Moorish War.

[Prepared by our Special Correspondent, at St. Louis, thence by Express to St. Joseph's, thence by Pony Express to Carson City, thence by telegraph to San Francisco, for the *Alta California*.]

[PER ST. JOSEPH, PLACERVILLE AND ALTA LINES,]

CARSON CITY, APRIL 22, 1860,
The Overland Pony Express, from St. Joseph, Missouri, arrived here at 4:10 this morning, with dates from St. Louis to the 12th inst. The Express was detained six hours at Roberts' Creek, by reason of the horses having been driven off by the Indians.

The Pony Express in St. Joseph.
ST. LOUIS, April 12, 1860.
The departure of the last Pony Express was an important event in St. Joseph. The Express was detained two hours and a half by the failure of the New York messenger to make the connection. The ceremony of inaugurating the event was performed by the Mayor of the city, who put the letter-bag on the horse, and accompanied the act with a speech.

the center of the continent was superior to the oxbow route.

The first rider out of St. Joseph was Johnny Fry, who, rather ignominiously, was delayed in starting by some two hours. (A special messenger bearing the mails from the East had missed a train connection.) When Fry actually left at around 7 p.m.—armed with 49 letters, some copies of Eastern newspapers specially printed on tissue, five private telegrams and numerous telegraphic dispatches for California newspapers—his eastbound counterpart had already achieved a three-hour headstart.

The westbound mail reached Sacramento at 5:25 p.m. on April 13, about two hours faster than the promised 10-day schedule. The final relay rider, William Hamilton, was welcomed warmly to California's fast-growing capital with a cannon salute, marching bands, clanging church bells and flag-waving crowds. The state legislature adjourned to join in the celebration. A half-continent away, the last eastbound relay had reached St. Joseph and set off another outburst of rejoicing there.

Almost from the outset, Pony riders gained wide renown for their casual heroism in the face of danger. Tales of their escapades gave them larger-than-life status, and made them riveting figures not just to newspaper readers at home and abroad but to the people who lined their route. "Pony Bob" Haslam, waylaid by Indians in Utah Territory, completed his 120-mile run with his jaw broken by an arrow and with one arm shattered by bullets. Howard Egan, finding that his way through a narrow canyon was blocked by an Indian encampment, refused to make a long detour; he spurred his horse straight through the camp, scattering the warriors in all directions.

Worse than the Indians—worse than anything, the riders said—was a mountain run through a blizzard in sub-zero cold with snowdrifts higher than a man's head. Warren Upson spent more than a day blindly struggling through a white maelstrom to a station he normally reached in a couple of hours. But all the riders brought the mail through.

The Pony riders' greatest asset was sheer speed. Their horses—grain-fed rather than grass-fed—could outrun any Indian pony. Perhaps the most eloquent testimonial to this fact was the experience of Pony Bob, who made what was probably the longest one-man run in Pony Express history.

Assigned to the Nevada run between Friday's station, at the foot of Lake Tahoe, and Fort Churchill, 75 miles to the east, Haslam started his celebrated ride on May 11, 1860. Twenty miles out, he reached Carson City, expecting to get a fresh mount there. But all the stock in town had been commandeered by local residents bent on killing Paiutes. It turned out that, four days earlier, the Indian tribe had attacked several stations between Carson City and Fort Churchill, killing some of the occupants and stealing or scattering the stock. As a result, Haslam had to whip his tired horse past one abandoned station after another, all the way to Fort Churchill.

His relief rider at the fort, however, refused to risk taking the mail to the next home station, Smith's Creek, 115 miles farther east. Pony Bob grabbed a fresh horse and made the run himself, changing mounts at Sand Springs and again at Cold Spring. He arrived at Smith's Creek early on May 12, having ridden 190 miles in 18 hours.

But Haslam's odyssey was far from over. After knocking off for eight hours' sleep, he was back in the saddle again. Riding, changing mounts, riding again he sped on through hostile Indian land eventually arriving back at Friday's station on May 13. In 36 hours of riding "Pony Bob" Haslam had covered the astonishing distance of 380 miles.

Despite such prowess—and the overall determination that was the hallmark of the Pony Express—the company's fortunes were destined to be as brief as they were glorious. Scarcely a year after the first rider slapped a specially designed lightweight saddle kit on his mount and galloped off, the life of the Pony Express started to ebb. The horses were simply no match for a telegraph line that would soon link East and West. By late August, one wire-stringing crew had advanced westward 90 miles beyond Fort Kearney, Nebraska, and the Pony soon abandoned service east of that point. Another crew made rapid eastward progress from Carson City, sometimes advancing 25 miles a day. The fast-dwindling gap between the telegraph poles was finally closed in Salt Lake City on October 24, 1861.

Soon autopsies were being performed on the Pony in the public prints. But the valiant firm refused to die quickly. Here and there, riders continued to make short local runs—almost as if the habit were too strong to break. On November 20, 1861, the last rider on the last run handed over the mail in San Francisco and began looking for a new job. During their 18 months of glory, he and his fellow riders had transported no fewer than 34,753 precious pieces of mail and pounded out a total mileage equal to 24 times around the globe.

In its brief life the Pony Express had also conclusively proved the superiority of the central route, roughly marking out the path later to be followed by the transcontinental railroad, and provided countless stories of dedication and courage for a people badly in need of such relief and reassurance. The Pony had profited no one, but it had immeasurably enriched the whole country.

The California *Pacific* said it as well as anyone: "We have looked to you as those who wait for the morning, and how seldom did you fail us! When days were months and hours weeks, how you thrilled us out of our pain and suspense, to know the best or know the worst. You have served us well!"

While the Pony Express was faltering in its battle with technology, the stagecoach was just hitting its stride as the most popular means of carrying people, mail and valuables across the West. For the next several decades, almost anyone who had to go anywhere in the West went by stage. But the choice of lines was limited: sooner or later, most travelers found themselves paying their fares to a coach service owned and imperiously operated by a single individual, Ben Holladay.

As brilliant in business as he was ruthless, Holladay had been born in 1819, one of seven children of a hardscrabble Kentucky farmer. At 16 he ran away to Weston, Missouri, and while still in his teens was operating his own tavern. By the time he was 21 he owned a drugstore and a dirt-floored hotel. Six years later, in 1846, Holladay came to grips with the destiny

THE GREAT CONCORD COACH

Concord coaches, including this model owned by Wells, Fargo, weighed more than a ton, stood eight feet high and cost from $1,200 to $1,500. They could accommodate as many as 21 passengers—nine seated inside on three upholstered benches and a dozen more on the roof. The driver's seat, or box, was shared by an express messenger riding shotgun over precious cargo. The boot, a leather-covered receptacle under the driver's seat, held mail and a strongbox of valuables. Express parcels and personal baggage went into a bigger rear boot.

The teams that drew the Concords—four or six horses—had their task made easier by the sturdiness of the vehicle itself. The most ingenious design feature was the suspension of the carriage on two thoroughbraces, three-inch-thick strips of leather that served as shock absorbers. The rocking motion created by the thoroughbraces bothered some passengers, but moved Mark Twain to lovingly describe the Concord as "a cradle on wheels."

Rear Boot

WELLS FARGO & CO.

U.S.

Brake Shoe

168

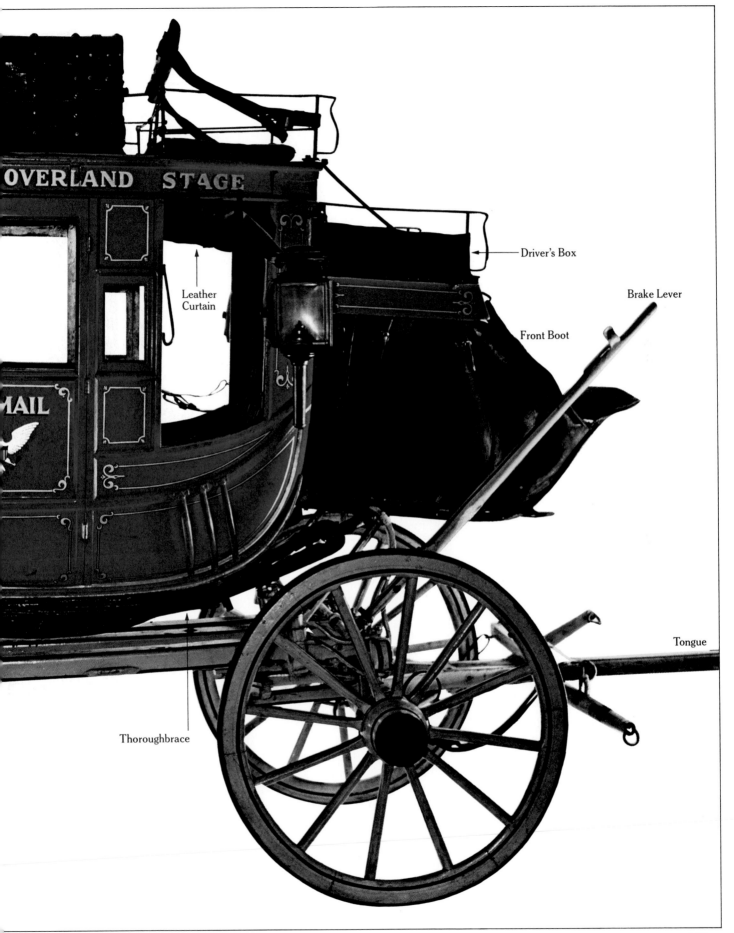

OVERLAND STAGE

MAIL

Leather
Curtain

Driver's Box

Brake Lever

Front Boot

Tongue

Thoroughbrace

that was to make him the master of a transportation empire. He mortgaged his holdings, bought 14 wagons and 60 mules, took on a cargo of trade goods and set out for Santa Fe where he unloaded 28-cent tea for $1.50 a pound and garnered comparable profits on other commodities.

In the next few years, Holladay dealt aggressively in distilleries, packing plants and freighting, and bought into Nevada's fabulous Ophir Mine. Then, in 1859, he initiated an alliance with William Russell of Missouri, of the great freighting firm of Russell, Majors & Waddell.

No love was lost between them. Russell had once refused to lend Holladay money at a time when he was trying to get started in freighting. Still, Holladay figured he could turn the alliance to his advantage. But after turning a handsome profit for two years, Holladay closed in on his erstwhile collaborator. Though he had never forgotten Russell's original refusal to lend him money, he had ostensibly turned the other cheek. Now, however, he found himself, no doubt to his relish, in the role of Russell's creditor.

From time to time Holladay had lent Russell, Majors & Waddell money to buoy up the sinking Pony Express and the Central Overland stage line. Waiting until his partner spiraled hopelessly into debt, the rapacious Holladay foreclosed on the loan. After a series of devious maneuvers he acquired sole possession of Central Overland, a stagecoach system extending 1,200 miles from Atchison to Salt Lake City.

Very little in Holladay's freighting experience had prepared him for stagecoaching—a far more different and more complex pursuit. But big money was there to be made, and the ever-shrewd Holladay had every intention of making it. He dressed his stage drivers like dandies. His coaches were equally eye-arresting, painted bright red and lettered in gilt with the legends "Holladay Overland Mail & Express" and "U.S. Mail."

The company harvested sums of up to $140,000 each month from shipments of gold dust, bullion and other valuable cargo. Carrying the United States mail ensured further profits—almost two million dollars over five years. In addition, passenger prices often resulted in gross revenues of $60,000 a month.

Considering the quality of service on the line, passengers must have cringed at the steep prices they paid for the dubious pleasure of traveling by stagecoach. The journey was an adventure into the unknown, to be approached with either trepidation or calm but always with a tingle of anticipation. A mechanical breakdown, a passenger's illness, an unseasonal blizzard, a sudden, lethal onslaught by bandits or inflamed Indians—any of these and more could turn a trip into a nightmare. On the other hand, the time might pass without incident and the travelers arrive at their destination on schedule.

A typical stage departure had something of an air of ritual about it. The team of six glossy horses would pull up in front of a designated hotel at dawn. Then, stamping and flicking their tails impatiently, they would wait as the coach was loaded. Leather pouches crammed with mail went into the front boot below the driver's seat. On top of the mail went an iron strongbox containing the most valuable items going west. Lumpy canvas bags of printed matter, express packages and passenger baggage were stowed in a second, larger boot behind the carriage. As the loading proceeded, the nine passengers, fortified by a hearty hotel breakfast, came out into the cool morning air for a look at the rig that would be their world for days to come.

Once on the road, the stagecoach rolled along at an average speed of eight miles an hour. About every 12 miles, the horses were changed, and at every 40- or 50-mile interval the coach would pause at a home station. Sleep was a luxury. Passengers were informed that they were expected to sleep bolt upright in the coach.

To help while away the endless discomforting hours, passengers told stories, played word puzzles and indulged in the odd game of poker. But nothing was likely to prove as interesting as the terrain itself. Travelers from east of the Missouri were always struck by the immensity of the prairie and the abundance of unfamiliar animals, including buffalo and prairie dogs.

Travel in the Rocky Mountains was equally awe-inspiring, though perilous. One passenger recalled that upon sweeping suddenly around a mountain curve "we found nothing but blue sky. We streamed around the curves, at one moment swinging over the abyss and next, swinging back easily toward the bank. In some places we would lose sight of the lead horses around the curves." Yet they were probably in less danger than they imagined; stage drivers invariably had an intuitive feel for what the animals might do and could speak to the horses "through the ribbons."

A time always came on the long journey westward when the sleep-starved stage travelers began to wish devoutly for its end. Passengers would doze, drop into deeper slumber, fall against their neighbors, awaken with a start and begin to doze again. Under such conditions people abraded each other's nerves, and tempers often flared. Passenger friction could be deadly serious. In March 1866, a passenger on the overland route went berserk, stabbed a fellow traveler, then drew a pistol, killed a second passenger and wounded a third before he himself was shot to death—all within the narrow, rocking confines of the coach.

When, at the end of a trip, the joltings were at last over, the passengers headed for a hotel, a bath, a barber and a bed. The long journey was over and the travelers were glad of it. But inevitably, after the irritation had worn off, the view in retrospect was one of pride of participation in an unforgettable exploit.

For five years, from 1862 through 1866, Holladay enjoyed a virtual monopoly of the eastern half of the central overland route, maintaining his advantage with methods verging on piracy. To Denver's *Rocky Mountain News* he was "a nuisance to be abated by Congress." A competitor branded him "wholly destitute of honesty, morality and common decency." On the other hand, no less a journal than *Harper's Weekly* rated him as "the greatest organizer of transportation the West has produced." Both his critics and admirers were right.

At the climax of his career, on November 1, 1866, Holladay suddenly sold out, and turned his ambitious gaze toward creating a rail and steamship empire. In order to finance these ventures, as well as his own thwarted political aspirations, Holladay floated a complex structure of bonds and debentures. This proved to be a fatal mistake; on September 18, 1873, the New York stock market plummeted. In the ensuing panic, Holladay's empire collapsed.

When Holladay's luck ran out, it ran all the way out. His beloved wife, Ann, died on the same day her husband defaulted on a major bond issue for his brainchild, the Oregon & California Railroad. One after another, their four grown children fell away. Daughter Jenny died in childbirth. Son Joe drank himself to death. Daughter Polly died aboard a ship. Holladay's surviving child, Ben Jr., bitterly contested with his father for title to the few properties that remained in the family, and died, like his brother, an alcoholic. None

of the children lived to middle age. A second Mrs. Holladay, however, gave him two children and renewed zest. Holladay tried for a comeback with the fragmentary holdings that were left, only to be stopped, this time by one of his brothers, Joe, who claimed title to them. There was more battling and disappointment until, in his 68th year, the Stagecoach King finally succumbed.

Dying as he did in 1887, Holladay had nonetheless lived long enough to witness the evolution of a company that swiftly became a household name in the West. The firm of Wells, Fargo—to whom Holladay had sold out in 1866—enjoyed a unique position in life beyond the Missouri. Its success was legendary and its honesty and reliability so proverbial that miners swore "by God and by Wells, Fargo." But precisely because the company was so far-flung and so preeminent in so many different activities, no one could sum it up easily. Possibly the best epitome was delivered by a long-time admirer of the company, who wrote: "Wells, Fargo went everywhere, did almost anything for anybody, and was the nearest thing to a universal service company ever invented."

Once a steamboat operator, Vermont-born Henry Wells got a foothold in the business by carrying mail and packages between Albany and Buffalo using the available stagecoach and rail services. In 1843, business was good enough for him to hire a messenger—William Fargo, a frugal, hard-working New Yorker. Two profitable years later, Wells made him a partner.

Efficiency was the keynote of their expanding operations: they managed to get the job done faster and cheaper than their competitors, even turning a profit delivering letters at six cents when the U.S. Post Office charged 25 cents. By 1850, Wells and Fargo were big operators—and eager to get even bigger. The way to do it, they decided, was to merge their two firms with another express company. When the deal was struck, the resulting firm was named American Express.

American Express was an instant giant, its very name reflective of the founders' ambition to make it a nation-wide enterprise. But Wells and Fargo met stubborn resistance from some of their fellow directors when they decided to set up shop in California. Unable to budge the others, Wells and Fargo decided to invade California on their own. Without relinquishing their positions or financial stake in American Express—since a connection east of the Mississippi River was vital to their plans—the two men met with seven other financial backers and formed a new express company to serve California and the Western frontier. The new firm, founded on March 18, 1852, was christened Wells, Fargo & Company.

The first Wells, Fargo office was in a narrow, red-brick building at 114 Montgomery Street in San Francisco. Behind the green, specially cast, iron window shutters stood a well-planned office with an array of strongboxes waiting to receive consignments of gold. Customers immediately liked what they saw and, within a short

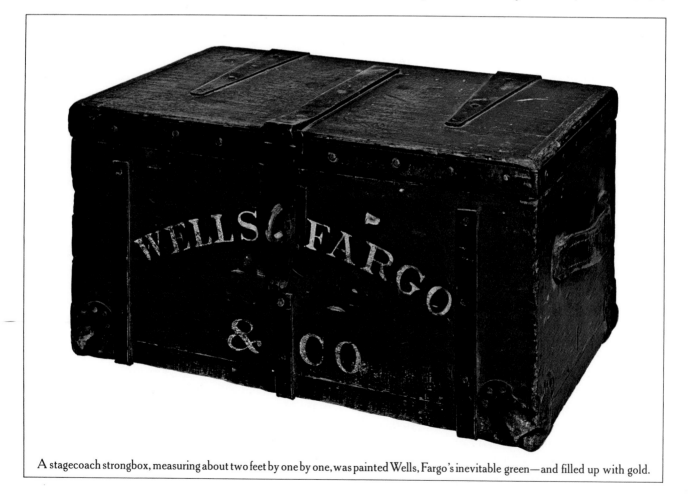

A stagecoach strongbox, measuring about two feet by one by one, was painted Wells, Fargo's inevitable green—and filled up with gold.

Wells, Fargo founders Henry Wells *(left)* and William Fargo *(right)* used acumen gained in the East to build a giant company that controlled virtually all stage lines between the Missouri River and California.

time, found themselves relying more and more on the speed and efficiency of Wells, Fargo's private mail service. By the end of the first year the company had branches in a dozen communities up and down the state.

By 1859 there were 126 Wells, Fargo branch offices—with more to come as new mineral strikes created pockets of settlement in the frontier wilderness. Transporting gold, silver, mail—indeed, anything of value (including wines and *pâté de foie gras* all the way from France), the company gained quickly in stature. It branched into staging, absorbing, among other lines, the Butterfield Overland Mail. Then, with the sell-out by Ben Holladay in 1866, the company finally realized the dream of William Russell and other expressmen: they now possessed a monopoly on long-distance staging and mail service west of the Missouri River.

Staging brought a spate of hold-ups by men with names like Rattlesnake Dick and Black Bart. The company came up with ingenious ideas for discouraging would-be robbers. Extra guards were added to the coaches, live rattlesnakes were stashed in strongboxes, silver was cast into virtually unliftable 700-pound cannonballs. The ultimate solution, however, turned out to be the formation of a private force of police and detectives, its unofficial motto "Wells, Fargo never forgets."

Wells, Fargo's greatest loss, however, did not come from theft. It came from a shrewd entrepreneur named Lloyd Tevis, who had speculated on the completion of a transcontinental railroad and, in anticipation, had obtained the rights to carry mail and bullion under the title Pacific Union Express Company. The railroad was completed on May 10, 1869. On October 4, at a meeting with Tevis in Omaha, Wells, Fargo's fate became painfully clear. The company was obliged to pay Tevis five million dollars for the piece of paper that had granted Tevis' firm exclusive express rights on the railroad. That agreement terminated the short life of Pacific Express and guaranteed that Wells, Fargo would survive. But Tevis had further news. Wells, Fargo's unhorsed and railless plight had caused stock to plummet from $100 a share to as low as $13—and Tevis had quietly been buying it up at depressed prices. In that room in Omaha, the directors were forced to concede that Lloyd Tevis now controlled Wells, Fargo.

Though Wells, Fargo took to the rails and continued to grow, it had changed irrevocably. Indeed, everything had changed irrevocably. An important and hard-fought era had come and gone, slipping into the pages of nostalgia. The glorious days of the expressmen were over forever.

High-chimneyed paddle wheelers crowd the St. Louis levee in the 1850s, when steamboating was beginning to hit its stride.

A 3,000-mile waterway west

"A great spiral staircase to the Rockies" was one 19th Century traveler's memorable metaphor for the Missouri, whose tortuous bends led canoeists, keelboaters and eventually steamboatmen from the Mississippi all the way to Fort Benton, Montana—nearly half a mile above sea level and 3,000 miles from the river's mouth.

For generations of explorers and exploiters, the Missouri was the key to the West. It excited the imaginations of 16th Century geographers as a possible avenue to the Orient; later, it provided access to the fur riches that drew the first frontiersmen into the wilderness; and after the Civil War, it conveyed thousands of prospectors to Rocky Mountain gold.

The river's orneriness matched its promises. "The broad current," wrote journalist Albert Richardson in 1857, "is unpoetic and repulsive—a stream of flowing mud studded with dead tree trunks and broken by bars." Yet hundreds of steamboats ran this gauntlet to earn profits that might repay the vessel's entire cost in a single voyage.

Eventually technology overtook the rivermen. Beginning in 1859, railroads began to intersect the Missouri, siphoning off water-borne traffic. By 1890, when the last packet boat departed from the deserted levee at Fort Benton, the only reminders of the steamboat's glory days were river bends with names like Malta, Sultan, Diana and Kate Sweeney—each honoring one of the Big Muddy's paddle-wheeled victims.

The Missouri River constantly challenged pilots by shifting
its course within the confines of steep bluffs. In this stretch
east of Fort Benton, the river has retreated (at right) from
the flank of the main trough to form a narrow channel—further constricted by the treacherous sand bar at the left.

A stern-wheeler rests on wooden ways at Bismarck in 1886. Boats were winched up by steam engine allowing workmen to repair hulls, rudders and steering mechanisms. In winter, as many as five steamers could be hoisted and stored side by side, safe from the Missouri's crushing ice.

8. Rivermen and railroaders

As a veteran traveler on the treacherous Missouri River, the stern-wheeled steamboat *Montana* had survived many a peril. Yet one day in 1884, while peacefully plying its trade near St. Louis at the eastern terminus of the 3,000-mile waterway, the *Montana* was caught by a capricious current and sent crashing into the stanchion of a railroad bridge—one of several such structures that by then spanned the Big Muddy as part of a system that reached all the way to the Pacific. Some of the cargo was saved, but the old boat itself settled into the muck of the river's bed. The *Montana* had made its final journey.

Although celebrated in neither song nor story, the death of the *Montana* somehow symbolized the waning of one era and the ascension of another.

For a host of traders and settlers, soldiers and prospectors, preachers and gamblers, the Missouri River had long been the way to the West. Since the first paddle-wheel voyage on the river—in May 1819, when the little steamboat *Independence* wended 250 hesitant miles upriver with a cargo of flour, sugar, iron castings and whiskey—some 700 different paddle wheelers had worked the Missouri. Of those, about 300 fell fatal victim to a whole catalog of calamities—impaled by snags, consumed by fire, crushed by ice, battered by violent winds and, not least, blown to smithereens by boiler explosions. But since the profits of a single voyage might repay the entire cost of a vessel, the traffic continued—until, at last, the steamboat was overtaken by a technology that ran on highways of steel.

Even in the early 1860s, the notion that a railroad might soon traverse the country's dizzying breadth seemed utterly fantastical to some. "A railroad to the Pacific?" scoffed a prominent government official. "I would not buy a ticket on it for my grandchildren."

Yet before the end of the decade, the job had been done. It required an outpouring of human endeavor by a gaudy cast of characters—rock-climbing surveyors, brawling Irish construction workers and their sober Chinese counterparts, engineers with their striped caps and red bandannas, sooty-faced firemen and, at the top of the heap, corporate promoters who combined vision and daring with a high degree of venality. By the time the *Montana* met its inglorious demise, three railroad lines crossed the continent; before the turn of the century there were five.

By then, the doughty steamboats had all but vanished. In 1880, some river cities still maintained the illusion of growth. That year, 30 million tons of freight had been landed at Fort Benton, a booming river city in the Montana Territory only 200 miles from the Rocky Mountains. A mere decade later, the last packet departed from Fort Benton's deserted levee. Soon, the sight of a steamer's plume of smoke and the sound of her mournful whistle would survive only in the memory of those who lived along the rivers of the West. The Golden Age of steamboats had come and gone.

The Missouri was the great watercourse of the prairies—and the longest river on the North American continent. A broad if changeable and dangerous stream, it swept from sources on the Continental Divide to a junction with the Mississippi 23 miles north of St. Louis. Tracing an enormous elliptical course, the Big Muddy enclosed a system of tributaries watering more than half a million square miles of the Dakotas, Nebraska, Montana, Wyoming and Colorado.

The Missouri rose twice a year. One period of high water began in April, when spring rains and prairie

From his station in the wheelhouse, 40 feet above the water line, the pilot of a riverboat could plot his perilous course up a river. The inevitable groundings were shrugged off; any pilot worth his salt soon developed ingenious ways to free his boat.

snowmelt often drowned the main valley under endless vistas of rushing brown water. The second rise occurred in May or June when the sun began melting the snowfields of the Rockies. Littering sand bars in low water were thousands of uprooted trees that were released like javelins when the water level climbed. "I have seen nothing more frightful," wrote French explorer Jacques Marquette in 1673. "A mass of large trees enter with branches interlocked—a floating island. We could not, without great danger, expose ourselves to pass across."

Worse yet was a submarine forest of trees that grew waterlogged, sank at the heavy root end, and hung in the river to form a hidden abatis that could tear the bottom out of a hull in seconds. Each year, scores of steamboats spitted themselves on such snags, and sank in the narrow channels at river bends, becoming impediments to navigation themselves. The river not only sent steamers to the bottom, but filled their hulls with mud and sand so rapidly that efforts to raise them or retrieve machinery and cargo were always difficult.

To negotiate the deadly Missouri, rivermen developed a special kind of boat—a flat-bottomed, multitiered structure that was designed to slide over the water rather than move through it. To save weight, the decks, floor, timbers, bulkheads and upper works were made of pine instead of sturdier but heavier oak. The craft's wedding cake-like superstructure—main deck, boiler deck, hurricane deck, officers' quarters and pilothouse—eliminated the need for a deep hold. In all, wrote a newspaper man from Council Bluffs, Iowa, the Western steamer was put together from "wood, tin, shingles, canvas and twine, and looked like the bride of Babylon." Yet the vessel did its job, if only because its draft might be as little as 14 inches.

Although the lower Missouri was frequently graced by the side-wheeled steamboats that had become familiar on the Mississippi River, the Big Muddy's upper reaches were mostly the domain of toilers whose single paddle was placed in the stern. This arrangement made up for its lack of aesthetics by saving weight, rendering the paddle less vulnerable to snags, and permitting a broader-beam hull with more cargo capacity.

Wherever they were located, the paddles were driven by the most powerful, albeit the crudest, simplest and most dangerous engines then known to man. Steam was generated for the engines by batteries of two, four or more cylindrical wrought-iron boilers. Their fireboxes

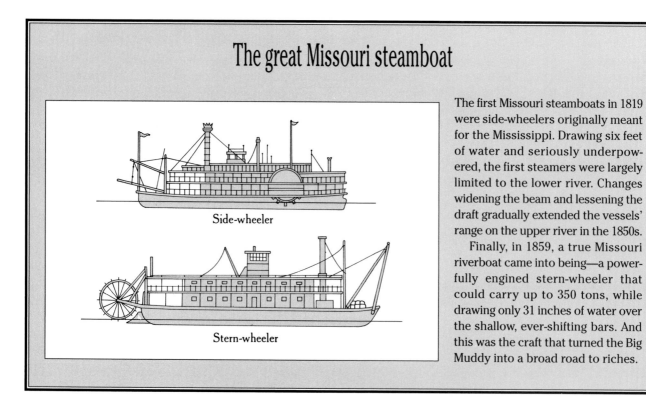

The great Missouri steamboat

Side-wheeler

Stern-wheeler

The first Missouri steamboats in 1819 were side-wheelers originally meant for the Mississippi. Drawing six feet of water and seriously underpowered, the first steamers were largely limited to the lower river. Changes widening the beam and lessening the draft gradually extended the vessels' range on the upper river in the 1850s.

Finally, in 1859, a true Missouri riverboat came into being—a powerfully engined stern-wheeler that could carry up to 350 tons, while drawing only 31 inches of water over the shallow, ever-shifting bars. And this was the craft that turned the Big Muddy into a broad road to riches.

were surmounted by a pair of iron chimneys (never called stacks or funnels) that rose up through the vessel's superstructure and towered as much as 100 feet above the upper deck.

During much of the period of the steamboat's popularity, water and pressure gauges were not in general use; engine-room crews relied largely on instinct to detect when boilers were building steam to dangerous levels. Coupled with this was the proclivity of pilots to call for more boiler pressure whenever trouble lay ahead; as rivermen put it, there was nothing like a "wad of steam" to get a boat through rapids or propel it across a sand bar. In consequence, Missouri River steamboats blew up by the dozen—as witness the tragedy of the paddle-wheeler *Saluda*, which produced perhaps the loudest and certainly the most lethal bang of them all.

It occurred during the spring flood of 1852, when the river fed an angry, ice-littered torrent down a channel that boats used to skirt a wide promontory above Lexington, Missouri. On April 7, Captain Francis Belt fired *Saluda* hard, but the boat's power plant was simply incapable of coping with the raging stream. Time and again *Saluda* tried, hung in the current and was slowly washed astern. Finally, Belt fell back on Lexington and tied up.

After another foiled attempt, Belt walked into the engine room early on Good Friday, April 9, and demanded to know how much more pressure the boat's boilers would stand. "Not a pound more than she's carrying now," replied the second mate. Belt ordered water injection shut off and the safety valve locked down. "Fill her fireboxes up," he ordered. "I want more steam. I'm going to round that point or blow her to hell trying."

Saluda had splashed through only two paddle revolutions when the boilers exploded. Captain Belt's lacerated corpse took a high, parabolic course inland along with the bell on which he had placed one elbow in the seconds before his death. Both landed high on a bluff above the river and rolled downhill together, the bell clanging wildly. A 600-pound iron safe, the ship's watchdog (which had been chained to its door) and second clerk Jonathan F. Blackburn were flung 200 yards from the river. Ashore, a local butcher was dismembered by a flying boiler flue.

Townspeople rushing to the river found, according to the *St. Joseph Gazette*, "the mangled remains of other human beings scattered over the wharf, and human

183

blood, just warm from the heart, trickling down the banks and mingling with the water of the Missouri River." The bodies of more than 100 crewmen and passengers were recovered and about the same number were believed to have washed down the river. It was recorded as the worst disaster in the history of steam navigation on the Missouri.

For the crews who manned the steamboats, there was little time to enjoy the scenery on the way to such upper Missouri towns as Sioux City, Yankton, Bismarck and Fort Benton. On the whole, the rivermen doubtless fit the description offered by an 1838 government report as roughnecks "of coarse habit, recklessness, and uneducated mind." Yet in their exertions they made their rackety vessels the key to development of the northwest.

The roustabouts—or roosters, as they were called—led a harsh and exhausting life. Firemen stood four-hour watches, but deck hands remained on call day and night, slept whenever they could grab a few minutes, and were expected to carry cordwood, bales and crates at a run over narrow, limber gangplanks that were often slippery with rain or ice. The crew's food was frequently execrable, though bigger packets sometimes served them pans of passenger leavings which they scooped up with their hands when summoned by the cry, "Grubpile!"

Negro roosters—often, in pre-Civil War days, slaves whose owners charged wages for them—were considered the most amenable to toil. German immigrants rated next in dependability. Missouri farm boys were thought to be too independent. Irishmen were scorned as being of little account. "Oh, hell," cried one pilot, continuing to steam even after being informed that a deck hand had fallen overboard, "it's only an Irishman!"

Overseeing the work of his crewmen was the least of the many crucial responsibilities that fell to the Missouri pilot. In the words of an experienced riverman, a pilot had to "know the river as a schoolboy knows a path to the schoolhouse, upside down, endways, inside, outside and crossways."

With no buoys, beacons or maps to go by, a Missouri pilot had to memorize the Big Muddy's endless bars, bends, rapids and chutes—and also the cliffs, dead trees, clearings, hills and cabins that served as landmarks at which a steamer was aimed when negotiating such hazards.

Peering through the window of his wheelhouse, the pilot had to recognize recent shifts in a stream that could change with bewildering rapidity. Eternally, a pilot also had to "read water"—to guess at a glance the speed of a current in a bend, and to decide from surface swirls and ripples whether the river concealed rocks, sand bars or snags. Wind sometimes helped him by ruffling the deep water. But rain dappled the whole surface and laid a blur of tiny splashes over the river's mysteries. Surface glare masked them, too, when the sun lay lower than 45 degrees above the horizon.

Drifting ice was another menace, although every captain did his best to get back downstream by late autumn and owners usually delayed upstream voyages until the worst of the river's winter burden had washed away. Still, ice could do terrible damage even in down-river ports.

An entire fleet of steamboats was ground to kindling at St. Louis during "The Great Ice Gorge of 1856." Rising water broke the solid, heavy ice near the city in late February, piled huge sections of it into vast, noisy hills and ridges and moved these grinding masses slowly downstream, along with every movable object they encountered. Dozens of boats were ripped from their moorings at the St. Louis levee, then solid with steamers for 20 blocks. Reported *The Missouri Republican*, "The steamers *Australia, Adriatic, Brunette, Paul Jones, Falls City, Altoona, A.B. Chambers* and *Challenge* were all torn away from shore and floated down with the immense fields of ice. The first obstacles with which they came into contact were a large fleet of barges and canal boats, about fifty in all, which were either sunk, broken or carried away. *Bon Accord* and *Highland Mary* were carried off, both total losses, and after them *Lamartine, Westerner* and *Jeanie Deans. Gossamer, Luella, Alice* and *Badger State* were forced ashore only slightly damaged, but *Shenandoah* was wrecked."

If the steamboat faced a list of obstacles almost without inventory, it still often managed to endure the worst the Missouri had to offer. For decades, boats multiplied faster than they went down. In 1859 alone more than 100 vessels plied the river regularly, splashing over the bones of their predecessors in bend after bend. The steamboat's record of accomplishment, all things considered, was astonishing. In the final analysis the catalog of its mishaps is significant only as a measure of the

odds surmounted and the price paid by the men who created for it such a strategic role in Western history.

The captains learned the fundamentals of their craft as lowly deck hands or cabin boys. Piloting skills were honed during a period of grueling apprenticeship that might last as long as five years. Above all, a helmsman needed consummate coolness, judgment and skill. All earned renown for their ability to cope with Indians, unreliable machinery and roisterous crews as they guided their boats, according to an entry in the log of one ship, "just a little beyond no place."

Of all the many talented river pilots who plied their trade during the second half of the 19th Century—some earning the then-princely sum of up to $1,500 a month—two dynamic men dominated the field. One career spanned the era of the Rocky Mountain fur trade; the other peerless pilot began his years on the upper Missouri during the Montana gold boom of the 1860s.

The first of the great river pilots was Captain Joseph Marie La Barge. A handsome, muscular man of French-Canadian extraction, La Barge started his career as a riverman in 1832, when few but keelboatmen had ever ascended the Missouri. He had an intuitive sense of water and an uncommon feel for the vessel beneath his feet. Having also been a fur trapper, he was confident of his ability to deal safely with Indians—so confident, in fact, that in 1847 he took his wife, Pelagie, with him on the steamboat *Martha* to regions of the upper Missouri where no white woman had ever been before.

During that voyage, there was indeed a confrontation with the Indians. At Crow Creek in Dakota Territory, hostile Sioux shot a deck hand, swarmed aboard, and then—having learned something of steamboats from observing them on the river—used buckets of water to extinguish the embers under the

A crowd of curious Mandans — one of a dozen tribes served
by trading posts on the upper Missouri — lines the riverbank
at Fort Berthold to watch a steamboat arrival. The Indians
were so awe-struck by the smoke-belching behemoths that
they sometimes accompanied them along the shore for miles.

vessel's boilers. La Barge, however, was unruffled. In complete control, he helped rig a pulley to haul the boat's brass cannon to the deck above the engine room, where the weapon had been undergoing repairs. Then he calmly lighted a cigar and held it close to the cannon. "Tell them," he said to a companion, "that if they don't get off the boat I'll blow it all to hell!" The horrified Indians—along with members of *Martha's* crew—departed in full flight.

During the 1840s and 1850s, such an Indian threat was the exception rather than the rule. But over the next decade, the belligerency of the Missouri tribes grew, and was altered dramatically by the 1862 discovery of Montana gold. Gold drew an increasing number of miners to camps like Virginia City and Last Chance Gulch and threatened the last, vast Indian domains as a few scattered trappers had never done. This invasion turned bands of Sioux and Northern Cheyennes into impassioned enemies who harassed steamers and Army posts alike.

Even though Joseph La Barge had a much better understanding of Indians than the Army officers and Indian agents who were given the task of dealing with them, the Sioux remained a continual source of danger. In the summer of 1863, one particularly persistent band engaged in a 600-mile running battle with La Barge's chartered vessel, *Robert Campbell*. The chase ended only when La Barge and his crew swept the attackers with a storm of cannon and small arms fire, felling nearly 40 Sioux and 20 horses in all.

By June of 1866, rich gold strikes, coinciding with the surrender of Robert E. Lee at Appomattox, had triggered waves of invasion and exploitation such as the northern Rockies had never known. That spring, 31 steamers had reached, or were approaching, the head of navigation at Fort Benton—though not more than a half dozen had done so in any previous year—and they lay bow to stern along a half mile of riverfront. Among them was the *Luella*, a survivor of the 1856 St. Louis "Ice Gorge." *Luella* was now captained by 34-year-old Grant Marsh, making his first run on the upper Missouri.

Marsh may have been new to the upstream reaches of the Big Muddy, but he already was a veteran of the Ohio and Tennessee rivers, and the lower Missouri. It took him no time at all to make his mark among the miners swarming around Fort Benton. Although captains made a habit of hurrying downstream from Fort Benton to avoid the shallow water of midsummer, Marsh decided to delay until September, risking freeze-up, in order to accommodate miners who wished to stay at their diggings as long as possible. When *Luella* finally did leave, she carried with her the most valuable cargo ever borne downstream: $1,250,000 in gold dust. Working *Luella* as few boats had ever been worked on the upper river, Marsh handily disposed of an Indian war party, and made a profit of $24,000 in the bargain—all of which earned him a respect rarely accorded new captains on the Missouri.

Marsh was guided by impressions formed during 1862, when he had served as mate of the New Orleans packet *John J. Roe* that supported General Ulysses S. Grant's forces at the Battle of Shiloh on the Tennessee River. He admired good soldiers and felt a sense of duty to them; he believed in the efficacy of resolution and daring during moments of stress or danger. Accordingly, his career on the river was punctuated with outlandish attempts and spectacular successes.

The year following the ambush of *Luella*, Marsh was compelled to cope with a more serious attack while in command of the steamboat *Ida Stockdale*. On his way to Fort Benton, he was confronted by a big Sioux war party. The only escape, as Marsh saw it, was to risk a fast, narrow chute previously unattempted by a steamer. He headed into the quickening water of the chute, scraped across a sand bar with bullets clanging on his boiler plate, put his wheel hard down to avoid a jutting snag, ground along the bottom for awful seconds—and glided into open water with the sound of Indian musketry dying into frustrated silence astern.

There was a curious inconsistency about these brushes with Indians and, indeed, about the whole pattern of their reaction to whites. Almost all bands took recesses in enmity at times, and the captain who came downstream with bullet holes in his upper works might find himself starting back with cargo for the very warriors who had put them there. Marsh attached less importance to his adventure on the *Ida Stockdale* than to the fact that he had made a hefty profit during the voyage on which it occurred.

The next decade proved to be a decisive one for the rivermen's way of life. St. Louis lost its position as supplier and citadel of the Missouri when railroads reached new ports (Sioux City, then Yankton, then Bis-

marck) a thousand miles and more above it on the upper river itself. All three river ports were launched on a contest for commercial dominance of the Missouri—a contest led by William J. Kountz and Sanford B. Coulson. These two Pennsylvanians were the biggest boatline operators of their day, transporting hordes of settlers and miners upriver, and increasingly supporting the Army in its campaigns against the Indians.

By 1873, the U.S. Army prepared to quell the rebellious Sioux. It was obvious that the Yellowstone River, which watered the heart of the Indians' remaining hunting grounds, would be a key to military operations. Yet though generations of explorers and trappers had trudged along the banks of the Yellowstone, no one knew whether the stream was navigable for more than a few miles above its mouth.

Marsh was chosen to find out, and he achieved results in two monumental voyages. One expedition, that same year, took him and the Coulson steamer *Key West* 460 miles to the mouth of the Powder River. Another, in 1875, thrust Marsh and *Josephine* farther up the Yellowstone's higher reaches to within 60 miles of present-day Yellowstone Park. Little did he know at the time that he was conducting a rehearsal for tragedy—and for the astonishing climax the next year of his own career.

On May 17, 1876, Colonel George Armstrong Custer's 7th U.S. Cavalry Regiment rode out of the Dakota Territory's Fort Abraham Lincoln as part of a three-pronged expedition that was aimed at subduing the Sioux once and for all. Grant Marsh was selected as captain and pilot of the 190-foot stern-wheeler *Far West*, which steamed up the Yellowstone as the Army's supply boat, hospital ship and mobile command post.

One after another, the Yellowstone's tributaries—the Powder River, the Tongue River, Rosebud Creek—fell behind *Far West's* wake. Then Marsh steered up the Bighorn River, where no steamboat had ever dared before, and anchored near its junction with the Little Bighorn at noon on June 26. At almost that same moment, only eleven miles away, Custer was making his foolishly fatal approach to a waiting Indian horde. Five of the companies personally led by Custer were obliterated, but elements of seven other companies survived the terrible fighting—and Grant Marsh was soon ordered to take the wounded, along with word

of the catastrophe, back to Fort Abraham Lincoln.

It was axiomatic among pilots that every river had to be "learned" twice—going up and going down. No steamboatman had ever seen the Bighorn going down. Still, Marsh ordered the *Far West's* lines to be cast off, rang up the engine room—and began reacting in a daze of concentration to the kaleidoscopic succession of chutes, islands, rocks and rapids that were flung across his field of vision by the boat's startling speed in the narrow waterway.

"*Far West* would take a shoot on this or that side of an island as the quick judgment of the pilot would dictate," wrote a newsman who was along. "Down the Yellowstone the stanch craft shot, and down that river sealed to pilots she made over twenty miles an hour. The bold captain was taking chances, but he scarcely thought of them. He was flying under orders. Lives were at stake. The engineer was instructed to keep up steam at the highest pitch. Once the gauge marked a pressure that turned his cool head and made every nerve in his powerful frame quiver. The crisis passed and *Far West* had escaped a fate more terrible than Custer's. The rate of speed was unrivaled in the annals of boating. It was a thrilling voyage!"

Fifty-four hours after her wild journey had begun, *Far West* arrived at the Bismarck wharf, directly across the Missouri from Fort Abraham Lincoln, and Marsh rang down FINISHED WITH ENGINES. Even including several necessary stops, he had averaged an incredible 13 1/7 miles an hour over a distance of more than 700 miles.

In the end, *Far West* represented something more than this ultimate triumph of steampower and human nerve. The course of history had begun changing even as she tied up at Fort Lincoln. The Sioux had sealed their own fate by their bloody victory over Custer. The U.S. Army was moved to intense exertion in response, and within a year Indian resistance was broken forever. The long, brave day of the Missouri rivermen declined thereafter, for nothing now impeded railroad construction in the wilds. *Far West*'s voyage had brought an age to a stupendous climax; no American vessel ever approached her record and she remained the queen of speed when the steamboat had vanished from the rivers of the West.

In the early spring of 1864, Mr. Collis P. Huntington of Sacramento and Dr. Thomas C. Durant of New York City had gone to Washington, with government money their aim and bribery their game. Huntington was a member of the so-called Big Four of the Central Pacific Railroad (C.P.R.), which had begun laying track eastward from Sacramento. Durant was the guiding light of the Union Pacific Railroad (U.P.R.), whose route pointed west from Omaha. Although the men and their fledgling railroads were fierce competitors, they had one thing in common: they were in serious trouble.

Behind them lay a generation of bitter debate and broken dreams, of seething regional rivalries and cunning political maneuvers. As early as the 1840s, Missouri's powerful Senator Thomas Hart Benton had proposed a railroad that would link the two halves of the continent—with St. Louis as its natural eastern terminus. But

against the railroad were arrayed Eastern interests championed by Massachusetts' renowned Daniel Webster. "What," asked Webster, "do we want with this region of savages and wild beasts, of deserts, of shifting sands and whirlwinds of dust, of cactus and prairie dogs?"

Gradually, however, the idea of the railroad prevailed, if only because the imagination of America was captured by the immensity of the challenge. The distance from the Missouri River to the Pacific was 1,600 miles. Within that expanse lay not one but two mountain chains—the Rockies and the Sierra Nevada; in both ranges, peaks thrust above 14,000 feet and winter snows piled up in the passes to depths of more than 40 feet. Equally formidable, between the mountain ranges lay the arid wastelands of the Great Basin, where water for men and locomotive boilers was scarce and corrosively alkaline, and wood for fireboxes and for railroad ties was almost as rare as a rainy day.

Prospects for a railroad were enhanced, however, by a scheme that seemingly offered something to everyone. The U.S. owned land in almost measureless quantity, and it was suggested that the government might give some of it to the railroads in a sequence of sections lying alternately north and south of the proposed right of way. The government would thus be providing a commodity that the railroads could sell to pay for construction, while at the same time increasing the value of the sections it reserved for itself.

So alluring was this logic that in 1850 President Millard Fillmore signed the nation's first railroad land-grant act. But that, in a sense, was putting the caboose before the locomotive. Although there were plenty of differing opinions, no one at the time had any real idea as to the best route for the railroad. In fact, it was not until 1853 that Congress sent an appropriation of $150,000 to Secretary of War Jefferson Davis—a Mississippian who favored a line leading west from Texas that would link California to the economy of the South—instructing him to survey within ten months the principal paths to the Pacific.

As it turned out, Davis' army engineers surveyed no fewer than five routes and produced volumes of information on the flora and fauna of the West, on the weather, the fisheries and on life among the Indians. Sadly lacking, however, was the hard engineering data that would be necessary to build a railroad.

Among those unsatisfied by the reports was a young civil engineer and railroad visionary from Bridgeport,

Connecticut, named Theodore Dehone Judah. In 1860 Judah took his theodolite, and went looking for his own route across that intimidating range. His efforts were sufficient to interest a group of investors led by a quartet of Sacramento merchants who would become known as the Central Pacific's Big Four—Collis Huntington and Mark Hopkins, partners in a hardware business; Leland Stanford, a wholesale grocer and politician; and Charles Crocker, who dealt in dry goods.

They were an unlikely team. Huntington, whom a newsman once called "ruthless as a crocodile," had forsaken New York for California's gold fields, where he shoveled gravel for exactly one morning before setting himself up as a trader in hardware. His sidekick, Hopkins, was a frail, mousy man whose main interests lay in growing peas and carrots for his meager vegetarian diet, and in driving a shrewd bargain.

In contrast to the hard-driving Huntington, Leland Stanford was a heavy, slow-moving man whose habit of pausing gravely between words gave the impression of wisdom. Although Huntington privately considered him "a damned old fool," Stanford rose steadily in politics and in 1861 was elected California's first Republican governor. In that capacity, he not only coaxed the legislature into helping finance the Central Pacific but also envisioned the day when the railroad would turn Sacramento's muddy streets into something resembling the fabled marketplaces of the Orient, teeming with "the busy denizens of two hemispheres."

Charles Crocker, the fourth member of the combine, was cast in an altogether different mold. As a purveyor of ladies' calico and ribbons, Crocker had been hopelessly miscast. But as the profane and bullying construction boss of the Central Pacific, he would be worth his 265-pound weight in gold. Once, when lambasted by a business rival as "a living, breathing, waddling monument to the triumph of vulgarity, viciousness and dishonesty," Crocker was so impressed by the man's eloquence that he hired him for the railroad.

Railroad promoters received a boost in 1862, when Congress passed the Pacific Railroad Act, thanks partly to the blessings of the new President of the United States, Abraham Lincoln, a knowledgeable railroad enthusiast since his days as a sometime lawyer for the Rock Island Railroad line.

By then it was clear that the railroad should follow the basic path of the old trail that was still being used

by wagon trains of emigrants. Sticking close to rivers and generally following the easiest grades, the Emigrant Trail went up the Platte River Valley, over the Continental Divide via South Pass and then across the Great Basin to Oregon or California. It also was determined that two roads would be built, one from the West Coast and one from mid-continent; they would meet someplace in between.

Under the charter granted to the Central Pacific, the company would be given 10 miles of land on either side of its right of way for each mile of track laid, plus loans of $16,000 a mile on the plains, $32,000 through the Great Basin and $48,000 through the Rockies and the Sierra.

There was, however, one major catch: the company would receive its awards only in increments based on sections of track it had actually laid. Undiscouraged by that technicality, the Big Four broke ground on their railroad in January, 1863. But as they soon learned, it was one thing for Governor Stanford to make a grandiose speech about their railroad as a "great highway of nations" and quite another to extend their tracks much further than a good buggy ride east of Sacramento. One major obstacle was the inflation that accompanied the Civil War. The price of a ton of rails, for example, had soared from $55 to $115 since 1861—and that was just the cost at the Boston wharf, with freight charges for the trip around Cape Horn still to come.

Unlike the heavy-handed Californians, Thomas Durant was a smooth operator. Although he had forsaken a medical career in favor of railroading, he was still called The Doctor, and he had few peers at dispensing financial snake oil. Durant's splendid manners and his princely wardrobe, his French-speaking friends and his love of fine wines, the rococo elegance of the statues and potted palms and caged canaries that crowded his office left no room for doubt that The Doctor was a virtuoso to be reckoned with, if not necessarily trusted.

He was also an old hand at railroad promotions. Moving west as early as 1851, he had helped build the Michigan Southern and the Chicago & Rock Island lines. And it was while with the Rock Island that his destiny became closely tied together with that of a young surveyor named Grenville M. Dodge.

A New Englander by birth, Dodge was a Westerner by disposition, and he never ceased marveling at the "lands wild and uncultivated that have been subdued, fenced and cultivated." Employed as a surveyor for the Rock Island, he was delighted when Durant, who was already formulating plans for a transcontinental railroad, assigned him to start running a survey westward from Council Bluffs, Iowa, as far as the Rockies. For the next five years, Dodge explored the great valley of the Platte River, returning to Council Bluffs in the late 1850s with a detailed map.

Soon after the outbreak of the Civil War, Dodge entered the Union Army as a colonel. Although he later became a major general with a formidable reputation as an Indian fighter, he never forgot his civilian passion: once, while chasing a band of Crows through Evans Pass in the Laramie Mountains, he recognized that the defile would make a perfect passage for his railroad.

Meanwhile, staking their future on Dodge's survey, Thomas Durant and some financial associates had formed a new railroad and given it the patriotic name of Union Pacific. Granted a charter similar to that of the Central Pacific, it broke ground in Omaha in December, 1863—and soon ran into the same problems afflicting California's Big Four, most notably a lack of cash.

Thus, at the time Durant and Huntington went to Washington to procure further government assistance, the Central Pacific had laid only 20 miles of track and the Union Pacific had yet to get outside Omaha's city limits.

With their dwindling funds, the two men spread their largesse widely among Congressmen later described by Huntington as "the hungriest group of men who ever got together." Although the behavior of both aspirant railroad barons was (as an anonymous wit said of Huntington), scrupulously dishonest, they were in fact no more than men of their time, an era when business ethics, and morality itself, were in a state of upheaval.

At any event, their efforts paid off: land grants to the two lines were doubled; eventually, the C.P. and U.P. would get a total of more land than Vermont, Massachusetts and Connecticut put together—almost 21 million acres. More significant, instead of having to wait until they had actually laid track before receiving their federal funds, they would get two thirds of the money as soon as each 20 miles of the roadbed had been prepared.

The Central Pacific quickly qualified for its first loan. Durant's Union Pacific, however, remained bogged down

An elegant detachment of soldiers fires cannon salutes as the *Best Friend of Charleston* clatters along the track in South Carolina.

From puny puffers to transcontinental workhorses

On January 15, 1831, as pretty girls tossed flowers onto the track and the gentlemen in the rail coaches — mainly stockholders — cheered, America's first passenger locomotive wheezed out of Charleston, South Carolina. For six months the machine *(above)*, named the *Best Friend of Charleston,* rattled at 20 mph between the city and nearby towns. Then one day its fireman, annoyed by the hiss of escaping steam, fastened down the engine's safety valve, thus ending its vital protective function.

Friend and fireman blew up together.

America's other early engines had sadly similar records. Called puffers for the sound they made, they spewed sparks, jerked people off their seats when the cars crashed forward at stops, and tended to jump the track when their rigid drive wheels hit a sharp curve.

But as the locomotives on these pages show, improvements came quickly. By 1833, engine design incorporated a swiveling front wheel assembly, a truck, to help ease a locomotive

around a bend. A funnel-shaped casing with a wire screen inside was fitted atop the stack to hold in cinders *(right)*.

Four years later Henry Campbell united these and other improvements in an eight-wheel design like that below. Railroaders classify engines by wheel arrangements; this engine was a 4-4-0, meaning it had four wheels on its lead truck, four drivers and no wheels underneath the cab. It was this engine that, combining speed and power, conquered the first transcontinental route.

A prototype of later engines, the *Philadelphia,* a 4-2-0 with a lead truck and funnel-shaped stack, was built by William Norris in 1836. The only major feature it lacked was an enclosed cab to shelter the engineer.

A triumphant 4-4-0, *Engine 30,* was built in Jersey City in 1856. Refinements included a cowcatcher, a headlight, a smokestack that killed sparks by pulverizing them, an enclosed cab and a snappy brass trim.

Fierce rivalry between C.P. and U.P. crews gave rise to track-laying competitions such as this one involving Irish and Chinese laborers, who toil furiously within sight of a land-clearing blast.

until, just a few weeks before Lincoln's assassination, the President came to its rescue. Lincoln summoned to his office U.S. Representative Oakes Ames, a 60-year-old millionaire from Massachusetts. Referring to the U.P.'s difficulties, Lincoln said simply: "Ames, take hold of this."

The appeal had an electric effect: Oakes Ames and his brother Oliver put up $1 million of their own; their example soon attracted the first transfusion of solid Boston capital to the tune of $1.5 million more. The money did not, however, go directly to the Union Pacific. Instead, it was channeled to a corporation called the Credit Mobilier (borrowed from a French company, the name meant movable goods trust company), which would become one of the century's great bonanzas—and scandals.

The Credit Mobilier was set up by the U.P. directors to raise money for the physical task of building the railroad—grading roadbed, digging tunnels, laying track and so on. Since the railroad directors were also directors of the Credit Mobilier, they would, in effect, be doing business with themselves. Such an operation was of course open to padding construction costs, manipulating stock and other wonderfully lucrative abuses. Knowing a good thing when they saw one, the Central Pacific's Big Four made similar arrangements through a firm named the Contract & Finance Company, C. Crocker, President.

In the summer of 1872, such shenanigans would blow up in a scandal of enormous proportions, tarnishing not only the names of the railroad barons but of politicians who had been allowed to participate in—and profit from—the schemes. Among those implicated to one degree or another were Vice President Schuyler Colfax; James G. Blaine, a future Presidential candidate; James A. Garfield, a future President; and even President Ulysses S. Grant. Oakes Ames, who had started it all by doing Abraham Lincoln's bidding, suffered the disgrace of an overwhelming vote of censure by his fellow Congressmen; a broken man, he went home to Massachusetts and died a few months later.

But all that lay in the future. For now, the money was pouring in, and the rival railroads—operating on the

194

tenable assumption that whoever laid the most rail was going to own the most railroad and thus collect the most amount of government bonds and land grants—had begun their great race across the Western half of the continent.

In overall command of the Union Pacific field force was Grenville Dodge, who left the Army to become the railroad's chief engineer. In charge of actual construction, however, was Brigadier General John Stephen Casement, an Ohioan of five feet four inches in height who stood tall as a giant when it came to handling men. Using a system based on loyalty rather than fear, Casement took whatever raw material he could find—Irish immigrants, discharged soldiers, fed-up farmers, disillusioned prospectors and even a few Indian women. He drilled them into a quasi-military army that could not only spike down track with the speed and precision of a close-order drill team but was ready to repel Indian raiders with the Spencer rifles stocked in the work train.

For the Central Pacific, Charlie Crocker was in his element as the line's bulldozing boss contractor. Crocker's right-hand man was James Harvey Strobridge, a gangling 37-year-old New Englander with a spectacular fund of profanity and a merciless conviction that his men—ultimately 10,000 of them—were as "about as near brutes as they can get." Strobridge drove himself as hard as his crews, and his impatience while monitoring a black-powder blast cost him his right eye; he now wore a patch over the empty socket, and his Chinese roustabouts fearfully called him "One Eye Bossy Man."

The Chinese themselves had been a subject of contention. Confronted by a chronic shortage of manpower, Crocker repeatedly urged their employment. But Strobridge possessed in full measure the white man's contempt for Celestials, as he and other Californians called the strange little men with their dishpan straw hats, floppy blue pajamas and pigtails. Strobridge argued that they were too frail for the work—and besides, who could provide them with their outlandish diet of cuttlefish, bamboo shoots, mushrooms, rice, even seaweed?

The Chinese had an early opportunity to dispel Strobridge's lowly opinion of their courage—and also to demonstrate the amazing reserves of their sinewy strength. Fifty-seven miles out of Sacramento, the Central Pacific's construction crews ran up against a rocky spur of the Sierra that came to be known as Cape Horn; towering high above the gorge of the American River, to which it descended at an angle of 75 degrees, it seemed to forbid all passage. Yet the surveyors had decided that the rails must go along a ledge—where no foothold existed—1,400 feet above the thread of green water.

Strobridge set the Chinese to it. Armed with sledges, iron hand drills and kegs of black powder, Celestials were lowered down the face of the cliff in large wicker baskets. With their natural love of fireworks, they soon learned to cut their fuses so that an entire round of charges would go off at once; the louder the noise, they believed, the more likely it was to scare off devils and imps. Work on the fearsome ledge around Cape Horn was completed without the loss of a single life—and never again did a job come up that Strobridge believed his Chinese could not or would not do.

The winter of 1866-67 caught the Central Pacific crews at work on Summit Tunnel, highest, longest and most exposed of the six bores needed to get up and through the Sierra before the line reached the steep pitch down the eastern slope. Just below the rugged crest of Donner Pass, a bore 20 feet high had to be punched through 1,659 feet of solid granite, 7,032 feet above sea level. It would have been a brute in the best of weather, but during that savage winter the blizzards piled cuts and canyons with drifts 60 feet deep and set off avalanches that roared down on roads and camps.

Living and working literally under the snow, the Chinese had to cut passageways between the tunnel entrance and their barracks. Inside the bore, crews labored around the clock, but progress was a mere eight inches each 24 hours. Strobridge wanted to use a newfangled European invention, nitroglycerin, which was eight times as powerful as blasting powder. But when an accidental explosion of the unstable stuff in San Francisco killed 12 persons virtually all shipments of it were suspended.

Desperate for progress, Strobridge hired a Scottish chemist named James Howden and prepared a kitchen for him at the summit of the majestic Sierra. There, like some Merlin of the snows, Howden set about brewing a fresh batch of nitroglycerin every day to blow the guts out of the mountains. Yet though work thereafter proceeded at twice the previous pace, the job of laying rail through Summit Tunnel was completed only in November 1867. From then on, the going was progressively easier for the Central Pacific.

A temporary trestle, 1,100 feet long by 130 feet high, spans May Creek in western Washington with a maze of wood beams and iron bolts. One newspaper reported such bridges would "shake the nerves of the stoutest hearts when they see what is expected to uphold a train in motion."

A worksheet for April 29, 1869 lists the names of the C.P. tracklayers who, on that day, lifted 1,000 tons of iron to lay a record 10 miles of track in 12 hours. For their feat, they were given four days' pay.

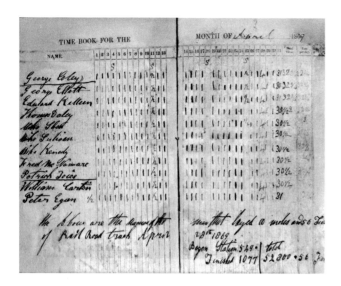

Compared to the terrible toiling of the Central Pacific in the Sierra, the job faced by the Union Pacific, with its starting point in the flatlands 680 miles east of the jagged Rockies, had seemed like a lark—at first. Once Casement got his people in rhythm, it went like this:

As many as 300 miles out in front of the rust-eaters (as the men who handled the rails called themselves), roustabouts graded a roadbed with horses, mules, scrapers, hand dumpcarts, Ames shovels (produced by a company owned by the Union Pacific's great benefactor, Oakes Ames) and sweat. Far to their rear, but still 20 miles ahead of track, bridge monkeys erected trestles across rivers and gullies with timber felled in Minnesota, floated down the Mississippi, barged up the Missouri to Omaha, and then mule-freighted to the site.

Behind the bridgebuilders came crews whose horse-drawn wagons were piled high with ties. Obtaining ties was an endless aggravation on the barren high plains, where the only timber was often the pulpy cottonwood that fringed the rivers. The U.P. made do with such inferior material by "burnettizing" the logs, a method of preservation devised by a Scot, William Burnett, in which wood is impregnated with a solution of zinc chloride.

Then came the tracklayers in their ballet of muscle and iron. On and on they went, five men and 28 or 30 spikes to the 500-pound rail, three blows to the spike, two pairs of rails to the minute, 400 rails to the mile in what a marveling reporter called "a grand Anvil Chorus."

Following the freshly laid track was the work train—the perpetual train, as it was known, because it

never stopped for long—which served as the nerve center, heart and stomach for the entire operation. It was pushed, rather than pulled, by an engine so that the leading flatcars, bearing tools and a blacksmith shop, were closest to the point of construction. Next came three barnlike boxcars, 85 feet long and lined with triple tiers of bunks. These rough mobile barracks were followed by a dining car that could accommodate 125 men at a time at a table that ran its full length. Finally, there was a car partitioned into three sections—kitchen, storeroom and engineers' office. Hanging spiked on hooks along its outside flanks were quarters of beef, freshly killed from the contractor-supplied herds that grazed beside the tracks.

As the Union Pacific thrust westward, makeshift towns such as Julesburg, Cheyenne and Laramie sprang up every 60 miles or so along the right of way. They were populated largely by fast-dollar saloonkeepers, gamblers, con men, pimps and whores who followed the railroad workers downtrack, thereby giving birth to the phrase "hell on wheels." From Julesburg, a U.P. construction chief wrote to his wife: "Vice and crime stalk unblushingly in the mid-day sun."

Yet if the riffraff was a bother, other forces were a blight to the Union Pacific. In particular, the notorious summer storms of the Platte River struck with shattering violence upon U.P. work crews on the open prairie. One such tempest, observed by photographer William Henry Jackson, "came down raging and howling like a madman. It rocked and shook us and started some of the wagons on their wheels. The roaring thunder and the flashing lightning were incessant, reverberating through the heavens with an awful majesty."

And then there were Indians, a problem that the Central Pacific's Charlie Crocker succeeded in circumventing by issuing lifetime passes that permitted tribal chiefs to ride the passenger cars. Out on the Plains, however, the Union Pacific found that the Sioux and many Cheyennes were not to be bought off so cheaply.

Some of the Indian attempts to fight off the encroachments of the Iron Horse were simply ludicrous. For example, one mounted war party of 50 or so warriors actually tried to capture a locomotive by stretching lariats across the track and attaching the ends to their saddles. When a train hit the rawhide barrier at 25 miles an hour, several of the Indians were swung along with their ponies into the pounding drive wheels and dismembered.

A gold spike used to link the U.P. and C.P. bears a prayer: "May God continue the unity of our Country as this Railroad unites the two great Oceans of the world."

That story, of course, afforded amusement to idlers in the jerkwater stations west of Omaha, but other Indian attacks were no laughing matter. That fact was tragically demonstrated at Plum Creek, Nebraska, on the night of August 6, 1867, when a war party of Cheyennes, led by Chief Turkey Leg, piled a barricade of loose ties on the Union Pacific track and lashed it with wire ripped from nearby telegraph poles. Then they waited.

When the wires went dead back at Plum Creek, the linesman on duty, a young Englishman named William Thompson, loaded five section hands, a spool of new wire, repair tools and six Spencer rifles aboard a hand-pump car and set out to find the break. In the darkness, they never saw the barricade. They hit the ties and went flying through the air; within minutes, five of the six men were dead at the hands of the Cheyennes. Although clubbed down, Thompson managed to creep away and escape.

Yet despite all natural dangers and human depredations, the railroads were under a full head of steam; in 1868 the C.P. built 360 miles of track and the U.P. racked up 425. On April 28, 1869, the Central Pacific spiked an incredible 10 miles and 56 feet of track in 12 hours, a new record. In addition, both lines graded far ahead of their own rail until, in the great American desert, the grading gangs met and passed each other so closely that one crew sometimes had to dodge the flying debris from the other's blasting charges—the timing of which both gangs neglected to announce before lighting their fuses.

The government finally ended the grading war by decreeing that the rails of the two lines would be joined at Promontory Summit, 56 miles west of Ogden, Utah. The date was set for May 8, but had to be put off when Dr. Durant, on his way to the ceremony, was kidnapped at Piedmont, Wyoming, by his own tie cutters, whose wages the U.P. had neglected to pay. An embarrassed Durant

wired for enough money to bail himself out; the historic Promontory observance was held two days later.

It proved to be more farcical than solemn. As Chinese workmen lifted the last rail to the roadbed, a photographer shouted to his assistant: "Shoot!" The Chinese dropped the rail and fled. When the rail was finally put in place, Governor Stanford was supposed to drive home the last spike, which was ingeniously wired so that each blow would be telegraphed across the nation. Stanford swung mightily—and missed. Nevertheless, a telegraph operator flashed, "Dot. Dot. Dot. . . . Done." Guns boomed in Sacramento, San Franciscans danced in the streets and Mormons prayed in Salt Lake City.

The impossible had been achieved, and the awesome breadth of the continent had noticeably shrunk.

Only five days after the joining of the rails came the announcement that the first transcontinental railroad was initiating regular passenger service. Once a day, the Pacific Express would head west from Omaha for Sacramento. And once a day, eastbound passengers would board the Atlantic Express in Sacramento for a run of about 2,000 miles to Omaha.

The railroad offered two lures that travelers could hardly resist—speed and comfort. In 1870, the first full year of operation, nearly 150,000 passengers availed themselves of the service; a dozen years later, their number soared to almost a million.

Such statistics, of course, attracted other entrepreneurs. Thus, in steady succession, came the completions of the Southern Pacific and the Northern Pacific, both in 1883; the Atchison, Topeka and Santa Fe in 1885; and the Great Northern in 1893. "The prairie schooner has passed away," exulted a newspaper report, "and is replaced by the railway coach with all its modern comforts."

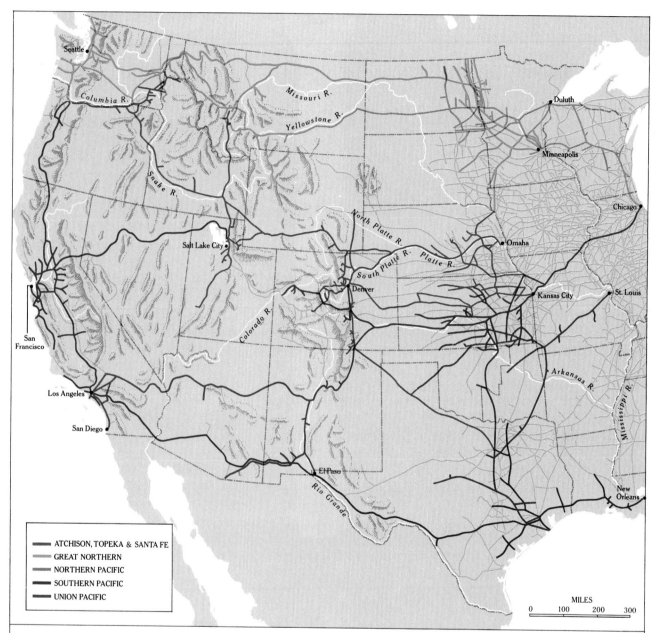

THE GREAT RAIL SYSTEMS OF THE WEST

On January 6, 1893, when the last spike of the Great Northern Railway was driven home, the country's sprawling network of transcontinental rail lines was essentially complete. Five long ribbons of track now spanned the West, following the general routes of the first transcontinental rail surveys of the 1850s. The five great rail systems (color-coded according to the map legend) were complemented by an intricate web of other main lines, feeders and spurs (*light blue*). The Union Pacific had flung track north to Washington and south into Texas. The old Cen-

tral Pacific had been merged in 1885 with the Southern Pacific, which dominated rail traffic in California and included a transcontinental line east to New Orleans. The Santa Fe owned track from Chicago to Los Angeles, and the Northern Pacific and Great Northern ran from the Great Lakes to the Northwest coast. Altogether, some 40,000 miles of track had been added to the Western railroads in the 1880s alone. Now the building spree was over, and the wail of highballing locomotives penetrated the farthest reaches of the West.

To lure the carriage trade into taking the long trip west, railroads offered genteel comforts such as this reclining chair, designed in 1876 and adopted by George Pullman for his luxurious first-class cars.

Comforts indeed. Thanks largely to George Mortimer Pullman, an innovative builder of railroad cars, well-heeled travelers could lounge in reclining seats or sleep in a hinged berth that folded against the ceiling when not in use. Pullman's parlor cars were resplendent in plush upholstery, rich hangings and hand-carved inlaid paneling. His magnificent dining cars provided gourmet meals that on special occasions featured such delicacies as blue-winged teal, antelope steaks, boiled tongue, corn on the cob and, everywhere in the Rockies, fresh trout.

Second-class travelers, riding in day coaches, had a much less luxurious time of it. Typically, they were short-haul "way" passengers—cowhands, farmers, miners, hunters and Indians who traveled only a few, or perhaps a few hundred, miles down the line. By the early 1880s, they outnumbered through passengers in a proportion of six to one, and, according to one account, their destinations on the Omaha-Sacramento route were 230 stations, most of them in tank towns and whistle stops.

Yet no matter what the amenities, first- and second-class passengers shared alike the considerable risks of travel by train. They were marooned by deep snows, stranded by floods, smitten by tornados, scorched by prairie fires that could engulf hundreds of square miles. They lost their shirts to cardsharps (by one estimate, more than 300 operated on the Union Pacific alone) and their wallets to a new breed of badman, the train robber; one Central Pacific train had the singular bad luck to be held up twice in two days at locations 400 miles apart.

For the employees who spent their lives on the trains—engineers and firemen, conductors and porters, brakemen and switchmen—the perils were compounded. Locomotives blew up on whim, brakes failed on steep grades, hastily built trestles buckled under the weight of 50-ton locomotives, railway cars had a disturbing habit of coming uncoupled and careening off the tracks in several directions. In 1888, the first year in which such statistics were compiled, 2,070 railroad men were killed on the job and 20,148 were injured.

Still, there never was any dearth of either railroaders or passengers, and between them they populated the Old West. To the railroad magnates, an increase of citizenry along their rights of way was simply added up to good business. James Jerome Hill, the creator of the Great Northern, put the proposition in the form of an epigram: "Population without the prairie is a mob, and the prairie without population is a desert." He hardly need have mentioned that the railroads could turn huge profits by selling off the land the government had given them.

And so the railroads launched a massive propaganda campaign designed to attract settlers. In 1874, an office set up by the U.P.'s General Grenville Dodge spent $105,000 to advertise its lands in 2,311 newspapers and magazines. Other lines followed suit in language that often waxed poetic; one brochure spoke of the plow "tickling the Plains and producing in return the laughter of bountiful harvests." Even after awful droughts turned Kansas to dust, the Rock Island Railroad assured one and all that the state was "the garden spot of the world."

The effort brought dramatic results: the 1870 population of Kansas had been 364,000; in 1887, more than a million and a half people lived there. Inevitably, the population surge benefited mainly the railroad tycoons, and a rascally bunch they were. Jay Gould, for one, was a stock swindler who amassed an enormous fortune after buying out the Union Pacific. Edward Harriman, for another, avariciously grabbed 75,000 miles of track and lived to be described by President Theodore Roosevelt as a "malefactor of great wealth." Even the most enlightened of the lot, the Great Northern's Jim Hill, who had lost an eye in a boyhood accident, more than lived up to his nickname of One-eyed Old Sonofabitch.

Knaves they may have been, but the barons were part of a grand arrangement. Picking up where the rivermen had left off, and together with the men who worked the railroads and the travelers who rode on them, they stitched together a nation that spanned the continent.

A notorious showman, Custer was depicted at center stage by artist Charles Schreyvogel in this painting titled *Custer's Demand*. While General Sheridan *(right rear)* waits with the troops, Custer tells Kiowa war chiefs in sign language that they must go peacefully to a reservation. They went.

IV. ASSERTING A MANIFEST DESTINY

The faces of a proud people

Who were the Indians of the Old West? Everyone knows them—the hawk-faced men with braided hair and war feathers, their copper skin stretched over high cheekbones, their expressions penetrating and fearless. The tribal names are familiar too: Comanche, Cheyenne, Sioux, Kiowa, and others—all resonant of fierce valor, calling up images of painted horsemen with lances and bows. These tribes and their warriors, like the Comanche at right, dwelt on the Great Plains. To most whites they represented the model of all Western Indians—the men trained from birth to hunt and fight, measuring manhood by their boldness in battle; the women raised to sustain the warriors, sharing in celebrations of victory or slashing their bodies in moments of grief.

For some tribes these images were true, but only partly true. For the Western Indians as a whole they were only the most visible and spectacular manifestations of a broader, more complex story. From the Mississippi to the Great Basin on the far side of the Rockies lived more than 30 distinct tribes, each with its own language and way of life. Some were nomadic hunters who followed the buffalo. Some were primarily farmers who tended peach orchards or raised corn and melons in the fertile river valleys.

Some were pirates of the plains, who raided other tribes for horses, corn and tobacco. The Indians' realm was culturally diverse, but the far-flung villages were connected by a network of trails over which flowed such goods as Pacific seashells in exchange for deerskins.

All of these Indians, whether they were warriors or farmers, shared a common destiny—to be forced aside by the white man. By the middle of the 19th Century they were being pushed from their lands by white farmers, miners, cattlemen and the U.S. Cavalry.

The outcome of the confrontation with the whites was never really in doubt. Although they won some key battles, including one as late as 1876, the Indians were too few, too fragmented and too poorly armed to fend off the waves of intruders. In 1840, before the onslaught had fairly begun, no more than 300,000 Indians roamed the West. But although their battle was hopeless, pride and defiance shone in their faces and rang in their words. As Kiowa Chief White Bear said in 1867, "I do not want to settle down in houses you would build for us. I love to roam over the wild prairie. There I am free and happy." Nine years later White Bear committed suicide in a prison hospital.

Otter Belt, Comanche

A Navaho boy, name unknown

Two Hatchet, Kiowa

Particular Time of Day, Pawnee

Nalin, Apache girl

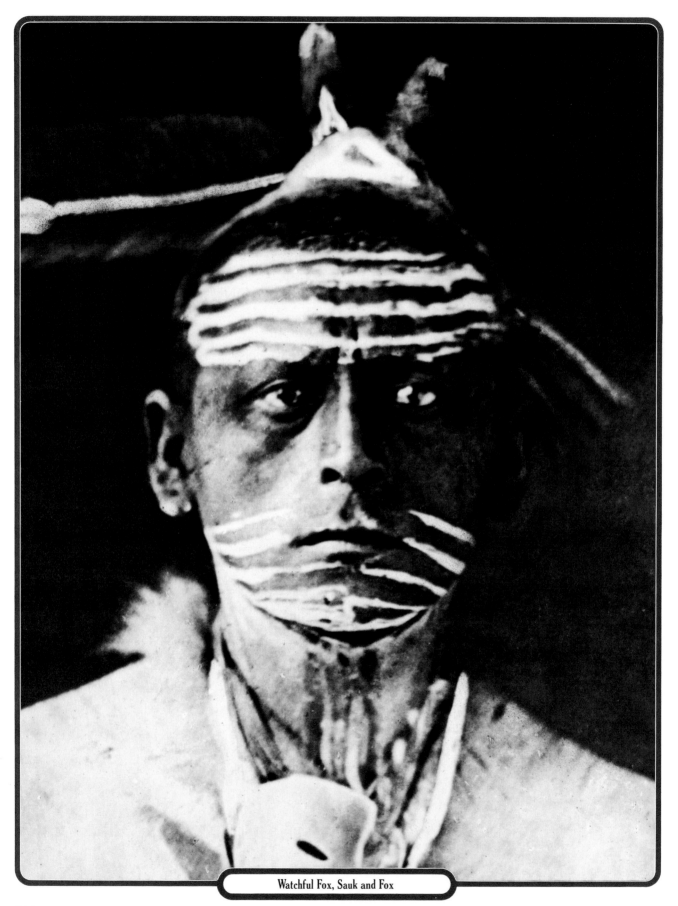

Watchful Fox, Sauk and Fox

Spotted Eagle, Sioux

9. The last stand of the plains tribes

It was the time of year when the buffalo have shed most of their long hair and the sun bears down hot on the high plains. A great Indian peace council was gathering in that summer of 1840, and some 5,000 men, women and children traveled over hundreds of miles of treeless grasslands toward the river they called the Arrowpoint (and the white man knew as the Arkansas) in present-day Colorado. For years, the Arrowpoint had served as an ineffective dividing line between tribes at war, with the Cheyennes and Arapahos allied against the Kiowas and the Comanches. Now, for a variety of reasons, peace was desired by all.

Coming down from the north, Cheyennes and Arapahos were the first to arrive. Three days later, they began to see the distant silhouettes of lone riders—scouts—on ridges along the southern skyline. Then gray dust clouds began to rise, and finally the earth trembled beneath a thunder of hoofbeats. The newcomers were Comanches and Kiowas, and they were bringing with them 8,000 horses, more than the Cheyennes and Arapahos had ever dreamed of.

At any Indian conclave, the bestowal of gifts was an important institution, and it was in a mood of high expectancy that the Cheyennes and Arapahos waded across the shallow Arrowpoint in response to an invitation from their erstwhile enemies.

To make the giving a solemn and orderly ceremony the southerners distributed small sticks as counters. The first to move along the long rows of guests was a slender, graceful Kiowa war chief, Sitting Bear, his left arm holding a big bundle of sticks, his black hair and long drooping mustache gleaming with grease. Many times he had led war parties against the Cheyennes and the Arapahos. Now, as indicated by the number of sticks he passed out, he was giving them 250 horses from his own herd.

In the years that followed, the four tribes never broke the peace they had reached on the Arrowpoint. Instead, both separately and together, they warred against the white intruders who were steadily taking over their hunting grounds. Yet theirs was a hopeless struggle, and so it came to pass that more than three decades after he had handed out his little sticks—in 1871—Sitting Bear was arrested after returning to the Kiowa reservation in Oklahoma from a raid into Texas, where his band had killed seven whites and captured 41 mules.

He was 70 now, an old man with a doleful voice, loose hair and a mustache the color of cotton twine. Yet he was still Sitting Bear, war chief of the Kiowa, and he had no intention of ending his days with a white man's noose around his neck.

On the morning that Sitting Bear was to be transported from his dungeon at Fort Sill to a Texas court, where he would stand trial for murder, he began chanting shrilly. The words were those of a warrior of the Kiowa Kaitsenko—the Society of the Ten Bravest, which Sitting Bear led.

Kaitsenko ana obahema haa ipai degi o ba ika. Oh, sun, you remain forever, but we Kaitsenko must die.

Kaitsenko ana oba hemo hadamagagi o ba ika. Oh, earth, you remain forever, but we Kaitsenko must die.

With his wrists and ankles shackled, Sitting Bear was placed in a wagon with two soldiers carrying carbines, while five troops of cavalry rode escort. As the wagon trundled toward Texas, Sitting Bear repeatedly ducked his head under his blanket, gnawing the flesh from his hands until they would slip through the handcuffs. A short distance south of the fort he got them free and,

This painted buffalo robe chronicles the history of one Indian tribe—the Dakota Sioux—from 1800 to 1871, the major period of white invasion. The calendar, painted by a warrior named Lone Dog, is read from the center outward, with a significant picture or symbol for each year.

brandishing a hunting knife that he had somehow obtained and hidden, slashed at one of the soldiers and wrenched away the man's carbine. Both soldiers jumped onto the dusty road.

Sitting Bear stood up—no longer a doddering old man but now an armed Kiowa warrior.

He pointed his gun at members of the escort, but it failed to fire, and he was screaming his war cry as the soldiers' bullets cut him down. Again he rose, aiming the useless gun with his bleeding hands. Again his body jerked at the impact of bullets, and again he fell to the floor of the swaying wagon. This time he stayed there—dead, as he had wished.

In his full and highly honored life, he had been a demigod—the most respected warrior of a proud, fierce tribe. In his death, he was mute testimony to the inability of the Indians of the Great Plains to control the long sweep of Western history.

By 1840, when the four tribes smoked their pipes of peace on the Arrowhead, the Plains Indians had attained the pinnacle of their transient power. Already, they were remarkably few: probably no more than 300,000 Indians lived in what is now the Western United States. Theirs was a diverse population; in their origins, their manner of living, the form of their worship and their rites for the dying, the Plains Indians varied as greatly as the colors they daubed on their faces.

The Blackfeet, for example, were the original inhabitants of the areas on both sides of the Canadian border, where they had been scourges to the early whites who called themselves mountain men. Similarly, the Crows were native to the country along the Yellowstone and its tributaries. Indeed, they had taught the ways of Plains Indian life to the Kiowas, who had come out of the upper Missouri region and moved to the Black Hills realm of the Crows before migrating south.

From the cloistered woodlands of the upper Mississippi and the Great Lakes had drifted two of the tribes that would play leading roles in the Indians' struggle for survival on the open plains.

Cheyennes had once farmed in Minnesota and western Wisconsin, but they were driven out by neighboring tribes that had obtained guns from white traders. Somewhere in the course of their western migration they had, as they put it, "lost the corn," meaning that

The tribes and their territories

Formidable both as fighters and as hunters, 13 nomadic warrior tribes (*red italics on map*) dominated the heart of the grasslands during the early and middle decades of the 19th Century. But the world they lived in was in swift and violent transition; the tribal locations for the year 1840 shown on this map were very different from what they would have been only 50 years earlier—or later. Some of the fiercest of the warrior tribes, among them the Cheyenne and Sioux, had moved to the wild plains from the wooded territory around the upper Mississippi and Great Lakes. Other, less powerful Indians, such as the Iowa and Missouri, had been forced by white pressure out of the regions that carried their names.

The horse-borne nomads who roamed the Great Plains subsisted mainly by hunting buffalo. They fought hard among themselves and sometimes found the grasslands contested by tribes like the Pawnee and Mandan, who for the most part lived and farmed in permanent villages but hunted buffalo during the summer and sometimes raided the nomads for horses.

To the southwest were the Pueblo Indians, sophisticated farmers who lived in huge apartment houses of adobe or stone and shrewdly traded horses and corn to the southern nomads for buffalo robes and other products. Nearby were the deadly Apaches, once dwellers of the southern plains but by now mostly driven to the region that would become New Mexico, where they were periodically harassed by their powerful enemies, the Comanches.

Through the central and northern Rocky Mountains, the Utes, Shoshonis, Nez Percés and others occasionally sallied out into the buffalo country. Every summer, for example, the Nez Percés rode eastward over the high passes to hunt buffalo and to trade with, or raid against, the plains tribes.

By the 1840s tribe-against-tribe fighting had less effect on the Indians' settlement patterns than the growing incursions of white men. As white pressure upon the West increased, only the largest and most powerful plains tribes—among them the Sioux, Cheyenne, Blackfoot and Comanche—could hold out for any length of time; smaller tribes, such as the Arikara and the Crow, often became allies of the whites against warrior nations that had been their traditional enemies.

they had almost entirely ceased farming in favor of a more active life. Now they were buffalo hunting, fur trapping—and waging war.

Like the Cheyennes, the Sioux had been forced from their homeland in the upper Midwest. Though many clung to their sedentary way of agricultural life, the members of one major branch—the Teton Lakota, or Western Sioux—became the nomadic masters of the immense tract of territory that was encompassed by the Platte valley, the upper Missouri and Yellowstone and the eastern slopes of the Rockies.

Sometime between 1840 and 1845 a certain baby boy was born to a woman of the Lakotas. His name was Crazy Horse, and he would eventually take his place among the great chiefs in whose hands the destiny of the Plains Indians was placed. Yet in the melancholy march of history, neither the tactical brilliance of a Crazy Horse nor the doomed patience of a Black Kettle, neither the tigerish ferocity of a Geronimo nor the spirits awakened by a Sitting Bull, could preserve a culture based on use of the horse and pursuit of the buffalo.

Ironically, the Indian's most prized possession was an unintended gift from the white man. In the early 17th Century, as Spaniards moved northward to exploit the region that would be Mexico and the Southwestern United States, they brought with them large numbers of horses. Many of them strayed and were captured by Indians; others were simply stolen. At first, the Indians of the Southwest were the major beneficiaries, but those to the north gradually acquired horses through intertribal raiding and trading.

To the Comanches, the horse became known as a god dog, to the Sioux a medicine dog, and to the Blackfeet a big dog. The canine comparison was by no means coincidental: Until the arrival of the horse, the scruffy Indian dog was the only beast of burden—other than women, who carried whatever the dogs did not. Indeed, the Sarsis gave to the horse a name—seven dogs—that provided a specific measurement of working ability. The Indian work dog could carry approximately 50 pounds on its back and pull about 75 pounds with a pole drag, or travois. So loaded, a train of dogs could move five or six miles a day. A horse could be packed with 200 pounds or pull a 300-pound burden with the travois and make as much as 10 or 12 miles a day. Thus the work ratio in favor of the horse over the dog was, in fact, roughly 7 to 1.

In short order, the horse became the essential instrument by which the Plains Indians hunted the buffalo that gave them the meat that they ate, the hide for their clothing and tipis, the sinew for their bowstrings, the bone for their arrowheads, the horn for their spoons and even the dung for their fuel. Before the horse, Indian hunters had generally been forced to stalk the beast on foot, a slow affair that often resulted in meager kills. Now, however, mounted Indians could surround an entire herd, sometimes slaying every animal within as little as 15 minutes.

But other changes were less predictable. Among the earliest was the size of dwellings. In the past the limit on loads had made it impossible to transport a large, heavy tipi cover or a set of sizable poles. In consequence, the tipis had been small and cramped, usually no more than five or six feet tall. With bigger beasts of burden, the Indians could build lodges 12 to 15 feet high, with more room inside for family, visitors and for storing possessions.

Within the intimate social structure of each tribe, the horse was responsible for certain fundamental alterations. The status of women improved—at first—if only because they were relieved of some of the burdens they had carried on their backs. But the betterment of the women's lot was of brief duration. Their time was soon fully occupied by dressing, tanning and working the increased number of buffalo hides brought in by the hunters. Partly because of the braves' need for this kind of assistance, polygyny, which had previously been practiced in a modest way in various tribes, became popular among affluent males. As noted by a Blackfoot chief whose practicality may have outdistanced his arithmetic, his "eight wives could dress 150 skins in the year whereas a single wife could only dress ten."

But only the affluent could afford such spousal profusion—and horses were a basic standard of exchange, not only in the form of gifts to the lodge of a prospective wife but in many other transactions. An ordinary riding horse might be worth eight buffalo robes, three pounds of tobacco or 15 eagle feathers; a speedy racing horse carried a ten-gun price tag, while a fine buffalo horse could be bartered for several pack animals.

There was a lively trade in stolen horses, and the Comanches were considered matchless as horse

How the tipi was constructed

Warm in winter, cool in summer and sturdy enough to withstand gale-force winds, the tipi was a remarkably serviceable dwelling—and yet it was so easy to assemble that two women could erect it within an hour.

Although certain details of design differed from tribe to tribe, the tipi was basically a cover made of dressed buffalo hides that were stitched together with sinew and stretched over a framework of poles. Most tribes used a tripod of especially strong poles for the main support. These primary supports were tied together at the top and raised *(bottom, left);* then all but one of the remaining poles were leaned against them, tied in place and,

in windy weather, anchored to a single peg in the ground within the tipi. The frame was not a true cone, but was tilted slightly. This asymmetry served several functions. It provided more headroom in the rear of the dwelling; it permitted better ventilation with an off-center smoke hole; and, since tipis almost always faced east, the greater slant of the front side helped brace the structure against the prevailing west winds on the back.

When the poles were in place the folded hide cover *(below, center)* was fastened to a stout lifting pole and hoisted into position. It was relatively easy at this point to unfold the cover around the poles, peg the bottom edge

down, close the vertical seam with wooden pins and attach the door flap. (In warm weather the bottom edge could be raised for ventilation.) Finally, two lighter poles outside the tipi were inserted in the pockets of the smoke flaps; by moving these poles the flaps could be adjusted to compensate for changes in wind direction, or the flaps could be closed in case of rain or snow. Now complete *(bottom, right),* the tipi was ready for the furnishings. Usually about 15 feet in diameter at the base, it had ample room for beds, back rests, a stack of firewood and other articles of equipment, sometimes arranged according to the scheme shown below, center.

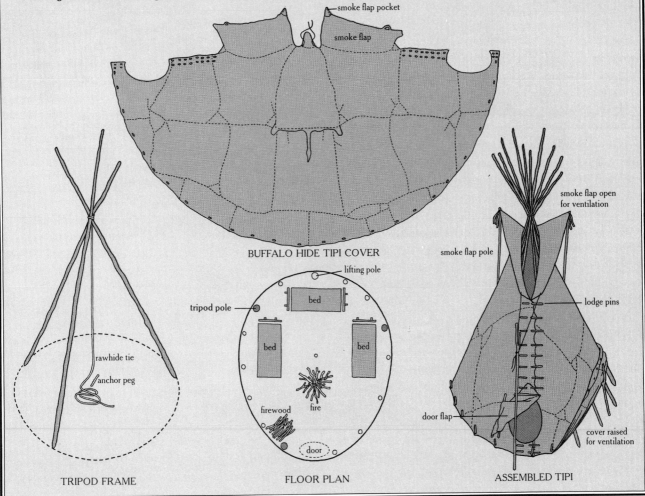

BUFFALO HIDE TIPI COVER

TRIPOD FRAME

FLOOR PLAN

ASSEMBLED TIPI

thieves: one observer wrote that a Comanche could crawl into a "bivouac where a dozen men were sleeping, each with a horse tied to his wrist by a lariat, cut a rope within six feet of the sleeper, and get away with the horse without waking a soul." The Comanches also gloried in large-scale, far-ranging raids, and on one memorable expedition they thrust so deeply into Mexico that they saw brightly plumed birds and "tiny men with tails" climbing around in trees—an indication that they may have reached the Yucatán Peninsula.

On the back of a horse a Comanche warrior was poetry in motion. "I doubt very much whether any people in the world can surpass them," wrote artist and Western explorer George Catlin. "A Comanche on his feet is out of his element, and comparatively almost as awkward as a monkey on the ground, without a limb or branch to cling to; but the moment he lays his hands upon his horse his *face* even becomes handsome, and he gracefully flies away like a different being."

But pure horsemanship does not always equate with prowess in war, and although the Comanches were certainly formidable antagonists, it was the Sioux who were considered by General George Crook (perhaps the U.S. Army's most competent Indian fighter) to be the greatest light cavalry the world had ever known.

The skill of the mounted Sioux warrior was honed from childhood, especially in a game called throwing-them-off-their-horses, in which boys would strip naked and choose up sides, then charge each other on horseback, the animals rearing and plunging. The youngsters used no weapons but tried to wrestle their opponents off their mounts. A boy on the ground was "dead," out of the game. The sport inevitably produced many lumps and bruises—and many expert horsemen and toughened fighters.

As with all else in the existence of the Plains Indians, such games were part of an ordered pattern of human relationships, institutions and values. And despite the many differences in detail among the customs of the various tribes, the birth-to-death passage of the Cheyenne may be considered typical.

When a Cheyenne baby first opened its small dark eyes it faced a world shaped to ensure the preservation of the tribe and to foster, though not to guarantee, a satisfying life.

A sprawling encampment of Sioux is thronged with horses, some used in hunting or war, others to haul possessions on simple drags or, in later days, on the white man's wagons. So crucial were horses to the Plains Indians' way of life that the U.S. Army made killing them a major objective.

Two Kiowa girls hold up an infant strapped to a cradleboard, which was usually made by a female relative of the father, often in return for a horse.

The infant's skin was greased and powdered with finely ground dried buffalo manure, decayed cottonwood pulp or ripe, dry spores of the star puffball—especially favored for the umbilical cord. Later, when the cord had dried and dropped loose from the navel, the mother would sew it into a small buckskin bag, shaped like a turtle or a lizard, to be worn by the child as a charm to ensure long life.

The mother gave her baby much affection, allowing it to nurse at will until, in some cases, it was four or five years old. But crying was not tolerated, partly because a bawling baby might give away a camp position to enemy raiders. If a baby persisted in crying, the mother took it out alone in its cradleboard and hung it on a bush; only when the howling stopped would she return it to human company. After a few such experiences the baby learned that crying was useless.

Cheyenne children quickly became tough, inured to the extremes of a life lived close to nature. A frontiersman named Jacob Fowler once saw Indian children, probably including some Cheyennes, playing on the ice of the Arkansas River. "The weather is now cold," he wrote, "the river frozen up, the ice a great thickness, and the Indian children that are able to walk and up to tall boys are out on the ice by daylight and all as naked as they came into the world. I doubt that our white children, put in such weather in that situation, could live half an hour."

Cheyennes were strict about sex, and as children approached their teens, boys and girls were no longer allowed to play together. The time had come for the family and tribe to prepare the members of each sex to function as adults. At 12 or 14 a boy went on his first real hunt. When he killed a buffalo—the first was usually a calf—his father cried out the news to the whole camp and perhaps announced the gift of a good horse to a deserving poor person. In his early teens a boy might go on a raid with a war party, and although he was seldom permitted to do much more than gather wood or hold the warriors' horses, he began to take on the dignity of a man.

Cheyenne girls went through a formal puberty rite. At a girl's first menstruation, her father called out to the camp that she had become a woman. The girl unbraided her hair and bathed herself; the older women painted her body red. She then wrapped herself in a robe and sat near a fire. A coal from the fire was sprinkled with sweet grass, juniper needles and white sage, and the girl bent over the coal, surrounding it with her robe so that the smoke passed over all her body. Then she went to a special lodge, where women spent their menstrual periods. There her grandmother cared for her and gave her instructions on womanly conduct. Finally, before returning home, the girl once again passed through the smoke to purify her body.

Women of the Cheyenne tribe were noted for their chastity. A young unmarried woman customarily wore a leather or rope chastity belt that was tied around her waist, knotted in front and wound down between her thighs. One Cheyenne woman later recalled the admonitions of an aunt: "You must always be sure to take great care to tie the hide (the chastity belt). You must remember that when a man touches your breasts he considers that you belong to him. And in the event that he does not care to marry

Adorned with health symbols, this yard-high painting depicts the rites attending an Indian girl's attaining puberty. It was painted in vegetable dyes on doeskin.

ha dance. On such occasions the husband, holding a stick in his hand, would dance alone. Advancing to a drum, he would strike it a mighty blow, throw the stick into the air, or toward a crowd of men, and shout: "There goes my wife; I throw her away! Whoever gets that stick may have her!"

No such public humiliation, however, was heaped upon the man whose wife was bent on divorce. Instead, she merely moved back to her parents' lodge, usually taking her children with her. If as a young woman she had been given horses by indulgent relatives, she retained property rights in them and in their increase, and upon divorce she took the animals with her.

A good wife was one who kept plenty of parfleches (rawhide bags) filled with dry meat and other provisions. She was also skilled in the making of clothes and of gear for horses, as well as a mother who reared mannerly children, respectful to their elders and thoroughly trained in Cheyenne ways.

The gathering of wild plants was one of a wife's major tasks, and the women assumed it proudly. The most widely used plant was the prairie turnip, which grew throughout the high plains and was gathered in the spring. Growing to as much as four times the size of a hen's egg, it was eaten raw or in soups and stews, and it could be sliced and sun-dried for storage.

When Cheyenne women and girls neared camp after digging prairie turnips they often engaged in ceremonious horseplay, making believe that they were a war party and the men of the tribe were their enemies. One woman would wave her blanket and give a challenging war whoop, whereupon any men who were in the mood for a frolic would rush from the camp. With much fierce yelling, they would charge the women's position, to be

you he will not hide what he has done to you, and you will be considered immoral. And you will not have a chance to marry into a good family."

Courtships might last for as long as six years. During much of that time, a young man would wait near a spot where his favored girl might pass, hoping for a few words or a smile. And while alone on the plains—scouting, traveling, herding horses—the words of love would come to his lips in song: "My love, it is I who am singing. Do you hear me?" Or: "My love, come out on the prairie, so that I may come near you and meet you."

Once such moonstruck reveries were transformed into the realities of marriage, however, the man became the boss of his household. He lived in a male-dominated society, and in some cases he treated the woman in a cruel, even inhuman manner. A routine punishment for infidelity was cutting off the wife's nose. And if a Cheyenne man wanted to divorce his wife, he could "throw her away" at a tribal ceremony called the Oma-

met with showers of sticks and buffalo chips. The rules of the game permitted any man who had a proven war record or who had lost his horse in battle to capture some of the roots for himself if he could make it through the barrage without being hit.

Fun was fun, but for the most part the lives of men were consumed by the deadly serious jobs of fighting and hunting.

Among the Indian's techniques for waging war, white men were understandably impressed by his habit of taking scalps, which were kept as trophies. But to the Western Indian, scalps were distinctly secondary in importance to the scoring of coups by touching or striking (sometimes lethally) an enemy with hand or weapon. Coups struck within an enemy camp ranked highest, and the bravest man was the one who entered such a camp armed not with a lance or a bow and arrows, but with a tomahawk or whip. Better still, he might carry only a stick.

Less dramatic but far more vital to the life of a Cheyenne man was hunting. He hunted deer, elk and bighorn sheep by stalking or by ambush as they came to a water hole; antelope by an organized method of surrounding, then driving them into a camouflaged pit so that they could easily be slain by a ring of bowmen. To catch an eagle, valuable for its feathers, the hunter hid in a pit and waited for the mighty bird to come down to a meat bait; then he reached up, seized the eagle and killed it with his hands.

His greatest game was the buffalo, which he preferred to kill, even after the advent of the gun, with lance or bow. For a buffalo hunt a brave stripped down to a breechcloth and moccasins, tucked a sheath knife in his belt and carried a short lance or a three-foot bow with a quiver of about 20 iron-tipped arrows. Around the neck of his horse was a trailing rawhide thong, which a rider would grab if he fell, to slow the horse with his dragging body so he could remount.

Once a herd had been surrounded by mounted Indians, an individual would close on his quarry and try to puncture its diaphragm and collapse its lungs by hitting a spot just behind the last rib. Even if the arrow or lance was accurate, the powerful beast usually took at least three hits before it fell—and a wounded buffalo was as dangerous an animal as ever lived. Unhorsed, trampled and gored, men lost their lives every year during buffalo hunts.

And so they passed their lives, these Cheyenne nomads of the plains, until, at last, they were graced by the coming of death. A dead person, regardless of age, was dressed in his or her finest clothing, wrapped in a blanket or robe and placed in a tree, on a scaffold, or on the ground and covered with rocks. A man's favorite horse might be killed at his place of burial, and his weapons, pipes and other treasured belongings were left with him. A woman was buried with her utensils, her digging stick and sometimes her hide-fleshing tool.

Relatives wailed at the grave. Women mourners, especially the mother and wife of the dead person, cut off their hair; if they mourned a man who had died of wounds or in battle they gashed their foreheads and legs and might even cut off a finger.

The Cheyennes believed that there was no burden of guilt to be borne beyond death. According to their faith, the spirit of the departed traveled up a Hanging Road, the Milky Way, to the abode of Heammawihio, the Wise One Above—there to follow the Cheyenne way and to live forever among long-lost loved ones.

To the Plains Indians, death from hunger, killing weather or marauding enemies was never far away. To survive properly in such a world they felt a need for some powerful assistance. They got it from a host of spirits that inhabited the natural world.

The spirits were thought to be everywhere and were always identified with some visible object, animal or phenomenon. They were said to dwell in the sun and earth, in rivers and hills, in thunderstorms and rainbows, and within creatures ranging from the dragonfly to the buffalo. These sacred beings had the power to bring success in the hunt and war, protect the young, heal the sick, guarantee fertility and generally assure the welfare of the tribe and its individuals. But this power would be shared only if humans performed a steady round of ceremonies aimed at enlisting the help of the supernatural forces.

The religious rituals took many forms. Some were simply small gestures of respect. When, for example, an Apache hunter skinned a deer, he turned the head of the animal toward the east—the sacred direction where the life-giving sun arose and whence would come new life for other game. When a Comanche sat down to a formal meal he often cut off a tiny morsel of his food,

Galloping up to a bull, a mounted hunter draws his bow for the kill. Although an estimated 50 million buffalo lived in the mid-1800s, the white man and his repeating rifle soon decimated their numbers, slaughtering up to 150 animals per hunter per day. Lamented Sioux Chief White Cloud, "Wherever the whites are established, the buffalo is gone, and the red hunters must die of hunger."

held it up toward the sky as a symbolic offering to a heavenly deity, and then buried the tidbit in the earth.

Major ceremonies were far more complex—and sometimes excruciating. Among them was the sun dance, practiced by 20 or more plains tribes to prevent an expenditure of the underlying energies of nature that would cause animals to gradually disappear, plants to wither and humans to starve.

Although there were some variations from one tribe to another, enough overlapping elements existed so that the sun dance may be seen as one ceremony. The ritual was conducted over a period of several days during late summer or early autumn, when the earth was deemed most bountiful. The ritual was sponsored by a person known as a pledger. He did not have to be a priest or medicine man, but was often merely an ordinary individual who had some urgent need for a spiritual favor or had been told in a dream to take on the role.

The most dramatic feature of the dance was self-mortification. The participants, usually young warriors, would go without water and food, dance to exhaustion and sometimes slash their flesh or cut off fingers. In certain tribes a young man who had vowed to undergo self-torture in the ceremony would have a medicine man cut two small holes through the skin and flesh of his upper chest on either side. The medicine man would stick wooden skewers through the holes and secure them to two ropes, the ends of which were fastened to the top of a pole. Next the young warrior would then begin to dance, straining against the ropes. If he did not break free, the medicine man would finally cut his flesh to release him.

The pain that was experienced in the sun dance was considered well invested. When the ceremony was over the Indians counted on enjoying health, fertility and food. The world seemed renewed and ready once again to work for the welfare of the tribe.

Among all the plains tribes, the spirits most frequently called upon were those that dwelt within animals. The bull elk, for one, was considered an effective helper in love (Indians were much impressed by the elk's ability to call females). The bear was hard to kill and was thought to heal its own wounds; therefore it was felt that it might mend human injuries as well. Eagles and hawks with their powerful claws were good allies in

wartime. The skunk was thought to have much supernatural power; its tail was used to hold medicine, and its image was often painted on lodges and even on the seeds employed by women in gambling.

But there was a catch to all this: Powers from the spirits were hedged with taboos that, if violated, would render the supernatural aid ineffective. Often the beneficiary of the power would have to refrain from eating certain foods—perhaps the entrails or brain of a buffalo. A man whose supernatural helper was an eagle could not let another person walk behind him when he was eating, for the Indians believed that eagles were disturbed by such an act.

Within every tribe there were certain leaders who had served long apprenticeships in priestlike functions and had memorized every detail of major ceremonial performances. A priest did not wield supernatural powers by himself; he simply guided the participants through the rites that summoned spiritual aid. There were, however, other prestigious individuals in the Indian community who were thought to exercise strong supernatural powers on their own. These were the medicine men.

Such a one was a Hunkpapa Sioux who was born in 1831 at Grand River in what is now South Dakota. At first his father, Returns-Again, named his son "Slow" because he was so deliberate in his ways.

As it happened, Returns-Again was not only a warrior but also a mystic who could sometimes communicate with animals. One night, while on a hunt, Returns-Again and three other braves were squatting over a campfire when they heard strange noises. As the sounds came nearer the Indians saw that they emanated from a lone buffalo bull that had approached their fire. After brief puzzlement, Returns-Again understood that the bull was repeating four names: Sitting Bull, Jumping Bull, Bull Standing with Cow and Lone Bull. Returns-Again concluded that he was being offered a choice of new names to take for himself. He promptly adopted the first name on the buffalo's list—Sitting Bull.

Meanwhile, even as an adolescent, his son Slow had also become aware of special ties to the spirit world. Once, at a lake in the Black Hills, he heard a call from high on a rocky crag. He climbed the butte and found an eagle perched there—an experience that he interpreted as meaning that he would one day rise to lead all his people.

Animals held an important place in Indian spiritual beliefs and rituals. Depicted below by Swiss artist Karl Bodmer, a lone Mandan worshiper wrapped in a buffalo robe prays to the sun and moon idols made out of animal skin, grass and twigs.

When Slow was 14, he counted his first coup by striking a Crow with a stick during a raid to capture horses. Back in camp, his father was so proud that he formally divested himself of his own new name and bestowed it on the boy. "My son has struck the enemy," he cried. "He is brave! From this time forward his name will be Ta-tan-ka I-yo-ta-ke"—Sitting Bull.

And it was as Sitting Bull that the erstwhile Slow became a famous medicine man and, fulfilling the prophecy of the eagle, was named chief of the Hunkpapa Sioux in the 1860s. During the dark years then approaching, he would need the most powerful medicine the spirits could offer.

Sitting Bull lived in an era of great chiefs—soaring eagles whose feathers were earned through their bold exploits. They were as disparate as the tribes that bred them. Some resisted the white invasion of their homelands with unrelenting ferocity; others invested their hopes in cooperation with the powerful intruders. Some were brutes, others idealists. Some died in battle, as they would have wished; others lingered long past their prime and were treated as sideshow freaks by their conquerors. But they had one thing in common: All were victims of an alien culture that they little understood and were powerless to withstand.

Ever since the first trappers and traders had penetrated into the West, Indians had killed white men and white men had killed Indians. But those were mostly random, isolated incidents—until the 1850s, when the conflict began to take on patterns of organized violence.

Since 1840, white movement into the West had been accelerating. Steamboats churned up the Missouri; ox-drawn wagons rolled across the plains; and in 1848, with the discovery of gold in California, the stream became a torrent. To protect the emigrants the U.S. government dotted the West with Army posts, and the brisk tattoo of "Boots and Saddles" became as much a part of the plains as the cooking fires of Indian women. The soldiers were greatly resented by the original inhabitants of the land they invaded; the incidence of violence rose, and major confrontations were obviously in the offing. To forestall them, the U.S. Congress agreed to fund a conference at Fort Laramie in the autumn of 1851.

Amazingly, some 10,000 representatives of nine Indian nations (notably excepting the Comanches and

Curative art for a bed of pain

In some Southwestern Indian tribes when special help was needed from the spirits medicine men prepared beds of sand decorated with mystical designs, such as the one at right reconstructed from 19th Century reports of a secret Navajo ceremony. Crowds of tribesmen came to watch the ritual and to feast on corn meal, soup and roast mutton—all supplied by the patient. The rite began with the medicine man spreading a light layer of sand across the floor of the patient's lodge. Then, from a traditional repertory of symbols varying in size from one foot to 20 feet in diameter, he decided on the suitable motif. The one here symbolizes the gods of planting and harvest, and would have been executed in spring or fall to help bring abundant crops as well as to heal the patient. Using pigments ground from rocks, charcoal, root bark, crushed flowers and pollen, the shaman created his design by trickling the colored powders between his thumb and forefinger. When the picture—called a sand painting, or dry painting—was done, the shaman and his assistants put the patient in the middle of it, while they chanted exhortations to drive evil spirits from the body. Spectators picked up handfuls of sand to keep as talismans. When the ceremony was over, the shaman erased the last traces of the design with a long wand.

This dry painting pays homage to the Navajo gods of the four main compass points. The principal god of the east, at top, is painted white. Like the others, he suspends from his right hand a number of magic symbols, including a rattle, a Y-shaped good-luck charm and a swastikalike basket symbolizing the harvest; and he raises his relatively unencumbered left hand to protect a sacred plant, in this case the corn. The god of the south and his beanstalk are blue-gray, the god of the west and his squash plant are yellow, while the god of the north and his tobacco plant are black. If this were a true ceremonial medicine painting, the god of the east and the opening of the encircling rainbow would be at the sacred right-hand, or easterly, side of the painting. But in keeping with tribal tradition that no outsider should ever see a perfect dry painting, the shaman altered the design.

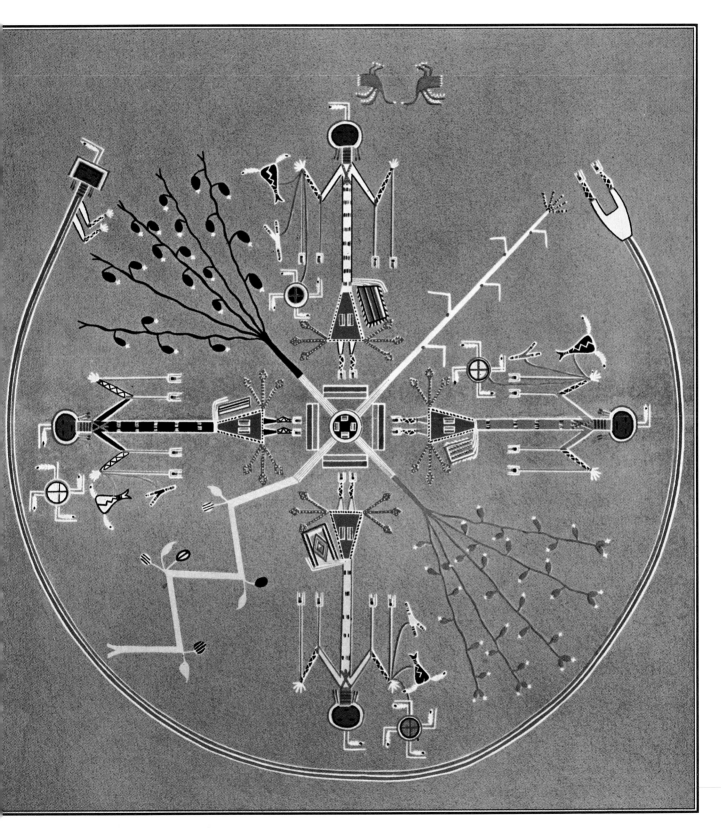

An outstanding warrior, a revered spiritual leader and a wily politician, Sitting Bull parried every attempt by the white man to reduce the Sioux lands for as long as he could.

Kiowas, who said there were too many horse thieves around Laramie) attended the greatest assemblage of Indians ever seen on the North American continent. Equally astonishing, the Indians agreed that the government might establish roads and Army posts in their territory. As recompense they would receive annuities to the value of $50,000 per year for 50 years. (A cheeseparing Senate later cut the number of years to 10.)

For the United States government, treaties with Indians were old hat. The first one had been signed in 1778 with the Eastern Delawares, whose domain once stretched from the Atlantic to Ohio; in return for help against the British, the government promised to recognize the Delawares as head of a newly organized Indian state. Such assurances notwithstanding, the Delawares were steadily pushed into and out of Indiana, into and out of Missouri, into and out of Kansas, then finally into Oklahoma. In all, during the first century of its national existence, the U.S. would sign 370 treaties with Indians—and nearly all of them proved to be worthless.

The Laramie pact was no exception. Despite good faith on both sides, whites still thought of the lands of the Plains tribes as territory to cross; they did not anticipate how many thousands of their own kind would cross it in the years ahead—and, indeed, how many whites would finally decide to settle on it. For the Indians' part, they were willing to tolerate a few Army posts and a few travelers, but not the onrush of great crowds of people onto their beloved Mother Earth.

It took only three years and a minor incident to rend the Laramie treaty asunder. In the summer of 1854, as the tribes gathered at Laramie to collect their annuities, a Sioux brave shot and slaughtered a lame cow that had either strayed from an emigrant train or had been abandoned. Its white owner complained to the Laramie commander, who dispatched a 30-man party under a hot-headed young lieutenant, John L. Grattan, to arrest the offending Indian. When the Sioux declined to turn over the guilty party, Grattan ordered a volley fired. A major chief was mortally wounded, and in the battle that followed Grattan and all his men were wiped out.

Naturally, the Army sent out punitive expeditions. And naturally, the Indians retaliated. The peace that had been promised by the treaty at Fort Laramie was now destroyed, and the destruction would continue.

The smolderings of Indian resentment burst into a feverish flame eight years later. The flash point was reached after the Santees, an eastern branch of the Sioux Nation, failed to receive the annual payment that had been promised them in return for their birthright—24 million acres of hunting ground they had ceded to the white man. Racked by a winter of near starvation, the Santees burst from their reservation along the upper Minnesota River and killed more than 450 settlers in the region before they were defeated by a hastily assembled force of raw recruits. Thereafter called the Minnesota Massacre, the event was described by the Episcopal Bishop of Minnesota as "the most fearful Indian massacre in history." The Indian wars that would buffet the West for many years to come had begun full force.

Half a continent away, a savage guerrilla war that would last for 26 years in the mountain fastness of the Chiricahua Apaches in the Southwest was already under way.

Issuing out of their rock strongholds, the Apaches for more than 200 years had ruthlessly preyed on the villages, the haciendas, the herds and the pack trains of Mexico. For the most part, however, they had caused little trouble to Americans; in 1860, the great Chiricahua chief Cochise even signed what was probably the first commercial deal ever made by an Apache—a contract to cut firewood for a stage-line station.

That same year, however, a ne'er-do-well white man named John Ward, who was living with his Mexican mistress near Apache Pass in southern Arizona, accused Cochise's braves of abducting his 10- or 11-year-old son. (The lad had, in fact, been taken by a band of Pinal Apaches who were not under Cochise's control.) The Army accepted Ward's view and in response, sent second lieutenant George Bascom along with 54 men to Apache Pass to recover the kidnapped boy.

Hearing that the detachment was camped in a nearby canyon—and entirely unaware of the reason for its presence—Cochise decided to pay a formal visit. When the Apache sat down for a polite discussion, however, Bascom accused him of the boy's abduction. And when an astounded Cochise denied the charge, Bascom grew abusive and laid down an ultimatum: Unless and until the boy was produced, Cochise would be held prisoner. At that, Cochise instantly sprang to his feet, drew a knife from his moccasin legging, slashed the wall of the tent, plunged through and disappeared into the canyon rocks.

The U.S. could hardly have made a worse enemy. In his appearance, Cochise was the very picture of the noble red man—"a fine-looking Indian," wrote a white Army officer who knew him, "straight as a rush, six feet in stature, deep-chested and roman-nosed." He was also sagacious in council, deeply concerned for his people's welfare, and absolutely implacable once he had made up his mind to fight—as now he had.

According to one estimate, Cochise and his Chiricahuas killed 150 whites during the next two months. Year after year, they were continually in action in small parties, swooping down on travelers, prospectors and settlers living on remote, unprotected ranches. Troops who went after them returned to their base empty-handed, only to learn that the Apaches had hit half a dozen places in the opposite direction.

This was a war that defied statistical accounting. A Cochise raid would claim one or two or a half-dozen lives, but wild rumors would count the casualties in dozens or scores. Conversely, a good many transients undoubtedly died with no one to mark their deaths but their killers and the vultures. Although hard to pin

In a lurid portrayal of the Minnesota Massacre, an Indian squaw cuts the legs of a young captive white girl in the presence of her mother *(left)*. Captured by a band of the rampaging Sioux, Julia Smith tries to protect her mother from being shot *(right)*. Both died from the same bullet. These paintings are from a series by a local artist, John Stevens.

Protection on the warpath

Since war was the climax of the Indian's life, he brought to it all the supernatural aids that he could muster. War paint sometimes symbolized past deeds; the hands adorning the chief at right are an example. But more commonly a warrior decorated his face and torso with designs intended to protect him as he went into battle. In fact, according to some sources, it was the warrior's red paint that originally caused the Europeans to call the Indian a red man.

Perhaps the most fascinating insight into the warrior mentality was the act of touching a live or dead enemy; this act was called counting coup, after the French word for blow. To the Indian, contact with a live enemy was the supreme act of his existence as a man. In Comanche tradition the first warrior to touch a fallen foe would cry, "A-he!" meaning, "I claim it." A second and a third warrior could also count coup on the same body, each earning a lesser honor. Some warriors carried special coupsticks like the one at right. Others used guns, whips or their bare hands. However it was done, the man who counted coup most often and most daringly was the hero of the battle.

Magic charms, like these stuffed kingfishers decorated with beads and feathers, were worn into battle. The agile kingfisher symbolized quickness, and the warrior hoped this charm would help him dodge arrows.

Coupsticks such as this elaborate, brass-studded bat were used by warriors to tag their opponents in battle.

Indians dabbed on war paint both before and after a battle. This portrait shows a Pawnee warrior after a victory, with hands painted on his chest as a sign that he had killed an enemy in hand-to-hand combat.

down, the toll taken by Cochise was certainly sufficient to cause the nation deep concern. In 1870, General William Tecumseh Sherman, commanding the Division of the Missouri, wrote only half-jokingly: "We had one war with Mexico to take Arizona, and we should have another to make her take it back."

The end of Cochise's war was almost anticlimactic. In 1872, President Grant sent a pious, one-armed Civil War officer to make peace with the Apaches. General Oliver O. Howard sought out Cochise and spent 11 days in negotiations. As a result, the Chiricahuas were allowed to keep their weapons, their way of life and their own traditional range; they were granted a reservation that enclosed the Dragoon and Chiricahua mountains where they had lived, hunted and fought since time out of mind.

"The white man and the Indian are to drink of the same water, eat of the same bread and be at peace," Cochise said when the pact was sealed. He was not privileged to enjoy this new era of coexistence for long: in 1874, taken mortally ill, he predicted his own death by 10 o'clock the next morning. The hour came, and the prophecy was true.

But, as it turned out, Cochise was wrong about a prolonged peace for his people. About two years after his death, increasing numbers of Apaches were using the reservation merely as a sanctuary: They raided in Mexico, stealing horses and cattle, and returned when pursuit threatened. Their exemplar was a scarred warrior who had been born to the Mimbres Apaches but had joined the Chiricahuas to fight under Cochise.

In his youth and early manhood the leader had been named Gokhlayeh (One Who Yawns) and though he possessed the two cardinal virtues of the Apache warrior—toughness and cunning—he was also known for his gentler qualities as an affectionate husband and doting father. That changed, however, during an Apache expedition south of the border, where Mexicans warmly greeted the Indians and then set treacherously upon them with cavalry. As many as 130 Apaches were killed, including Gokhlayeh's wife, mother and children. Henceforth, fellow tribesmen noted that Gokhlayeh had turned quarrelsome and was prone to unpredictable outbursts of wild violence. Many warriors came to fear and dislike him.

Both as a Mimbres and as a Chiricahua, Gokhlayeh would give Mexicans abundant cause to rue the day of his family's deaths. Years later, in talking about the humans he had slain, he would say that Mexicans were "not worth counting. We kill Mexicans with rocks."

One day about a year after his bereavement, Gokhlayeh was part of a large war party that engaged in a pitched battle—lance against bayonet, war club against saber—with Mexican soldiers. Gokhlayeh was everywhere, reckless, almost berserk. Watching him in awe, an unknown Mexican shouted "Geronimo!" The connotation is beyond explaining—in Spanish, the word is the equivalent of "Jerome"—but from that moment on, Gokhlayeh would be called Geronimo, and it was as Geronimo that he would strike fear into the hearts of a generation of Mexicans and American whites.

But his greatest hour of renown—such as it was—still lay in the future. For the moment, he left the Mimbres band, took a Chiricahua wife and placed himself under the leadership of Cochise.

He looked like a formidable opponent—about five feet seven inches tall, with a barrel chest and a fierce countenance of overhung brows, prominent cheekbones, and a hawk's-beak nose above a thin, straight mouth. Later, one of his eight battle wounds would cause the right corner of his mouth to droop in a permanent sneer.

And he lived up to his looks: Capable of frightful barbarities, he became feared and hated even by some of his fellow Apaches. Yet there were always a few—never more than 100—warriors to follow him, and in the years after the death of Cochise, his activities fell into a bloody pattern. Either because of grievances, both real and fancied, or out of simple boredom, he repeatedly broke away from the reservation, holed up in Mexico and raided over the border. Then, when things got too hot, he returned to the reservation.

Apprehension grew among the Indians, and in 1885 Geronimo provoked severe action by the white man. He again decamped from the reservation, this time taking with him 42 men and 92 women and children. Collecting supplies on the way south, Geronimo attacked the ranch of a man named Phillips and killed him, his wife and an infant. He also hanged their five-year-old daughter on a meat hook. She was still alive when a white posse arrived, but died a few days later.

At that, the U.S. Army under General George Crook mounted the heaviest campaign so far in the Apache

wars, with 20 cavalry troops and more than 200 Indian scouts. Thrusting into Mexico's Sierra Madre, they hounded Geronimo's little band until, in March 1886, its weary members persuaded their renegade leader to meet with Crook a few miles south of the border. When the general arrived, he took a hard look at Geronimo and his retinue. "They were in superb physical condition," he recalled later, "armed to the teeth,

fierce as so many tigers." After two days of negotiations, Geronimo agreed once more to return to the reservation. "Do with me as you please," he said. "Once I was free as the wind. Now I surrender to you, and that is all."

Despite the chief's submissive words, he departed. On a dark and rainy night before Crook could convey him north of the border, Geronimo took with him the last coterie of desperate Apache fugitives: 20 warriors and 18 women and children—38 in all.

Upon being reproved for letting Geronimo escape, Crook disgustedly asked for a transfer. He got his wish and was replaced by General Nelson Miles, who promptly arranged for all Chiricahua, Apaches and Mimbres on the reservations to be exiled to Florida. Then Miles put 5,000 men on horseback and set off into the mountains of northern Sonora.

But even in a countryside swarming with soldiers, Geronimo remained as elusive—and as lethal—as ever. In April of 1886, he and his warriors crossed the border into Arizona, murdered a cattleman's wife, her 13-year-old child and a ranch hand. A few weeks later, the Apaches killed two men outside the town of Nogales, Arizona, then ambushed pursuing soldiers and took two more lives.

Yet the end was near. That same year, Lieutenant Charles Gatewood, an emissary sent by General Miles, trailed Geronimo into the Sierra Madre and arranged for a meeting. During the encounter Geronimo deliberately sat so close to Gatewood that the lieutenant could feel the revolver on his hip. Geronimo asked what the U.S. government would offer if he gave himself up. Gatewood replied that he could only accept unconditional surrender and that Geronimo would be sent to exile in Florida. Geronimo bristled. "Take us to the reservation," he demanded. "Or fight!"

Then Gatewood told Geronimo that his family (the renegade had remarried into the Chiricahuas after the death of his first wife) had already been removed to Florida. All at once, the fighting spirit seemed to drain out of the old warrior. He gave himself up.

In the years after his imprisonment in Florida, Geronimo was turned into a human exhibit, paraded in President Theodore Roosevelt's inaugural procession in 1901 and at the St. Louis World's Fair in 1904. He also eked out a living of his own: He made and sold bows and arrows, and peddled his autographed photographs. But even in his degradation, he could always remember that it had taken 5,000 whites to subdue his 38 Apaches.

During the years that Cochise and Geronimo waged their long, lonely wars in the Southwest, the struggle on the Northern plains had intensified. In the early winter of 1864, readers of Denver's *Rocky Mountain News* rejoiced in a report from Colonel J.M. Chivington, a former Methodist minister, now commander of the Military District of Colorado.

Chivington claimed that troops under his command had attacked a Cheyenne village populated by "from nine hundred to one thousand warriors strong" on Sand Creek in eastern Colorado. He reported having killed between 400 and 500 of these redoubtable savages. Of his soldiers, Chivington said: "All did nobly."

But the facts, as they seeped out during ensuing weeks, told a different story. The chief of the Cheyenne at Sand Creek had been one Black Kettle, who for several years had been trying to persuade his people not to go on the warpath against the whites. In fact, he had pitched his camp at Sand Creek in accordance with Army instructions, and had believed that he and his followers were under government protection.

Thus, at dawn on the cold morning of January 30, when Black Kettle saw U.S. troops approaching, he hoisted an American flag above his tipi and raised a white flag below it. The soldiers, however, began firing cannon into the Cheyenne tipis, then rushed the camp. Robert Bent, a half-Cheyenne who had been forced to guide Chivington's expedition, later described some of the frightful things he witnessed: "I saw one squaw cut open with an unborn child lying by her side. I saw the body of [Chief] White Antelope with the privates cut off, and I heard a soldier say he was going to make a tobacco pouch out of them."

Instead of the formidable band of braves claimed by Chivington, the village had contained no more than 500 people—two thirds of them women and children. And, after the battle, an observer who said he had counted the Indian dead put the total at 123, including 98 women and children. Black Kettle, among others, had escaped.

The reaction of other plains chiefs to Sand Creek was quick and violent. By late December, 2,000 Cheyenne, Arapaho and Sioux warriors had gathered in villages on the Republican River, where one chief said, "We have now raised the battle ax until death." And death to the whites it was. In January a war party lured a cavalry detachment out of Fort Rankin and slaughtered 45 troopers. Indians then ravaged every white man's ranch for 80 miles west of Fort Rankin, killed eight

more people and stole 1,500 head of cattle. Finally, they ended their spree by sacking Julesburg, where chanting warriors danced to the light of a bonfire made from torn-down telephone poles.

In the ensuing years, one Indian who declined to participate in the bloody succession of reprisals and counter-reprisals was the forgiving Black Kettle, who continued to preach peace with the whites. Yet despite his efforts, tragedy would be inevitable.

On the morning of November 27, 1868, Black Kettle and his Cheyenne people were camped on the upper Washita River in what is now western Colorado, where snow blanketed the cottonwood groves and the plains. Just as the first light of a chilly dawn was making the tipis of the quiet camp visible, there was the sound of a shot, followed by the notes of a bugle. The United States 7th Cavalry, led by an officer named George Armstrong Custer, was charging from four different directions.

As he armed himself, Black Kettle must have thought of Sand Creek. But this time he was to die, and Custer's Osage scouts lifted his scalp. Some 40 Indian women and children were also killed. Called the Washita Massacre, this was not a major engagement; it served as another brutal reminder that the white man would strike hard at any Indian tribes that showed the slightest semblance of armed resistance. Survivors—if there were any—were destined for the reservations, which would confine the Indians to a sedentary life and leave the remainder of the West wide open for settlers.

By 1868, the U.S. government had offered the Sioux Nation, along with some northern members of the Cheyenne and Arapaho tribes, a spacious reservation encompassing the entire western half of present-day South Dakota, including the Black Hills, which the Sioux regarded as a dwelling place of spirits. Many chiefs accepted the terms. Among those who refused was the leader of the Hunkpapa Sioux—Sitting Bull himself. "I

235

Corralling a proud, nomadic race

The placing of troublesome—or inconveniently located—Indians on reservations began long before the beginning of the Indian wars. Between the years 1790 and 1834, Congress passed numerous acts aimed at guaranteeing the Indians a safe homeland, supposedly free from white preemption or trespass.

In the end, the iron-clad guarantee of reservation lands proved more fiction than fact. Time and time again, the government found ways to induce the Indians to give up territory that had been described to them as a permanent home for their people.

Underlying these actions was the conviction that the only way to pacify the warrior Indians was to transform them into steadfast farmers. Peaceful husbandmen were what they should become, turning from the red man's ways of war and hunting to the white man's plow and furrow, thereby facilitating the peaceful settlement of pioneers and townsmen in the West.

But few warriors, however, were interested in the plow and furrow; they believed that was woman's work. Moreover, even if they had been willing to farm, the Indians learned Eastern agricultural techniques that proved hopelessly inadequate on the arid Western plains.

Serving as the liaison between the reservation-bound Indians and the U.S. government was the Indian agent. Working under his supervision were blacksmiths, millers and schoolteachers to abet the Indians in the various arts of civilization. The Indian agent was also responsible for distributing annuities of food and supplies which the Indians received in exchange for land and a promise of docility.

In theory, this policy was benevolent; in practice, the annuity system encouraged indolence on the part of the Indians. It also occasionally led to starvation when the annuities failed to arrive, either through bureaucratic mismanagement or outright theft by white officials or traders.

Reservation policy called for the Indians to govern themselves. But their own cultures rarely had equivalents to the police force and courts they were required to set up. Nor did they see the worth of the white man's law which prohibited a wide range of formerly accepted practices, from brewing beer to slicing off the nose of an unfaithful wife.

Perhaps the greatest hardship of all was coping with boredom. Women and children were busy with tasks such as gathering hay, but the erstwhile warriors were idle—reduced to whiling away the hours gambling, singing and comforting one another with wistful tales of an unfettered life in the past.

By 1889 the corralling of the Indians was firmly in practice; Western tribes had been persuaded to sign away 61,000 square miles of land for as little as 50 cents an acre.

As an old Sioux expressed it, "They made us many promises but only kept one; they promised to take our land and they took it."

Families queue up for their weekly rations of flour and beef, which were seldom sufficient for more than four or five days.

wish all to know that I do not propose to sell any part of my country," he declared, "nor will I have the whites cutting our timber along the rivers, especially the oaks. I am particularly fond of the little groves of oak trees."

Only a few years passed before the Sioux who did retire to the reservation had cause to regret it. In 1874 reports began to circulate that the Black Hills were rich in gold. The Sioux were a proud, conquering people. What warrior would follow a plow or do women's work because some white man said he should?

And what white gold seeker would let savages stand between him and riches? By the middle of 1875, nearly a thousand prospectors were illegally digging and panning on the Sioux's sacred ground. In March of the following year, the U.S. Army took to the field in force to subdue the Sioux once and for all.

Sitting Bull prepared to greet the white troops. Calling a council, he said, "We must stand together or they will kill us separately. These soldiers have come shooting; they want war. All right, we'll give it to them." He sent couriers to every Sioux, Cheyenne and Arapaho camp, both on reservation and off, summoning them to a rendezvous on Rosebud Creek about 60 miles south of its confluence with the Yellowstone River.

Now, in June, they were joined in a single great Indian army. Meanwhile, their opponents drew inexorably closer, marching towards destiny—and a stunning defeat that would rock the country from ocean to ocean, and the Indians' way of life forevermore.

The day was hot and dry with a layer of thin clouds hanging in the sky. The U.S. 7th Cavalry, under the command of a soldier the Indians called Long Hair, was advancing toward an Indian encampment along the banks of a meandering river in the southern part of Montana Territory. Timber-lined in places, the stream wound along the east side of a valley. To the Indians it was known as the Greasy Grass River; to the bluecoated troops, who were barely more than a rifleshot away in the early afternoon of June 25, 1876, it was called the Little Bighorn.

Among the thousands of Sioux and Cheyennes camped by the stream were 1,500 to 2,000 warriors. Foremost among them was a chief of the Oglala Sioux named Crazy Horse. A brave fighter and a brilliant tactician, Crazy Horse had long been a burr under the Army's saddle blanket. His most dramatic encounter with white troops resulted in the massacre of an entire detachment of 77 men under Captain William Fetterman in December 1866. Now, still in his early 30s, he was a lithe and sinewy five feet eight inches tall, quiet and dignified, with a reflective, melancholy face.

The first attack came at midafternoon to the south of the encampment on the west bank of the Greasy Grass River; it was quickly repulsed by an overwhelming number of Indian braves. The white men retreated pell-mell toward a bad ford over the stream, where the east bank and the hills above were steep. The Sioux swarmed around them as they fled, showering them with arrows and bullets as the retreating horses scrambled up the gray slopes to a defensive position. The fleeing force left at least 30 men dead or dying.

Crazy Horse and the war chief Gall then turned downriver and sped back through the camps in pursuit of the main body of the white forces which had already forged north. While Gall crossed to the east side of the river, Crazy Horse forced his tiring pinto past two and a half miles of wickiups and willow and brush shelters, motioning as he went to the warriors still in camp to join him. By the time he arrived at his own Oglala circle, an army of Sioux fighters was following him, cheering and yelling war cries: "Hoka hey, Lakotas! It's a good day to die!"

Riding well past the camps they turned east, forded the river several miles beyond where Gall had crossed and climbed a broad ravine. Crazy Horse had no difficulty in locating the bluecoats, who had already been struck by Gall and his warriors. A decisive moment had arrived: If Crazy Horse could attack quickly the white soldiers would be crushed by an attack on two fronts, with no possibility of escape.

Crazy Horse galloped towards the troops. The dust rose thicker, mixed with the darker, dirty powder smoke. The midafternoon seemed like twilight; under the pall gunflashes winked like fireflies. At times, the blast of rifles and carbines sounded like the ripping of a giant canvas down the wrinkles of the hills. The white men's horses screamed above the din. They clawed at the gray slopes like cats; they whinnied as the arrows and bullets entered their bodies, as they bled, as they struggled against the weight of the troopers on their backs or dragging from the stirrups.

The whites tried vainly to regroup but it was futile: The warriors had completely encircled them. The only protection was an occasional swell of ground or the carcass of a horse, and every small group or line of cavalry found itself defending in one direction as an attack came from another. At the last, most of the work was done with lances or war clubs, as the whites' guns jammed or their ammunition ran out.

It was over in a matter of minutes. Near the top of a hill lay the body of Long Hair—Lieutenant Colonel George Armstrong Custer. Around him, strewn over the gray and sere landscape, lay the corpses of the men he had led to disaster—dead, all 215 of them.

For the triumphant Sioux, the battle on Greasy Grass River—known to the whites as the Battle of the Little Bighorn—was the beginning of a preordained end. Far from being a decisive Indian victory, Custer's catastrophe brought only more U.S. troops and relentless pressure. Within a year, even a discouraged Crazy Horse surrendered himself. He did so with style, leading 1,500 followers bedecked in their war paint and feathers into a reservation.

But it was a forlorn gesture: Later that year, hearing rumors that Crazy Horse was planning more trouble, authorities ordered him locked up in the guardhouse at Fort Robinson in the Nebraska Territory. When soldiers tried to seize him, the war chief resisted. Crazy Horse was stabbed in the abdomen with a bayonet and died a few hours later.

Among the few who held out was Sitting Bull, who led his followers into Canada in May 1877. He stayed there for four years, all the while watching his homesick people trickle back to their native land. Finally, Sitting Bull led the last pitiful remnant—185 people—toward Fort Buford, 70 miles south of the border near the Dakota-Montana line. Still, in his proud heart, he conceded nothing. "The land I have under my feet is mine again," he told an officer of the U.S. Army. "I never sold it; I never gave it to anybody."

Sitting Bull had nine years of life left to him. He spent part of it on the road with the Wild West show run by Buffalo Bill Cody, with whom he became fast friends. But his heart was still in his homeland, and he was there in 1889, when a Sioux mystic named Kicking Bear arrived with word of a miraculous new religion

Proof of daring in battle is everywhere visible among this war party of Oglala Sioux, the tribe to which Crazy Horse belonged. Although some of the warriors have guns, most are carrying coupsticks to strike an enemy directly. The eagle feathers in their war bonnets signify their past coups.

that had arisen in Nevada and was spreading fast. Its followers believed that sometime within the foreseeable future the Indian dead would rise, the buffalo would return in their millions, and the white oppressors would disappear. Whites, who also heard of the new faith, called it the "ghost dance religion" after the simple, shuffling dance that was part of its ritual.

Sitting Bull was skeptical. "It is impossible for a dead man to return and live again," he told Kicking Bear. But because he respected faith in all of its guises, he refused to interfere with those who performed the ghost dance, and his people soon added a wrinkle of their own: They began dancing in loose shirts adorned with cabalistic designs that, they believed, would render them impervious to the white man's bullets.

Naturally, this sort of thing was disturbing to the white authorities, and just as naturally they suspected Sitting Bull, who had given them a great deal of trouble in the past, of being the ghost dancers' guiding genius. Determined to arrest Sitting Bull, they decided that the job could best be done by Indian policemen, and so they turned it over to Lieutenant Henry Bull Head, a Sioux.

Thus, in the cold and cheerless dawn on December 15, 1890, a party of some 40 Sioux police burst through the door of Sitting Bull's Grand River cabin. At first, Sitting Bull agreed to submit to arrest; but then he changed his mind and shouted, "I am not going." At

Troopers of the 7th Cavalry survey the corpse-strewn field at Wounded Knee, blanketed by the first blizzard of the season. Three

240

that, one of his followers fired a rifle at Lieutenant Bull Head; as the officer fell, badly wounded, he managed to put a bullet into Sitting Bull. In the shooting affray that followed, six policemen and eight of Sitting Bull's people were killed. So was the old medicine man who had once had a vision of white men hanging their heads in defeat.

Now it was nearly over. Nearly, but not quite. The last tragic act of Sitting Bull's heritage and destiny still had to be played out.

In the days after Sitting Bull's death, authorities decided that a certain Big Foot, a chief of the Miniconjou Sioux about 100 miles to the south, was also a potential troublemaker. Big Foot and his bedraggled band of some 350 men, women and children were taken into custody and started on their way to Fort Cheyenne with a guard of 450 soldiers. On the evening of December 28 they camped at Wounded Knee Creek in the South Dakota Badlands.

Next morning, when soldiers started searching the Indians for weapons, a young brave pulled a gun out from under his robe and fired wildly. Instantly, the soldiers retaliated with a point-blank volley. By the time the slaughter had stopped, about 180 Indians, including Chief Big Foot, lay dead. For three days their corpses were left to lie where they fell while a winter blizzard swept over them—and over the last pathetic remnant of the Indian cause.

days after the engagement, the white soldiers pried the victims out from under a shroud of ice and snow for an unceremonious burial.

Sudden fury in a long, slow war

The stark vulnerability of a skirmish line at the height of battle is vividly portrayed in this work by Charles Schreyvogel.

Like shafts of lightning, the savage battles that shattered the monotony of a soldier's life in the Indian wars were hard to fix in the memory, even for the survivors. The re-creation of those violent moments called for the artistry of such painters as Frederic Remington and Charles Schreyvogel.

Schreyvogel's canvases capture the quintessence of battle on the Plains.

The fact is that he never saw an Indian fight; born in New York, Schreyvogel painted most of his major works on the rooftop of his home in Hoboken, New Jersey. To bridge the distance from Hoboken to the West, he drew upon a lifetime of exhaustive research. He was a fine horseman and crack shot, and had traveled extensively through the West, sketching and collecting Indian artifacts.

He combed archives and corresponded with old soldiers.

In tribute to his labors and art, *Leslie's Weekly* called him "the greatest living interpreter of the Old West," and defined his achievement in these words: "He has seized the significant thing out of the lives of the staunchest band of soldiers that we have produced yet, and has transferred that life to canvas."

243

Behind a falling trumpeter an unhorsed warrior runs for his life through the midst of a cavalry charge.

A beleaguered garrison defends its stockade. Attacks by massed warriors were rare but bloody.

10. Battered cavaliers of the Indian wars

At about four o'clock on the afternoon of September 16, 1868, a column of 50 men led by Major George A. Forsyth rode through a ravine and onto the flood plain of the Arikaree River in what is now eastern Colorado. They were all seasoned troopers, wise to the frontier. Forsyth, a young man with brown hair and a round, boyish face that belied his aggressive nature, had served during the Civil War as the trusted aide to the Union cavalry hero General Philip Sheridan. After the war, Sheridan had been assigned to the most important military command in the nation, the Division of the Missouri, and Forsyth was once again his aide.

Indian warriors had been striking all over the Great Plains, burning settlements, wagon trains, ranches and telegraph stations. Sheridan was ready to retaliate. Forsyth had proposed to assemble a small force that could travel fast, hunt out the Indians and force them to fight. The plan was now being put to the test.

The cavalrymen halted in the valley of the Arikaree. A shallow stream coursed through the center of the riverbed, parting to pass Beecher's Island, a strip of land 60 yards long by 20 wide. Forsyth's men made camp, thinking they had not been detected. But at an encampment 12 miles upriver Indian warriors—Sioux, Cheyennes and Arapahos—began collecting their fighting ponies, and dressing and painting themselves for war.

Among them was one of the greatest of all Indian fighting men. Known as Bat to the other Indians, he was a Cheyenne, large and muscular, with a broad, handsome face dominated by a distinctive hooked nose. To the whites he was known as Roman Nose, and his commanding presence ensured that what might have been a skirmish would become a deadly battle.

At dawn of the next day 600 Indians were poised on the bluffs overlooking the cavalrymen's camp. The engagement began when eight overeager young Indians made an ineffectual attempt to stampede the Army horses. Pickets beat off the attackers, while the main body of soldiers hastily saddled their mounts.

Concerned that his small force would be overwhelmed and slaughtered on open ground, Forsyth ordered his men to break for the small island. The Indians charged, but the soldiers opened such heavy fire with their repeating Spencer rifles that at the last moment the wall of horsemen broke in the center, parted and surged down both sides of the island and beyond it. The Indians wheeled, regrouped and charged again, but the repeating rifle fire broke them once more. As Forsyth would learn later, Roman Nose had not yet entered the fight—convinced, for some reason, that he would die if he fought that day. But when an Indian with the singularly appropriate name of White Contrary accused him of cowardice, Roman Nose elected to lead the next charge.

His appearance had a galvanic effect on the warriors. They galloped in a boiling mass down on the little island. Forsyth's men, hidden in tall grass, waited until their targets were a mere 50 yards away. Their volleys crashed like cannon fire, and bullets cut down men and horses. By the sixth volley, Roman Nose was over the position where the hidden marksmen lay. One of them fired point-blank and knocked him and his horse down.

When the warriors saw their leader fall, mortally wounded, the charge faltered and passed by. The Indians continued to attack sporadically and riflemen on the surrounding bluffs held Forsyth's men under siege for more than a week. Meanwhile, two pairs of scouts slipped away and walked to Fort Wallace, 110 miles distant, for help. By the time a relief column finally reached Beecher's Island more than 20 of Forsyth's men had been killed or wounded, and the survivors were subsisting on the putrid flesh of dead horses. But they were holding their own. The major, who had been wounded three times, was coolly reading *Oliver Twist* when rescue arrived.

This regimental flag was carried through the Indian wars by all U.S. troops. While the cavalry version measured a modest five square feet, the flagmen of the infantry staggered under a 40-square-foot behemoth.

The Battle of Beecher's Island was one of the most celebrated in the annals of the Plains. In Forsyth, soldiers all over the West saw a vision of their own plight as Indian fighters: outnumbered and surrounded, but heroic under fire, steadfast under prolonged siege.

The troops on Western duty had little enough to cheer about: Service on the frontier was arduous and thankless. Few of the men had been fully trained, and many were neither good horsemen nor good riflemen. Their pay was miserly—only $16 a month for a private at the end of the Civil War, later reduced in 1871 to $13 by a parsimonious Congress. To make matters worse, the food was about on a level with their pay: The hapless soldiers subsisted mainly on beans, hardtack, bacon, coffee and coarse bread, with an occasional meal of low-grade range beef or game.

The posts they manned often were hundreds of miles from the nearest railhead. The soldiers reached their remote stations on foot or horseback, marching in long columns under constant danger of Indian assault. Not all of these establishments were permanent installations. Hastily built forts, thrown up in the middle of nowhere, stood as the advance guard for the moving tide of civilization that quickly engulfed the trans-Mississippi wilderness.

A painting by Robert Lindneux depicts the wounded Major George Forsyth *(center, holding pistol)* and his besieged command on Beecher's Island, Colorado, awaiting the climactic charge of Cheyenne warriors. Their leader, Roman Nose, was felled by a bullet, and the Indians withdrew.

251

Robt. Lindneux

The amenities of a typical early frontier fort were minimal. Officers occupied private quarters, but enlisted men were crammed into poorly constructed, badly ventilated barracks where rows of bunks or cots stood head-in to walls. Privies were outside and bathhouses were virtually nonexistent. Southwestern posts were afflicted with centipedes, tarantulas and snakes. Soldiers on the Northern Plains were no better off. At Fort Randall, in Dakota Territory, the cottonwood-log buildings were so full of rats and other vermin that the men preferred to sleep outdoors. Fine dust blew through cracks in the log or adobe walls and log roofs of post buildings in summer, and snow sifted through in winter.

As time went on, however, the forts were improved. Mess halls were painted; bunks were equipped with springs and cotton mattresses; kerosene lamps replaced candles. Officers were given two-story frame houses with well-tended lawns in front.

The one thing that did not change was the routine of Army life. Serving as a soldier at a frontier post meant a fixed and monotonous grind of guard mount and fatigue details that included building roads and bridges, repairing telegraph lines, filling water barrels, disposing of garbage and cleaning stables.

Companies were ordered to assemble every day to drill, if the weather permitted. This official policy, however, was widely ignored, often because Western posts were undermanned. Though a few officers—notably that proud martinet George Armstrong Custer—turned their troops into good riders and excellent shots, many others simply did not care about the prosaic task of training soldiers. Their indifference stemmed partly from an ill-founded opinion that Indians were unskilled in the martial arts and that chasing after a bunch of redskins was an almost insulting comedown after the glorious setpiece battles of the Civil War.

Such misunderstanding was typical of the enmity that characterized relations between the two races. For his part, Civil War hero General William Tecumseh Sherman, Commanding General of the Army, considered Indians as "a class of savages." His prescription for them was quite simple. "I suppose they must be exterminated," he said.

But not all senior officers were completely without sympathy for the Indians' struggle. Although he was as tough and uncompromising as Indian fighters came,

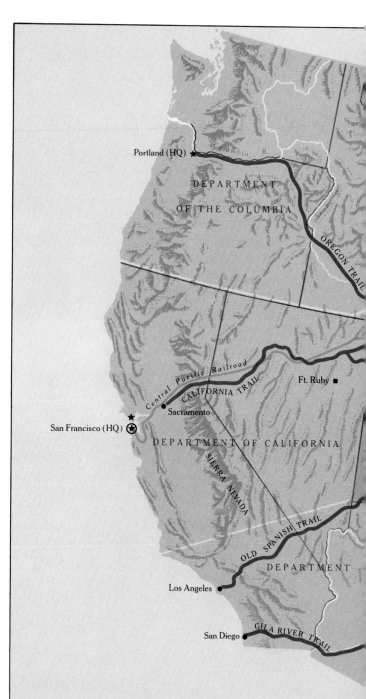

A SOLDIER'S MAP OF THE OLD WEST

During the decisive years of the Indian wars, from 1865 to 1876, the Army's troops were strung out in isolated forts (the major ones are shown here) across the 2.5 million square miles from the Mississippi to the Pacific. Rarely more than 15,000 men, they had a mission that seemed impossible: to protect trails; to defend miners, settlers and cattlemen; to survey railroad lines and guard construction crews; to engage the enemy in battles of extermination like those indicated on this map. But they managed, winning more often than they lost—and in the end, they secured the West for white settlement.

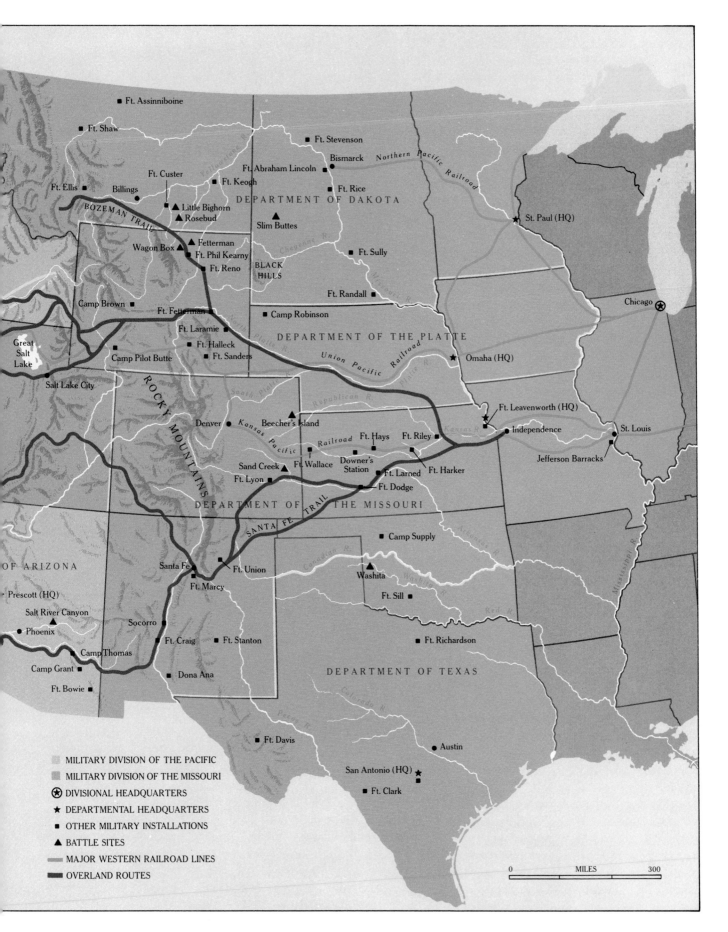

■ Ft. Assinniboine

■ Ft. Shaw

Ft. Custer

Ft. Ellis ■   ● Billings
BOZEMAN TRAIL

■ Ft. Stevenson

Ft. Abraham Lincoln ■   ● Bismarck   Northern Pacific Railroad

St. Paul (HQ) ★

▲ Little Bighorn
▲ Rosebud

■ Ft. Keogh

■ Ft. Rice

DEPARTMENT OF DAKOTA

▲ Slim Buttes

▲ Fetterman
Wagon Box ▲   ■ Ft. Phil Kearny
■ Ft. Reno

■ Ft. Sully

Camp Brown ■

Ft. Fetterman ■

BLACK
HILLS

Chicago ⊛

■ Ft. Randall

Great
Salt
Lake

Ft. Laramie ■

■ Camp Robinson

DEPARTMENT OF THE PLATTE

Camp Pilot Butte ■

■ Ft. Halleck
■ Ft. Sanders

Union Pacific Railroad

Omaha (HQ) ★

Salt Lake City ●

ROCKY MOUNTAINS

Denver ●

Beecher's Island ▲

Kansas Pacific Railroad

Ft. Hays ■   Ft. Riley ■

Ft. Leavenworth (HQ)
★
■   ● Independence

● St. Louis

Sand Creek ▲
Ft. Lyon ■

■ Ft. Wallace

Downer's
Station

Ft. Larned ■   Ft. Harker ■

Jefferson Barracks ■

OF ARIZONA

Santa Fe ■
■ Ft. Union
Ft. Marcy ■

DEPARTMENT OF THE MISSOURI

SANTA FE TRAIL

■ Ft. Dodge

■ Camp Supply

▲ Washita

Prescott (HQ)

Salt River Canyon ▲

Socorro ●

Ft. Sill ■

● Phoenix

Camp Thomas

Ft. Craig ■   ■ Ft. Stanton

■ Ft. Richardson

Camp Grant ●

● Dona Ana

DEPARTMENT OF TEXAS

■ Ft. Bowie

■ Ft. Davis

● Austin

San Antonio (HQ) ★

■ Ft. Clark

MILITARY DIVISION OF THE PACIFIC
MILITARY DIVISION OF THE MISSOURI
⊛ DIVISIONAL HEADQUARTERS
★ DEPARTMENTAL HEADQUARTERS
■ OTHER MILITARY INSTALLATIONS
▲ BATTLE SITES
MAJOR WESTERN RAILROAD LINES
OVERLAND ROUTES

0   MILES   300

General Sheridan was still able to admit: "We took away their country, broke up their mode of living, their habits of life, introduced disease and decay among them, and it was for this and against this that they made war. Could anyone expect less?"

Indian tribes, on the other hand, usually saw themselves as naturally superior not only to all white men but to other Indians as well. Most tribal names meant, in translation, something like "The People."

That exalted self-image was scant defense against a well-organized, well-supplied adversary. The Indians were better horsemen and more fanatical fighters than the soldiers; they also knew the terrain perfectly and could move as silently as the dust. But they could not hold what they had won. Most battles ended with the Indians in retreat—regardless of whether they had won or lost—because their supplies were exhausted.

The Indians were, in fact, essentially a stone-age people, recently introduced to the technology and social structure of the whites but having neither the capacity nor the desire to reproduce either one. Their own concept of society was as a diffused collection of tribal groups acting autonomously. They saw life itself as controlled by numerous spirits, and they sensed no god-mandate to improve themselves or to conquer the wilderness around them.

To many white men who met them in battle on the Plains and in the desert, the Indians' mystical culture was nonsensical and contemptible. In the eyes of privates and generals alike, the red man was a heathen who stood in the way of a pre-ordained westward expansion of white Americans. In the vanguard of that

Early Western campaigns: The Mexican War

A generation before the Indian wars, the U.S. Army embarked on its first major venture west of the Mississippi.

It began as a brazen bit of saber rattling by President Polk, who sent 10 regiments to the Rio Grande in 1846 in an attempt to force Mexico to sell California and the Southwest to the United States. Since the Rio Grande was in disputed territory, Mexico regarded the act as an invasion, and war quickly broke out—notwithstanding "all our efforts to avoid it," as Polk self-righteously claimed.

In the initial clash of armies in early May, 1846, General Zachary Taylor's 2,000 regulars, although outnumbered, routed the overconfident Mexicans by superior marksmanship and expert use of artillery.

Facing total forces of more than 30,000 men, Taylor could not drive into Mexico without reinforcements. But volunteers proved easy to come by: within a few months 50,000 recruits had signed up for glory and adventure in the Halls of Montezuma. Raw but eager, these "wild volunteers," as General Taylor called them, massed in Texas, where they soon grew impatient with drills in the blazing summer sun and spent much of their time drinking, brawling and earning the contempt of the regulars.

But when Taylor thrust into Mexico, the new soldiers fought ferociously. The fortified city of Monterrey (right) fell on September 25 at a cost of almost 500 casualties. Taylor ended his campaign with a narrow victory at Buena Vista—won when a cavalry charge broke the surrounding Mexican lines. The charge was led by a colonel named Jefferson Davis, whose comrades in arms included such other young West Point graduates as Robert E. Lee, Ulysses S. Grant and George McClellan.

While Taylor bludgeoned his way southward General Stephen Kearny's Army of the West marched from the Missouri to California. He did not encounter significant resistance until he approached San Diego, and within a month the province was secured. In the main theater of the war, the crushing blow was delivered by General Winfield Scott, who attacked inland from Veracruz and on September 14, 1847, captured Mexico City.

The swift victory over Mexico heaped glory on the Army, and two of its generals—Zachary Taylor and Franklin Pierce, who served under Scott—would become Presidents in the next decade. But it cost 13,000 American lives, the great majority of them lost to diseases such as dysentery and smallpox. And after the war the Army had the additional burden of protecting the half-million square miles of territory it had won. The Indian tribes of the area—Navaho, Apache and Ute—would keep U.S. soldiers busy there for 40 more years.

movement stood the U.S. Army—the protector of a chosen people who were destined to displace the original inhabitants of an untamed land.

It was a tragic clash of cultures; Indians and soldiers blundered on toward the final bloodletting. Even in the end, neither side would understand the world of the men they fought and killed.

Following the Civil War, the Army was reduced to a small core of regulars. Generals dropped back to colonels and lower, and colonels to lieutenants. (Major Forsyth had been a brigadier general during the war; his first sergeant, William McCall, had held that same rank while commanding a regiment from Pennsylvania.) After 1870, the entire force rarely totaled more than 25,000 men. Only a small portion of these went to posts scattered across the hostile immensity of the West; at one point in 1868 the total was no more than 2,600. Some outposts counted fewer than 50 men; many had a mere three companies, perhaps 200 or 300 men in all.

While the Army shrank in size, the territory it was required to cover expanded, and when U.S. troops sallied forth to do battle, they were usually outnumbered. The vast expanses of the West were populated by the toughest, most ferocious warriors in North America—part of a total Indian population of 200,000 between the Mississippi and the eastern slopes of the Sierras.

During the long tragedy of America's Indian wars, all sorts of battles took place—foolish battles, battles well fought, ambushes laid and ambushes foiled, extended marches in which disease and weather took as great a toll as did bullets. But the common characteristic of

Charging through cannon fire, Zachary Taylor's troops fight their way up the steps of the Bishop's Palace in Monterrey, Mexico.

It was under Civil War cavalry hero Philip Sheridan, appointed commander of the Army's enormous Division of the Missouri in 1869, that the final subjugation of the Plains Indians was carried out.

the infantry back up the slope, and the cavalrymen swung back up the hill on their left. Indians swarmed up the slope. As the cavalrymen's ammunition dwindled to a round or two per man they bunched close together.

Fetterman had once boasted that with 80 men he could cut through the entire Sioux Nation. By a curious coincidence he had gone into battle against Crazy Horse with exactly 80 men. Now he discovered how tragically wrong his headstrong claim actually was.

The surrounding Indians were so close that some arrows overshot and killed warriors on opposite sides of the embattled troops. Then, all at once, the Indians leaped over the rocks and dashed among the soldiers with lances and war clubs. As they came, Fetterman and Captain Fred Brown stood up, face to face, with their pistols at each other's temples. The two men must have counted down and fired simultaneously, killing each other and leaving clear evidence of their act by the positions of their bodies and the powder burns on their temples.

The Indians then moved about the field killing any survivors, stripping and mutilating the stiffening bodies, tearing out the eyes, cutting off noses and ears, bashing out teeth, ripping out entrails and scooping out brains, in what came to be known as the "Fetterman Massacre."

these engagements was the total hatred with which they were undertaken and the intent of the antagonists to annihilate one another.

The point was made with terrible force on December 21, 1866, near Fort Phil Kearny, Wyoming. That bitingly cold day, 80 infantrymen and cavalrymen under Captain William Fetterman moved out to rescue a detachment of wagons on its daily mission—bringing timber back to the fort. Indian attacks had long been a threat to the wood train, and this day was no different—or so it appeared. As Fetterman's men approached, a party of Sioux under a young Oglala named Crazy Horse was attacking the wood train. The warriors broke off the attack and rode down a slope onto the flats of a creek, and the soldiers followed. They were following a decoy.

The Indians crossed the creek, split into two groups and then swung back toward each other. At this signal, an enormous force—2,000 warriors in all—rose from the grass almost at the soldiers' feet. Bows twanged, arrows skittered through the air and soldiers began to fall. Indian battle cries rang so loud in the cold air that the soldiers probably could not hear their officers. Fetterman started

In their battles against the U.S. soldiers, the Indians had an advantage in their intimate acquaintance with the country. They always knew where they were going, and the ins and outs of every water hole, canyon and bluff. Simply following them would have been all but impossible for the soldiers had they not had the assistance of scouts. Most of the scouts were former fur trappers who had learned how to survive in the wilderness. They knew the country, Indian ways and how to bring down plenty of game to keep their employers fed.

On the march, the scouts chose the route and selected river-crossings. They also picked campsites, always with a canny eye for animal forage, drinking water and fuel for cookfires. Able to converse with the Indians in their tribal tongues, the scouts tracked the enemy on his native ground, made knowledgeable estimates of his strength and aims, and often ventured into hostile villages to parley with the chiefs and attempt to divine their intentions.

But it was as couriers that the scouts showed the fullest measure of their skills. Operating in a vast region served only sparsely by telegraph, the scouts were frequently called upon to bear military dispatches across hundreds of miles of hostile territory. Traveling alone at night, they were the vital communications link between far-flung Army commands.

Men with the ability to excel in this demanding and dangerous task were rare. Among the greatest was Christopher Carson, better known as Kit. Carson had a reputation among his fellows for courage, trustworthiness and honesty. He also embodied a spirit of brotherhood unusual among scouts, who commonly looked out for themselves first.

After working as a messenger during the Mexican War, Carson attempted to settle down; at 40 he considered himself too old for life on the open trail. But the frontier was not yet ready to let him lead a quiet existence. The army called on him frequently to lead one detachment or another in pursuit of hostile Indians. During the Civil War, Carson guided a force that killed or captured 9,000 Navajo, permanently breaking the power of that tribe. Following the war he was brevetted brigadier

general for "gallantry and distinguished services."

The scouts' knowledge of the West was as vast as it was invaluable. Trapper-turned-scout Jim Bridger, for example, was a walking atlas. The expanse of wilderness from the headwaters of the Missouri to the Rio Grande, down the Colorado River and across the Sierra Nevada to California, lay in his memory like a panoramic mural. Moreover, his eyesight was almost unbelievably acute, as he demonstrated on an Army expedition in pursuit of Indians in 1865. Scouting ahead of the column one day near the Tongue River in Wyoming Territory, Bridger drew the attention of his companion, a Captain Palmer, to smoke "over there by that saddle." The scout was pointing to a saddle-shaped depression in the hills nearly 50 miles distant. Palmer could not see the smoke even when he used field glasses. But soon other scouts rode up and reported an Indian village with campfires where Bridger had seen the smoke.

Early frontiersmen Carson and Bridger brought the scouting profession to a high art, and Buffalo Bill Cody and Wild Bill Hickok glamorized it to a public hungry for heroes. Both men had the knack of mixing fact with fiction; yet beneath the romantic haze of hyperbole that

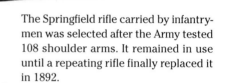

The Springfield rifle carried by infantrymen was selected after the Army tested 108 shoulder arms. It remained in use until a repeating rifle finally replaced it in 1892.

The lethal tools of the Indian-fighter

In 1873, the frontier forces received their first standardized arms issue. This belated action provided a boost to the fighting capabilities of Western soldiers by ending an impossible situation in which they had to make do with a chaotic diversity of small arms: repeating rifles, various kinds of handguns, plus some leftover Civil War weapons that had been converted to load through the breech—the back of the barrel—rather than the muzzle.

It was true that the saber issued to cavalrymen after 1873 was an 1860 model whose function was mainly ceremonial. But the single-action Colt revolver and the new Springfield rifle and carbine—all employing .45-caliber ammunition—were first-rate arms.

The Springfields were single-shot breech-loading weapons. They could not be fired as rapidly as repeating shoulder arms like the seven-shot Spencers used by Major Forsyth's men at the battle of Beecher's Island in 1868. But they were less prone to misfires and had greater accuracy; their maximum range was 3,500 yards—at least twice the Spencer's.

Most soldiers and many civilian critics agreed with the campaigner who said "We could have been better armed." This opinion was based on the belief that a repeating arm would make up for their woefully poor marksmanship and give them a better crack at hitting their moving targets, but the Army stuck to these single-shot guns throughout the Indian wars. Aside from accuracy, the Springfield's range on many occasions kept Indians at such a distance that their muzzle-loaders, less powerful repeating weapons or bows and arrows were useless.

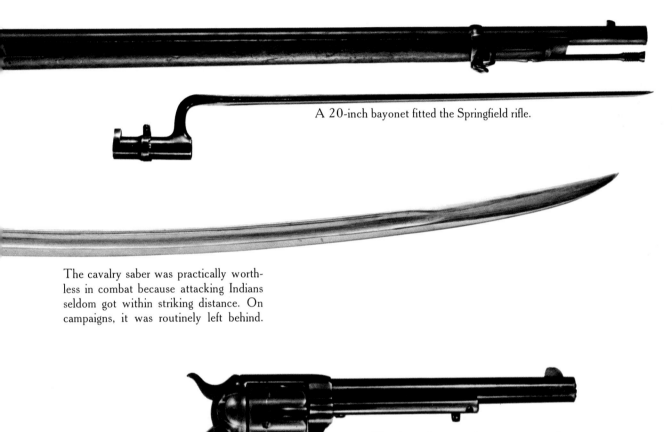

Issued to cavalrymen, the Springfield carbine was lighter and shorter than the rifle, and its metal cartridges contained 55 grains of powder as opposed to the rifle's 70.

A 20-inch bayonet fitted the Springfield rifle.

The cavalry saber was practically worthless in combat because attacking Indians seldom got within striking distance. On campaigns, it was routinely left behind.

The Army-issue revolver was so popular for its rugged efficiency that throughout the West the terms "Colt" and "Forty-five" were nearly synonymous with handgun.

surrounded them, both Hickok and Cody were plains-men of genuinely high caliber.

James Butler Hickok and William Frederick Cody first met in Leavenworth, Kansas, in 1861. Hickok, an ex-constable, was working as an Army wagon boss and he took Cody on as his assistant. The next year, Hickok was serving as both a scout and a spy for the Union Army. He was assigned to infiltrate enemy lines in southwestern Missouri to gather information. Cody's war service was less distinguished; one day after having been under the influence of bad whiskey, he awoke and discovered that he was a soldier in the 7th Kansas, following which he served 19 lackluster months as a cavalryman.

At the end of the Civil War, Hickok got a job as a civilian scout with the Army at Fort Riley in Kansas. In the spring of 1867, he was assigned to accompany George Custer and the 7th Cavalry on a campaign against the Cheyennes and the Sioux in western Kansas. It was a hazardous job that entailed carrying dispatches through the night, scouting ahead of the main columns and staying alive by outguessing, outriding and outshooting the Indians. Custer was so impressed that he later eulogized Hickok as "a Plainsman in every sense of the word, yet unlike any of his class. Whether on foot or on horseback, he was one of the most perfect types of physical manhood I ever saw."

Hickok helped Buffalo Bill enter the scouting business, and in 1868 Cody was hired on as a scout at Fort Larned in western Kansas. That summer, he was sent on a one-man 65-mile ride north from Larned to Fort Hays, to warn General Sheridan that the Kiowas and Comanches were on the warpath. He then rode 95 miles southwest to Fort Dodge, carrying orders from Sheridan. After resting for six hours, he went back to his own post at Larned, rested another 12 hours, then rode to Hays again with a message for Sheridan. In all, he covered 350 miles in less than sixty hours. Sheridan retained him at Hays and made him chief of scouts for the 5th Cavalry.

Three years later, when a band of Cheyennes led by Chief Tall Bull went raiding in central Kansas, the 5th Cavalry and scout Cody quickly launched a pursuit of the Indians and their two women captives. By mid-July, Cody had tracked down Tall Bull's recently abandoned campsites. The regimental history would subsequently record that in the sand hills south of the South Platte River, Cody "guided the 5th Cavalry to a position whence the regiment was enabled to charge the enemy and win a brilliant victory." Only one of the captives was found alive.

That same year, Hickok sustained a leg injury at the hand of a Cheyenne warrior that put an end to his scouting career. Desperate for employment, he and a few friends set out for the gold diggings in the Black Hills in 1876, and it was on this excursion that Cody and Hickok met for the last time.

Cody was on temporary duty with the 5th Cavalry when Hickok's train pulled up at a ranch in eastern Wyoming. What passed between the two men is not known, but farewells would have been in order: Within a month, Wild Bill Hickok was dead, shot in the back of the head by an enemy as he was playing out a poker hand.

Buffalo Bill later turned to the life of a thespian. His five-act melodrama "The Red Right Hand or Buffalo Bill's First Scalp for Custer" was such a success that Cody plunged into a career as a performer and theatrical entrepreneur, becoming a composite image of the Western scout—half true, half fictional—and entertaining audiences throughout North America into the 20th Century.

In the final conquest of Indian lands by whites, the scouts who played one of the most crucial roles were, in a strange twist of fate, Indians themselves. By capitalizing on animosities between tribes, the Army found it easy to recruit Plains warriors as scouts. Indians from small, more or less pacified nations—Pawnees, Crows and Arikaras—welcomed the chance to seek revenge against powerful enemies like the Sioux and Cheyenne.

Nowhere did the actions of scouts prove more pivotal than in the sere, hostile country of the Southwest. In New Mexico and Arizona, there was a small Apache population; they were fierce fighters, masters of trickery and treachery. Typically, the warriors darted down from mountain strongholds, killed and were gone. Lieutenant Colonel George Crook, whom General Sherman would eventually call "the greatest Indian fighter and manager the army of the United States ever had," was determined to strike at these remote bases. Since no white men knew how to penetrate the distant reach-

es of the mountains, Crook relied on a band of friendly Apaches that he had enlisted as scouts.

The job of recruiting such scouts was not especially difficult, for the Apaches were not a single cohesive tribe, but a loosely organized confederation of diverse bands. A number of bands, in fact, had long since cast their lot on the side of the white man.

In the fall of 1872, some 220 of Crook's men from the 5th Cavalry set out under the command of Major William Brown. One of their Apache scouts, named Nantaje, had once lived in a naturally fortified cave in Arizona's Salt River Canyon—a place now suspected as being an Apache base and refuge.

The canyon was 1200 feet deep; the cave could be reached only from above. At the cave mouth itself a natural parapet of smooth stone rose 10 feet high, making the interior nearly impregnable.

The soldiers wore moccasins stuffed with hay to ensure silence. At midnight they reached the chasm's edge. The Indian scouts ranged ahead. At dawn a single file of 100 men started down into the canyon. Nantaje and Lieutenant William J. Ross crawled to within 40 yards of the cave and spied warriors singing and dancing as their women prepared food.

Ross signaled his marksmen to follow. They eased themselves behind stones. Then, as Ross whispered the command, they fired in unison. Six warriors fell dead. A call to the Apaches to surrender was greeted with derisive shouts. A stalemate developed until someone noticed that the roof of the cave sloped downward to the back. A hail of lead splattered deep into the cave, and cries of frightened Indians, including women and children, were heard. The Apaches rushed forward to crouch behind the parapet, but the ricocheting, shattering slugs continued to pour down on them. Brown ordered his men to lay the heaviest possible fire against the cave roof.

On the mesa directly above the cave, boulders as big as cannonballs lay everywhere. Some of the soldiers rolled them to the edge and tipped them over on a signal. A mass of stone rolled down and into the cave, smashing bodies and setting up a cloud of dust. The soldiers dashed across open ground, surmounted the parapet and entered the cave to face a terrible sight. Crushed bodies, some hardly recognizable as human, were everywhere. In all 76 Apaches were killed that day in what came to be known as Skeleton Cave.

In the afternoon the soldiers moved on, taking along 18 captives, most of them wounded. As the soldiers marched away they carried the solemn knowledge that they had passed through a pivotal episode in a war that had flickered meanly for more than 20 years. Brown and his men had proved that soldiers could find and kill Apaches in their deepest retreat. Now denied the cover of the mountains, the Indians gradually gave way under the grinding pressure of the Army campaign. Never again would the Apaches pose a serious threat to their white adversaries.

Far to the north, tough Phil Sheridan had already achieved considerable success with a tactic designed to destroy the warrior tribes on the Plains. Called the winter campaign, it was based upon the assumption that the Indians were most vulnerable when they were immobilized by the bitter weather and their ponies had grown thin and weak. The general decided to go out in winter, find their villages, kill as many as possible, burn their food and their shelter, kill their horses, then drive the survivors out onto the frozen Plains on foot. The strategy was to be aimed not only at the warriors, but also at women and children.

The man who first carried out Sheridan's directive was his favorite young officer, George Armstrong Custer. Custer's career up to that point had been meteoric but erratic. A West Point graduate, he had finished 34th in a class of 34, with a reputation for slovenliness and a record number of demerits. But he was a superb horseman with a commanding presence and a flair for the dramatic. Going immediately into the Civil War, Custer caught the eye of powerful officers, and in a single year made perhaps the most extraordinary series of leaps in rank in U.S. Army history. Between July 1862 and July 1863, he rocketed from first lieutenant to brigadier general. And in 1865, at age 25, Custer was commissioned a major general in command of one of Sheridan's cavalry divisions. After the Civil War, as was to be expected, Custer was reduced to captain. But within a year, he had scrambled back up to lieutenant colonel in the 7th Cavalry, not least because he had attracted the personal attention of President Andrew Johnson.

Custer became a popular hero of the Indian wars, yet by almost any rational definition, he was a fool and a bad commander. Most of his men disliked him, distrusted him and feared him—with good reason. He was personally undisciplined, but to those who served under him, he was a martinet. He cared little for his men's welfare on campaign, and could be murderous toward them when he felt he had been crossed. In 1867, he was court-martialed and convicted on seven counts for disobeying orders, ordering some deserters shot and then deserting his own command to visit his wife at Fort Riley, Kansas. He was sentenced to a year's suspension without pay. But Philip Sheridan, wielding his lieutenant general's rank to override the court, soon rescued Custer from even that lenient sentence by calling him back to the 7th for a winter campaign.

Burning with ambition, utterly ruthless, as heedless as always, Custer soon made his mark in a way that Sheridan approved—by annihilating a hapless band of Cheyennes in their encampment on the Washita River. As Custer's 7th Cavalry came out of the dawn, bugles blaring, the Indians poured from their lodges, some armed, many naked and simply running for the icy river, herding their women and children before them. It was over in just a few minutes. Custer reported that 105 Indians had been killed, and 53 women and children taken captive. The clear implication was that the Indian dead were warriors; in actuality, fewer than 40 warriors had been killed; most of the slain were women and children.

But the Indians gained one small measure of revenge. Since Custer had not bothered to reconnoiter, he did not know that the camp was only the first of several strung out along the Washita. And when a group of 20 cavalrymen set out in pursuit of some fleeing survivors, they were ambushed and cut down to a man. When the detachment failed to return, Custer ordered only a perfunctory search; his main concern was burning the Cheyenne lodges and all their belongings, and slaughtering their 600 ponies.

Then, driving his captives before him, he returned in triumph to his headquarters at a place called Camp Supply. Sheridan was elated, and Sherman, commander of the entire U.S. Army, wired congratulations.

The Cheyenne band was broken. Naked, starving, their shelter destroyed, the winter stretching before them, those who had survived the bullets and the cold eventually crept into the post to surrender. This was a pattern that was repeated again and again all over the Western Plains until the Indians' power was permanently eradicated. It took a decade of brutal warfare, and before the Indians went down there were a few battles in which the soldiers, not they, were trampled into the ground.

The greatest of the battles—and the climax of Custer's career—commenced on June 22, 1876, when the brass bugles of the 7th Cavalry rang out in the clear morning air at a point in eastern Montana where Rosebud Creek ran into Yellowstone River. In perfect columns of four, 600 mounted men wheeled, lined up and saluted a group of officers that included Alfred Terry, the commanding general.

At Terry's side was Lieutenant Colonel George Armstrong Custer, his flowing yellow hair newly trimmed, wearing buckskins, a white wide-brimmed hat and high boots. As the last notes of the trumpets died in the wilderness, the 7th moved out. The battle they were heading into would be one of the most dis-

In the words of one Army officer, troops and Indian scouts "pour in lead by the bucketful" on the Apaches crouching below in Skeleton Cave.

263

Soldiers on winter campaigns were allowed to purchase supplementary clothing against the cold but it is doubtful that this undergarment lived up to the sweeping claims made for it in the Army & Navy Journal.

cussed, pondered and analyzed in all of U.S. history.

Setting a brutal pace aboard his sorrel gelding, Custer rode for the valley of the Little Bighorn River. The 7th Cavalry made 12 miles up the valley of Rosebud Creek that first day, then stopped for the night in some of the last rich pasture they would find for their horses. The men unsaddled, rubbed their horses down and started small cookfires. At dusk, the officers gathered at Custer's tent. They found their commander in a strange mood, nervous, tense, irritable. The officers understood that Custer was under unusual pressure, and one of them remarked after hearing him discuss the forthcoming campaign, "I believe General Custer is going to be killed, because I have never heard Custer talk in that way before."

What his officers were observing was a man grown half-mad with desire. Ahead of him, George Armstrong Custer envisioned a glory such as his soul had screamed for ever since his days as the dashing "Boy General" of the Civil War. There had been a flicker of fame with his devastation of the Cheyennes on the Washita. But that had been eight long years before. It was time to renew the glow. And Custer's mentor, General Philip Sheridan, was providing the golden opportunity.

The situation had started to develop in the previous year when Sheridan decided to complete his destruction of the Northern Plains Indians—primarily the Sioux, most numerous and warlike of the tribes. Many of the Sioux had been infuriated when hordes of miners and settlers invaded their reservation in the Black Hills. As a result, Indians now clustered in great numbers, ever more warlike, in eastern Montana and Wyoming, where the plains became mountains.

Sheridan's plans were simple. General George Crook would lead a column north to Montana from Fort Fetterman, in Wyoming. Colonel John Gibbon, who had led the

ATTENTION BATTALION!

DRAWERS, $8.

SHIRTS, $8.

Attention to Orders!

GENERAL ORDERS, No. —. I. The commander-in-chief having discovered the wonderful properties contained in the PERFORATED BUCKSKIN UNDERMENTS, patented by Colonel Hamilton E. Smith, as a cure and preventive of Rheumatism, besides being the greatest preserver of health ever presented to the Army, recommends their use to his subordinate officers and men for the following reasons:
They are indispensable to all suffering from colds,
They will prevent sudden cold;
They will positively cure Rheumatism;
They are indispensable whenever and wherever the wearer is exposed to the inclemency of the weather;
They keep the body in a uniform degree of heat;
They are patented and warranted;
They received the first premium and medal at the American Institute Fair of 1869;
They are recommended by the Medical fraternity.
II. With such an array of evidence in regard to the sterling qualities these garments possess, their use is generally recommended, and it is hoped the Army will adopt them whenever possible.
By order of ———
Manufactured and sold by
ANDRUS BROS. & ADAMS,
AMERICAN EXPRESS BUILDING,
55 to 61 HUDSON ST., New York.

famous Iron Brigade and later been a corps commander in the Civil War, would bring a column east from Fort Ellis, in Montana. And a column led by Custer would drive westward from Fort Abraham Lincoln in Dakota Territory. The Indians would be caught by one column or another, and their power would be permanently broken, for Sheridan believed that any one of his columns could crush any conceivable Indian resistance.

As planned, Gibbon came from the west, and Custer, with General Terry, from the east. When they met on the Yellowstone River, Terry took control of both columns. There was no liaison with Crook, who was supposed to be working his way north from Wyoming, nor was there any serious attempt to determine the Indians' numbers; instead, the Terry-Custer column scouted the rivers it crossed as it moved toward the rendezvous. On June 14 a 7th Cavalry scouting party led by Major Marcus A. Reno found a heavy trail going up Rosebud Creek, between the Tongue and Bighorn rivers.

What no one in the Army knew was that the Indians would fight with a force they had never mustered before and would never muster again. Camped on the Little Bighorn (a tributary of the Bighorn) was one of the greatest concentrations of Indians ever gathered on the North American continent. They may have numbered as many as 12,000, with perhaps 2,500 warriors. Even more important, many of them were going to fight not in their usual individual fashion, but as a striking force of cavalry. The soldiers of Terry's columns were unaware that the Indians had already engaged Crook on the upper Rosebud and had sent him reeling back into Wyoming.

Ignorant of everything except the Indians' approximate location, which had been deduced from Reno's scouting report, Terry divided his forces. Custer would take the 7th up the Rosebud along the trail Reno had found, then turn westward and cross over the divide to the valley of the Little Bighorn. Terry and Gibbon would go up the Yellowstone to the Bighorn, and up that river to the Little Bighorn. There the Gibbon and Custer columns would be in a position to trap the Indians between them.

Everyone agreed that the Indians' best chance of escape was to head south to the Big Horn Mountains, where they could split into small groups and be difficult to pin down. Custer was not to rush to the attack, but was to block their escape route. Terry's instructions were clear, but they were issued to an officer who was often insubordinate, whose ego was immense and who believed that success always lay in striking hard and immediately.

The regiment was marching by 5:00 on the morning of June 23, and Custer set his usual awful pace. As the sun climbed high, the air dried and the heat grew intense. The soldiers passed one deserted campsite after another. They came to an enormous camp circle where a framework of lodgepoles still in place showed that a great sun dance had been held. Custer had no way of knowing it, but at this point three weeks earlier Sioux Chief Sitting Bull had had a vision of soldiers falling into his camp, signifying that they would attack and be killed.

At first the pony droppings had been dry, but as the command moved along, the droppings became fresher. The men began to notice the remains of fires so recent that ashes still flew in the wind, and roasted buffalo ribs, though gnawed clean, had not yet dried.

With their strung-out horses laboring along the ever-freshening trail, the troopers went more than 30 miles over hard terrain on June 23. The next day they continued about 28 miles before they stopped at sundown on the upper reaches of Rosebud Creek. Custer sent three of his Crow Indian scouts ahead to follow the Indian trail. At about 9 p.m. they returned: As expected, the trail had turned westward to cross the divide between the Rosebud and the valley of the Little Bighorn.

The trail spread more than a half-mile wide in places, leaving the ground broken as by a cattle drive. Since the scouts had spent their lives tracking animals and men, they knew that there was more than one trail here, and that it must involve several tribes of Sioux as well as some Northern Cheyennes. They felt certain that there would be more of the enemy up ahead than anyone had ever seen together at one time. On the first night out the half-breed scout Mitch Bouyer, who had roamed the country for 30 years, asked a young officer if he had ever fought the Sioux. When the officer confidently answered that the 7th could handle them, Bouyer said, "Well, I can tell you we are going to have a damned big fight." Custer's favorite scout, Bloody Knife, grimly warned the cavalry commander that there were more Sioux ahead than there were bullets in the belts of the soldiers.

Custer rejected the scout's warning; he was supremely confident of the 7th's capacity to defeat any Indians it met. The greater the number, the greater would be the scope and fame of his victory.

He instructed his troops to prepare to march at 11 p.m., thereby clearly disobeying the orders that he had received: Terry had told him to swing well to the south, then double back to prevent any possibility of an Indian escape. Instead, Custer had pushed his command at such a brutal pace that he was far beyond the point Terry would have expected him to reach. Now he prepared to attack immediately on his own. Waiting for Terry and Gibbon to come up would have meant sharing the victory. Continuing south as instructed would have risked a meeting with Crook's column, which Custer wrongly supposed was still heading north—and that would have reduced Custer to a subordinate again and made the victory Crook's.

Custer had made his decision. He started the exhausted men and their exhausted horses on a night march of 10 miles up the divide between the Rosebud and the Little Bighorn. At 2 a.m. the column reached a deep wooded ravine. Some of the men unsaddled and rubbed their horses' lathered backs with dry grass and dust, but many merely wrapped their horses' reins around their arms and fell to the ground to sleep. Then, six hours later, the troops took up the march again. After 10 more grueling miles, they stopped in another wooded ravine, just below the crest of the divide.

During the previous night Custer had sent Lieutenant Charles Varnum and a party of scouts ahead to a knob later called the Crow's Nest, perched high on the divide. From that lookout, as the dawn broke, they

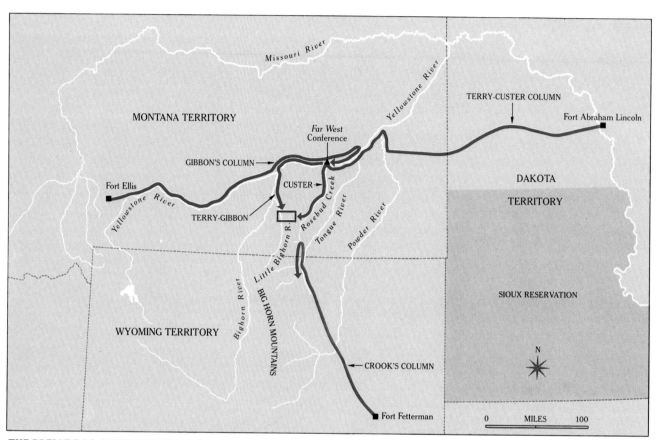

THE PRELUDE TO CATASTROPHE was General Philip Sheridan's three-pronged offensive against the Sioux. In 1876, Sheridan sent separate columns converging on Indians in the Powder River region. One column was led by General George Crook, one by Colonel John Gibbon, and one by General Alfred Terry, whose lieutenant colonel was George Custer. An Indian force turned Crook back on Rosebud Creek. Meanwhile, aboard the steamer *Far West,* Terry formed a plan to join Gibbon's column and move south to a Sioux camp on the Little Bighorn. To block the Indians' escape route Custer was told to ride to the Rosebud headwaters, then north; instead, he followed an Indian trail leading toward the Little Bighorn and the battleground shown opposite.

could see the valley of the Little Bighorn about 15 miles away. What they saw astonished them: On the eastern side, from which the scouts were looking, the river cut against steep bluffs 80 to 100 feet high. On the western side lay a flat plain, in some places as much as two miles wide. In the growing light, the scouts began to sense that the hills beyond the flat, about 20 miles from where they watched, looked wrong somehow. Then they realized that they were looking at horses, 20,000 or more of them, covering the hills like a brownish carpet in the distance.

A message was sent to Custer, and he rode forward to the observation point. The sun was climbing and the day promised to be scorching by the time he arrived, but even with glasses he could not make out the horses that the scouts had seen in the clarity of early morning with the sun at their backs. The scout Mitch Bouyer told him that the camp here was the biggest village he had ever encountered in his three decades among these Indians. But Custer did not care how big the village was. The night before, he had told several officers: "The largest Indian camp on the North American continent is ahead and I am going to attack it." Custer was famous for his luck. He relied on it. He evidently considered the presence of so many Indians the greatest luck of all.

Custer returned to his regiment. Varnum remained behind, and from his post he saw a group of Indians moving downstream. Assuming that the Indians were starting to escape, he sent a runner galloping after Custer. In fact,

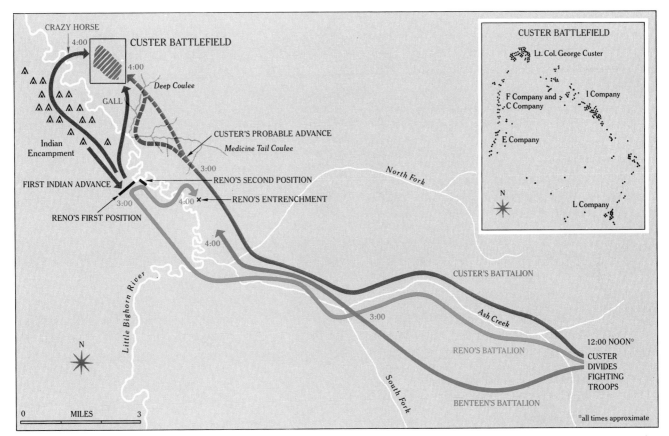

THE FATAL DECISION that precipitated disaster was Custer's order to divide his force. Having found the Sioux encampment, he sent one battalion, under Captain Frederick Benteen, to scout the hills to the west. Another, under Major Marcus Reno, was dispatched to the southern end of the encampment, while Custer himself rode on to attack from the north. Reno was soon turned from his first position in the valley, and retreated to a second. Finally he fled across the Little Bighorn to a bluff, to be joined by Benteen, who had come back after finding no Indians. As for Custer, he headed into Medicine Tail Coulee. He and his five companies were then forced up some hills away from the river, and there annihilated. The inset shows the positions in which they fell.

the Indians had sighted the soldiers and were hurrying toward their camp.

The cavalry commander immediately set his regiment in motion toward the valley of the Little Bighorn. The encampment lay on the far side of the river, which ran between banks from five to ten feet high in places. Three fords were available to Custer: One lay upstream, in the direction from which the cavalry was coming; one was near the center of the Indian camp, and the other lay farther downstream.

Custer decided to split his force. He assigned three companies of about 125 men to Captain Frederick W. Benteen, the regiment's senior captain with the brevet rank of colonel, and told him to sweep the bluffs well south of the valley, scouring them thoroughly for

Indians. Then he assigned three more companies to Major Marcus A. Reno, instructing him to cross the river and charge upon the southern end of the camp. Custer, with a five-company main force of 215 men, would support him. Reno supposed that Custer would be riding behind him, to follow up the initial collision with the great Indian community that lay ahead. But instead of trailing Reno across the ford, Custer remained on the other side of the river, and rode downstream, parallel to the Little Bighorn.

Clearly, Custer's mind was focused more on preventing the Indians' escape than on the strategy of fighting them. Reno rode on. His total force amounted to 134 officers and men and 16 scouts. He took his three companies to the ford at a trot. They halted, the horses

267

One of the most accurate reconstructions of Custer's Last Stand at the Battle of Little Bighorn on June 25, 1876, Edgar Paxson's

1899 canvas was painted after 20 years' research. Custer wields a saber at center, left.

Named a brevet general at 23 during the Civil War, George Armstrong Custer felt by 1876 that the magic of his "boy general" reputation was fading. He died at 37 while trying to recoup with a spectacular victory over the Sioux.

drank briefly, then they crossed the 25 to 30 feet of belly-deep water and re-formed on the other side.

Reno galloped down the valley toward the village three miles away. Warriors came out of the village afoot and on horseback to meet the threat and then fell back toward the village so fast that Reno suspected a trap. Ahead Reno saw—or thought he saw—a shallow ravine from which hundreds of warriors swarmed against him. Suddenly he ordered his men to halt and dismount. He instructed every fourth man to take four horses to a stand of timber near the river. The remaining men, about 80 in number, formed a skirmish line, its right end anchored in the timber.

Reno had now shifted from the offense to the defense. The mounted Indians soon swept around his flank and had him in a deadly crossfire. He began to order the men to retreat to the woods, and some who had received no orders began to yield to pressure.

The Indians set fire to dry river-bottom grass and buffalo-berry brush, and the flames spread through the undergrowth. Reno peered upriver, searching for Custer's promised support, but Custer was miles away on the other side of the Little Bighorn. As more and more Indians surrounded Reno's little force, he ordered a move to the far side of the river.

Reno galloped for more than a mile parallel to the river and away from the village, making for a high bluff on the far side. As the cavalrymen struggled to cross the river, many horses toppled backward in the water. Meanwhile, Indians were coming along the bluffs and shooting down the soldiers as they scrambled up from the stream.

The fight in the timber and the flight across the river had cost Reno a third of his men. The survivors straggled to the top of the highest bluff and lay there, exhausted, demoralized and awaiting another onslaught. But as they stationed themselves to meet the next attack, they could see that the Indians were leaving, galloping toward the center of the encampment.

No one knows exactly what happened to Custer. Soldiers studied the evidence of the battlefield afterward, and over the years the Indians gave their conflicting accounts. According to the most generally accepted theory, Custer led his men down the river to Medicine Tail Coulee. His next move, then, would have been toward the central ford on the Little Bighorn. The Indian camp—huge beyond any expectation—lay directly across the river.

There may have been a thousand warriors facing Custer's 200 men. They were led by Crazy Horse, one of the few great battle leaders among Indians. Custer and his men moved to high ground in good order. Crazy Horse crossed the river at the lower ford, and moved to meet them head on. In the meantime, the Sioux chief Gall, leading the attack on Reno, heard the firing and galloped downstream with hundreds of warriors. Crossing the center ford, Gall's men hurled themselves at Custer's rear.

Custer dismounted L Company, commanded by his brother-in-law, and I company. The men moved backward step by step, firing as they went, covering the rear. Like hammers, Crazy Horse's men crashed into Custer and his three forward companies. In the rear, Gall's warriors dismounted and crawled close to L Company, picking the men off one by one, mostly with bows and arrows. A warrior thus armed could hug the ground and shoot without sound or smoke to reveal his position. He would fire up into the air, the arrow arching high on its trajectory and falling to strike a soldier in the back with appalling effect. Many a soldier died that way, and in death lay face down, an arrow rigid and upright in his back.

Coming closer, Gall's men stormed over L Company. No soldiers broke; they fought and died in place. And the Indians moved on I Company.

Up above, Custer organized his defense. The men worked their carbines amid the sweat, smoke and fear, until the weapons fouled, and then they fired their pistols. They were brave men, and the Indians knew it. A year later, Sitting Bull would say, "I tell no lies about dead men. These men who came with 'Long Hair' were as good men as ever fought."

Down below, Gall's men rolled over I Company as they had over L. Crazy Horse, his warriors behind him like a tide, swarmed over Custer and his men, cutting them to the ground. A handful of white men ran downhill, but the Indians galloped behind them and killed them. And then it was over. Custer and the soldiers—to a man—were dead. The ground suddenly became quiet, and the Indians, as they said later, were as surprised as men are when a tornado passes and leaves quiet behind its awful roar.

The Battle of the Little Bighorn was the U.S. Army's worst defeat during the Indian wars. The question as to what had gone wrong reverberated throughout the nation. Custer idolaters charged Reno with "gross cowardice" and blamed him for the catastrophe. Reno demanded an Army court of inquiry. The court convened in Chicago and heard evidence for 26 days, filling 1,300 pages with testimony. Reno was exonerated, but he was haunted by the accusations for the rest of his life. And Americans never stopped being haunted by the notion that with Custer's death they had been cheated in the loss of a hero.

But if the Little Bighorn was a calamity for the country and the Army, it also sealed the fate of the Indians. From then on, there was no way whatsoever for men of good will to bridge the gaps that separated Indians and white men. After the deaths of Custer and his soldiers, the national mood hardened; in Washington and in the field, government officials and military leaders addressed themselves to the task of crushing Indian resistance once and for all. Companies of cavalry were expanded from 64 to 100 men each, and recruits hurried to join up as "Custer Avengers." That winter, soldiers dressed themselves in warm buffalo coats and swept across Sioux lands without mercy; columns slashed into Indian camps from all sides. The Sioux ammunition was exhausted and no replacements were to be had. The warriors were slain, the villages destroyed, the food supplies burned, the women and children left homeless in terrible cold. Though fighting flared periodically for 15 years, there was never again a real war, nor a battle on the scale of the Little Bighorn.

Custer's death marked the end of an era. New railroad lines continued to thrust through the West, towns and cities mushroomed, and settlers filled the land. And as the country changed, the role of the frontier soldier changed, too, but as always, many of the hardest and most dangerous jobs were his.

Soldiers still lived in drafty barracks on tiny faraway posts, unwelcome in many towns and invariably frozen out of the town's pleasures by its prices. They still responded to Indian alarms, but now they also faced white desperadoes who struck isolated towns or stopped and robbed trains, then rode into the deep reaches of the badlands that dotted the West. The bright notes of "Boots and Saddles" still rang out in the posts and the soldiers still mounted and moved out within the hour, a few days' ration of 'tack and bacon and coffee in their saddlebags, dust rising from their horses' hoofs, hoping that the water hole ahead held water, fearing that the turn concealed a rifleman.

Skillful *vaqueros* drive a herd of longhorns in a trail scene painted in the 1870s. Mexican riders for King and other Texas ranchers were

zealous guardians of their employers' cattle, and some *vaqueros* even went hungry during trail drives rather than butcher a single steer.

V. PUTTING THE OPEN SPACES TO WORK

11. An empire of longhorns and woollybacks

ometime during the mid-1850s, Lieutenant Colonel Robert E. Lee, the epitome of a Virginia gentleman, reportedly offered some words of wisdom to a rough-and-tumble young rancher named Richard King, with whom he had become friendly while on U.S. Army duty in Texas. "Buy land," Lee is supposed to have said, "and never sell." The precept was one that King followed to the end of his days—and in so doing he became the archetype of a new breed of businessmen on horseback who stamped an indelible brand on the West.

These were the ranchers who set up their spreads on rolling plains and watered uplands from Texas to Montana and from Kansas to California. Some built empires of land and livestock that gave them feudal powers at home and influence far beyond their domains. Others scrabbled for bare survival against the numbing isolation and relentless rigors of the hard land. Yet between them, big and small, baron and bitter-ender, they produced the beef and mutton Americans ate, the leather and woolen goods Americans wore, and the horses Americans rode.

It never was easy. The ranchers had to defend their lands and their livestock not only against Indians but also against rustlers, squatters and one another. They also had to cope with winters of killing cold, summers of wasting drought, and market prices that veered wildly out of control.

Yet somehow they persevered. In their heyday from 1866 to 1886, Western ranchers shipped more than 10 million cattle and one million sheep to market in the East. They created jobs for 40,000 cowboys and herders, founded communities inhabited by half a million people and kept another million busy in the East and Midwest processing and transporting meat products.

If any one ranch was a blueprint for success it was a legendary establishment in the south of Texas prairie between the Rio Grande and the Nueces rivers. It became the world's largest stock-raising operation and the only American ranch to develop a new breed of beef cattle, the cherry-red Santa Gertrudis. But above all else, it was the mirrored reflection of its extraordinary founder—none other than Richard King.

He stood nearly six feet tall, was broad-shouldered and heavily muscled, with piercing blue eyes and a big, determined jaw. He fought with his fists as well as his nimble mind, and he enjoyed both kinds of contests. Ferociously ambitious, he could still wait patiently for years to attain his goals; a risk-taking innovator, he was nonetheless as careful as a Boston banker. All in all, said a friend, "I never met a rougher man, nor a better one."

King had come far—the hard way. The son of poor Irish immigrants, he escaped New York City's slums as a boy of 11 by stowing away on a ship bound for the Gulf of Mexico. During a brawling career in Southern waters and on Texas docks, he earned his pilot's license, the title of captain and enough money to go into the riverboat business with a friend named Mifflin Kenedy. King and Kenedy prospered by ferrying goods up and down the Rio Grande from Brownsville, the southernmost town in Texas.

Although already a success by most men's standards, King was restless and ready to take a stab at some risky enterprise that might make him a major capitalist before he turned gray. And so, on a spring day in 1852, the 27-year-old riverman mounted a horse—awkwardly, since he rode very little—and set out with friends on a 170-mile trip from Brownsville to Corpus Christi, which was promoting a fair to attract businessmen to the area. About 45 miles short of their

Square-jawed Richard King (*seated*) and his partner Mifflin Kenedy, photographed in Brownsville during the 1850s, were both successful riverboat captains before they pioneered Texas cattle ranching.

Midday dinner is a bountiful spread of home-grown beef and corn for the William Parmenter family of Colorado in 1889. But their faces betray the toil of providing it. Eating well was important, for the ranch workday began at sunup, continued until sundown and included chores for everyone.

277

destination, King's group paused to drink the clear, cool water of Santa Gertrudis Creek. There, King looked beyond the live oaks and anaqua trees that shaded the stream and saw the prairie rich with waist-high grass and splashed with red, blue and gold wild flowers. The place seemed a rancher's paradise.

At Corpus Christi, King ran into a friend named Gideon Lewis, a Texas militiaman who knew the Santa Gertrudis area and was enthusiastic about its possibilities. A curious partnership evolved: King would finance and set up a cattle camp on Santa Gertrudis Creek; then, while King continued his profitable riverboating, Lewis and his militia would guard and supervise the fledgling ranch. But hardly had the enterprise begun than Lewis, a dedicated womanizer, was shot to death by the husband of his latest paramour. King then took on two new partners: Mifflin Kenedy, his riverboat associate, and James Walworth, a steamer captain.

Although it was customary for ranchers simply to occupy and use vacant lands (an informal practice that would later cost many of them a pretty penny in lawsuits), King went to the trouble of seeking out the heirs to an original Spanish grant on the Santa Gertrudis and purchasing their 15,500 acres for $300. A little later, he paid $1,800 for 53,000 adjoining acres of prime grassland.

Early in his ranching career, King hit upon a novel way of staffing his spread. During a purchasing trip south of the Mexican border, he bought all the livestock available in a drought-stricken village below the town of Camargo. Then, realizing that the villagers were left without a business to sustain them, he made them an offer: If they would come to work on the King Ranch, they could build homes of their own.

And so they came, more than 100 men, women and children in a long, noisy caravan, riding rickety two-wheeled *carretas* and pushing wheelbarrows that bore all their worldly goods. They found King to be firm and demanding but—unlike the typical *patrones* they had known before—always fair and even kindly. They gave him their unqualified loyalty and became the nucleus of *Los Kineños*—the King People.

The contentment of *Los Kineños* was enhanced in December 1854, when King took as his bride Henrietta Chamberlain, the pretty daughter of a Presbyterian minister in Brownsville, whose spunk had kindled King's interest when she scolded him for his profane language. As mistress of the King Ranch, Henrietta looked after *Los Kineños*, tending their needs and nursing their sick, and the ranch people came to adore the woman they called *La Patrona*.

To King and others, the cattle business offered some irresistible enticements. Cattle being fecund, a herd normally doubled in size in three years, and up to 1,000 head could be tended by a single cowhand who earned perhaps $25 a month. Beyond that, mature longhorns valued in Texas at three dollars a head might bring $30 at distant cattle markets—but only when the day came that they could be delivered swiftly, cheaply and reliably.

That day was still years away. Beef could not be preserved well enough to ship to distant population centers, and driving live animals to markets 1,000 or more miles away along trails beset by Indians and outlaws was a shaky way of doing business.

But Richard King could wait, and while biding his time he could improve his herd. Although the Texas longhorn was a hardy, nimble beast that drank little water and was ideally suited to its surroundings, it produced less beef than low-slung Eastern breeds of English origin. On the other hand, the Eastern cattle had trouble traveling on rugged ground, and were more vulnerable to disease, drought, insects and heat. To combine the longhorn's toughness with the meatiness of Eastern breeds, King began importing blooded Durhams to cross with his best native stock. Slowly but steadily, his breeding experiments improved the quality of his stock.

During the Civil War, in which King served the South by transporting cotton on his steamboats, most Texas cowboys went off to fight Yankees. They left behind them thousands of young bulls that would ordinarily have been castrated. They bred at a fearful rate, and at war's end the state was drowning in cattle—six million animals with no place to go.

The Texas ranchers were saved, however, by the coming of the railroads, most notably the Atchison, Topeka and Santa Fe, which in 1868 swung south from St. Louis and passed through a succession of prairie hamlets in southern Kansas. These ramshackle waystops, especially Abilene and Dodge City, immediately became trail's-end for immense cattle drives. In 1875, Richard King, who had by then bought out his partners, shipped no fewer than 60,000 head to Kansas markets.

A portrait of Richard King, together with a drawing of Texas longhorns bearing the Running W brand of the King Ranch, graces the letterhead used by King's wife, Henrietta, after his death.

He might have sold even more had it not been for an onslaught of rustlers who stole more than a million dollars worth of his stock before they were squelched in 1875. They were mostly Mexican outlaws operating from hideouts south of the Rio Grande, and some of their raids against the hated Texans turned into orgies of bloodletting. According to one federal report, "Old and young were subjected to every form of torture, dragged at the hooves of horses, burned and flayed alive, shot to death or cut to pieces with knives."

Of his frequent business trips to Brownsville, King later recalled, "I had to travel fast. My life depended on it." In his usual careful way, he posted expert riflemen at small relay stations, built at 20-mile intervals along the 125-mile route and stocked with fresh horses. For each trip King concealed his funds—sometimes as much as $50,000 for payrolls and purchasing land—in a steel safe built into his stagecoach; he rode inside with a shotgun at the ready and was escorted by half a dozen armed riders.

Helpless against the thieves, many of King's neighbors abandoned their ranches and moved to nearby towns. But King grimly held on, defying the outlaws, who had vowed to hang him. In February 1875, a large force of Mexicans attacked his ranch, killed several hands and stole a large herd of horses. Next month, *Los Kineños* beat off a determined siege. At about the same time, 50 brigands swooped down on a village 12 miles from Corpus Christi, killing one man, hanging another, and stripping and torturing several prisoners.

Finally, the state government took action by reestablishing the Texas Rangers, disbanded since 1860 because of certain high-handed activities. The Rangers killed bandits, and displayed their bodies in Brownsville's market square as warning to their Mexican comrades; the Texans even invaded Mexico to recover stolen cattle. Such activities soon had a pacifying effect, and by the end of 1875 most of the rustlers had found safer ways to make a living.

With the rustler troubles behind him and with the

cattle market now booming, King during the next several years built up his ranch into a 600,000-acre empire worth, by his estimate, about $6.5 million. Yet for all his affluence, and despite his advancing age, Richard King remained Richard King, swapping rough jokes with his cowboys, keeping a jug of Rose Bud whiskey close at hand and, when it seemed advisable, using his fists to make a point. One day a big ranch hand named Kelley objected to a reprimand from King. "If you were not such a rich man and a captain," he declared, "you wouldn't cuss me as you do." Replied King: "Damn you, forget the riches and the captain title and let's fight!"

Fight they did, as the story goes, for half an hour, wrestling on the bloody floor of a ranch slaughterhouse. Then, exhausted, they shook hands in mutual admiration and walked away.

Sometime in 1882, at age 57, King began suffering from a stabbing pain in his gut—it turned out to be stomach cancer. King patiently started to set his affairs in order, designating as his successor a son-in-law, Robert J. Kleberg. Not until early 1885 could King finally be persuaded to place himself under the care of a San Antonio doctor. As he left his beloved ranch, King issued instructions for one of his managers about a matter involving some nearby land. "Tell him to keep on buying," the ailing rancher advised.

Never again would Richard King see the clear waters of the Santa Gertrudis.

Far different from Richard King and other Texas ranchers, who had launched their careers by acquiring immense tracts of land, were the early cattlemen of the Northern Plains. There, in the mid-19th Century, a few individuals known as road ranchers had realized that there was business to be done with the rising stream of families heading west along the pioneer trails. By the time the wagon trains reached the North Platte and Green rivers, the travelers were desperately short of almost every necessity.

Their needs were provided for by the road ranchers, whose facilities frequently consisted of little more than a wagonload of trading goods and a small corral for cattle and horses. Many a family cow, unfit for the hardships of the trail, never made it to the West Coast but instead was turned in at a road ranch for a sack of flour. Often a road rancher would trade a healthy steer

from his own stock for two exhausted ones from the trail, which he would then fatten up and trade again.

For those shoestring ranchers, opportunity rose sharply in the early 1860s, when a succession of gold strikes brought thousands of miners to the Montana hills. Yet even as they increased their herds to meet the soaring demand, their lives remained bleak. Almost as hot as Texas in the summer, the Plains in winter were fiercely cold. As protection against the elements, most ranchers lived in one-room shacks whose leaky roofs often required the occupants to wear hats and boots even while indoors during the rainy season; in winter, driving sleet and snow penetrated the chinks in log walls.

Many cattle could not endure the frozen winters and died when vicious storms pounded out of the north, driving them across unprotected range and covering their forage with layers of impacted snow. Their numbers were further reduced by predators of various kinds. Timber wolves ravaged the calves; Indians augmented their dwindling supply of buffalo meat by plundering the ranchers' stock. An even more serious threat to property was the renegade white man who built illegitimate herds by rustling cattle and blurring the brands.

Singular among the men who fought the odds to establish themselves in Northern ranching was Danish-born Conrad Kohrs, whose dappled background included youthful stints as a cabin boy, sausage salesman, grocery clerk, river raftsman and apprentice butcher. Arriving in Montana's Deer Lodge Valley in 1862, Kohrs originally planned to pan for gold but quickly decided that providing beef to the miners was a surer, if slower, way to wealth. After starting as a butcher in the mushrooming town of Bannack, Kohrs soon set up shops in Helena and in the Alder Gulch district around Virginia City, and then began acting as a wholesaler for other butchers.

Kohrs rode hundreds of miles a month between widely separated road ranches looking for cattle to buy. By 1868, he was affluent enough to install his bride in a house described by a Virginia City newspaper as "by long odds, the finest in Montana." In truth, that said very little. "There were no carpets," Kohrs later admitted. "We had an old homemade bed; strings of rawhide stretched across in place of springs, a straw tick for a mattress."

Brands of Conrad Kohrs' Pioneer Cattle Company are illustrated in the *Montana Brand Book*. Kohrs retained the D-S brand of the firm's former owners, and added brands with his initials, numerals and a frying-pan symbol.

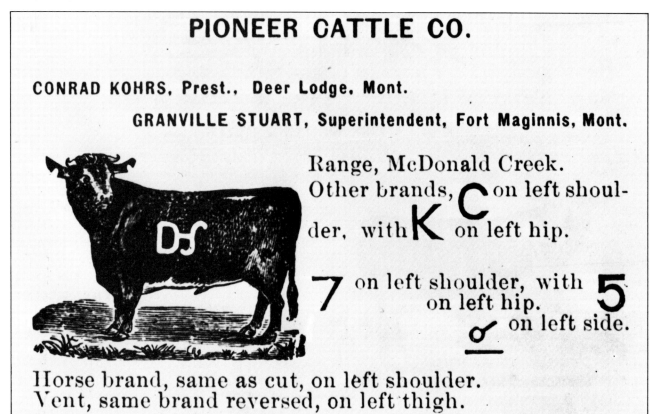

PIONEER CATTLE CO.

CONRAD KOHRS, Prest., Deer Lodge, Mont.

GRANVILLE STUART, Superintendent, Fort Maginnis, Mont.

Range, McDonald Creek. Other brands, C on left shoulder, with K on left hip.

7 on left shoulder, with 5 on left hip.

σ on left side.

Horse brand, same as cut, on left shoulder.
Vent, same brand reversed, on left thigh.

Even though Kohrs was by then recognized as one of the region's top livestock men, his herd was tiny by Texas standards. That situation began to change, however, with the arrival of a man named Nelson Story and the first large herd of longhorns from the Southwest.

As an Ohio-born prospector in Montana, Story had noted the trouble Kohrs and others were having in finding enough meat to supply the expanding market. Story realized that if he could somehow get cheap Texas beef to Montana he could make a financial killing. It so happened that Story had hit a small bonanza, taking $30,000 worth of gold out of Alder Gulch, and in the spring of 1866, while in Dallas, he used part of his grubstake to buy 600 longhorns at $10 apiece. Six months later, Story's herd reached Virginia City after an epoch-setting drive of 1,500 miles.

Although it took several more years for other Texas cowmen to follow Story's example in significant numbers, they eventually flooded the trails with their herds. The cattle business boomed, and by 1883 an estimated 600,000 cattle were grazing on the open ranges of Montana and of Wyoming to the south.

In that year, Kohrs acquired as a partner a complex, contradictory man named Granville Stuart. A self-taught scholar who loved books more than anything in life (he collected a personal library of 3,000 volumes), Stuart nonetheless chose an unlettered Indian woman for his wife and lived for years in isolated valleys where books were rarer than gold. He was also a peaceful man with a profound respect for the law, yet when he deemed it necessary he would grasp the law in his own hands and become the incarnation of Death on Horseback.

From the beginning, the Kohrs-Stuart combine flourished. Yet success in the West seldom was undiluted, and in this case it attracted large bands of rustlers. In the spring of 1884, after thieves had twice raided his ranch, Granville Stuart convened a secret meeting of 14 stockmen who also had suffered losses. As a result of that session, the rustlers were in for some unpleasant surprises.

Late in June, a ranch owner named William Thompson came upon two armed men, Narciss Lavardure and Joe Vardner, who had in tow seven horses that Thomp-

In his career as a pioneer cattleman in Montana, Granville Stuart fought Indians, hanged rustlers, started a school, collected 3,000 books and wrote some himself.

son recognized as belonging to a neighbor. When the outlaws tried to flee, Thompson shot Vardner dead and captured Lavardure, who was placed in a stable under guard. At 2 o'clock in the morning, the guard was "overpowered" by a group of armed cowmen. Lavardure was dragged from the stable, lynched, and left to twist in the wind with a rudely lettered sign on his coat that said, "Horse Thief."

During the next few weeks, numerous other corpses, similarly adorned, were found dangling at the end of nooses, and word got around that "Stuart's Stranglers" were bad men to steal from. The climax of the campaign came at Bates Point, 15 miles below the junction of the Missouri and Musselshell rivers. There, early on the morning of July 8, Stuart and nine vigilantes deployed around a tumbledown shack in which John Stringer, a notorious outlaw known as "Stringer Jack," was holed up with 11 other rustlers. When several of the thieves tried to shoot their way out, Stringer Jack was cut down but five others escaped. As for the men who remained inside the cabin, they were either shot to death or perished in a fire ignited by the vigilantes.

Later, the gang's five survivors were arrested by soldiers at a government post 200 miles eastward on the Missouri. A deputy U.S. marshal was sent to bring the prisoners back to Montana, but he returned empty-handed. Along the way, he said, he had been intercepted by armed cowboys who relieved him of his charges. A makeshift gallows was rigged by placing a log across

the roofs of two cabins that stood close together, and Stuart's Stranglers strung up their last victims.

No law-abiding citizen could argue with the results of Stuart's effort, but there were plenty who could—and did—criticize his methods. "There was a lot of bitterness in the country against Granville Stuart after the raids," wrote one of Stuart's cowhands. "But he never denied anything, nor did he tell who was with him. Once I heard a woman accuse him of hanging thirty innocent men. He raised his hat to her and said: 'Yes, madam, and by God I done it alone.'"

Although Stuart's cleanup ended horse and cattle stealing in Montana for many years, catastrophe was approaching on a scale that would dwarf the work of the thieves.

In 1886, hardly a drop of rain fell during the spring, and none at all in the summer. By July the ranges were parched and hot winds shriveled the stunted grass. Cattle became lean, then gaunt, as they foraged for tufts. Then, as autumn came, there were ominous portents of a hard winter. Wildfowl and songbirds started south early. Muskrats built their lodges twice as large and thick as usual and their hair grew long and heavy.

True to its harbingers, the winter of 1886-87 came to be called The Great Die-Up, with relentless blizzards and unusually bitter cold from Montana and the Dakotas to Texas. Cattle rubbed their noses blood-raw in futile efforts to break through the ice and crusted snow to the dead grass beneath. On January 9, a 10-day blow began; 16 inches of snow fell on Montana in as many hours. Thermometers registered 46 degrees below zero.

Robust cattle might have survived such conditions, but the weakened, half-starved cattle of Montana never had a chance. When spring warmth finally melted the snow and ice, it uncovered the carcasses of thousands of dead animals. Among others, Con Kohrs and Granville Stuart lost two thirds of their stock.

The Great Die-Up accomplished what the rustlers had failed to do—it drove Granville Stuart out of the cattle industry. "A business that had been fascinating to me before suddenly became distasteful," he wrote. "I never wanted to own an animal again that I could not feed and shelter."

But the determined Conrad Kohrs stayed on, rebuilding his herds at a measured pace and purchasing land at a rate that eventually made him the holder of a million acres. Still, no matter how wealthy he became, he could never forget the long, hard road he had traveled. "I guess," he once said, "I've been broke oftener than any man in Montana."

There had, in fact, been a surer way to make money from livestock—although it was one that no self-respecting cattleman would have chosen. According to a time-worn adage, "Wherever the foot of sheep touches, the land turns to gold." By most standards, sheep were easier and cheaper to raise than cattle: They could adapt to rough terrain, subsist on forage too sparse for cows, and get along on a fraction of the water. They also required fewer handlers. It took seven mounted cowboys to move 1,000 head of cattle any distance, but a similar number of sheep could be tended easily by a single herder, on foot, with the help of a good dog.

Yet for the cattlemen who believed they held exclusive claim to the open range, sheep were a plague. Wherever too many were crowded together or held too long, sheep ate grass down to the roots, and trampled what was left. It became axiomatic among cowhands that "everything in front of a sheep is eaten, and everything behind is killed." Indeed, according to one Western writer, the feeling against the woollies was so pervasive in cattle country that if anyone ordered mutton in a restaurant "the very waiter girls had scorn in their voices when they called to the cook through the kitchen window for 'a plate of sheep.'"

Given such sentiments, it was perhaps inevitable that quarrels over grass and water rights should break out shortly after sheep in huge numbers began appearing on the High Plains in the 1870s; and it was equally unsurprising that those disputes soon escalated into violence of a particularly ugly nature.

The sheep had traveled far over a prolonged period of time. Christopher Columbus had bought some of the animals on his second voyage to the New World, landing with them on the island now called Hispaniola in 1493. Later, Spanish explorers and gold-seekers trailed them into the region that became the U.S. Southwest, and by the end of the Mexican War the region was flocked with the hardy little *churros* that Americans called "Mexican bare-bellies" for their scruffy, top-sided coats.

For Southwestern sheepmen, confronted by a glut that forced prices down to less than a dollar a head, the mid-19th Century gold strikes in northern California meant salvation in the form of hungry prospectors who were willing to pay up to $25 a head. Among those making the drive was the famed scout Kit Carson, who purchased 6,500 sheep in New Mexico in 1853 and drove them to Sacramento, where he sold them for a profit of $30,000—enough to enable him, for the first time in his life, to build a ranch of his own.

In the flood that followed, more than a million sheep were herded to California by the end of the Civil War. Busily devouring every blade of grass they could find, the animals were far more abundant than the West Coast could sustain, and sheepmen soon began seeking new grazing land in the vast plains that lay eastward beyond the Rockies. In 1880 alone, apparently almost 600,000 sheep crossed the mountains.

Upon arriving at their destinations, they found not the empty, unclaimed range they needed but a land already occupied by hundreds of thousands of cattle, with millions more moving in. As the range filled up, cattlemen and sheepmen rushed to beat each other to what was left of the grasslands and good water, and neither side was interested in accommodating the vital interests of the other.

Among the mounted knights of the Plains, the sheepherder was a lowly pedestrian, and a peculiar one at that. He generally spoke little English and came from other than Anglo-Saxon stock—perhaps Mexican or Indian or Basque. Or he might be a Mormon, which made him almost as much an alien.

Unlike the cowboy, who took an extravagant pride in flaunting his wide-brimmed hat, decorated chaps and tooled-leather saddle, the sheepherder rarely worried about finery. After all, for long periods of time he had nowhere to go and no one to get dressed up for. One sheepman, Robert Maudslay, said his shoes were "run down so much on one side that the uppers were constantly threatening to become lowers, and the soles seemed always aspiring to become uppers on the opposite side." If his trousers suffered a rip, Maudslay repaired them with a mesquite thorn. "But there always came a time," he admitted, "when a patch became imperative, and this I would put on with a needle and thread. If the patch wore out, I would patch

Sodbusters in the heartland

Thousands upon thousands of emigrant wagons had traveled through the great central prairies and plains before pioneers thought of actually settling there. And, indeed, the vast region —stretching from the Missouri to the Rockies and from the Canadian border to the Texas Panhandle—abounded in reasons for pressing on. It was treeless, matted with dense sod in its eastern reaches, arid farther west, and everywhere possessed of a climate that ran to brutal extremes of hot and cold.

But after the Civil War, pioneers swarmed onto this desolate expanse —and they stayed. The conquest was spurred partly by the growing shortage of arable lands elsewhere and partly by a relentless stream of propaganda. Newly built railroads, eager for business, wooed settlers with promotional campaigns. They were joined in their hard-sell tactics by transatlantic steamship companies hoping to tap a huge pool of land-hungry foreigners.

The new land the settlers called home was essentially an ocean of grass with scarcely a tree to distract the eye. Though poor in almost every essential, including timber and sometimes water, the land was inexpensive and there were hundreds of acres of it. Even so, some homesteaders packed their families into wagons and hastened away soon after they arrived. In that would-be home, said one, "it rains grasshoppers, fire and destruction."

For those who stayed on, living in

On a homestead set in the immensity of western Kansas, pioneers present their Sunday best outside a house built of sod. In two

the prairies meant being resourceful and flexible as well as trusting in providence. The most pressing task at hand was providing shelter—at first often a dugout hollowed out of a prairie knoll. But as soon as possible, most pioneers managed to build a drier, sturdier, aboveground sod house.

The building material for this classic of prairie architecture lay all about in limitless quantity. Sod blocks were laid grass-side down, in staggered layers like brickwork. Two rows were gener-ally placed side by side, resulting in walls as much as three feet thick. When equipped with windows and doors these houses could almost be considered cozy. Outside the home, however, there were fearsome threats that could bring an end to many a homesteader's dream—droughts, blizzards, prairie fires and the dreaded Indians.

The most terrible scourges of all were swarms of locusts. Nothing escaped their appetite, from crops and prairie grass to leather boots and harness straps. The insects blanketed the ground in a writhing layer as much as six inches deep; the combined weight of their bodies could snap the limbs off cottonwood trees.

But despite the awesome obstacles most settlers held on to the prairie as stubbornly as the matted grass beneath their feet. This bleak country would remain their home and slowly, inexorably, they transformed it into some of the most productive farmland the world has ever known.

decades after the Civil War, more new U.S. terrain was brought under cultivation than in the previous two and a half centuries.

A Nebraska couple's cornfield covers every arable inch of land and almost engulfs their sod house. With the corn-hog ratio profitably figured at one bushel of feed to 12 pounds of pig, Nebraskans needed no urging when a state agriculturist wrote in 1876: "We cannot raise too much corn."

the patch, and if that wore out I would even sometimes patch the patched patch. But I never allowed myself to go further than this."

One of the sheepherder's worst enemies was the utter loneliness by which he was afflicted for weeks and months at a time. "The wonder," said an old Dakota herder, "is not that some are supposed to go crazy, but that any of them stay sane."

To combat their solitude, many herders read voraciously—Shakespeare, dog-eared novels, back issues of the *London Illustrated News*. More than one immigrant herder taught himself to read English with the help of a Sears Roebuck catalog. For lack of anything better to read, another sheepman took a copy of *Webster's* dictionary to camp with him. He found it so fascinating that he pored over every word from cover to cover, then started again at *A*.

Some of the herders' most exasperating problems arose from the nature of the dim-witted, defenseless animals they tended. If sheep were missing when the flock returned to bed-ground in late afternoon, the strays had to be found before nightfall. A missing animal was almost always dead or in deep trouble, and trouble came in many forms. A sheep might wade into a bog and just stand there mute, stoically awaiting rescue or death, whichever came first. Merely wading in a stream or pond, a heavily fleeced sheep could become too waterlogged to climb out. Bloat, caused by gorging on the first green foliage, could immobilize an animal and make it easy prey for wolves or coyotes. (A seasoned herder knew exactly where to stick the point of his knife to safely deflate the sheep's stomach.)

While a sheepman gradually learned the limitations of his charges, his dogs apparently knew about them all along. Most sheep dogs belonged to breeds in which the herding instinct was deeply ingrained—they were descendants of collie-sized Australian shepherds or of smaller black-and-white Border collies originally imported from Scotland and Australia. For such animals, obedience to the herder and loyalty to the flock were absolutes; carefree diversions such as chasing rabbits were sternly discouraged; barking was permitted only when essential to warn of danger or discipline recalcitrant members of the flock. Few sheep dogs needed to be punished physically. "The worst thing you could do to them was to scold," recalled a herder.

"When you scolded, the dog reacted just like it had a whipping. He would never do it again."

A well-trained dog in action was a joy to watch, sensing any restlessness in the herd, and eagerly anticipating the herder's spoken or whistled commands, which were frequently accompanied by hand signals. A smart dog never nagged or "drove" his sheep but simply persuaded them with his self-assured leadership—a quality few sheep possessed.

A herder and his dog were inseparable. When a sheepman died on the range, his dog might refuse to leave his body or even to take enough food to sustain its own life. The attachment was reciprocal. As one chronicler put it, "A sheepherder will sigh to lose his friend; groan if his wife or child dies; but if his dog is lost by death, his grief is overwhelming and his anguish cannot be assuaged."

The two brief periods when a herder had the companionship of other sheepmen came during the seasonal exercises of lambing and shearing.

Lambing time came first, in late winter or early spring, and one participant called it "a month-long hell of worry and toil" because the very future of a sheep ranch depended on the number of ewes that gave birth to live lambs and on the number of those lambs that could survive their first critical weeks. Pregnant ewes had to be segregated into "drop bands," watched day and night and attended quickly. If they had difficulty giving birth, the herder became the midwife.

A sheepman also functioned as a sort of adoption agency. A lamb born to a "dry" ewe could be saved by introducing it to a foster mother or by feeding it formula—milk, water and molasses—from a bottle. The care of such rejected or orphaned lambs, known as bummers, was a major preoccupation of the herder, for every survivor represented a future return in wool and mutton.

The true social season of the sheep industry came later in the spring, after lambing, when the shearing gangs arrived to remove the heavy coats the adult sheep had grown during the winter. On any sizable ranch, the shearing was done by itinerant crews of specialists who followed the market northward from Mexico to the Canadian border. A good shearer could handle 100 sheep a day, an expert perhaps 150. The shearers were generally a flamboyant lot, and their arrival always signaled a major break in the tedium of sheep-ranch

Members of a shearing crew in Umatilla County, Oregon, present a view of their work in several ongoing stages. A good shearer was expected to fleece up to 100 sheep per day, which led sheepmen to remark that "A shearer is a herder with his brains knocked out."

life—an excuse for feasting, drinking, gaming and perhaps a few good fights.

The final chore of the shearing season entailed the conversion of most of the male lambs into wethers by castrating them. This procedure had two purposes: to produce better mutton (just as steers made better beef than bulls) and to improve the herd by ensuring that the ewes would be bred only with prize rams. The most effective method of wethering was perhaps the ultimate test of a sheepman's devotion to his calling: While a sheep was being held by all four legs in an elevated sitting position, the herder would extract the animal's testicles with his teeth, which were considered more precise than a knife.

Despite—or perhaps because of—the hard and lone-

ly life that they led, sheepmen were often fiercely proud of their vocation. "For God's sake," one of them admonished a writer of a later era, "don't picture a sheepherder with a longhandled crook and a face like Jesus Christ. And don't give him so few as a dozen sheep crowding close to him and licking his hand. Give him a sizable flock of at least two thousand and let them keep at a respectful distance. He was a sheepherder, not a shepherd."

As sheepmen reached the end of the eastbound trails they did not always find the empty, unclaimed ranges that an earlier generation of trail drives had passed through. Instead, they found cattle—some already there and millions more moving in. As the range filled up there was no more virgin land to trail to; a collision

was inevitable. The cattleman's angry unwillingness to share what he considered to be his rightful and exclusive domain would lead to decades of brutality and terror on the range.

As early as the 1870s, some cattlemen had begun promulgating "deadlines"—arbitrary boundaries on public lands that sheepmen were ordered not to cross. For example, one Montana sheep owner, edging his herd toward what was predominantly cattle country, received a pointed message from local cowmen: "If you take sheep to Powder River bring your coffin along. You will need it."

Sheepherders ignored such warnings at their peril. Poisons such as saltpeter—toxic to sheep but not to cattle—might be spread in the path of a flock, or grain laced with strychnine might be scattered near the sheep's bed-ground at night so the animals would eat it as they moved out in the morning.

Over the years, as grass ran out and tempers grew even shorter, cattlemen resorted to more direct means of intimidation. Teams of club-swinging cowboys would ride through helpless flocks, smashing skulls until they grew arm-weary. When such methods became too time-consuming, resourceful cowmen turned to dynamite charges fitted with percussion caps. In a tightly bunched flock a few accurately thrown sticks could kill or maim dozens of sheep. Fire was even more diabolically efficient: One or two woollies ignited in a closed corral would soon touch off a whole flock.

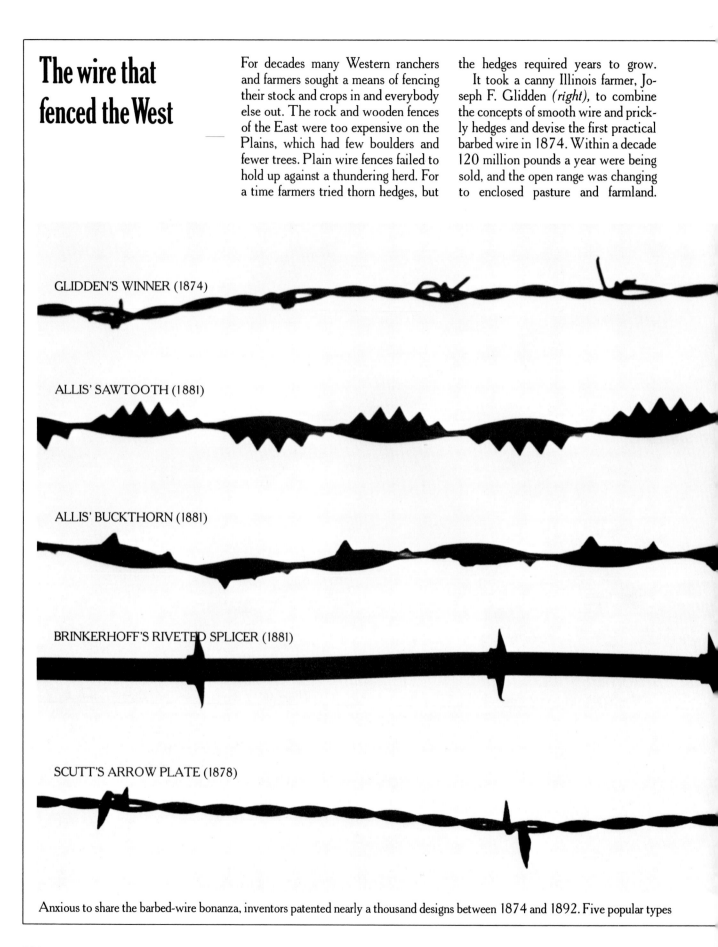

The wire that fenced the West

For decades many Western ranchers and farmers sought a means of fencing their stock and crops in and everybody else out. The rock and wooden fences of the East were too expensive on the Plains, which had few boulders and fewer trees. Plain wire fences failed to hold up against a thundering herd. For a time farmers tried thorn hedges, but the hedges required years to grow.

It took a canny Illinois farmer, Joseph F. Glidden *(right)*, to combine the concepts of smooth wire and prickly hedges and devise the first practical barbed wire in 1874. Within a decade 120 million pounds a year were being sold, and the open range was changing to enclosed pasture and farmland.

GLIDDEN'S WINNER (1874)

ALLIS' SAWTOOTH (1881)

ALLIS' BUCKTHORN (1881)

BRINKERHOFF'S RIVETED SPLICER (1881)

SCUTT'S ARROW PLATE (1878)

Anxious to share the barbed-wire bonanza, inventors patented nearly a thousand designs between 1874 and 1892. Five popular types

In later life Joseph Glidden looked every inch the tycoon, but he was merely a prosperous farmer in 1874 when he took out a barbed-wire patent. He got the idea from a crude prototype he saw at a fair and barely beat an Illinois neighbor to the draw.

The original working model of Glidden's barbing machine was an old-fashioned coffee mill with its casing cut away and its grinder altered to cut and coil small lengths of wire. The barbs were strung by hand between strands of plain wire.

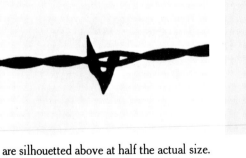

are silhouetted above at half the actual size.

Night-raiding cattlemen destroy defense-less sheep. In Colorado and Wyoming such slaughter sometimes annihilated entire flocks while the sheepherders were held at gunpoint.

The most devastating attacks were those that exploited the sheep's own flocking instinct and made them destroy themselves. Shouting, shooting raiders had only to start a flock moving toward some nearby natural hazard; the panicked sheep would push the animals in front to death and then follow mindlessly along. Sometimes quicksand was the fatal trap. In 1884 alone, four thousand head died in the bottomless sands under the Little Colorado River in Arizona.

The virulence of the range wars continued well into the 20th Century and was finally checked only after the murder of two sheep owners and a young French herder in 1909 turned public opinion against the escalating violence. Although isolated skirmishes occurred for another decade, the sheepman-cattleman wars were drawing to a close.

In ironic fact, cattlemen eventually learned to their vast surprise that sheep could actually improve the grasslands. If the animals were not overstocked and were afforded well-spaced water holes, no part of the range would be "sheeped." Instead, their hoofs harrowed the soil rather than tramping it—and cattle

The major markets for the barons' cattle were stockyards such as this one in Kansas City, Missouri, which teemed with more than 100 acres of solid beef on any given day and handled more than half a million head in a year in the 1880s.

seemed to prefer the rich, rank grass that had been fertilized by the droppings of the despised woollies.

Even before the conflict between cattle owners and sheepmen had faded, an entirely different sort of competition for control of the Western lands was well under way. It was waged not on the range by cowboys and herders but in banks, board rooms and financial markets of the Eastern U.S. and Europe.

By the mid-1880s, cattle represented by far the biggest business in the Old West—with perhaps no more than three dozen rangeland rajahs controlling more than 20 million acres of U.S. soil. Some, to be sure, were veteran ranchers who had amassed their holdings after the fashion of Richard King; many others, however, were men who had never toted a Colt and would hardly have recognized a branding iron.

Attracted by prospects and promises of huge profits, Eastern investors included the varied likes of William Rockefeller, brother of John D. and himself an organizer of Standard Oil; William K. Vanderbilt of the railroading Vanderbilts; Nelson Morris, a Chicago packer who never even bothered to visit his 250,000-acre

ranch; and, not least, a wealthy young New Yorker named Theodore Roosevelt.

Along with the rich Eastern investors came a horde of money-heavy Scots, Englishmen and other Europeans who had heard reports of huge profits to be made from ranching. Although such tales were often grossly exaggerated (sometimes by Western ranchers, who were by no means above hornswoggling gullible foreigners), the Europeans persisted. In the process they created some of the greatest cattle spreads of all time.

Thus, the Maxwell Cattle Company, Ltd., which straddled the New Mexico-Colorado border on 1.75 million acres, was so vast that the Atchison, Topeka and Santa Fe Railroad had to put in six stations on the track that crossed the property. Then there was the Texas Land and Cattle Company, which owned and leased an area in 1885 bigger than Long Island.

Perhaps the most impressive operation of all, the XIT Ranch in the Panhandle country of Texas, was controlled by English capital. Extending for 200 miles, the ranch occupied parts of ten counties and employed as many as 150 cowboys who rode 1,000 horses, herded 150,000 head of cattle and branded 35,000 calves a year. "Rounding them up," mused a veteran cowhand, "was like a farmer in Massachusetts turning out a cow to graze and finding her months later in Delaware."

In the late 1880s, the XIT in partnership with another company put together a second ranch complex that was almost as big as the original in Texas. This one, in Montana, sprawled over an area covering 200 miles by 75 miles between the Yellowstone and Missouri rivers. A long, long trail connected the two ranches, like the bar in a giant dumbbell. Thus, herds of XIT cattle could traverse no fewer than seven states—Texas, Oklahoma, Colorado, Nebraska, South Dakota, Wyoming and Montana—on the trail drive between their two giant pastures. This was the kind of security and control that any good cattle baron might long for. And there was unmistakable pride in the voice of XIT General Manager A.G. Boyce when, down on the Texas ranch, he issued to his northbound trail hands the order for what must surely have been the longest series of marches ever to begin and end on private property: "Keep your eye on the North Star, and drive straight ahead until you can wet your feet in the waters of the Yellowstone."

A trail boss gives the cattle sign to an Indian by imitating horns with his upraised arms, indicating that the brave may take an animal to eat from a herd crossing Indian land.

A sweaty little man, tall in the saddle

In the mythology of the Old West, the American cowboy appears as a hard-drinking, hard-swearing, Injun-fighting, rootin' tootin' romantic son of a gunslinger. At times, he was all of that. But mainly he was a sweaty little man—overworked, underpaid and ill-fed—who fried his brains under the prairie sun, and rode endless miles in wind and rain to mend fences and recover lost calves.

He was the man who made the great ranches into what they were—and the ranchers into tycoons. He lassoed and broke the wild mustangs, rounded up thousands of Texas longhorns and drove them north on the long, often tedious and sometimes hazardous trails to market. It was a jolting, young man's job; most ranch hands started punching cows in their early 20s and quit before

they were 35—and too crippled to ride.

Two well-known Old West artists, Frederic Remington *(above and page 300)* and Charles Russell *(page 298)*, rode with the cowboys, recording every detail of their lives. The artists knew the reality. And they knew, too, that in the largest sense, the cowboy did indeed ride tall in the saddle, the hero of his country's boldest legend.

Helping to trap wild horses, a cowboy who has roped a mustang rises onto his left stirrup, putting all his weight there to keep his saddle from twisting to the right and overturning his horse. This is a typical Russell work — correct in each detail but stressing the drama in a working cowboy's life.

Running blind alongside cattle stampeded by a nighttime thundersquall, a cowhand gallops toward the head of the herd to turn the animals by riding in against the leaders.

301

12. The hard-working hombres who rode the range

"Deer sur," began the report of a ranch hand to his absentee employer back East, "we have brand 800 caves this roundup we have made sum hay potatoes is a fare crop. That Inglishman yu lef in charge at the other camp got to fresh and we had to kill the son of a bitch. Nothing much has hapened sence yu lef. Yurs truely, Jim."

Within that laconic catalog of life and death, toil and tedium, reposed the soul and substance of an American hero—the Western cowboy. Even during his brief heyday, which lasted but a bare generation between the end of the Civil War and the mid-1880s, the number of cowboys who rode the cattle trails across the Great Plains totaled no more than 40,000. As men of a particular time and place, they lived by a code compounded of harsh frontier realities and Victorian-era social values, performing body-punishing jobs and pitting themselves against a land of sweeping grandeur that offered prodigious helpings of misery. They were surprisingly young—their average age was only 24—but they swiftly grew old in the saddle, and the usual cowpunching career lasted only about seven years.

In some ways, the cowboys were a wildly mixed lot. About one in every six or seven was Mexican; a similar proportion was black (most of the blacks had learned how to ride and rope while serving as slaves on Texas ranches), and there were even some representatives of those erstwhile lords of the plains, the Indians. Many cowboys were former Rebel soldiers seeking new stakes and release from the frustrations of the lost cause; they rode alongside former Yankee soldiers who were unwilling to return to the rocky farms of New England or the dullness of Midwestern homesteads.

Others were English remittance men, scapegraces paid by their families for enduring voluntary exile to the Western wilderness, or saddle bums who regularly took advantage of the Western custom of offering food and tobacco to anyone who happened to show up at a ranch. There were even a few sailors who had exchanged the sea for the arid plains. They brought with them a favorite chantey: *O, bury me not in the deep, deep sea, Where the dark blue waves will roll over me.* And they remodeled it to go: *O, bury me not on the lone prairee, Where the wild coyotes will howl over me.*

The common denominator for all those diverse types was the service they paid to the unlovable, thickheaded, panic-prone creature whose name was attached to the cowboys. Actually, the term "cowboy" is of uncertain derivation. During the Revolutionary War it was applied to armed Tories who tinkled cowbells to lure farmer patriots with lost cows into the brush—where the Tories ambushed them. Later the name referred to Texas bandits who stole cattle from Mexicans. Only after the Civil War did the term come to signify anyone who tended cattle in the West.

In performing that chore, the cowboy's most useful instrument was the horse, an animal that greatly augmented the muscle power and mobility of the rider. Distances on the range were too great for a pedestrian, and without horses it would have been impossible to round up and drive millions of cattle over the plains.

Moreover, the act of sitting high in the saddle gave the cowboy a sense of majesty and power, and most cowboys were resolute in their judgment that "a man afoot is no man at all." Indeed, a cowpuncher named Jo Mora once went so far as to admit that a dismounted cowboy was "just a plain bowlegged human who smelled very horsey at times, slept in his underwear and was subject to boils and dyspepsia."

A second tool, indispensable to both the cowboy's

Despite their steely gaze and the guns they tote, these five cowboys in Montana still betray a youthful awkwardness and innocence.

302

work and his image, was the rope, or lariat. Expertly thrown, a rope could snare a cow's horns or a horse's neck, or the hoofs of either, enabling a 140-pound man to capture and subdue a 1,000-pound animal. A rope could be transformed into an instant corral when it was stretched taut by several men. It could be used as a hobble to keep a horse from straying away in the night. Hitched around a saddle horn, a lariat served to pull a mired cow out of a bog. And, not least in the legend of the West, a rope could be looped into a noose to serve up justice quick and hot when someone was caught in an unforgivable crime such as horse stealing.

Another proud cowboy possession was the gun—although not always the celebrated Colt. In fact, when a cowboy went hunting for antelope or jackrabbits he was as likely as not to leave his notoriously inaccurate

revolver back in the bunkhouse and carry a rifle or a shotgun. The Colt was, however, handy for killing rattlesnakes, finishing off a horse that had a broken leg, or turning aside a stampede by firing the revolver directly in front of the leading cattle.

There were, of course, occasions when cowboys used their six-shooters against other humans. Cowpokes on a trail's-end spree might succumb to both liquor and a desire to show off their manhood by shooting up a cattle town. The cattle trade also embraced a fair number of outright thugs who doubled as cowhands when not rustling or working as enforcers for autocratic ranch owners. During the course of one such rowdy career, a so-called cowboy named Scharbar killed no fewer than 32 persons. But he was unusual, and Homer Grigsby, a cowhand who spent many years on the Southwestern

The original American cowboy, a California vaquero of the 1830s, throws a bull with the style of a latter-day rodeo showman.

range, declared that he never saw a gun drawn on another man except by a feverish greenhorn who had heard that courage in the West was proved with a Colt.

Still, a cowboy was certainly aware that guns gave him an aura of lethal manliness, and he weighed himself down with firearms whenever he wished to impress a girl. Pride in his image was also reflected in the clothing he wore. A cowboy would spend as much as four months' wages on a hat with a fancy sweatband. His boots were custom-made, sometimes costing more than $50 a pair. The vamp of the boot had to be skintight so that his feet would look small—a point on which cowboys were particularly sensitive, not wishing to be confused with some big-footed groundling. Heels were high, narrow and undersloped to hold the stirrup firmly. The pointed toe enabled a rider to insert his foot easily into the stirrup,

and to slip out of it if he was thrown. Even so, the most common form of death among cowboys was to be dragged by a horse.

Left to his own devices, with very little law and no social arbiters, the cowboy developed an unwritten, roughhewn code of behavior that was understood by nearly everyone. A man's word was his contractual bond, the end of a noose awaited a horse thief, hospitality to visiting cowboys was a sacred obligation—these were among the cardinal principles of the code, but there were a great many more.

Some of the finer points dictated horsemen's etiquette. No one borrowed a horse from another man's string without his permission (which was rarely given). One did not whip or kick a borrowed horse. When two mounted cowboys approached each other on the trail,

The cowboy's elegant Spanish ancestry

A good half century before the Western beef-cattle industry blossomed in Texas, a singular breed of professional horsemen calling themselves vaqueros had already set the style, evolved the equipment and techniques (left), and even developed much of the vocabulary that would become the stamp of the American cowboy. The range of the vaquero was Spanish California; there, a unique pastoral society evolved, founded on Christ but ultimately flourishing on the cow.

When Franciscan missionaries first arrived in California around 1769 they brought with them a few modest herds of domestic cattle for dairy and brood stock. In the warm, grassy valleys of California and along the lower Rio Grande, the cows thrived and became an unexpected source of profit to the missions. The padres utilized the inedible parts of the animal—selling hides and tallow to New England factories for the manufacture of leather goods, candles and soap.

Before long, the mission fathers were saving as many pesos as souls, and local Indians found themselves learning as much about cattle as about the Trinity. For as the business and the herds increased the priests needed help handling the cows. The only laborers available were their Indian converts; those selected by the padres became skilled horsemen able to handle big herds of cattle on an open range.

The Indian horsemen were taught how to snare a steer on the run by throwing a loop of braided rawhide rope, known in Spain as *la reata* and later Americanized to "lariat." Once a steer was caught, they learned to bring the animal to a stop by taking quick turns of the lariat around the saddle horn. This they called *dar la vuelta* (to make the turn), which became the American cowboy's "dally."

To protect their legs while riding through chaparral thickets, the mission hands wore heavy leather trousers called *chaparreras*—subsequently abbreviated to "chaps." The cowhands, themselves, came to be called vaqueros (an extension of the Spanish *vaca*, meaning cow), which their American heirs later changed to "buckaroo."

Mexico broke away from Spain in 1821, and later took the mission range away from the Spanish padres. The holdings were then snatched up by private rancheros, the first real cattle barons of the West. The vaquero threw off his peonage and then went to work for the ranchero, becoming in the process a proud and independent range hand.

His day, however, was short. In 1846, when Mexico and the United States went to war, Mexican troops retreated below the Rio Grande, leaving the ranchos at the mercy of marauders, both Indian and white. Cattle were slaughtered and driven off by the thousands.

When the herds recovered decades later, the emphasis of the cattle business had changed from hides and tallow to beef. And the center of the industry had moved to Texas, nearer the railheads leading to Eastern markets. The men who worked beef cattle spoke English and called themselves cowboys. Yet whenever they swung a lariat, held a rodeo, or pulled on their chaps they were paying mute tribute to the vaquero who had started it all.

a friendly word was appropriate but a wave of greeting was considered bad form—it might spook a horse. If one man dismounted, the other did too, so they would meet on equal terms. A man on foot did not grab the bridle of a mounted man's horse, for that could be taken as an intrusion on the rider's control.

Other rules governed the practicalities of rangeland housekeeping. Cowboys were expected to close pasture and corral gates behind them, and to remove their sharp-roweled spurs when they entered another man's house. On roundup a cowboy did not wait for his fellow hands to arrive before beginning a meal; he helped himself and began eating at once so he would be out of the way when other punchers came to dip food from the common pots and pans.

One activity that did not submit to any restrictions was swearing. Cowboy talk assayed somewhere around one third profanity, which was either directed at horses and cattle or used as the salt and pepper of ordinary speech. "Son of a bitch" in particular seems to have been part of every other sentence. But blasphemy was also common, if only because most cowboys did not want themselves to be thought of as Sunday-schoolish. One cowpuncher commented of his acquaintances that "ninety per cent of them was infidels." Documentary support for that assessment still survives in period pamphlets bearing such titles as "Help the Heathen Cowboys of the West."

In matters of money, most cowboys bound themselves to be trusting and trustworthy. One North Dakota hand gave back part of his wages for digging postholes because he realized later that he had dug one of them too shallow. At payoff time, bosses might dump sacks of money on the ground and leave them there, unmolested, for days at a time until the boys came by to pick up their wages.

The cowboy's code observed a special reverence for womankind—or, at least, for the nice-girl portion thereof. It was, however, a remote kind of reverence: Marriage was a mode of life that most cowboys had to shun because they were always on the move. In any case, nice girls were few and the cowhand's pay was too low to support a family. Yet even while he rode the trails, consorting with an occasional cattle-town prostitute, a lonesome young cowboy would yearn for the company of a virtuous woman. And when the opportunity arose, he would,

by one account, travel for miles "just to sit on a porch for an hour or two and watch some homesteader's red-faced daughter rock her chair and scratch her elbows—and not a smack or a hug."

But there was also an ugly side to the cowboy, one seldom seen in the glorifying dime novels of the Old West. Most of the white majority of cowhands were unabashed racists. Blacks were "niggers," Mexicans were "greasers," and the attitudes behind those words were sometimes expressed in deeds. There was also a surprising amount of cruelty to animals. During the early days of cattle tending in Texas, punchers sometimes adopted the brutal Mexican practices of making a sulky cow move by rubbing sand in its eyes or by twisting its tail until the bone snapped.

Yet for all his faults, the cowboy redeemed himself by the pride he took in his work—and even in the prowess of his fellow punchers such as Ed Lemmon, who knew every important brand in the West, saddle-handled more than a million cattle in his lifetime, and set the record for the most cows—900—cut out of a herd and branded in a single day.

Based on that pride in his calling, the cowboy became fully convinced that he was the aristocrat of the West. An Englishman visiting a ranch in Wyoming discovered this quality when he inquired of the foreman, "Is your master at home?" The foreman looked at him levelly and replied, "The son of a bitch hasn't been born yet." It was that vinegary self-esteem that would carry the cowboy through the vicissitudes of his daily life.

In the spartan setting of a Western ranch, the most comfortless place of all was the bunkhouse where the hired hands lived. Typically, it was a shack made from weatherboard or cottonwood logs. In some cases, the cowboys themselves put in board ceilings over a single main room, creating an attic reachable by ladder. At the T-Anchor Ranch in Texas, cowboy Harry Ingerton slept in an attic and pronounced it "the coldest place I ever saw." Little help could be expected from the few blankets available. "If I owned a ranch," grumbled cowhand Peter Wright, "I would buy these blankets and use them as a refrigerator in the summer."

Always, the bunkhouses were distinguished by their smell. The aroma that assaulted the senses was a composite of sweaty men, dry cow manure, old work boots,

the licorice in chewing-tobacco plugs and the smoke from lamps that were burning coal oil or perhaps even tallow rendered from the generous supply of skunks that scavenged around the ranch. There was a chronic look of untidiness around these places. Clothes were "hung on the floor," as one historian of the cowboy era said, "so they wouldn't fall down and get lost." And amid the filth were some unwelcome guests. Cowpuncher Charlie Siringo recalled that his bunkhouse pals "made an iron-clad rule that whoever was caught picking grey backs [lice] off and throwing them on the floor without first killing them, should pay a fine of ten cents for each and every offense."

On the premises around the ranch house, cowboy work often tended to be downright undignified, especial-

ly if it had to be done on foot. Over a three-week stretch, Texas cowhand Blue Stevens did nothing but gather dried cow manure for fires. C.H. Hanbury, on the huge XIT Ranch, was equally far removed from the image of the tall-in-the-saddle cavalier when he was assigned the task of building traps for turtles that had overpopulated a lake used to water livestock.

Yet cowboys were generally able to apply a basic range-land stoicism to the discomforts and displeasures that were their lot. For everyone knew that a ranch was set up for the care and well-being not of people but of cows.

Out on the range cattle had to be watched and worried over to keep them healthy—or even alive. Throughout the summer, for example, cows by the thousands had to be doctored for blowflies. These insects laid eggs

307

On a Western saddle each part *(identified on the diagram at right)* evolved to meet a specific cowboy need, from the horn for roping to the broad stirrups in which the cowboy stood when he was riding down steep slopes or trotting along the trail.

The functional beauty of the saddle

The single piece of equipment that the cowboy was fussiest about was his saddle. And small wonder. For months at a time he sat in it all day and sometimes half the night as well. And when he finally lay down to rest at the end of a long day's work on the range he pillowed his head on it. So indispensable was it to his life and livelihood that the phrase "he's sold his saddle" came to mean of a cowboy that he was finished in the profession.

Unlike the horse, which was supplied by the employer, the saddle was the cowboy's own personal property. A saddle like the typical Western rig shown at left, turned out in 1875 by master craftsman E.L. Gallatin of Denver, cost a cowhand a month's pay or more. But the $30 or so was money well spent, for the saddle could serve him well for as much as 30 years or even longer.

The Western saddle, as it evolved on the plains, was a direct descendant of the 16th Century Spanish war saddle, pictured above, on which the Spanish conquistadors rode into Mexico. This war saddle (itself descended from one devised by the Moors a few hundred years earlier) weighed up to 40 pounds, had a wooden frame, or tree, was well padded and was covered with brocaded silk velvet.

The pommel at the front of the saddle is at left in the illustration; the cantle, at the back, was sharply curved to prevent the rider from sliding off. They were made of ornately chased silver, as were the long plates descending from the pommel on either side. The plates served two purposes: They shielded the rider's thighs and prevented an enemy lance from getting under the rider and unseating him. The saddle had stirrups, not shown, that hung low; the rider sat with his legs hanging almost straight down.

When the war saddle moved into cattle country in the early decades of

A 16th Century Spanish war saddle held a lancer secure between its pommel and sharply curved cantle, at right.

the 19th Century, the cowhands kept the tough wooden tree that was its foundation, and they retained the general notion of a high pommel and cantle. But from there on they made a number of drastic changes. The curved cantle was tilted well backward for the rider's comfort and lowered for easier mounting and dismounting. The ornate velvet gave way to long-wearing, readily available leather. The high metal pommel was modified in size, tilt and material until it became the horn needed to secure a lariat. And the metal thigh guards, or braces, disappeared altogether. If a cowboy wanted anything extra to steady himself in his seat, he rolled up his slicker or some other piece of the gear that he carried and tied it into place with the leather strings that hung from the saddle.

Carefully crafted and lovingly maintained, a fine saddle was at least as important to the horse as to the cowboy. A rider with a gentle hand and a good rig could travel 70 miles in one day and still have a healthy horse. But a thoughtless tyro in a poor saddle could make a horse sore in an hour's time.

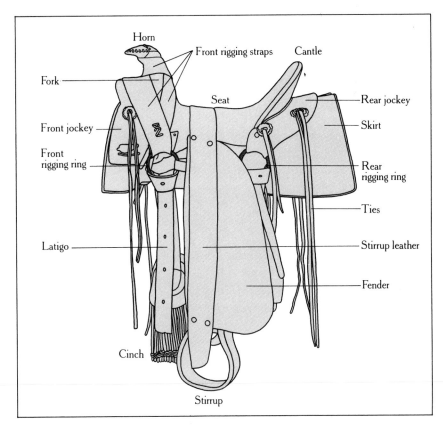

in open wounds, such as fresh brands and castrations. The eggs developed into screwworms—maggots about three fourths of an inch long—which inflicted agonizing pain, and sometimes death, on the animals. To daub the wounds and kill the screwworms, the men carried bottles containing a powerful mixture of carbolic acid and axle grease, among other ingredients.

Such crude remedies occasionally turned out to be more lethal than the ailments. A cowboy named J.W. Standifer got orders to treat a bunch of cows suffering from a skin disease that was similar to the mange. He did, by dousing them with kerosene from a garden sprinkling can. This was the standard cure, and it should have worked, but one cow ran through a branding fire that turned it into a living torch. The flaming cow fled back to the others and ignited the whole bunch. That day, twenty head died.

In summer, when the sun baked the treeless range, cattlemen had to keep a steady watch for fire. A blaze could sweep over entire counties, killing cattle and wiping out the grass. To curb the fires, cowboys got behind

plows and made firebreaks—sets of furrows 75 to 200 feet apart, with the grass in between purposely burned off. Foreman Ira Aten estimated that in a single summer he had plowed 150 miles of firebreaks.

When a fire or drought or overstocking made a range unusable, the cattle had to be moved to better grasslands, and the drives to new ranges were often fraught with difficulties. Trail boss S.P. Conrad reported on a few of the problems he encountered while trying to move some cattle across the Bitterroot Mountains in Montana: "I went as far as the Summunt & Made up my mind that we could never drive the Cows with Their Calves & returned & sold Them [the calves] at $4.50 per head." Having virtually given away the calves, Conrad was then able to get the rest of the herd to Missoula, Montana, still in the middle of the mountains. By then, some of his men had quit and others were malingering. But, he wrote, "I apprehend no Trouble I intend to hire a full crew & kick out every son of a Bich that has the belly ache."

In later days the coming of windmills and barbed wire largely eliminated any need to move cattle from range

310

to range. A rancher would fence off an area to keep the animals from wandering off and then provide them with an adequate supply of water from a windmill-pumped tank. But though the cowhands were saved a lot of hard driving, the wire presented a new set of duties.

"A whole lot of sorry things can happen to a fence," one oldtimer said. Riders called pliers men went out to patrol the fences, equipped with a pouch full of staples, a roll of spare wire, and a tool that served as both nippers and hammer. One man usually was assigned 10 to 15 miles of fence. Besides repairing wire he often had to reset the "deadmen," buried boulders to which were attached guy wires that kept the fence taut but which tended to wash out in storms. On any given round of fence patrol, a pliers man might also have to chivy weak, starving cattle to a haystack or pick porcupine quills from some sad calf's nose.

At least once a year, a cowboy drew the utterly monastic duty of line riding. Most large Western ranches were too big to be manned from their central buildings alone. Like small nations, they needed outposts. The Millet Ranch on the Brazos River, for instance, had such outposts spotted every six or eight miles around the 60-mile perimeter. In the days before barbed wire (and sometimes in the days after it, if the boss was a wire hater or had fence-cutting neighbors) the line riders patrolled between their stations, forming a kind of living fence around the owner's range.

In addition to ceaseless efforts to prevent cattle from straying off the home grass, the line rider performed such multifarious chores as shooing calves away from alkaline water, watching out for rustlers, and hunting or poisoning wolves, mountain lions and even eagles, which were thought to attack calves on occasion. The line rider was also expected to take note of pasture conditions for the boss' information. On a ranch located near a rail line, a hand would be assigned to patrol the tracks, chasing cattle off the right of way and keeping a record of cows that were run down so that a carefully itemized bill could later be presented to the railroad.

Life at the line camps was even more primitive than in the lowliest bunkhouse; sometimes, in fact, such camps consisted of no more than a dugout scratched from the side of a hill. When a man was alone in a crude dwelling for weeks at a time, the boredom became unbearable. Veteran hand John Hendrix remembered a cowboy who spent an entire winter alone in a shack papered with old newspapers and farm journals; fighting mightily against ennui, the man read the north, south, east and west walls "and was just starting to read the ceiling when they called him to headquarters." Other hands passed the time memorizing the labels on tomato or condensed-milk cans.

When two men were in a line camp for prolonged periods, they could wear terribly on each other's nerves. An old story told of a pair in a lonely camp who heard bellowing noises in the night. One of them suggested: "Bull." The other said: "Sounds like an old steer to me." Not another word was spoken, and the two went to bed. The next morning one of the cowboys started packing up his horse. "Leaving?" asked his companion. "Yes," came the answer. "Too much argument."

The slowest time around a ranch was winter. By late November, two of every three ranch hands were laid off until the workload picked up again in spring. Most of the newly unemployed housed up with buddies in town and took temporary jobs like bartending or blacksmithing.

For those who remained on the ranch, the most important job was the grueling business of going out from time to time to be sure that cattle were not starving or freezing to death, or both. Cattle had a stubborn, mindless tendency to stand, shivering and hungry, in deep snow rather than attempt to find food. Bundled in their bulky buffalo coats, men on horses tramped out trails to hillsides where wind had blown snow off the grass, then returned to drive the cattle to the cleared spots. The cowboys also had to chop through snow crust and ice so the cattle could drink, because most cows lack the instinct to eat snow for water.

One wintertime assignment did offer some excitement—and even reward. In cold months, when the pickings were slim among natural game on the range, wolves became particularly bold in stalking cattle. Moving in packs, they would disable a cow by severing the hamstrings in its hind legs; then they moved in to finish off the cripple. R.M. Dudley was hired by a ranch in Texas to shoot wolves at a salary of $35 a month plus the $5 bounty offered by the county government. The rancher, in addition, paid him with food, four to eight horses, two rifles, a Colt .45 and all the ammunition he needed.

For the most part, however, the wintertime chores of a cowboy were pure drudgery. Firewood had to be gath-

ered; the men dragged tree trunks with ropes made fast to the horns of their saddles. Texan J.W. Standifer recalled once being assigned to "cutting dead cottonwood into stove wood. It was like cutting sponge—every time my ax hit it bounced back." And Bob Haley spent an entire winter rendering the suet of 11 slaughtered beeves for tallow. He reported that the stuff gave "a purty good light" in lamps. Furthermore, he solemnly advised, sourdough biscuits could be rolled in it just before baking for extra flavor.

In dozens of such make-work ways, the cowboys whiled away the tedious winter weeks—until the coming of spring, when the range sprang again to life.

Especially in the North, the annual rite of spring was the roundup, in which cowmen scoured the range and then sorted out the cattle that had wandered and intermingled during the winter. In the Southwest, with its dry, sparsely vegetated plains, cattle tended to group themselves around water holes and rarely strayed across the intervening parched country to join other herds; there, ranchers needed only to search their own holdings to find their cows. But on the Northern plains, which became overstocked and overgrazed after 1880, cattle were forced to cross divides and mix with other herds to find new grass and water. In that vast land, a roundup required planning almost as intricate as a major military campaign.

And so, in mid-April 1886, it came to pass that 175 members of the Montana Stockgrowers Association gathered in Miles City, Montana Territory, to map out that spring's roundup. Also on hand was a military band from nearby Fort Keogh, which led a parade, along with more than 100 whooping, hat-tossing cowboys, many of them resplendent in new, pearl-gray California pants from Orschel Brothers Clothing Store right up the street.

For all the festive atmosphere, this was a serious affair. It would be one of the most extensive roundups in the history of the cattle industry, and in its sweep and complexity it served as an exemplar of all the problems, strategy and techniques of roundups as they occurred in the high time of the Old West.

North, east, south and west of Miles City, in an area as big as Pennsylvania, nearly every coulee, gulch and box canyon contained cattle, for a total of more than a million head. As at all roundups—even the smallest— these animals had first to be gathered together. Next, the

increase in new calves would be tallied and branded. At the same time, most of the males among them would be castrated to make them gentler (a relative condition, considering the wildness of some steers) and to help them gain weight. Ailing stock would be doctored, and some healthy ones would be dehorned. Finally, all the strayed cattle would be separated into individual groups and driven home—a monumental job, since some 4,000 different recorded brands were mixed more or less higgledy-piggledy.

At the Miles City meeting, the attendees cut up the range into 17 districts, some of them huge. At the eastern end of the area, for example, lay District 8, a 130-by-30 mile swath of land extending along the north shore of the Yellowstone River, and bounded on the north by the divide between the Yellowstone and the Missouri. Some of the most powerful outfits of the northern range would be working District 8: the Circle Dot, the J Lazy J, the Bow and Arrow. The area also contained 12,000 cattle and 300 horses of the L U Bar, a new ranch stocked by four herds driven up from Texas the year before. Among the L U Bar cowboys in Miles City was 18-year-old Luke Sweetman, who in later years would write with detailed clarity about his recollections of the great Montana roundup of 1886.

As it turned out, the roundup was delayed for almost a month. Rain was desperately needed to green up the range enough for cows to graze out of the ravines and hidden bottom lands. It was not, therefore, until late May that Sweetman and eight other L U Bar hands rode up to the designated meeting place of District 8 on the north bank of the Yellowstone across from Miles City. There, the benchland teemed with nearly a hundred men and more than 500 horses.

For three days, while awaiting latecomers, the cowboys amused themselves by racing horses or by sneaking over to Miles City to sample the pleasures afforded by the likes of Connie the Cowboy Queen, who sported a $250 dress embroidered with the brands of every outfit from the Yellowstone to the Platte.

On the third night, however, the roundup crews got all the rest they could. They knew that for at least the next six weeks they would never get enough sleep. And they were right: In the predawn darkness of the next day the L U Bar cook, for the first of many mornings, roused the men with a call that began with a trill and ended in a

The heraldry of the branding iron

Arizona cowpuncher Evans Coleman once remarked that he knew cowhands "who could neither read nor write, but who could name any brand, either letters or figures, on a cow." A brand was the key to ownership in a business where ownership was everything. Many cattlemen, in fact, named their ranches after their brands and held the symbol in as proud esteem as did any knight his crest. Branding was an ancient practice before the first cow came to America. Certain 4,000-year-old tomb paintings show Egyptians branding their fat, spotted cattle. Hernando Cortés burned crosses on the hides of the small herd he brought with him to Mexico. The vaqueros passed the custom on to U.S. cowboys, who developed and refined their own calligraphy.

On any 19th Century ranch the greenest cowhand quickly mastered the three major elements of the branding alphabet *(below)*. He learned to read the components of a brand in correct order: from left to right, from top to bottom, or from outside to inside (a T inside a diamond translates as Diamond T, not T Diamond). In time he could pick out any one of hundreds of markings in a milling herd; a good cowboy, said Coleman, could understand "the Constitution of the United States were it written with a branding iron on the side of a cow."

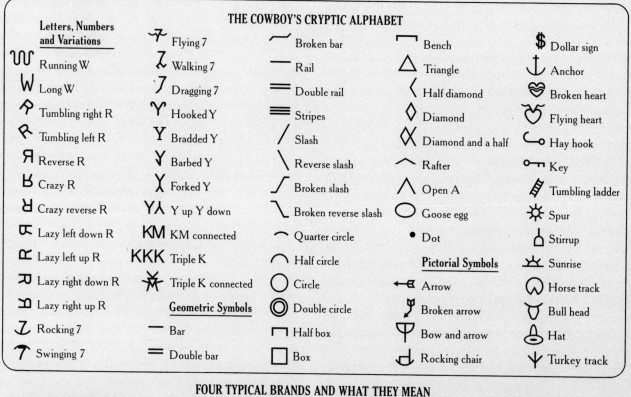

THE COWBOY'S CRYPTIC ALPHABET

Letters, Numbers and Variations

Running W
Long W
Tumbling right R
Tumbling left R
Reverse R
Crazy R
Crazy reverse R
Lazy left down R
Lazy left up R
Lazy right down R
Lazy right up R
Rocking 7
Swinging 7

Flying 7
Walking 7
Dragging 7
Hooked Y
Bradded Y
Barbed Y
Forked Y
Y up Y down
KM connected
Triple K
Triple K connected

Geometric Symbols

Bar
Double bar

Broken bar
Rail
Double rail
Stripes
Slash
Reverse slash
Broken slash
Broken reverse slash
Quarter circle
Half circle
Circle
Double circle
Half box
Box

Bench
Triangle
Half diamond
Diamond
Diamond and a half
Rafter
Open A
Goose egg
Dot

Pictorial Symbols

Arrow
Broken arrow
Bow and arrow
Rocking chair

Dollar sign
Anchor
Broken heart
Flying heart
Hay hook
Key
Tumbling ladder
Spur
Stirrup
Sunrise
Horse track
Bull head
Hat
Turkey track

FOUR TYPICAL BRANDS AND WHAT THEY MEAN

Monogram

Charles Goodnight's simple and famous J A brand spells out the initials of his partner John Adair. The running curves have a practical purpose: sharp angles tend to blotch and blur the brand.

Phonogram

Rancher J. H. Barwise re-created the two syllables of his last name in symbolic equivalents that combine to form his brand. Read correctly from top to bottom, this puzzle works out as Bar Ys.

Pictograph

A gunslinger turned rancher arrived in the West with nothing but two .45-caliber pistols to his name. Later, when he made good as a cattleman, those two guns were memorialized in his brand.

Word Story

"A man's a fool to raise cattle," said Texan T. J. Walker, and he took the word for his brand. Fun-loving cowpunchers with running irons would sometimes rope his bulls and change the F to a B.

roar—"Come, boys, get up and hear the little birds singing their sweet praises to the Lord God Almighty; *damn your souls, get up!*"

The District 8 roundup was captained by Tom Gibson, foreman of the J Lazy J, a strong-faced man in a big silver-bangled Mexican sombrero. Although Gibson's long-term strategy was to divide his force between the eastern and western halves of the area, on this first day of work everyone stayed together to gather the cattle grazing close at hand. This happened to be on the range of the Bow and Arrow, and by custom Gibson turned his authority for the day over to that ranch's foreman, Buck Merritt.

Once the cows were collected, it fell to Buck to rope the first calf for branding. But how could the ownership be determined? The answer to that puzzle was provided by the calf's already-branded mother. A cow loves her calf, and when it is roped at a roundup she shows her concern by wild-eyed bawling. This simple fact was one of the bases of the cattle ownership system, and Buck Merritt used it now. Holding fast to the struggling calf, he read the brand on a flank of its hovering mother and shouted: "Bow and Arrow." The manager of the Bow and Arrow did first honors by burning his brand on the little animal's side—and by the end of the day the air was acrid with the smell of scorched hair.

After the relatively easy work of the first day, the roundup army split. The majority, which went off to the eastern section, included the L U Bar crew—all but Luke Sweetman, who was assigned to represent the ranch with the smaller group in the west. Under the direction of Al Popham, foreman of the L S Ranch, Sweetman and his fellow cowhands moved upstream along the Yellowstone.

Up every day at about 3:30 a.m., each cowhand selected from his string of six horses the long-legged distance animal he would use that morning. Still in the darkness, Popham mapped out the plan of the day's campaign by drawing on the ground with a stick. He picked a spot at the center of the day's activities, and as soon as he did so the L S Ranch's chuck wagon, the roundup's mobile headquarters, set off for that place at a smart trot. Then Popham divided his mounted men into two bands of a dozen each to cover the left and right halves of the terrain ahead.

As the sun threw its first long shadows across the range, the leader of each band led his men out of camp. In theory—and in practice if the land was flat—the men would ride at an angle to the chuck wagon's route, then go parallel to it and finally curve back toward it. Every couple of miles the leader would tell off—that is, station—a rider, so that the two groups together would block out a circle about 20 miles in diameter. Once some of the cows were in hand, all the men would head back for the center along lines like the spokes of a wheel, driving and concentrating the cattle. The maneuver was performed with each man coming nearer the next, so that by weaving their horses back and forth they could make a cowproof net.

But the country northwest of the Yellowstone was broken in many places, requiring frequent detours that added to the distance the cowboys had to travel. With a change of horses, the circle riders often logged 35 miles in the morning and as much again in the afternoon.

During the spring roundup of 1886, the men working the western section of District 8 had a special problem. Day after day a silent crew of six gun-toting cowboys ghosted right along behind them. The strangers belonged to the STV Ranch, which the Montana Stockgrowers Association had barred from participation in the roundup. It seemed that the STV had put 3,500 Texas cattle to graze on ranges north of the Yellowstone that were already close to the point of being overgrazed.

Boycotts like this took place all over the West as big cattlemen who had grabbed government land tried to prevent smaller newcomers from doing the same—or from sharing in grazing rights. But in the case of the STV the attempted freeze-out failed, largely because the outcast ranch's owner, John H. Conrad, decided to ignore it. Among other things, he instructed his boys to follow the roundup's riders on circle. When, for example, Sweetman found a steer wearing the STV brand, he had no legal alternative but to drive it away, whereupon the STV man shadowing him took it under control. Thus, without belonging to the roundup, the STV benefited from it. As Sweetman observed, there was no real way to prevent a man from riding a rod or two away from the circle, "especially when he is armed." And in any case, he added, "It all happened on Uncle Sam's land."

Ignoring the intruders as best they could, the roundup cowboys got on with their morning's work, and by the time it was done, they were ravenous. According to an unwritten law, a rancher killed one of his own beeves when the operation was working his land. A good chuck-wagon cook would barbecue the fresh beef, having already spent the morning preparing an assortment of puddings and pies.

After the meal, Sweetman and the others chose ponies specially trained for roping and separating, or cutting, certain cattle from the main herd. The best cutting ponies were so alert and intelligent that their riders had little need of reins. In fact, a mounted man would often drop the reins to the saddle horn and steer with knee pressure alone, aware that over-guidance might distract the horse and break its concentration—which was intense. As soon as the rider showed the pony what calf or steer he wanted to cut out of the herd, the horse's ears began to twitch, and its eyes would be glued to the pursued animal while it was being chased toward the branding fire.

The cutting out of a herd followed a strict protocol. Whatever outfit seemed to have the most cows in a herd (usually the ranch that owned the range being worked) got first cut and sent in two or three men to get its calves. Then Popham judged which brand was the second most numerous, and that outfit's cowboys moved into the herd. And so on. Finally, the reps such as Sweetman were waved in to pick out any remaining strays.

Whenever a calf or unbranded steer got reasonably close to the fire, the pursuing cowboy unlimbered his rope to capture it. This was the roundup's single most dangerous job. A line carelessly dangled around a saddle horn could nip off a man's thumb or fingers as some steer pulled the rope taut. In the hurly-burly, men went crashing to the ground with their mounts.

Toward the end of each afternoon, the L S Ranch chuck wagon trundled off to a night camp, and after the branding was finished the crew and the cattle followed. After the final meal of the day, a few unlucky riders prepared to guard the herds in shifts throughout the night, while the rest of the crew bedded down. Before turning in for the night, the cook pointed the tongue of the chuck wagon toward the North Star to give the trial boss a sure compass heading in the morning.

Although the cowboys were exhausted after spending 15 or more hours in the saddle, sleep was often elusive. On hard ground, cushioned by no more than a quilt, men restlessly tossed and turned. Near prairie sloughs in late spring, they covered their heads with tarps to fend off mosquitoes (which could settle so thickly on a roan gelding as to make him appear gray, then, flying away, leave him streaked with blood). Unfortunately, although the tarps left the men half suffocated because they kept out oxygen along with the insects, they were about as effective as sieves against driving rain.

So it continued, day after day and night after night, until at last Popham's crew reached the divide between the Yellowstone and the Missouri—where, instead of quitting, it threw in for many days with the roundup of District 9. As part of this work, Popham sent men with pack horses northwest to the Missouri tributaries called Squaw Creek and Hell Creek, which ran through country too rugged for a wagon. As Sweetman later recalled it, in the stiff prose of his later years, the cowboys "penetrated those variegated, inaccessible nightmares of disturbed earth and brought out cattle

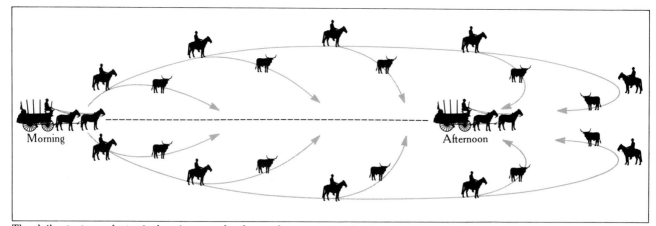

The daily strategy of a typical spring roundup focused on a moving chuck wagon from which the men fanned out in the morning and to which they circled back with the cattle for sorting and branding each afternoon.

The sky at night could tell a trailwise cowboy not only what direction he was facing but also the time: In every 24-hour period the Big Dipper made one full turn around the North Star.

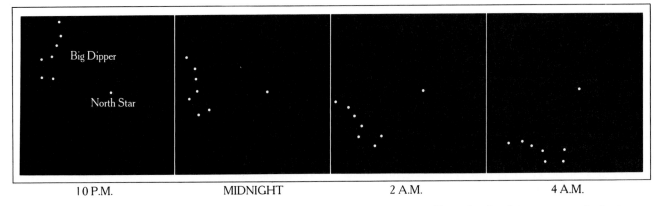

Big Dipper

North Star

10 P.M.   MIDNIGHT   2 A.M.   4 A.M.

that had not even been seen by man for over two years."

With that, the roundup ended. It had been, as Luke Sweetman proudly recorded in his journal, "a perfect job."

If the spring roundup (there would be another in the autumn) was an endless succession of bone-aching days for which not even the most dedicated cowboy could muster much enthusiasm, the phenomenon known as the long drive was altogether another matter.

It mattered not that to the profit-motivated cattle barons the long drive was only a means of moving masses of beef to market at the cost of a mere penny or so per mile per head. And never mind that the harsh realities of trail life could degrade a man to the point of forcing him to lick horse sweat from a saddle when the chuck wagon ran out of salt. Never mind, either, that in return for three to four months of dust, thirst, blisters, cold and danger the cowboy received a paltry $100 in hard wages. What really counted was the proud awareness of having passed the toughest test in the cowboy's trade and of being part of something grand and fundamental.

It was in response to that challenge that a 19-year-old redhead named Baylis John Fletcher hired out in the spring of 1879. His trail boss would be George Arnett, a former Confederate soldier and Indian fighter who had been employed to drive 2,500 cattle—an average-sized trail herd—from just north of Corpus Christi, Texas, to the vicinity of Cheyenne, Wyoming, a distance of 1,200 hard and perilous miles.

The drive began on April 11 to the rousing cowboy cry of "Ho cattle ho ho ho ho." This was a mixed herd of cows and calves, which tended to drive poorly because the mothers and their young wandered around looking for one another, calling in mournful groans like the notes

of a pipe organ. To make the drive more orderly, Arnett had brought along a few steers as leaders. Trail hands freely conceded it was the lead steers' initiative as much as the cowhands' prodding that kept the animals going.

Now, as the steers moved naturally to the front, the cows and calves followed behind them in a ragged line of march. While the trail boss rode ahead, other cowboys of the ten-man crew took holding positions on the herd's flanks. The worst job fell to the drag riders, who came at the rear, breathing dust through bandannas as they harassed lagging cattle.

Trouble came the second day out as the herd was passing through the town of Victoria and a splenetic old woman flapped her sun bonnet at the passing cattle to keep them off her roses. The lead steers stampeded, doubling back against their followers, and longhorns soon flashed in every street. No one was hurt, but it took Arnett and his boys several hours to stop the cattle, line them up and get them going again.

It was a bad start, made worse a few nights later. Young Baylis Fletcher and his night-guard partner, in dereliction of duty, were dismounted and warming themselves at a fire, when suddenly, the bedded cattle jumped to their feet and took off in another stampede.

Next morning 100 cows were missing. Four hard-looking men rode up and offered to find the missing animals for one dollar a head. George Arnett, correctly surmising that he was dealing with the very men who had started the stampede, offered 50 cents. The men accepted, but brought back only 60 head. Arnett's trail scouts rounded up another 20 strays, leaving 20 cows that had been successfully—but unprovably—rustled.

More than two weeks later, with the herd in central Texas, the sky opened up with a cannonade of hail-

A stern code for the XIT

In the turbulent early years of cattle ranching, cowboys had but one check on their behavior: loyalty to the rancher with whom they lived and worked. But when the big ranches came along, their absentee owners, needing to control scores of cowhands, brought in hard company rules limiting every aspect of life on the ranch. Below are only seven of the rules posted on the three-million-acre XIT spread in western Texas.

No employee of the Company, or of any contractor doing work for the Company, is permitted to carry on or about his person or in his saddle bags, any pistol, dirk, dagger, sling shot, knuckles, bowie knife or any other similar instruments for offense or defense.

Card playing and gambling of every description, whether engaged in by employees, or by persons not in the service of the Company, is strictly forbidden.

Employees are strictly forbidden the use of vinous, malt, spirituous, or intoxicating liquors, during their time of service with the Company.

Loafers, "sweaters," deadbeats, tramps, gamblers, or disreputable persons, must not be entertained at any camp, nor will employees be permitted to give, loan or sell such persons any grain, or provisions of any kind, nor shall such persons be permitted to remain on the Company's land under any pretext whatever.

Employees are not allowed to run mustang, antelope or any kind of game on the Company's horses.

No employee shall be permitted to own any cattle or stock horses on the ranch.

It is the aim of the owners of this ranch to conduct it on the principle of right and justice to everyone; and for it to be excelled by no other in the good behavior, sterling honesty and integrity, and general high character of its employees, and to this end it is necessary that the foregoing rules be adhered to, and the violation of any of them will be just charge for discharge.

stones as big as quail eggs, pelting birds and rabbits to death and raising welts on the men so bruising and numerous that the skin later sloughed off. The storm, of course, caused the herd to scatter, and it had to be rounded up again.

This was the only hailstorm of the trip, for which Fletcher was duly grateful. Working out on the prairie, with no natural shelter, cowboys dreaded hail; a man could protect himself only by quickly dismounting and covering his head with his saddle.

Four days after the hailstorm, the herd approached Fort Worth, the biggest town on the Chisholm Trail, that renowned avenue to the north that had been trampled smooth to a width of 200 to 400 yards by millions of clumping cattle. Beyond Fort Worth lay three weeks of easy going, with good grass and quiet weather. But then there was a barrier of critical importance to every cowboy driving north from Texas: the Red River, underlaid with quicksand and lined with trees bearing tangles of driftwood in their high branches, marking the high water mark of past floods. Here, a scattering of rude graves held the bones of men who had died while attempting to make the crossing.

Fletcher and the herd caught the Red River when it was low and fordable—but still ready to mete out a measure of trouble. In midcrossing, the cook stopped his wagon to fill the water barrel. The whole rig promptly sank to its axles in quicksand. The draft oxen, straining and twisting, ripped off the wagon tongue. Turning carpenters, the cowboys cut a cottonwood pole and sloshed into the water to bolt it to the wagon as a substitute pole. Then they borrowed two more yoke of oxen from another outfit that was waiting at the crossing. Together the six animals managed to drag the wagon across.

Now the men were in the Indian Territory. Though by 1879 the Indian hazard had waned, Baylis Fletcher was excitedly aware that they were heading across 300 miles of wild and lawless land belonging to savages, many of them still distinctly unfriendly. As a reasonably educated young fellow, Fletcher knew everything about Indians that could possibly be learned from the novels of James Fenimore Cooper. So he took his Winchester carbine, which had been stowed in the wagon, and stuck it into his saddle scabbard. The other boys rubbed their six-shooters bright and strapped them on.

"We marched on now, armed to the teeth for savage

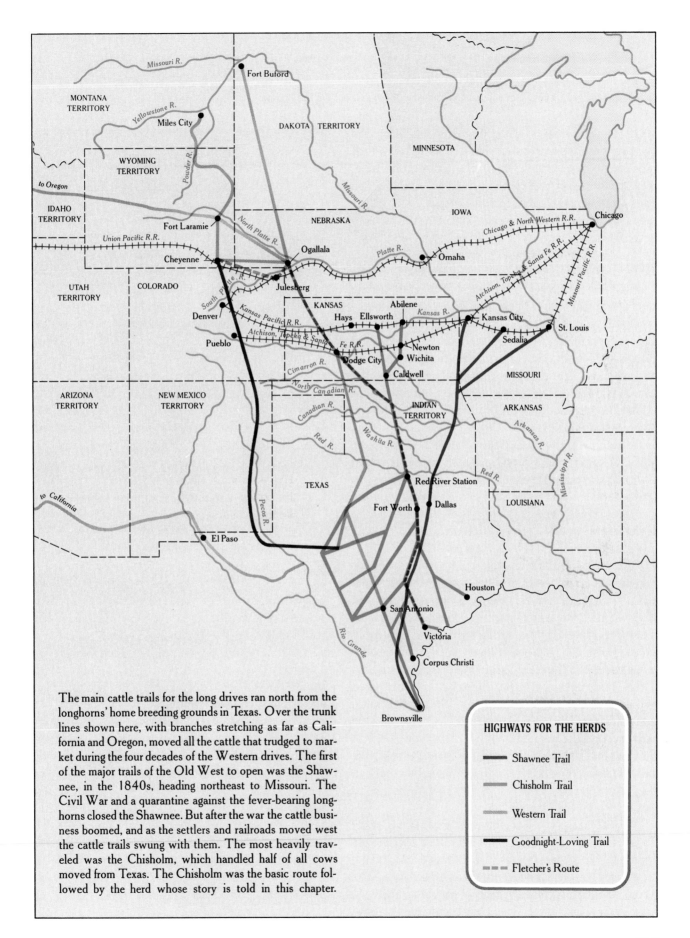

The main cattle trails for the long drives ran north from the longhorns' home breeding grounds in Texas. Over the trunk lines shown here, with branches stretching as far as California and Oregon, moved all the cattle that trudged to market during the four decades of the Western drives. The first of the major trails of the Old West to open was the Shawnee, in the 1840s, heading northeast to Missouri. The Civil War and a quarantine against the fever-bearing longhorns closed the Shawnee. But after the war the cattle business boomed, and as the settlers and railroads moved west the cattle trails swung with them. The most heavily traveled was the Chisholm, which handled half of all cows moved from Texas. The Chisholm was the basic route followed by the herd whose story is told in this chapter.

HIGHWAYS FOR THE HERDS

— Shawnee Trail
— Chisholm Trail
— Western Trail
— Goodnight-Loving Trail
- - - Fletcher's Route

foes." Fletcher wrote. Nothing much happened, and the boys vented their frustration with a running fusillade at rabbits and rattlesnakes. Then, on a mid-June morning, they spied riding in a circle around them . . . Indians! The chief approached. Fletcher, taking a wary stance as the Deerslayer might have done, bent to catch the warrior's fierce words.

"Mebbe-so white chief give Injun some beef?" the Indian begged. "Injun mighty hungry. Squaw mighty hungry. Papoose mighty hungry." Alas for romance, such was the typical trail encounter between cowboys and Indians.

The days that followed in Indian Territory passed almost hypnotically, the prairie unfolding before the trail riders in a slow, majestic panorama. For mile upon mile the cowboys could see nothing but an undulating expanse of seared brown grass. The only sounds were the muffled crack-crack of the cows' ankle joints, the steady thudding of hoofs.

By the end of June the trail riders made their last crossing of the Cimarron River on the border of the sovereign state of Kansas and embarked on a detour leading to Dodge City. The new route had become necessary a few years before when the state's government had bowed to pressure from settlers who feared that Texas cattle would infect their own livestock with tick fever.

With their animals now excluded from south-central Kansas, the trail drivers now faced a grueling 100-mile push to the Arkansas over virtually waterless country. At the herd's normal trailing speed, 100 miles would have taken eight days. By then, Arnett knew, the parched cattle might be dying or dead. He decided, therefore, to make the run in four days of double-speed driving.

The cattle went on the trail at sunrise on July 1, rested and grazed during the noonday sun, then marched on until after sundown. The harsh routine was followed the next day and the next. Then the cowboys got lucky: A providential rain squall provided a few puddles along the trail to relieve the cattle. And by the time they reached the Arkansas River near Dodge City they were able to water without overdrinking.

Had it not rained, they might have suffered two possible consequences. First, the cattle might have become ungovernable after three or four days without water, and the crew would have discovered that the animals had gone blind, a common effect of thirst. Or second, the cattle, unable to smell water ahead, might have turned back to the last drink-

Lullabies for jittery cows

Many cowboy ballads originated as a means of quieting stampede-prone cattle at night. Composed impromptu by cowhands riding around the herds, the often atonal songs took their rhythm from a horse's gait. Some had mournful tunes but no words and were termed "Texas lullabies." Others had standard verses that, like those excerpted below, became favorites.

Little Joe the Wrangler

Little Joe, the wrangler, was called out with the rest;
Though the kid had scarcely reached the herd,
When the cattle they stampeded, like a hailstorm
long they fled,
Then we were all a-ridin' for the lead.

❧

The next morning just at daybreak, we found where
his horse fell,
Down in a washout twenty feet below;
And beneath the horse, mashed to a pulp, his spur
had rung the knell,
Was our little Texas stray, poor Wrangling Joe.

The Old Chisholm Trail

I'm up in the mornin' afore daylight
And afore I sleep the moon shines bright.

❧

No chaps and no slicker, and it's pouring down rain,
And I swear, by God, that I'll never night-herd again.

❧

Oh, it's bacon and beans most every day—
I'd as soon be a-eatin' prairie hay.

❧

I went to the boss to draw my roll,
He had it figured out I was nine dollars in the hole.

❧

I'll sell my horse and I'll sell my saddle;
You can go to hell with your longhorn cattle.

At trail's end, the lead steers usually went the way of the other cows—straight into the loading pens for slaughter. But a few proved so valuable on the trail that they were spared to lead again.

ing place they remembered—perhaps three or four days behind them—and many would have perished.

Once a dry drive was over, it was customary for trail bosses to let a herd lie over for a couple of days while the men rested. But it so happened that the Texas owner of the herd was a blue-nose sort who did not like his hirelings even to curse, much less carouse. Acquiescing to the wishes of his pious boss, Arnett allowed Fletcher and the boys only a few hours to visit Dodge—and then just during the day, when the pleasure parlors of a town famous for its bacchanalian delights were in low gear. Having thus been spared by their employer's morals from all temptation to drink, gamble and dance with floozies, the crew put the herd back onto the trail on July 6 for the last leg of the drive, 380 miles through Kansas toward Wyoming.

A few days beyond Dodge City, the crew passed the carcass of a horse and, nearby, the grave of its rider. Both had been killed by lightning—one of the commonest causes of death on the trail and perhaps the prairie's most spectacular sight. Said one vivid account of the phenomenon: "It first commenced like flash lightning, then came forked lightning, then chain lightning, followed by the peculiar blue lightning. After that show it rapidly developed into ball lightning, which rolled along the ground . . . then, most wonderful of all, it settled down on us like fog. The air smelled of burning sulphur;

you could see it on the horns of the cattle, the ears of our horses and the brims of our hats. It grew so warm we thought we might burn up with it."

But the herd's luck held: It weathered July's thundersqualls with no casualties to either livestock or men. As it moved westward through the Platte River valley to Wyoming the land rose until the herd was traveling at an altitude of four thousand feet. Though the noon sun still bore down hard, the nights were becoming almost too chilly for Texans reared in the humid climes of the Gulf Coast.

With little more than 100 miles to go, they branched off the Platte Valley and began following a section of an old Mormon trail, from which they merged onto a broad plateau some 6,000 feet above sea level. And there, strung out in a distant line of stone and snow, lay the Rocky Mountains. Wrote Fletcher: "I feasted my eyes for several days on the backbone of America."

On August 15, 1879, Fletcher and his fellow riders, all tired, bearded, shaggy-haired and dirty, arrrived at their destination near Cheyenne and turned their herd over to its purchaser, the Swan Brothers Cattle Company, one of the most powerful outfits in the West.

When his odyssey had begun, Baylis John Fletcher was a boy who worked with cows. Now, after passing the supreme test of the long drive, he was a cowboy, fit to ride with the best into the history of the Old West.

At the Cosmopolitan Saloon in the affluent mining town of Telluride, Colorado, the marshal leans benignly against the gleaming mahogany bar as

VI. A ROUGH-HEWN SOCIETY

midafternoon gambling goes on apace across the room. Other diversions are suggested by the nude on the far wall—a portrait of a local Jezebel.

A splendidly wide main street—with the town's well in the middle—marks an ambitious beginning for Mullinville, Kansas, in the 1880s.

Making nowhere somewhere

"A new western village is truly indescribable in language. It can only be compared to itself." So wrote a young lawyer to his folks in the East after arriving in Kansas in 1858. His bafflement was understandable, for surely there was nothing back home quite so forlorn-looking yet so brimming with high hopes as the town he was helping to build beyond the Missouri.

The young lawyer was part of an army of men and women—doctors, merchants, millers, barbers, bankers and blacksmiths—who poured westward in the second half of the 19th Century to transform a near-wilderness into a thriving land, and as one frontier editor said, "to get rich if we can."

The new settlers were a sturdy and resourceful breed. A minister who settled in Nebraska in 1856 reported that they were endowed with "the three P's—poverty, providence and pluck." Beyond that they were equipped with boundless energy. They started towns by the thousands, mostly on the prairies and plains, where farming would support a stable population. They laid out broad streets, and achieved a touch of elegance with brave false-fronted structures. Then they battled fire, flood and pestilence, subdued the lawless, engaged in ceaseless boosterism—and sometimes went on to attain the dream of urban greatness that had inspired them as they put up the first building.

Some towns were built on false hopes. In 1868 the 200 citizens of Bear River City, Wyoming, were hastily setting up enterprises on the assumption that the Union Pacific would stop there and make their community important—but the railroad passed them by without even a sidetrack.

To establish a look of civic maturity—and in the hope of making their town county seat—the 700 citizens of two-year-old Marfa, Texas, saddled themselves with a $71,000 bond issue in 1886 and erected an imposing courthouse and a capacious jail *(at right)* on the outskirts of town.

13. The sprouting of cities and towns

It was a curious gathering. Thousands of anxious men stood poised at various points on the boundary of the region known as Indian Territory and, later, Oklahoma. No train was in sight, no august personality was scheduled to arrive. And yet all eyes were focused on a nearby watering stop on the Atchison, Topeka and Santa Fe Railroad known as Guthrie. In a few minutes—at the stroke of noon, April 22, 1889—a town was going to spring to life in this vast, open land. Not that the palpitating throng had gone to watch; they were there instead to engage in a frenzied bout of creativity.

The region had once been deeded to several tribes by treaty with the U.S. government. But early in 1889, responding to pressures by covetous farmers and townsmen, Congress acquired the District from the Indians and declared it open to white settlement. President Benjamin Harrison set the opening time for twelve o'clock noon on April 22—and also hinted that Guthrie would someday become a territorial capital.

As the magical moment approached, U.S. cavalrymen held the passel of Guthrie's prospective landowners in check until precisely noon. Then, as bugles sounded, the land rush began. Hordes of mule- or ox-drawn prairie schooners rumbled forward in clouds of dust. Some men wobbled along on high-wheeled bicycles; others sprinted toward the goal on foot or galloped ahead by horse—including four circus midgets on a single mount. Finally, to the toot of whistles, six trains steamed forth, quickly gaining the lead.

Even before the trains had come to a full stop, most of the passengers leaped off. They began furiously pounding the stakes they had brought along to claim lots that had been marked off by federal surveyors a few days earlier. Hard on their heels came the horsemen, wagon drivers, cyclists and runners. Among the stampeding hordes were several hundred railroad workers who contrived to get the jump on everyone by reaching Guthrie ahead of time, thereby earning them the label of "sooners"—a nickname that all Oklahomans were eventually to adopt.

By the time night fell a tent city was up and brawling. Within a day more than 10,000 people were calling Guthrie home; within a week, the frenetic genesis had already produced its first frame buildings—and 50 saloons. At the venerable age of a month, the city boasted a hotel, three newspapers, three general stores and numerous restaurants.

In a world of lightning changes, the once-somnolent outpost of Guthrie, Oklahoma, had become, quite simply, the fastest-growing town in the West.

The overnight metamorphosis that transformed Guthrie from nowhere to somewhere was unusual even by the exuberant standards of the Old West. But it was a story repeated in thousands of scenarios throughout the second half of the 19th Century. History has never recorded a social phenomenon quite like the mass impulse that filled the American West with cities, towns and hamlets. Like most movements, the shift westward in the United States began tentatively, but once it took hold there was no stopping the flood. Land-starved Easterners and European immigrants alike were captivated by a combination of glorious dreams and grandiose expectations. What started as a trickle early in the 19th Century became, within a few decades, a veritable tidal wave of humanity, determined to place their stamp on the prairies and mountainsides of the West.

The Civil War slowed the westward movement that had been forged by mountain men, then pioneers. But

Two of the busiest craftsmen in Guthrie, Oklahoma, take a break outside their shop in April of 1889. The town, having sprung up on newly opened government lands just a few days earlier, needed signs as fast as Walker & McCoy could turn them out.

after this national storm passed, the real rush began. Homesteaders and townspeople surged into the trackless void by the tens of thousands. In addition to the towns that proliferated to serve the needs of a permanent farm population, many other settlements came into being as lay-over points for people and goods in transit. By 1869 the way was paved with tens of thousands of miles of railroad track. Stretching across the grassland, the network now provided a transcontinental link that invigorated commerce in existing settlements and created towns every time a spur branched off.

Conceiving and selling the settlements was one of the hottest business angles of the time. A barrage of brochures and ballyhoo enticed people westward with calls like "Come! Rush! Hurry! Don't wait for Anything!" Easterners had only to open the door a crack to be battered by some boomer's appeal, delivered on paper or in person. Without a blush, speculators would dub the most rudimentary community a city. The practice was so common that *New York Tribune* correspondent Bayard Taylor complained on a visit to Colorado in 1866, "I only wish that the vulgar, snobbish custom of attaching City to every place of more than three houses could be stopped."

The faster the number of would-be towns outstripped the supply of settlers, the quicker promoters—those Pied Pipers of the 19th Century—were reduced to indulging in blatant puffery. As the claims grew so did the gulf between promises and reality. "On paper *all* these towns were magnificent," wrote journalist Albert Richardson, who crisscrossed Kansas during the 1850s and 1860s. "But if the newcomer had the unusual wisdom to visit the prophetic city before purchasing lots, he learned the difference between fact and fancy. The town might be composed of twenty buildings; or it might not contain a single human habitation. Anything was marketable. Wags proposed an act of Congress reserving some land before the whole Territory should be divided into city lots. It was not a swindle, but a mania."

Not everyone succumbed to the seductive selling spiels in brochures—what one disgruntled Easterner called a "chromatic triumph of lithographed mendacity." After all, many of the millions of settlers who crossed the Mississippi and Missouri rivers were only indirectly concerned with towns. They came instead to wrest a living from the region by tilling its soil, grazing cattle upon its almost limitless grasslands or extracting precious metals from its streams and mountains.

But along with them—or only a half step behind—came men and women who proposed to win their livelihood by providing goods and services for the rest of the population. These were the townsmen: the butchers, bakers, bankers, bootmakers and barbers, the teachers and tailors, the doctors and dentists, locksmiths and liverymen, the saloonkeepers and sheriffs of the Old West. Inevitably, their ranks also included desperadoes, shysters, prostitutes, professional gamblers and scalawags, but mostly they were serious men and women bound upon the honest mission of building a new society in the wilderness.

"The mother's milk to an infant town," as one journalist modestly put it, was a newspaper, and one of the first citizens of any community was the editor, often hired by the promoters of the place. His function, in the beginning at least, was not so much to report on local events as to sing the praises of his community for the benefit of any prospective settlers among the newspaper's out-of-town readership. "No better or more desirable place can be found in the state of Kans.," claimed the editor of the *Winfield Courier* in touting his community. "Situate on one of the most beautiful and romantic streams imaginable, on as pretty a site as could well be selected, built up with neat substantial, and some even elegant buildings. Composed of a class of people, who, for energy, enterprise, are not excelled."

An editor's performance as publicist was closely monitored by his fellow townsmen, for their future depended largely on the efficacy of his proselytizing. Just how strongly they might feel about lackluster work was discovered in 1878 by the editor of the *Barber County Mail* of Medicine Lodge, Kansas. Printed with worn out and broken type, the publication was so hard to read that dissatisfied residents invaded the editor's premises and hauled him outdoors. Coating him with sorghum molasses and sand burs, the editor's critics capped his punishment by riding him around town on a wooden rail. The hapless editor sold the paper shortly thereafter and left for parts unknown.

Any community that hoped to grow beyond infancy needed a hotel—to accommodate prospective towns-

PAWNEE
KANSAS TER.

COME ONE   COME ALL!

PUBLIC SALE OF LOTS!!

In consequence of numerous applications
from persons desirous of building immediately, the trustees are induced to announce

A SALE OF LOTS

to take place at an earlier date than that already advertised.

There will therefore be TWO Sales of Lots in PAWNEE, one on the 10th of APRIL and the other on the 15th of MAY next.

The situation of PAWNEE is such as scarcely to admit a doubt of its becoming in a short time a large and important place. Being at the head of navigation of the Kansas it is the most delightful starting point for persons emigrating to our more western territories. A Military road from Pawnee to Bridgers Pass in the Rocky Mountains affords the most direct route to Utah, California and Oregon, whilst the road to New Mexico is considerably shortened by a new one recently made. The Military post of Fort Riley is scarcely distant a mile from Pawnee and the government business connected with it will mostly be transacted here.

Ample accomodations will be ready for persons attending the SALES. These as above stated will be on the 10th of April and 15th of May next.

TERMS.--Half the purchase money in cash; the ballance on completion of the title.

PAWNEE, K. T., March 12th, 1855.   HERALD OFFICE PRINT, LEAVENWORTH, K. T.

Editor James Curren *(center)* works at a hand press to get out an issue of the first daily paper in Kingston, New Mexico, in 1886. A newspaper often preceded the town itself, and many a journal published early issues outdoors until a building became available.

men as well as transients—and a hotelkeeper was generally among the first arrivals. His hospitality was often crude. At one frontier hotel, a guest who expressed dismay at the condition of the roller towel was told by his host, "There's 26 men used that towel before you and you're the first one that complained."

Along with a newspaper and a hotel, a saloon invariably appeared on the scene to dispense the fiery potables—and sometimes a variety of entertainment—that made life in a hard land a little easier. Saloonkeepers were particularly numerous in towns whose prime customers were cowboys or miners. Abilene, Kansas, for example, boasted 11 saloons to accommodate the 5,000 or more trail-parched cowboys who arrived herding

Texas longhorns. In mining towns, the saloons often stayed wide-open 24 hours a day seven days a week to squeeze the last dollar out of the prospectors.

Few new towns were lucky enough to attract the full array of skills and talents that contributed to the convenience of life in the East, including saddlers, shoemakers, tailors, cabinetmakers and hatters. Given the lack of such specialists, the early townsmen often had to settle for second-rate work from untrained, inept or overextended practitioners of all kinds.

Most vexing was the scarcity of qualified doctors. Many of the practitioners who arrived in frontier towns were impelled there by a lack of success back East, which was sometimes directly traceable to a lack of

on average. Not surprisingly, most schoolteachers regarded their job as a way stop to marriage or some more comfortable line of work.

Far more common in frontier towns were lawyers—and understandably so. The pay was rewarding: Lawyers could earn anywhere from a few hundred to more than $1,000 a month simply by settling land claims or mining claims, two prime sources of frontier litigation. Another reason for the abundance of lawyers was the ease of gaining admittance to the bar in new territories. To qualify, the applicant simply had to be at least 21 years old, supply evidence of good moral character and pass an examination before a judge—who usually limited his quiz to a few vague and simple questions since he probably had little legal training himself. Before the Civil War earned him fame as a general, William Tecumseh Sherman gained admittance to the Kansas bar merely by showing that he had a rich fund of miscellaneous knowledge.

No town was complete without a blacksmith, whose services were needed to shoe horses and oxen, sharpen plows, repair wagons and perform a multitude of other maintenance tasks for the community and outlying areas. In fact, so essential was this craftsman that town founders often offered blacksmiths free building lots as incentives to settle in their communities.

But the most indispensable townsman of all was the merchant who ran the chief focus of a new town's commercial life—the general store. Called a shebang—a term that may have derived from the Gaelic *shebeen*, or speakeasy—the storekeeper dispensed liquor in bottled form, along with almost anything imaginable that a frontiersman might crave. Everyone within walking or riding distance called in at the shebang, hovered over the shelves of goods, loitered amid the deliciously mingled odors and the warmth of the potbellied stove, and came away with a heartening sense of well-being.

Any customer who entered that wonderfully self-contained world could not help being overwhelmed by the cornucopia it contained. Not an inch of space was wasted: On one side of the typical general store stood a counter for groceries; on the other, a counter and shelves piled high with dry goods. Hardware—along with the proprietor's high desk and stool—took up the rear. From the rafters hung the vague shapes of hams, slabs of bacon, cooking pots and stocking caps. Arranged

competence. But even the capable men did not always find greener pastures beyond the Missouri, where they were expected to preside over difficult births, perform operations without proper anesthetics on kitchen tables or remove Indian arrows—a surgical procedure not taught in Eastern medical schools.

Almost as rare as competent doctors were qualified schoolteachers. The standard offer of free room and board at the homes of pupils scarcely compensated for the rigors of teaching in a crude one-room schoolhouse for the low wages of $10 to $35 a month. And even that meager income was anything but steady: Wages were paid only when school was in session, and children on the frontier attended school for only five months a year

around the floor was a treasury of kegs and barrels brimming with sugar, vinegar, flour and molasses; canisters of condiments and spices; sacks of whatever produce the season offered; and big glass jars of striped candy sticks and peppermint balls.

Practically every male customer who came into the store spent some time in the rough circle of chairs around the stove and the cracker barrel, talking lazily about politics, the weather, anything that came to mind. The proprietor might offer a dram or two of whiskey from a barrel in the back room. Those who chewed tobacco used the pan of ashes in front of the stove for a spittoon—missing as often as they scored.

The women who came to the store were in the habit of taking up a bench near the front door, and in some ways their visit was even more important to them than it was to the men. For those who came from outlying areas it was a rare opportunity to be with other women and discuss everything from weddings to babies and frilly bonnets—and to fondle the calicoes and muslins and ready-to-wears they could ill afford to buy. It made no difference that the fashions were already a year old in the East and two years old in Paris.

One merchant understood the yearnings well: "I have often seen a hard-worked country lady come into a store and inquire after all the handsomest goods in the stock, and admire them, comment on them, take out great strips of pretty patterns and with her knotted fingers fold them into pleats and drape them over her plain skirt, her face illumined with pleasure at the splendor of such material. Bright, harmonious colors, and fine fabrics, over which she would draw her tired hands caressingly, soothed and gratified her. Who could grudge her such a privilege?"

Certainly not James and Robert Aull, who journeyed west from Delaware to the Missouri frontier and introduced the institution of the chain store to the American West. With four branches and a headquarters in Lexington, Missouri, James Aull made laborious pilgrimages East each fall to buy everything from stoves, axes and plows, coarse wool and cotton cloth, flour and feathers for feather beds, to cravats, green gauze veils, black silk gloves, bonnets and palm leaf hats, violin strings, music boxes, playing cards, chessmen, Pike's *Arithmetic*, Byerly's *Speller*, *Robinson Crusoe*, *Don Quixote* and the collected works of William Shakespeare.

TILTING WATER BASIN

The goods Aull bought in January might reach the Missouri stores in April. But all manner of costly difficulties were sure to be encountered en route—from Indian raids to shipwrecks, rough handling and outright thefts by riverboat roustabouts. Yet most of it got through eventually, and the Aulls, like their competitors, served their communities in many ways. They were friends, confidants and bankers of sorts, extending credit and accepting farm produce in lieu of cash. A customer named Aaron Overton paid off his account with barrels of home-distilled whiskey, while other customers brought in beeswax, honey, tallow, meat, skins, eggs, butter or cider in exchange for store goods. A few needy souls paid for their purchases by slaughtering hogs, chopping wood or cutting brush.

Most of these pioneer merchants were Americans, for whom the frontier was still a living memory in the East. But some were tradesmen who had come all the way from the Old World to join a society that was utterly unknown to them. One of the first and most enterprising was Michel "Big Mike" Goldwater, who was born into a family of 22 children in Konin, a town west of Warsaw in Poland. In 1847, when local unrest attracted the unpleasant attentions of the Russian Czar's Cossacks, he left home and journeyed first to Paris and then London, where he worked as a tailor, married a dressmaker and anglicized his patronym from the original Goldwasser. While there, he was joined by his younger brother Joseph and others of his kin.

In his mid-30s, Bob Wright had already founded Dodge City and prospered in the buffalo-hide trade. But his merchandising glory days lay just ahead, when cowboys began pouring into Dodge in 1876.

Feverish talk of California gold soon spread through Europe and brought the Goldwaters across the Atlantic in 1852. Their intention was not to pan for gold, but to employ their commercial background in catering to the men who did. Big Mike opened a saloon and billiard parlor in the town of Sonora, California, selling fruit and candy as a sideline. When the Sonora gold field petered out in 1857 he moved to Los Angeles and joined his brother Joseph in operating a saloon in the Bella Union Hotel. Together they used their profits to open two general stores in Los Angeles.

Craving new business, Mike began operating a traveling store, hauled by four mules, that made regular runs as far as the western edge of Arizona. During the next quarter of a century he built a far-ranging empire, operating better than half a dozen stores in California and Arizona. When he retired in 1885 he handed over the reins to his sons Baron and Morris. The younger Goldwaters carried on in the trailblazing footsteps of their father by opening the most prestigious store in Phoenix. There they became the fashion pacesetters and arbiters of taste—a generation after their father had sold knives, tobacco, belts and ammunition to a collection of gold miners, frontier soldiers and hardscrabble farmers.

While Big Mike Goldwater and his family roamed the West, one entrepreneur proved that you could stay at home and still make it big. For Robert M. Wright, a boyish-looking native of Maryland, home now meant Dodge City—a southern Kansas town he co-founded in 1872 to capitalize on the approach of the Atchison, Topeka and Santa Fe Railroad.

Trading in buffalo hides stoked the early fires of the town's financial success; but within a few years the prairies were picked clean of uncounted millions of the valuable beasts and the trade was exhausted. However, a replacement business was on the way. The great resource that was to make Dodge City the hell-roaringest town on the frontier—and Bob Wright's fortune—was Texas cattle, driven north by cowboys with money to burn.

Dodge City's destiny as the last, boomingest and most long-lived of the Kansas cattle towns was a gift implicit in its location. Situated in the "southwestern sixteenth" of the state, Dodge was a convenient point from which to ship Texas cattle. By the late 1870s it was also one of the few remaining railroad towns in Kansas still legally open to Texas herds, whose longhorns were host to the tick-borne splenic fever deadly to local cattle.

The Kansas legislature had decreed a quarantine line, running roughly north-south, designed to limit longhorn drives to the western parts of Kansas, which were largely unsettled. Year after year, with the continuing influx of farmers, the quarantine line was moved inexorably westward and southward. One by one the cattle towns were closed off behind the line, and the Texas cattle drivers were obliged to seek new shipping centers. Finally, only Dodge and a few lesser towns along the Santa Fe Railroad were left.

The rise of Dodge as the preeminent cattle town in Kansas created a bitter rift between two key elements in the community. Local farmers saw the cattlemen's business as threatening their livelihood. They already

had trouble enough wresting a living from the often-parched soil without having their grain fields ravaged by the hungry herds and their stock decimated by the imported fever. But the father of Dodge exerted all his growing business acumen and political influence to ensure that the rising tide of longhorns did not abate. According to Wright, the future of Dodge City—not to mention his general store—depended on a sure and steady influx of free-spending cowboys.

The herds increased year after year—from 300,000 head in 1877 to nearly 500,000 in 1882. And so did Bob Wright's fortune as he extolled far and wide the open hospitality that Dodge City merchants extended to those engaged in the cattle trade. By 1880 the town, with about 700 full-time residents, supported 14 saloons and 47 prostitutes. In the meantime, Wright's store took care of just about any material need that might arise—from a bowie knife to a portable house.

To be sure, Bob Wright's policy was "live and let live." Much to the chagrin of Dodge City's more sober citizens, this created a freewheeling atmosphere unfettered by the niceties of law and decorum. A rival town's newspaper characterized Dodge as "the rendezvous of all the unemployed scallawagism in seven states. Her principal business," the report added, "is polygamy without the sanction of religion; her code of morals is the honor of thieves and decency she knows not."

As Wright discovered, boosting economic growth was only one of the problems facing a new community; controlling lawlessness was an equally pressing concern. Frontier town settlers were not above turning over the task of maintaining law and order to groups of vigilantes, whose idea of justice involved more than a passing familiarity with the noose. In Dodge, as the public outcry for peace and quiet reached full voice in the early 1880s, local lawmen required all visitors to relinquish their shooting irons for the duration of their stay in town. Ever the eloquent defender of his

town's good name, Wright did admit tolerantly that Dodge after dark and south of the track tended to be somewhat on the hair-raising side.

By the time Wright became mayor in 1885 the town's saloons, gambling halls and dance halls were still going full blast. However, there were ominous portents for the future. The outcry of the town's conservative element against the drinking, gambling and whoring of the cowboys prompted state governor John Martin to warn that the town's continuing "depravity" had to stop.

Wright fired back a letter. "Let us alone," he advised, "and we will work out our own salvation in due season."

But Dodge City's fortunes as a cattle town had already begun to crest. The first year of Wright's mayoralty was one of unusually abundant rainfall. A fresh influx of farmers—responding to the promise of fertile fields—poured into the county. The state legislature, no longer able to withstand the farmers' call for protection, that year extended the quarantine line all the way to the western border of the state. After 10 riotous, heavy years, the cattle drives from Texas to Dodge were finally at an end.

Many businesses in Dodge failed within the following decade; Wright himself barely escaped bankruptcy. When Dodge at last recovered it was a very different place: The longhorns and cowboys were gone forever. But Bob Wright was still there when the hitching rail in front of his store was uprooted to make room for automobiles, and he was as proud as ever. "Hurrah for little Dodge!" wrote the tradesman who had built, boosted, guided, coddled and protected his town for so many years. "She has a bigger heart, for her size, than any town in Kansas."

The rainfall that helped to end Dodge City's life as the undisputed king of cattle towns also gave rise to orchards, vast acreages of golden wheat and lush, green

alfalfa. But weather did not always play such a beneficent role. Predictable only in its excesses, it could also
serve as a formidable opponent to the life of a townsman and his town.

Each season brought its catalog of miseries. Winter's
weapon was the blizzard, and in mountain towns residents were regularly snowed in for weeks at a time.
Townsmen on the plains had no easier a time; there,
snow was whipped by berserk winds that could rush
hundreds of miles without encountering an obstacle.

The situation scarcely improved as the weather
turned warmer. Erratic cloudbursts in spring or summer could bring a flash flood roiling down a creekbed.
Or a wet spring, combined with the snowmelt from the
Rockies, could send a river spilling over its banks. Such
an act of nature could devastate the works of the townsmen, who too often ignored the counsel of friendly
Indians against building a house in a watercourse. In
March 1881, when the Missouri River flooded, three
quarters of the town of Vermilion, Dakota Territory,
simply disappeared.

At the opposite extreme, great droughts periodically
afflicted the plains, causing intense suffering on the
farms and in the towns as well. In late summer and fall
the grasslands turned sere, and the land was at the
mercy of fire, caused by a lightning stroke or a single
man's carelessness. Since fields and weeds usually ran
well into the village limit, such prairie fires did not
spare the towns.

Considering the merciless vagaries of Nature it was
surprising that any Western towns survived at all. But
survive many did, a few even reaching the hallowed
rank of cityhood with astonishing brevity. In 1854,
Omaha, Nebraska, consisted of one log house 16 feet
square. By 1856 the town's population had grown to
1,600 and some of its choicest building lots sold for
$2,500. A year later the lots had catapulted to $4,000
and Omaha boasted 3,000 people.

Boulder, Colorado, was more typical in its rate of
development. Founded in 1859 as a supply town for the
nearby mining camps—and consisting of only a few
mud-roofed log cabins—the little settlement eked out
a humble existence in its first few years. But as time
went by more precious metals were discovered and
two local railroads entered the town. By 1880 it had
become the seat of Boulder County. Gateway to the
mountain mines and a popular summer resort, Boulder
now boasted a population of 4,000 with two banks, six
churches and two weekly newspapers.

Yet for every Omaha or Boulder, there were many
towns that stayed small. And there were many others
that did well for a time, then withered away when local
mineral deposits played out or the cattle herds stopped
coming. Thus, a townsman needed courage, particularly
in the beginning, when his chosen community seemed
so vulnerable. If his town failed completely he needed
the fortitude to put the past behind him; once again he
would have to begin his life anew.

As difficult as it surely was, the townsman's existence
was far from joyless. The good life for a hard-working
citizen meant money in his pocket, a place to hang his
hat, a square meal at day's end—and something more.
Every man on the frontier knew that his whole being
needed nourishment of another kind: fodder for the
spirit and relaxation for the mind.

Across the wide Missouri and over the mountains
and plains came a kaleidoscopic variety of entertainers, braving rough travel conditions and sometimes
even rougher audiences to offer the priceless commodity of amusement. The spectrum was colorful and vast,
ranging from cockfights and boxing bouts to Gilbert
and Sullivan operettas and the sonorous rhetoric of
Shakespeare. Spanning the gulf between lowly and lofty
were marching bands, song-and-dance acts in saloons,
tear-jerking melodramas, and just about every possible
escape from the workaday world ever imagined.

Local tastes differed, but certain types of entertainment were popular virtually everywhere. When John
Robinson's Great World Exposition rolled into Western
communities, all hearts thrilled to its triumphant
parade of "31 Chariots, 4 Steam Organs, 60 Cages, 8
Bands and 2 Calliopes." The circus itself offered one
breathtaking sight after another: "Lulu, the tattooed
lady," "Zola, riding a velocipede over a single wire sixty
feet above the heads of the audience," "Zenobia, hurled
200 feet by the ancient Roman war engine, the cata-
pult," and "28 female Siberian roller skaters!"

The patent-medicine show could be almost as
grand. To peddle his magical nostrums, the patent-
medicine man not only relied on his splendid spiel and
imperishable vocal chords, but frequently employed

A surprise breakthrough for the better half

The passage of the nation's first women's suffrage law *(opposite)* by the Wyoming territorial government in 1869 was intended as a public relations gesture. It was expected to add no more than 1,000 active voters to the electorate, and although it gave women the right to hold office, most men assumed that the ladies would choose to stay home where they belonged. But the newly enfranchised voters were following a separate scenario. They promptly demanded more active roles for women in government, a prospect so unnerving to the all-male legislature that in 1871 it tried—and failed by one vote—to repeal the suffrage bill.

Wyoming's first woman officeholder was 57-year-old Esther Morris, one of the territory's most renowned suffragists. Despite a lack of legal training, she was appointed justice of the peace for the mining town of South Pass City.

Esther Morris

She ran her court with an iron hand for nearly a year and never had a decision reversed by a higher court.

Even as Judge Morris was gaveling rowdies into the calaboose, other women were pioneering as members of juries in Laramie and Cheyenne. Although cartoonists were quick to lampoon them *(below),* the women jurors took their new duties seriously. In one notable Laramie murder case, a jury of six men and six women was locked up for two and a half days trying to reach a verdict. The men, three of whom favored acquittal, played cards, smoked and drank beer in one room, while the women, unanimously for conviction, sang hymns and prayed next door. Finally the impasse was broken with a compromise verdict: guilty on a lesser charge of manslaughter.

Wyoming's widely publicized example emboldened women throughout the region to seek the same rights. By 1896, women had won the vote in Utah, Colorado and Idaho, and had begun to play a major role in politics and professional life all across the West.

This all-female Wyoming jury was the fanciful creation of a New York magazine artist; actually, women jurors always served with men.

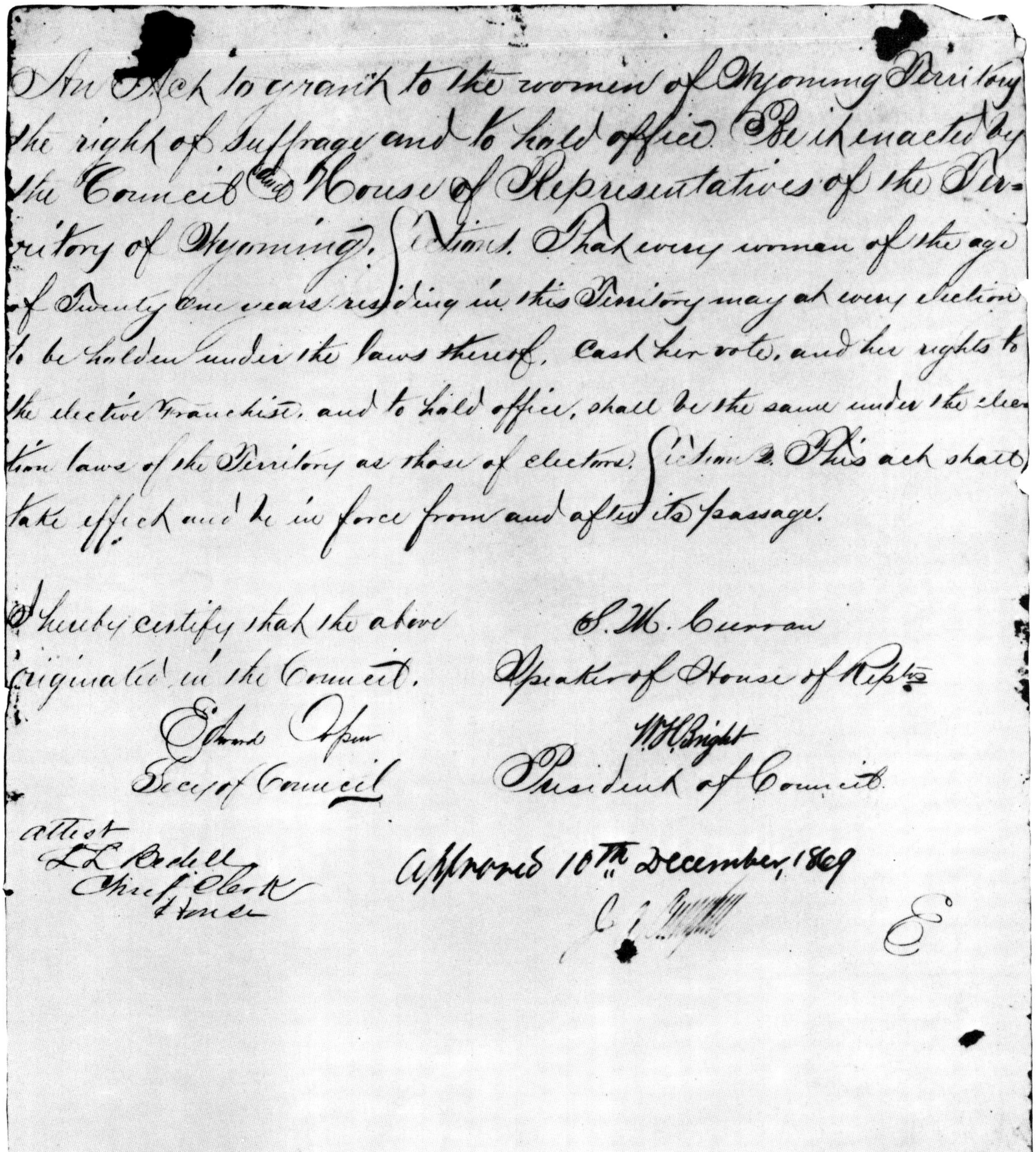

An Act to grant to the women of Wyoming Territory the right of Suffrage and to hold office. Be it enacted by the Council and House of Representatives of the Territory of Wyoming. Section 1. That every woman of the age of Twenty One years residing in this Territory may at every election to be holden under the laws thereof, Cast her vote, and her rights to the elective Franchise, and to hold office, shall be the same under the election laws of the Territory as those of electors. Section 2. This act shall take effect and be in force from and after its passage.

I hereby certify that the above originated in the Council.

S. W. Curran
Speaker of House of Repts

Edward Open
Secy of Council

W. H. Bright
President of Council.

attest
L L Bedell
Chief Clerk
House

Approved 10th December, 1869
J. J. Campbell

Recd at Governors office 6th Dec, 1869, 130 P.M.

Wyoming's historic law bears the signature of Governor John Campbell, a 34-year-old bachelor who had been widely expected to veto it.

Lillian Heath dressed like a man and toted pistols while studying under the only doctor in Rawlins, Wyoming. In 1893 she began work as the town's first obstetrician.

Grace Hebard was a civil engineer, the first woman admitted to the Wyoming bar, a university professor, a golf champion and the author of numerous Western histories.

Mary Lathrop showed herself a pace-setter as Denver's first woman lawyer and went on to achieve another first when she was admitted to the American Bar Association.

Susanna Salter, a housewife in Argonia, Kansas, became America's first woman mayor in 1887 after she was nominated as a joke and—irked—would not withdraw.

Estelle Reel, a Laramie, Wyoming, schoolteacher, was the first woman elected to a state office, winning the post of superintendent of schools in 1894 by a landslide.

Hired for three months in 1884 in an experiment by the Denver police department, Sadie Likens spent nearly a decade as the first full-time policewoman in the West.

A DEDICATED FEMALE VANGUARD

As the wave of emancipation rippled outward from Wyoming across the West, almost every town proved to have a share of women who aspired to positions that had been traditionally barred to their sex: doctor, lawyer, police officer, politician. Inevitably, most had to work long and hard to achieve the goal. Others, like Susanna Salter, mayor of Argonia, Kansas (*above*), became pathbreakers almost accidentally and later retreated to a homemaker's role. But everywhere they acquitted themselves so admirably that things would never be quite the same again.

Oskaloosa, Kansas, in 1888 chose Mayor Mary Lowman (*left, seated at center*) and five councilwomen to form the first all-female municipal government in the U.S.

Mary Lease (*right*), a teacher and self-taught lawyer, rallied Kansas farmers to the Populist cause in the 1890s with exhortations to "raise less corn and more hell."

troupes of fire-eaters, sword swallowers, tumblers and minstrels to rally a crowd of properly gullible townspeople. And just about everybody loved a good fight, whether between dogs or bears or badgers or men. The boxing matches were usually held in saloons, and they were not so much exhibitions of skill as tests of endurance—for participants and spectators alike. An 1867 prize fight in Cheyenne between John Hardey and John Shannessy for a purse of $1,000 ran 126 rounds. Each round lasted until one man or another was knocked down, at which point the boxers rested for 30 seconds. The referee, no doubt exhausted himself, finally allowed that Hardey had won on a foul.

As well as serving as an arena for boxing matches, the saloon provided the setting for many other forms of Western entertainment—including, of course, the most basic of all: drinking. When it came to seeking solace at the end of a weary day, the first recourse of most men on the frontier was beer or bourbon, or frequently a homemade beverage bearing the name Tarantula Juice, Skull Bender or Redeye. A few gulps of such potent potables were sufficient, as experienced swiggers put it, "to make a hummingbird spit in a rattlesnake's eye."

In addition to plying customers with alcoholic elixirs and offering them a place to gamble, many saloonkeepers featured another irresistible attraction—women, sometimes the only women in town. Unattached females seemed to arrive in the boomtowns in a dead heat with the saloons. There, typically, they danced with the cowboys or miners or railroad workers, sang a song or two if they were able, shilled drinks, enticed men into small back rooms for amorous interludes, and split all fees with the proprietor. More professional were the traveling taxi dancers: girls employed as dance partners for patrons who would pay a fee of 25 cents or so directly to the proprietor for each dance. Some dance hall girls were simply prostitutes, daring of dress and flexible of morals. But others could have passed muster at Sunday school—widows, married women with worthless or missing husbands, not a few with children, decent women whose job was merely to be pleasant to lonely men, nothing more.

Many saloonkeepers, anxious to try anything that would draw a crowd, added to their premises a stage for variety shows and short plays. One such temple of

the arts, in the gold camp of Georgia Gulch, consisted mainly of two shelves scooped out of the mountainside to serve as auditorium and stage. The most impressive appointment was a long bar with three bartenders who dispensed beer at 15 cents a glass and the hard stuff for two bits a shot. The performers' dressing rooms were screened off from the stage by bed sheets, and on opening night the box office was the crate in which the troupe's upright piano had arrived.

Despite the rough-hewn surroundings, these rude halls attracted not only home-grown amateurs but professional touring players as well—performers like Eddie Foy, who became one of the greatest stage personalities of his time. A wise-cracking song-and-dance man, Foy frequently relied on poking fun at local customs and customers, a practice that backfired on at least one occasion. In 1878, as a brash youngster of 22, Foy was booked into the Dodge City *Comique* ("Comikew," according to the cowpunchers)—a saloon, dance hall, gambling house and theater all in one. Having met such renowned gunfighting citizens of Dodge as Wyatt Earp, Doc Holliday and Bat Masterson, and finding them unexpectedly mild-mannered and soft-spoken, Foy was emboldened to joke about his audience from the stage.

As Bob Wright recalled: "He dressed pretty loud and had a kind of Fifth Avenue swaggering strut, and made some distasteful jokes about the cowboys." This led to their capturing Foy by roping him, ducking him in a horse trough, riding him around on horseback, and taking other playful familiarities with him—just to show their friendship.

Blessed with youthful resilience, Foy took the hazing in good part. "I was determined to be nonchalant," he later wrote, "and not let them see that they were worrying me, even if they broke my neck." His tormentors liked his spunkiness and, after playing several pranks on him—which Foy took with good grace—they accepted him and his friendly jibes. Foy played Dodge that entire summer and went on to tour the vast Western circuit of boomtowns.

Of all the entertainers who graced the Western stage during the latter part of the 19th Century, one of the unlikeliest performers—if not the most outrageous—

The great Eddie Foy, a variety-circuit hit as a wisecracking song-and-dance man, had this photo taken in 1882 at a Tombstone studio near the O.K. Corral, scene of the West's most famous gunfight the year before.

was Oscar Wilde. The Irish author arrived in 1882 on a lecture tour, a popular mode of entertainment during that period. Americans heard lectures from the likes of feminist Amelia Bloomer on practical attire for women, preacher Henry Ward Beecher on abolition, P.T. Barnum on temperance, and Victoria Woodhull on free love. Wilde's subject was Aestheticism—simply, the science of the beautiful, or art for art's sake.

Wilde was known throughout the country as the inspiration for the languid leading character in Gilbert and Sullivan's comic opera *Patience*, which mercilessly satirized the cult of Aestheticism. Lecture audiences soon discovered that the real Oscar almost outshone his caricature in elegance and refinement. His knee breeches were hailed as the most ridiculous attire ever seen in America. When he appeared on the Denver stage to discuss the niceties of interior decoration, his movement was described by a *Times* reporter as "a languid, dreamy sort of walk such as one would think a lovesick girl would have in wandering through a moonlit garden. A merry decorous laughter went up." Wilde, for his part, did not mind being laughed at. For one thing, he found the tour highly satisfying from a financial viewpoint: All of his travel expenses were paid, and his income at times exceeded $1,000 a month.

In Leadville, site of the Matchless Silver Mine, Wilde opened his talk with an injunction to the town's miners to study the Gothic school of Pisan art. Having thus won their somewhat baffled attention, he launched into a discourse on gold. He urged his listeners to follow the example of Renaissance sculptor Benvenuto Cellini in valuing gold not as wealth but as the raw material of fine art. Recounting events in this town later, he said that he read the miners passages from Cellini's autobiography, "and they seemed much delighted. I was reproved by my hearers for not having brought him with me. I explained to them that he had been dead for some little time, which elicited the enquiry, 'Who shot him?'"

Leadville's residents thought they would get the last laugh on their renowned guest by leading him on a wild tour through their town. During the protracted affair, the apostle of wit and manners watched dance hall girls and variety performers, gambled and consumed great quantities of liquor. The evening concluded with his companions suggesting that it was time for Oscar to have dinner—at the bottom of the Matchless Mine. Wilde found the idea charming, and soon he was climbing into an ore bucket in the No. 3 shaft to be lowered into the bowels of the mountain.

Down in the pit a reception committee of some dozen miners awaited their victim, each armed with a bottle of whiskey. Wilde chatted cheerfully with his hosts and partook of each bottle as it made the rounds. By the end of the first round some of the miners were a trifle dizzy, but Wilde seemed merely refreshed. It was nearly dawn before Oscar was hauled back to the surface in the ore bucket, showing neither fatigue nor the effects of drink. He was later asked what had transpired below. "Having got into the heart of the mountain, I had supper," the Aesthete replied in tones of complete satisfaction, "the first course being whisky, the second whisky and the third whisky."

When the miners recovered from Oscar's visit, they voted him an honorary life membership as one of them. And the Leadville *Herald*, heartily approving the way he played the gaming tables and held his liquor, paid the ultimate tribute, "There is no piousness in him."

Despite the financial success of the trip, the Western swing of Wilde's trip to America was not a notably aesthetic experience. The prairies, so somber and lovely at first sight, quickly lost their charm. "They reminded me of a piece of blotting paper," he confessed. The buildings

345

of the West did not fare much better in Wilde's estimation. The mammoth Mormon Tabernacle in Salt Lake City "has the shape of a soup-kettle and decorations suitable for a jail," he wrote. "It was the most purely dreadful building I ever saw."

But Denver was different. By the time Wilde passed through, the city was the richest community between St. Louis and San Francisco, boasting opulent mansions, opera houses and other tokens of culture. Only a decade after Wilde's visit, no less a cosmopolite than world-ranging journalist Richard Harding Davis hailed Denver as "a smaller New York in an encircling range of white-capped mountains." The mountains, in fact, were on just one side of the city—but Denverites forgave Davis his error, attributing it to a dazzlement that was only natural.

The city's early years were both auspicious and ominous. For the first dozen years after Denver was founded in 1858, residents of the Mile-High City swung between expectations of unlimited expansion and gnawing fear that everything would vanish overnight. Like many another Rocky Mountain burg, Denver grew from a dream of gold. But the first strike in the immediate vicinity, while not exactly an illusion, proved so thin that within a few months the hordes who had headed west in answer to the tocsin were plodding eastward again—threadbare, hungry and bitter.

In 1859 another discovery, 30 miles from the infant town, made a few early and lucky comers rich. But it also turned out to be a tough way for most of them to retrieve a few grains of gold with shovel, pan or sluice box. With almost nothing on which to pin their belief, a few obstinate holdouts clung to the view that one day Denver would strike it rich. They were right—not only gold but silver, and by the ton measure.

Meanwhile, it seemed that Denver had to do everything the hardest possible way. Even its location —alongside skinny Cherry Creek, where it flowed into the South Platte River—made life difficult. Neither the creek nor the river held enough water to bear boats of any appreciable size—except in moments of the most devastating floods. The close-looming Rockies presented an awesome 14,000-foot barrier to travel farther west. Ferocious Indians in the area were ready to defend the land they owned under an 1851 treaty. Local weather was capricious—capable of blizzards as late as May, yet not to be trusted for enough moisture to grow a crop without irrigation.

Despite man-made disasters such as the 1863 fire that burned out the city's center and natural calamities such as the 1864 flood that swept away half the town, Denver's irrepressible citizens forged boldly ahead. Any other town might have concluded that the gods were out to wipe it off the map for good. But Denver refused to think of hardship as anything worse than a temporary inconvenience on the road to destiny.

That road never appeared more tortuous than in 1868, when the Union Pacific announced that its new nation-crossing railroad would bypass Denver by 100 miles. The city's residents were aghast. They had assumed all along that, almost as a matter of divine right, the rail line would have to pass through Denver. But geography dictated otherwise; U.P.'s master engineer, Grenville Dodge, decided that Bridger's Pass in Wyoming offered an easier route through the Rockies.

The prospect for Denver's future without the rail line looked bleak indeed. Some fainthearts even moved their businesses north to the new town of Cheyenne on the U.P. main line. Company Vice-President Thomas C. Durant declared that Denver was now "too dead to bury." But the reports of the city's death turned out to be greatly exaggerated. Quickly, the money was raised to finance a branch line between Denver and Cheyenne. That was just the prelude to an orgy of railroad building; a network of rail lines pushing west and south and putting Denver back squarely on the map.

These new roads were pursuing a glittering new prize: silver. By the late 1860s the shine had gone off the gold-mining bonanza, leaving only the prospect of tremendous labor for moderate rewards. But just as Denver began to worry about this latest cloud on the horizon, its luck turned once again. In 1869, Colorado miners had discovered that a lot of the heavy rock they had been impatiently thrusting aside in their search for gold was high-grade silver ore. Railroads made fortunes hauling the ore out of the mining camps and hauling in everything from blasting powder to pianos.

By the centennial year of 1876, the frenzy had not abated, with strike after strike yielding richer and richer veins. That same year, much to the long-deferred satisfaction of its boosters, Colorado achieved state-

A big-city gift to a Montana boomtown

A ballad sung in the gold fields of Montana during the 1860s described the origins of certain local entertainments with disarming simplicity: "First came the miners to work in the mine / Then came the ladies who lived on the line." Although every Montana town had a "line"—a row of saloons that frequently offered dancing, gambling and female favors along with the liquor—few of them could claim ladies so enterprising as Josephine Hensley, who arrived in Helena in 1867.

Josephine had already served a long apprenticeship in the rawer forms of nightlife in Chicago by the time she took her talents to Helena at age 23. In this overwhelmingly male center of the gold-mining area, she acquired a modest log building and set up a hurdy-gurdy house—or dance hall—the first in the territory to be run by a woman.

The descriptive term "hurdy-gurdy" was left over from California gold-rush days, when dance hall music was provided by a wheezy hand organ. Josephine—given the affectionate nickname "Chicago Joe" by her customers—actually featured somewhat more sophisticated musical fare, supplied by a three-piece orchestra that occupied a small platform off to one side of the premises. At the rear was a well-stocked bar where customers could buy 50-cent drinks for themselves and their dance partners. The girls, imported from Chicago, received a share of both the bar receipts and the two-bit charge that was levied for dances, and they could augment their income by making other arrangements on their own. A touch of class was lent to Josephine's

CHICAGO JOE

establishment by the "Duke," a mysterious figure believed to be the black sheep of a titled British family, who helped to keep the patrons orderly and the dance hall staff disciplined.

Largely because her fresh-faced Chicago lasses outshone most frontier bawds, Josephine's place flourished. She moved into larger quarters in 1874, invested some of her growing capital in local real estate and formed alliances with influential figures in Helena's business and political worlds.

But in 1885, at the height of her reign as queen of the local underworld, Josephine's political friendship proved unable to protect her from the prospect of ruination. That year, under pressure from farmers and other family men who had begun to pour into the territory, the Montana legislature ordered the prohibition of hurdy-gurdy houses, and shortly afterward Chicago Joe was arrested. Her trial became the first test of the new law.

Conviction seemed certain after the police testified that she employed "lewd women to dance with male visitors" and that her establishment was a "typical hurdy-gurdy place." Then Chicago Joe's attorney, a former territorial governor named I.D. McCutcheon, offered his defense. The statutes of Montana, he noted, provided that "all words be interpreted according to their common use." This meant, he said, that a hurdy-gurdy house literally must be a house utilizing a hurdy-gurdy—a definition that hardly fitted Chicago Joe's place, where the music was supplied by a piano, a violin and a cornet. Impressed by the counsel's pristine logic, the jury found her not guilty.

But Chicago Joe could read the handwriting on the wall. Within a year, she altered her premises to include a variety theater—complete with heavily curtained stalls on the second floor where her girls could entertain between the acts and sometimes in lieu of them.

When the doors of her place finally closed at her death in 1899, a local paper pronounced a cool epitaph: "Her life in some respects was an eventful one." But Helenans accorded her a splendid funeral procession, and many of the city's leading citizens came to pay their last respects to this Montana pioneer.

hood. As the capital of the Union's newest and by all odds most glamorous state, Denver exploded: from a mere 4,759 people in 1870 to 35,629 in 1880. A decade later it had tripled to 106,713, a third of the state's total head count. That included a sizable chunk of the new state's richest citizens, whose increasingly lavish tastes were reflected in buildings like the Windsor Hotel.

By the time it was completed in 1880, the five-story, 300-room hotel had cost its builders $350,000. Another $200,000 was spent installing three elevators and a ballroom floor slung on cables to provide built-in bounce. Three thousand silver dollars studded a tap-room floor. All rooms had gaslights and most had fireplaces. For cleanliness addicts there were 60 bathtubs, a swimming pool and steam baths with areas denoted as "sudsatorium, frigidorium and lavatorium." In its main dining room, gourmets could order frogs legs, guava jelly, prairie chicken, trout, venison and bear meat, then top it all off with ice cream from the Windsor's steam-powered freezer.

With the depression of 1893 silver prices fell and times grew tough once again in Denver. Suicides and holdups were daily occurrences, and silver kings watched their empires collapse almost as quickly as they had built them up. But Denver's nine lives were far from over. The good years had fattened the city beyond starving. Blessed by the resources developed by farsighted men and permanent roots in agriculture and industry, the city weathered the financial storm. Before the century was out, the dreamers of Denver reached into their well of surprises and came up with one more fantastic boom: the Cripple Creek gold rush, which would surpass all previous bonanzas.

And thus to Denver—the Queen City of the Plains—came all the good things dreamed of, schemed for, struggled for by all those who had crossed the great rivers to found a new urban civilization. The community had many chances to vanish and become but a footnote to the history of the Old West.

But Denver was obstinate. It was also supremely fortunate in the quality of its citizenry—a rugged, resourceful breed of men and women. As a Congregational minister said about the townsmen he encountered in Kansas in the 1850s, "These people had not come as adventurers to see how they would like it. They had come to stay and see the thing done."

348

When Guns Speak, Death Settles Disputes was Russell's epigrammatic title for this rendition of a frontier clash.

The deadly brotherhood of the gun

Caught in the blaze of a midnight shoot-out, the men in this scene are instantly recognizable as specimens of the Old West's most flamboyant breed—the gunfighters. Whether they were lawmen, bandits or wanton killers, all of them shared a deadly purposefulness. Bat Masterson, a renowned peace officer among the breed, recalled that when it came to settling a dispute, any one of the numerous gunfighters he had known "would not have hesitated a moment to put up his life as the stake to be played for."

Here and in the following paintings, artist Charles Russell records the sudden violence that made these men legends in their own day—and thereafter.

His mount down, a horse thief blasts away at a posse as his partner starts to make a run for it in *When Horseflesh Comes High*.

In the wake of a card-game quarrel, a vengeful cowhand dispatches one player and mortally wounds another in *Death of a Gambler*.

14. Gamblers and gunfighters

When the cashier arrived at his Denver bank that morning in the 1870s, he found three weary-looking men sitting on the steps. They seemed too tired to be gunslinging bandits bent on robbing the bank, so he assumed they must be legitimate customers.

"Want to make a deposit, gentlemen?" he asked cheerfully. "Step inside."

"No, I want to negotiate a loan," replied one of the men, "and there ain't a minute to lose. I want $5,000 quicker than hell can scorch a feather."

The man explained that he and the others were involved in a high-stakes poker game at the saloon across the street. There was $4,000 already in the pot, and he needed the loan to stay in the game. As collateral, he proffered a sealed envelope containing his "hand"—the cards he was holding in the poker game.

The cashier ripped open the envelope and found inside four kings and an ace. By the rules of the day, before the ascendancy of the straight flush and royal flush, that was an unbeatable hand. Nevertheless, the cashier stiffly turned away the unusual loan applicant.

Back on the street, the disappointed gambler ran into the bank's president, who had just emerged from an all-night game of his own. The president took one look at the man's hand, then dashed into the bank, grabbed a bag of $20 bills and followed the trio to their game. Ten minutes later the president returned to the bank and tossed the bag and an extra handful of 20s for interest onto the counter.

He then gave the startled cashier a lecture on the nature of collateral. "Remember," he concluded, "that in the future four kings and an ace are always good in this institution for our entire assets, sir—our entire assets."

That tale, all but sworn to by storytellers in towns throughout the West, captured the excitement a game of chance could stir even in the breast of the stereotypical banker. Gambling was the frontier's favorite pastime, a sport exceeded in popular fervor only by a good gunfight. Never in American history had gambling been more widespread or more socially acceptable. Every riverboat and railroad town, every logging camp and cowtown, every mining boomtown had its game of cards or dice. And through all those towns moved the quick-handed professionals, those men who "seemed never to toil nor spin," as someone out in Deadwood, South Dakota, described them, "yet always were arrayed in fine linen and broadcloth fresh from the tailor's iron."

Wagering went with the territory. The act of going West was itself a gamble, and there was fertile precedent out there for gaming. Long before white men set foot in the West, the Indians bet on all manner of games of skill and chance—as an element in sacred rituals and also just to pass the time. A man might gamble any of his personal possessions, from his wife to the animal skin on his back, on contests ranging from foot races and lacrosse to the casting of special dice that, in contrast to the six-sided cubes of the white man, bore only two painted faces. The Dakota Indians even played dice at funeral ceremonies to divide up the possessions of the deceased. The Puyallups and other tribesmen of the Northwest sometimes stayed up for five days and nights without rest to play a gambling version of button-button-who's-got-the-button that required them to maintain a loud rhythmic chant the entire time.

Those early explorers, the Spanish conquistadors, introduced the Indians to the concept of playing cards, along with horses to race. Card games were "the first milk they sucked from the Christians," a Spanish missionary to the Apaches noted in 1795. Native Ameri-

Gaudy pictures of horses and lustrous abalone shell inlays decorate the rim of a seven-foot wheel of fortune. The agonizingly suspenseful slowing of such wheels attracted many a bet in boomtown gaming halls.

357

cans fashioned cards from ornately painted tree bark but had to await the arrival of poker-playing emigrants from New Orleans during the following century to learn what would become their favorite card game. One Indian, a native son of the Pacific Northwest named White-Geese-Sounding-on-Waters, proved so proficient at this new pastime that whites rechristened him Poker Jim. A diligent student and canny philosopher of the game, Poker Jim formulated with noble simplicity that principle dear to players everywhere tempted to bet on a marginal hand: "Two pair not much good."

For reasons more profane than sacred, gambling of all kinds appealed to white settlers of the West. To assuage the rigors, loneliness and boredom of frontier life, they bet not only on poker and dice but also on a dozen other different ways to lose their money—from card games such as keno and faro to roulette, chuck-a-luck and, toward the end of the century, those gaudy gangs of one-armed bandits known as slot machines. If anyone tired of those diversions, it was easy enough to find a dog or cock fight, a battle between bulls and bears, a horse race or a boxing match or some other event or situation where the outcome appeared to be in doubt and thus subject to a wager.

The fountainhead for the early dispersion of white man's gambling was the city of New Orleans. Beginning in 1812, the first steamboats from this haunt of gambling and other good times made their way north along the Mississippi River and westward along such tributaries as the Arkansas and Missouri, with stopovers at St. Louis and other early settlements. A third of a century later, no fewer than 557 steamboats were plying the Western rivers, each carrying its complement of con men and cardsharps. Their appearance sometimes was as crude as their morals. Fat and red-nosed, his waistcoat blotched with food stains, the gambler often affected the nondescript dress of an itinerant preacher or a hinterland farmer. Others came closer to the romantic image of the gambler as a gaudy dandy—resplendent in a knee-length, black broadcloth coat, brocaded vest and ruffled shirt, wearing high-heeled French leather boots, and sporting a diamond ring and a massive gold watch with heavy gold chain; one renowned Mississippi coxcomb boasted a watch chain 20 feet long that looped several times around his neck.

Not everyone among this vivid and varied lot was a cold-eyed crook. A gambler named Canada Bill Jones was a master of three-card monte, a variation on the old shell game in which the gambler manipulated three cards facedown and bet that the spectator could not identify the one called the "baby," which was usually an ace or a face card. But Jones was constitutionally

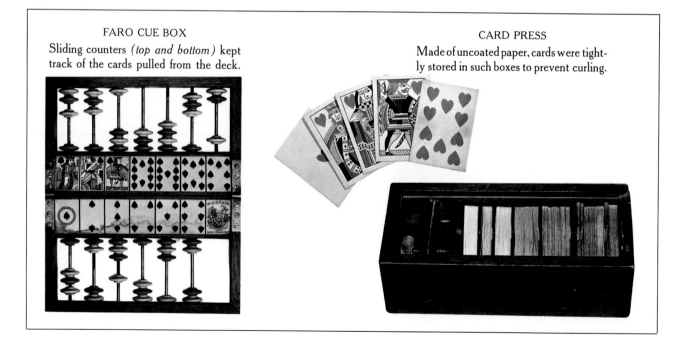

FARO CUE BOX
Sliding counters *(top and bottom)* kept track of the cards pulled from the deck.

CARD PRESS
Made of uncoated paper, cards were tightly stored in such boxes to prevent curling.

incapable of limiting himself to that game, and he almost always lost at others. "He loved gambling for its own sake," explained a confederate, "just as the moralists love virtue for its own sake." Canada Bill was losing at the card game of faro one night in a Mississippi river town when a friend tugged at his sleeve and asked, "Bill, Bill, don't you know this game is crooked?"

"Yes," answered Canada Bill, "but it's the only game in town."

By the same token, not every riverboat gambler lacked conscience or scruples. In 1858, a successful practitioner named John Powell engaged a young English traveler at poker and took him for everything he had. After the traveler shot himself to death, Powell was so remorseful that he sent all the winnings—$8,000 and his luggage—to the young man's family and forsook gambling for a year. Powell was worth half a million dollars and well could afford it. But he was still unnerved when he returned to his profession, and soon lost his entire fortune. He died broke, an example to his colleagues of the dangers of compassion.

For the most part, the professional gambler harbored little conscience—and no compunctions against loading dice, marking cards or otherwise improving the odds accorded him by chance. Cheating was especially prevalent on the riverboats. One authority held that, of the estimated 2,000 gamblers on Western waters at mid-century, only four were honest.

But cheating was also a way of life in the boomtowns. In San Francisco, nearly 1,000 gambling halls sprouted within a few years of the 1848 discovery of gold at Sutter's Mill. Inside the gilded walls of one of these sumptuous palaces, wrote the British diarist J.D. Borthwick, "Nothing was heard but a slight hum of voices, and the constant clinking of money." Here and in less exalted circumstances, "people wanted to be humbugged," con man James Pattee was quoted as saying. It was, he believed, his business to do it.

Professionals utilized their quick hands to stack the poker deck, deal crookedly or give their opponents the fast shuffle. "They'd just flutter them up like a flock of quail and get the aces, kings, queens, jacks and tens all together as easy as pie," Tom Ellison, himself a professional, observed of his colleagues. "A sucker had no more chance against those fellows than a snowball in a red-hot oven."

Poker-playing gamblers often teamed up to cheat unsuspecting opponents. One partner might deliberately deal his friend a series of winning hands, for example; or the confederate might stand near the table, posing as an interested spectator while signaling information about an opponent's cards. The signaling process, called "iteming," sometimes involved a series of puffs of cigar-smoke-like Indian signals, or the apparently casual but coded scratching of ears, nose or eyebrows. One gambler favored a walking stick, which he held at various angles to denote the cards; another, who pretended to be an affable half-wit, wandered through the saloon sawing out coded snatches of music on the fiddle.

The standard tool of the cardsharp was the marked deck, which enabled him to identify the opponent's hand and stack his own with high cards (pages 362-363). Cards known as "readers," with secret marks already printed on their backs, could be purchased by mail order from manufacturers such as E.N. Grandine of New York, whose catalog unblushingly advertised marked cards at $1.25 per pack. Many professionals preferred to mark their own cards with Braille-like punctures or by trimming the edges with razor-sharp blades so that they were slightly concave or convex. The ends of these so-called strippers felt correspondingly wide or narrow to the delicate touch, and a gambler who used such cards was said to be "playing both ends against the middle."

Taking advantage of marked cards required skillful manipulation. Like a surgeon, the cardsharp needed dexterity and nerve. He kept his hands uncalloused—"softer than a woman's," said the wife of one gambler—in order to be able to detect the smallest variation in the surface or shape of the cards. The famous woman gambler known as Poker Alice Ivers remembered dealers whose fingers were "sandpapered until the blood all but oozed through the skin" in order to read the cards they had marked.

For many cardsharps, the winning ace in the hole was provided by a device called a holdout. True to its name, the instrument secretly held out key cards until the time and pot were ripe for playing them. Holdouts ranged in complexity from a simple spring clamp attached to the underside of the table to ingenious contraptions worn under the clothing. One gadget allowed

Patrons of the Merchant's Hotel in Columbia, Nevada, place bets on faro *(foreground)* and roulette. The two fast-action games were popular in the Western boomtown casinos where gamblers were continually impatient for speedy results.

Clever devices for making dice more friendly

There were several kinds of delicately rigged dice that a Western cheater could use to boost his advantage at the craps table or in a casual game at the bar. Two popular styles were loaded dice, which were slightly unbalanced, and shaved dice, which were subtly misshaped. With both kinds, certain numbers would come up with more than the usual frequency. The rigging was done with odd-looking machines like the two below.

The edge shaver (*below left*) was used primarily to pare material off the edges of a die. If the gambler wanted to improve his chances of rolling, say, a 1, he could shave the edges off the 1 surface at an angle that increased the chances of the die landing with the 6 side (which is opposite the 1) down and the 1 up. To shave a die, the cheater laid it in the trough of the machine and passed it over a blade located beneath the slit in the trough.

A similar advantage could be gained with a dice loader (*below right*). To make the 1 come up, the cheater drilled out two or more spots on the 6 side of the die, filled up the cavities with a heavy metal such as lead or gold, then repainted the spots. Faithful to the laws of gravity, the heavy 6 side usually landed down leaving the lighter 1 side up.

The more the dice were shaved or weighted, the more reliable they were — and the greater the risk of detection. Prudent cheats used moderately rigged dice, which improved their chances by only 5 or 6 per cent, enough to be profitable for a few hours without inviting trouble.

Dice await rigging in a shaver (*left*) and a loader, also shown with its drill secured in its ivory handle (*foreground*) for storage.

the gambler to keep the winner up his sleeve, buckling around his bare arm and extending the desired card into his palm when he bent his elbow.

The most elaborate of the sleeve holdouts was invented by P.J. Kepplinger, a San Francisco cardsharp. Kepplinger tried out his new device on some of his professional colleagues in a series of games in 1888 with extraordinary success. Though these men were experts at spotting the slightest sign of such tools. "Kepplinger gave no sign of the employment of anything of the kind," wrote John Nevil Maskelyne, a 19th Century chronicler of cheating and chicanery. "He sat like a statue at the table, he kept his cards right away from him,

he did not move a muscle as far as could be seen; his opponents could look up his sleeve almost to the elbow, and yet *he won*."

Kepplinger's poker pals stood it as long as they could. Finally, during one of their games, they seized Kepplinger and laid bare his secret: a harness of pulleys, cords and telescoping silver-plated tubes that extended from his forearm to his shoulders and down both legs. Kepplinger needed only to spread his knees slightly to activate the mechanism and move the hidden card down between the two layers of a special double shirt sleeve toward his palm. The victims of his duplicity took their revenge by forcing Kepplinger to make a similar

Decks that "eliminated chance"

One cardsharp stares intently at the backs of his opponent's hands; another imperceptively caresses the cards as he deals; yet another idly thumbs the edges of the deck while shuffling.

These apparently innocent mannerisms were actually the mechanics of cheating with marked cards. The first gambler looked for secret marks on the backs of cards that revealed the sucker's hand. The second felt for punctured surfaces that gave away the high cards. The third found the aces, subtly trimmed to a wedge shape, and placed them on the bottom of the deck.

Nearly every cardsharp worthy of the name was a master of such trickery and utilized it, accepting the danger of exposure for the overwhelming advantage that the marked cards offered. "When successfully used," a reformed sharper observed, "every element of chance is eliminated from the game, and the play is practically reduced to a cutthroat contest, in which the professional alone carries the knife."

Blue-tinted spectacles enabled the wearer to detect marks made on the backs of cards with phosphorescent ink, which was invisible to the unaided eyes of his opponent.

This deluxe card trimmer, brass and steel with an ivory handle, could be used legitimately to renew frayed edges of a whole deck, or illegitimately for shaving certain cards to make them easy to find in a cut.

This corner rounder, ivory-handled companion to the card trimmer, could be employed to cut new corners on an entire deck after trimming or to mark particular cards by slightly altering their corners.

Special markings on the backs of these cards reveal their values to the dealer. The key is a dotted "7" *(enlargement)* printed in the upper right and lower left corners. The symbol revolves clockwise through eight distinct positions as cards increase in value from 7 through ace. Different marks divulged lesser cards. Suits, less important than card values in many games, were ignored by this marking system.

Depressing the plunger of this brass card pricker drives a needle into the face of the card and raises a Braille-like mark on the back. A crooked dealer could tell from the positions of these bumps what cards were passing through his fingers.

instrument for each of them. Only then, wrote Maskelyne, did "the temporary and short-lived discord gave place to harmony and content."

Kepplinger, with his cumbersome equipment, was in no position to conceal the evidence once his colleagues began to suspect him. Other operators were known to go to virtually any lengths to cover up. When a gambler in Dodge City, Kansas, realized that his opponents suspected him of secreting an ace up his sleeve, he nonchalantly ordered a sandwich, covertly slipped the card between the layers of bread and proceeded to chew and swallow the incriminating evidence.

Catching an opponent cheating, whether with a fast shuffle, marked cards or an ace up the sleeve, usually brought swift retribution. In the early days on the Mississippi, a steamer captain named John Russell became outraged when one of his passengers, a naïve clergyman, wandered off the docked vessel into the little community of Natchez-under-the-Hill and got bilked by the riverboat gamblers who hung out there between voyages. Russell armed his crewmen and led them into every gambling establishment in town, demanding the return of the minister's money. When the gamblers only laughed, Russell hooked up a chain to one of their dens and ordered full speed astern. Only after the house had lurched away from its foundation did the gamblers realize that the captain meant business and refund their ill-gotten gains to the clergyman.

Too often, a gambling dispute galvanized the adversaries into the event that exceeded even the excitement of the betting game—the gunfight. This was the greatest gamble of all in the Old West, for the gunfighter wagered his very life on his skill and quickness with a revolver, rifle or shotgun. Whether they were lawmen, bandits or wanton killers, and whether the dispute stemmed from gambling, lawbreaking or an old grudge, the gunfighters shared a common trait. As Bat Masterson, a renowned sheriff and sharpshooter put it, not one of the many gunfighters he had known would "have hesitated a moment to put up his life as the stake to be played for."

SMITH & WESSON REVOLVERS

Gunfighters comprised a distinct and deadly brotherhood. It was a special profession, and one practitioner, the Texas gunman Clay Allison, took pride in referring to himself by the specially coined title of "shootist." The sudden appearance of the shootist, or gunfighter, inspired awe and dread. When several showed up for a shoot-out, it was enough to send tremors through an entire region.

The most notorious shoot-out in the annals of the Old West took place one blustery day in October 1881, in the southeastern Arizona town of Tombstone. The battle pitted on one side the city marshal, Virgil Earp, his brothers Wyatt and Morgan, and their gambler friend, Doc Holliday, and on the other, a quartet of local cowboys, the Clanton and McLaury brothers. Because of the location—a vacant lot behind an old horse corral—their deadly showdown would be immortalized as "The Gunfight at the O.K. Corral."

In this lethal drama, the Earp brothers—long-legged and mustachioed—were cast as the good guys. Two of them, Virgil and Wyatt, had arrived in Tombstone two years previously accompanied by their eldest brother, James, a Civil War veteran with a game arm and a passive nature, who would become a saloonkeeper and play no part in the shoot-out. Virgil, 36, a former stage driver and part-time deputy sheriff, soon was appointed city marshal after the incumbent was gunned down by a cattle rustler. The ambitious Wyatt, 31, who had performed variously as horse thief, peace officer and cardsharp, bought into the gambling concession at the profitable Oriental Saloon, ran a faro game at the Eagle Brewery across the street and served as assistant marshal to Virgil. A few months later, they were joined by their youngest brother, Morgan, a 28-year-old hothead who found employment riding shotgun on the stagecoach to Tucson and as a part-time policeman.

The Earp clan soon had a cohort in Wyatt's friend from Dodge City days, John Holliday. An ardent gambler and sometime dentist who had once opened an office with the dubiously reassuring announcement that "where satisfaction is not given, money will be

WYATT EARP   MORGAN EARP   VIRGIL EARP

refunded," Doc Holliday was already alcoholic and tubercular at 28, a walking cadaver with a flash temper and a cold-blooded readiness to kill.

These new arrivals found in Tombstone a fledgling boomtown—a collection of dust-blown tents and shanties perched on a treeless plateau between the Dragoon and Whetstone mountains. Sustained by silver mined in the surrounding hills, the town soon boasted a population of 5,600. Early in 1880, it already had two dance halls, a dozen gambling places, more than a score of saloons and, according to a serious young attorney with a penchant for statistics, at least two Bibles. The editor of the Tombstone *Nugget* feared that things were getting out of hand when, one Sunday night, a bunch of "lewd women" and their men friends staged an impromptu street celebration with blazing six-shooters. "We live mostly in canvas houses up here," he wrote, "and when lunatics like those who fired so promiscuously the other night are on the rampage, it ain't safe, anyhow!"

Prominent among the troublemakers were the ranchers, cowboys and rustlers who rode into Tombstone periodically to raise hell. The most troublesome were the two sets of brothers, the Clantons and the McLaurys, who had been friends since the early 1870s, raising cattle along the San Pedro River west of Tombstone before the town was born. They came to town

regularly to sell the cattle they had raised and other beef that had been rustled in Mexico.

Their dubious livestock dealings helped spark the enmity that soon developed between this pair of clans and the Earp brothers. Billy Clanton appeared one day on a prize horse that had been stolen from Wyatt Earp. After mules turned up missing from a nearby Army post, a posse of soldiers and Earps led by Virgil, acting in his additional capacity as a deputy U.S. marshal, found the critters at the McLaury ranch.

The growing antagonism was not helped by John Behan, the sheriff of newly formed Cochise County, of which Tombstone was county seat. Appointed to office by Arizona's territorial governor, the explorer John C. Frémont, Behan had to run for election to keep the job, and he went out of his way to cultivate the cowboy vote. He became friends with the Clantons and McLaurys despite their shady reputations—and rivals with the Earps. He and Virgil, as chief law officer of the town, were bound to clash. And Wyatt not only coveted the sheriff's job but already had captured the affections of Behan's girlfriend, an attractive young actress.

All this hostility hardened into hatred. In July 1881, without any real evidence, Sheriff Behan arrested the Earps' crony, Doc Holliday, on suspicion of killing a stage driver during an attempted holdup. Two months later, Virgil Earp scored a double hit on the cowboys

John "Doc" Holliday was a dentist by trade and a gambler by choice, and fought beside the Earp brothers in Tombstone. A fellow gunfighter noted that he had "an ungovernable temper and was given to both drinking and quarreling."

and the sheriff when he ordered the arrest of one of Behan's deputies, Frank Stilwell, and a friend of the Clantons, Pete Spence, for holding up a stage. Frank McLaury came to town and, in a confrontation with Morgan Earp in the middle of the street, flung down the challenge, "If you ever come after me, you'll never take me."

On the morning of October 26, the tension mounted. Virgil Earp arrested Ike Clanton for carrying firearms within the city limits and then Wyatt and Morgan taunted Clanton. Minutes later, Wyatt got into an argument with Tom McLaury and pistol-whipped him. That afternoon, the Earps and Doc Holliday went looking for the Clantons and McLaurys, and after Sheriff Behan tried and failed to disarm the cowboy clans, Virgil vowed to do it himself. In the vacant lot at the rear of the open stalls of the O.K. Corral, the adversaries found themselves eyeing each other across a distance of no more than six feet.

"Hold!" Virgil Earp called out. "I want your guns." Then someone shouted, "Son-of-a-bitch"—and the next words were lost in the first exchange of gunfire.

Wyatt Earp whipped out his six-shooter and shot Frank McLaury in the stomach. Morgan Earp then pumped two rounds from his six-shooter into Billy Clanton, who slumped to the ground but kept firing. Then Ike Clanton, who had given up his rifle and revolver during his arrest, lunged barehanded at Wyatt and then fled. Tom McLaury, who was also unarmed, had taken cover behind his brother's horse. But then the horse suddenly bolted, exposing Tom to the blast of the shotgun Doc Holliday had borrowed from Virgil, and he went down mortally wounded.

Two of the wounded cowboys fought back. Billy Clanton put a bullet in the leg of Virgil, who had taken no part in the shooting. Frank McLaury exchanged shots with Doc Holliday, who was now firing with his own pistol. Holliday was hit in the hip; McLaury simultaneously took a fatal bullet below the ear from Morgan Earp. Billy Clanton caught Morgan Earp in the shoulder with his final shot, then slumped fatally wounded as

Morgan and Wyatt fired together and struck him below the ribs.

Suddenly the shooting stopped. As gun smoke drifted over the silent scene, a bystander crossed the lot to where Billy Clanton lay dying, still trying to cock his six-shooter. "Give me some more cartridges," Billy gasped. The man pulled the pistol from his weakened grasp.

The gunfight had lasted scarcely more than 30 seconds and though only two men—Ike Clanton and Wyatt Earp—had emerged without a scratch, the feud was far from settled. While Virgil and Morgan Earp were recovering from their wounds, Sheriff Behan jailed Wyatt and Doc Holliday for the murder of Billy Clanton and the two McLaurys. The judge acquitted them, calling their actions unwise but allowing for such mitigating circumstances as "the condition of affairs incidental to a frontier country, the lawlessness and disregard for human life and the many threats that have been made against the Earps."

The friends of the deceased cowboys embarked upon their own course of justice. Two months after the shoot-out, someone with a shotgun bushwhacked Virgil as he crossed Fifth Street in the dark, shattering his left arm. "Never mind," he told his wife, "I've got one arm left to hug you with." Three months later, in March 1882, Morgan was shot and killed as he bent over a billiard table with a cue in his hands. Witnesses saw three men running from the scene—the Clantons' friend Pete Spence, Sheriff Behan's deputy Frank Stilwell and a man who was reported to be an Indian.

The remaining Earps and Doc Holliday took quick retribution. Stilwell was found dead in Tucson, just after a train in which they were accompanying Morgan's California-bound casket, passed through that town. Returning to Tombstone, Wyatt gathered a posse of friends that hunted down and killed "the Indian"—actually a Mexican woodcutter. Then, with Sheriff Behan's deputies roaming the hills after them for Stilwell's murder, Wyatt Earp and Doc Holliday rode off into New Mexico. In that territory, they were safely out of reach of the Arizona

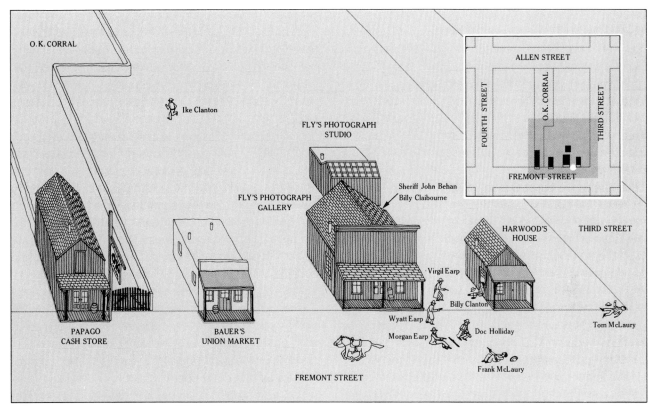

THE BLOODY CLIMAX OF THE SHOOT-OUT staged on Tombstone's Fremont Street near the O.K. Corral *(overview, inset)* is reconstructed in the diagram above. Frank McLaury, shot by both Wyatt and Morgan Earp, sprawls dying in the street, having just wounded Doc Holliday. Tom McLaury, blasted by Holliday's shotgun, lies at the corner of Fremont and Third. Billy Clanton, suffering two hits from Morgan Earp, slumps against a wall of the Harwood house; still shooting, he manages to wing both Morgan and Virgil Earp. Wyatt Earp stands unscathed. Ike Clanton, unarmed, sprints toward safety. Frank McLaury's spooked horse also flees. Sheriff John Behan and Billy Claibourne cringe under cover in Fly's photo gallery, powerless to aid their cowboy friends.

law. The daring of the Earp clan, if not their virtue, had been established beyond question.

Unlike the participants in the Tombstone shoot-out, many gunfighters were simply bandits. The most fearsome rode together in outlaw gangs and swooped down on banks, trains and stages to seize booty richer than any single gunfighter could have commanded. The prototype of the Western gang was the one put together after the Civil War by the James brothers, Jesse and Frank. During their 15-year heyday from 1866 to 1881, the James gang pulled off 26 jobs for a total take of about half a million dollars, while holding the citizenry of more than half the nation in fascinated thrall.

The James boys grew up on a Missouri farm, the sons of a Baptist preacher who did not live to see their exploits. Frank, the elder by three years, was quiet and bookish, an avid reader of Shakespeare and Francis Bacon. Jesse was the live-wire leader, blue-eyed and baby-faced but with the sudden energy of a coiled spring. Both served the Confederacy in the guerrilla bands that terrorized the Union forces occupying Missouri and neighboring states and territories. In these ragtag units of irregulars the James brothers learned such tactics as scouting the enemy, surprising him with swift attacks on horseback and then scattering into the surrounding countryside to hole up in refuges that they had planned in advance.

After the war, back home in Missouri nursing grievances against the former enemy, Jesse and Frank decided to put their wartime lessons to innovative use. They organized a group of ex-guerrillas, and on the afternoon of February 14, 1866, a dozen of them rode into the nearby town of Liberty. The men were muffled in long soldiers' overcoats, some with six-shooters strapped in plain sight. Three riders dismounted in the town square to keep watch while the others walked into the Clay County Savings Association.

One of the men went up to the counter and slid a $10 bill across the polished wood. "I'd like a bill changed," he said. Then, drawing a six-shooter, he broadened his request: "I'd like all the money in the bank."

As the robbers hurdled the counter, the young bank clerk William Bird backed away in disbelief. With the exception of a wartime raid on a small Vermont bank by a band of Confederate guerrillas, no one had ever robbed an American bank during business hours. The bandits made off with a bulging sack of $60,000 in currency, coins and other legal tender. Riding away through town, the James gang whooped and fired their guns into the air. A bystander, George Wymore, a 19-year-old student at the town's William Jewell College, got in their way and started to run for cover. One rider, in an awesome and cruel display of accuracy, pumped four bullets into Wymore, who died instantly.

The James gang was now in business, but the booty became smaller and more difficult to extract from the banks. The following year, they took $4,000 in gold from the bank in Richmond, Missouri, and in order to get away, they had to shoot down the mayor, the jailer and the jailer's son. Posses of irate townspeople pursued the outlaws off and on for months before catching three members of the gang and lynching them.

Early in 1868, branching eastward into Kentucky, the James boys enlisted George Shepherd, a friend from wartime guerrilla days. But their raid on the bank in Russellville near his home went awry, and they again had to shoot their way out of town. As they galloped off, Shepherd coolly took time to call to a spectator: "You needn't be particular about seeing my face so well you'd remember it again." It was a warning he would regret. D.G. Bligh, a Louisville detective hired by the town's bankers, tracked down Shepherd, who was forced to surrender after a gunfight and sent off to jail for three years. But Frank and Jesse went home to their mother in Clay County.

The James boys' pious mother persuaded Jesse to undergo baptism in the Kearney Baptist Church. Within a year, however, the brothers strayed from the path of righteousness and into the limelight. Tempted by the prospect of a fine haul from the Daviess County Savings Bank at Gallatin, Missouri, they tackled the job alone and risked their closest call yet. Jesse's horse, panicked by gunfire from a dozen Gallatin citizens, bolted just as he sprang into the saddle for the getaway. He was dragged along the street for 30 feet head downward before he could free himself. As the mare ran off, he was rescued by Frank, who had wheeled his horse and galloped back into the face of the townspeople's fire so Jesse could leap up behind him. Jesse's runaway mare was soon identified, and the James boys—up to now only suspected—were openly branded as outlaws.

The James family responded by launching a public-relations campaign as brazen as their daylight holdups. Jesse sent a letter to the *Kansas City Times* denying any part in the Gallatin bank job. In fact, each of the gang's subsequent exploits was followed by formal disclaimers, written by Jesse and sometimes personally delivered by his mother to the offices of Missouri newspapers. Frank and Jesse already enjoyed considerable moral support in the countryside, where people still revered the lost Confederate cause and detested bankers for their tight money policies and high interest rates. The James boys further embellished their public image by feats of showmanship such as seizing the cashbox from the ticket seller at the Kansas City fairgrounds and then spurring their horses defiantly through the middle of the throngs. A front-page story in that city's *Times* proclaimed this exploit "a deed so high-handed, so diabolically daring and so utterly in contempt of fear that we are bound to admire it and revere its perpetrators."

The effrontery of the James gang reached new heights when, after eight years of robbing banks, they expanded operations to the railroads. On January 31, 1874, at Gads Hill, Missouri, five masked men pulled a switch to send the southbound express onto a siding. They then plundered the baggage-car safe and, after examining the hands of passengers, robbed only "the soft-handed ones," as a member of the gang explained, the "capitalists, professors and others that get money easy." Before leaving, one of the boys handed the conductor a note and instructed him to give it to the newspaper. The note amounted to a press release. Prepared ahead of time by Jesse and headlined "The Most Daring Robbery on Record," it was deliberately misleading

Still neophytes at banditry, Frank and Jesse James flaunt their long-barreled revolvers. Frank *(left)*, the older of the brothers by three years, was quiet and bookish, while Jesse, as one friend put it, was "reckless and devil-may-care."

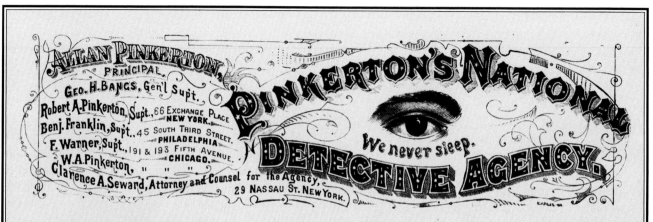

Allan Pinkerton in 1867

When the desperate bankers of the border states hired Allan Pinkerton to pit his army of sleuths against the James gang in 1871, they figured their troubles with holdups were over. In the detective business, Pinkerton had no peer. He once wrote to an aide, "I do not know the meaning of the word 'fail.' Nothing in hell or heaven can influence me when I know that I am right."

Pinkerton had honed his skills for this epic manhunt in a variety of secretive pursuits. In his native Scotland he had been a revolutionary agitator for workingmen's reforms, escaping arrest only by emigrating in 1843. Settling in Illinois, he turned

ardent abolitionist and smuggled many a runaway slave to safety in Canada. His relish for undercover work next prompted him to join the Chicago police force as its first detective; after cracking a counterfeit ring and scoring other successes, he formed his own detective force in 1850.

The agency quickly won fame for daring new methods, including a form of psychological warfare against its quarry. In one case, the murder of a bank teller in 1856, Pinkerton assigned a detective who startlingly resembled the dead man to shadow a suspect named Drysdale. Hounded day and night by this specter, Drysdale broke down, confessed and committed suicide. Such tactics caused criminals everywhere to fear Pinkerton. They dubbed him "The Eye," a name suggested by the agency's symbol (*above*)—and that later gave rise to the term "private eye."

Another innovation—supplying the Illinois Central Railroad with a guard force—led to a dream assignment for the agency chief. Pinkerton's contacts with the railroad included an ambitious executive and a backwoods lawyer, later better known, respectively, as General George McClellan and President Abraham Lincoln. Through their offices, a Major E. J. Allen—one of Pinkerton's many aliases—was ap-

pointed in 1861 to set up a secret service for the Union Army. He deployed his spies skillfully and, when they sniffed out a plot to assassinate Lincoln on a train from Baltimore to Washington, Pinkerton personally thwarted the attempt by putting the President on an earlier train.

In the wake of these activities, the Pinkerton agency came to be widely regarded as a minion of Northern big business and an unofficial branch of the federal government. The Pinkerton men were especially loathed by poor and unreconstructed Confederates of the border states, who balked the hunt of the James gang at every turn—and, for once, Allan Pinkerton learned the meaning of failure.

Despite the agency's inability to break up the James gang, its list of successes lengthened steadily, even after the founder's death in 1884. His sons William and Robert, whom he had trained to continue the detective dynasty, enjoyed a particularly satisfying triumph in 1896, when Pinkerton men bested the infamous Wild Bunch in a shoot-out; later, the leaders of the gang, Butch Cassidy and the Sundance Kid, would have to flee to South America. And the organization William and Robert left to their own sons in time was to serve as a model for a new federal agency—the F.B.I.

as to the robbers' physical appearance and understandably left the amount of the heist blank but was otherwise surprisingly accurate.

By then, the James boys already had wrought such havoc that the bankers had called in Allan Pinkerton's National Detective Agency *(page 370)*. Pinkerton agents combing Missouri's hills ran into a wall of silence and sometimes of bullets. Three died in shoot-outs in a single week soon after the train robbery, a pair of them at the hands of John and Jim Younger, two of the four notorious Younger brothers who were mainstays in the James gang. John himself was killed in the shoot-out. The surviving brothers—Cole, Bob and Jim—took temporary refuge in Dallas, where they sang in a Baptist choir and made periodic trips back north to take part in gang operations. Jesse and Frank also departed Missouri, returning only for special occasions such as their own weddings and a heist or two.

Early in 1875, the Pinkerton agents finally managed to get close to the James family's Missouri homestead. One investigator posed as a farmhand at the place across the road, and on January 26, a force of detectives brought in by special train surrounded the house. Their attack backfired when one of them tossed a round metal object—either a grenade or a flare intended to illuminate the interior of the house. It exploded, shattering the right arm of the James boys' mother, Zerelda Samuel, and killing her nine-year-old son by her second marriage. Zerelda let it be known far and wide that Jesse and Frank had not even been at home that night, and an outraged public saw the James boys in a new light—as martyrs.

All the same, Pinkertons' harassment of friends, neighbors and relatives helped Jesse and Frank decide to head far north to Minnesota—and the biggest shoot-out of their lives. On September 7, 1876, the James boys, together with the three Younger brothers and three other outlaws, rode into the town of Northfield. While three of them went inside the First National Bank to make their usual withdrawals, the others came under attack from townsfolk armed with rifles and shotguns commandeered from the two hardware stores. By the time Jesse and two companions came outside—Jesse wantonly dispatched the cashier on the way out—one outlaw was dead, and the street was blazing with gunfire. Another outlaw fell dead, and four suffered wounds before the gang made its exit. In a space of about 20 minutes, the aroused people of Northfield had virtually put out of action the gang that had held the nation spellbound for a decade.

A further reckoning impended. Still hounded by a posse more than a week after the shoot-out, the James gang split up. The Youngers and Charlie Pitts, another old Confederate guerrilla, were trapped a few days later. Pitts was killed and all three Youngers wounded, captured and then sent off to life imprisonment. The James brothers, riding together on a single horse, managed to break through a line of armed pickets. But a round from one picket passed through Frank's knee and lodged in Jesse's thigh. Though hobbled, they stole fresh horses and made it safely into the Dakota Territory.

Their old gang decimated and the glory days gone, Jesse and Frank went underground. Using pseudonyms, they settled with their wives around Nashville, Tennessee, and had children. Jesse, however, had lost none of his flamboyance. In Louisville one day he ran into D.G. Bligh, a detective hired to hunt the James gang, and had an amiable chat. He later sent the unsuspecting detective a postcard, informing him that he had met up with Jesse James at last.

In 1881, the James boys recruited a new gang and attempted to revive their old reputation in Missouri. They held up two different trains, killing a conductor and a passenger and beating a railroad agent senseless. Authorities tracked down several members of the gang, who talked freely about rivalries and disarray in the ranks. Missouri's Governor Thomas Crittenden set out to exploit this opportunity. He persuaded the railroads to put up a $5,000 reward for any member of the gang—with an additional $5,000 each for Jesse and Frank.

The offer soon attracted two recent recruits of the gang, Bob Ford and his brother Charlie. Bob Ford talked to the governor and agreed to tip off authorities on the time and place of the gang's next job. Then he and Charlie went to stay for a while with Jesse at his new home in St. Joseph, Missouri. On the morning of April 3, 1882, Jesse read in the newspaper that one of the gang had turned himself in. The man had been a friend of Bob Ford, and the news suddenly aroused Jesse's suspicions. "I had not fooled him," Ford later recalled. "He was too sharp for that. He knew at that moment as well as I did that I was there to betray him. But he

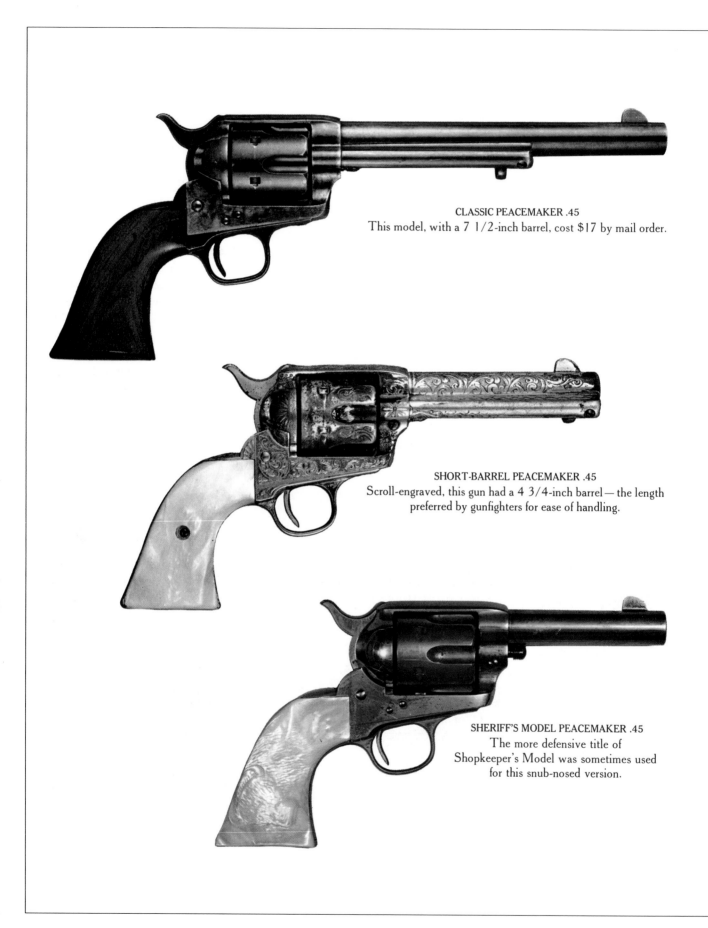

CLASSIC PEACEMAKER .45
This model, with a 7 1/2-inch barrel, cost $17 by mail order.

SHORT-BARREL PEACEMAKER .45
Scroll-engraved, this gun had a 4 3/4-inch barrel — the length
preferred by gunfighters for ease of handling.

SHERIFF'S MODEL PEACEMAKER .45
The more defensive title of
Shopkeeper's Model was sometimes used
for this snub-nosed version.

Tools of the gunfighters' trade

"God did not make all men equal," the Westerners were fond of saying, "Colonel Colt did." When it came to the use of shooting irons, however, some men were more equal than others—a fact that the gunfighters knew well. To improve the odds of landing on the right side of this equation, they exercised meticulous care in selecting their firearms from among the wide range of weapons available, some of which are shown on these pages

From service in the Civil War, thousands of frontiersmen inherited handguns like the three at left—revolvers whose rotating chambers could hold several rounds. They fired a kind of roll-your-own ammunition, which consisted of a ball, powder and a percussion cap. But the ammunition was all too fallible: Unless carefully loaded, it might misfire or even set off chain-reaction detonations of the rounds in the adjoining chambers.

The development of metallic cartridges soon solved these problems. The first metallic-cartridge revolver to be adopted as the standard sidearm of the postwar Army was the mordantly misnamed Colt's Peacemaker of 1873, three models of which are shown at left. Sold in enormous numbers on the open market as well as by mail, this single-action—i.e., manually cocked—pistol swiftly became the weapon most likely to be whipped from the holsters, waistbands or leather-lined coat pockets of Western gunfighters.

But the reliable Peacemaker, along with its imitators and successors, had a drawback. The relatively short barrel—eight inches or less—reduced the power and accuracy. While an expert might consistently hit a stationary man-sized target at 40 yards, an effective revolver range in the chaos of combat was less than half that figure. Most gunfighters therefore enlarged their arsenals with a rifle or a shotgun.

Even with one of these bigger weapons for deadly firepower, and revolvers for the close work, some gunfighters still felt less than fully equipped. So they added a vest-pocket pistol to their array of iron. Although it was woefully inaccurate, a small, hidden firearm possessed a matchless potential for surprise, and more than once proved a trump in the hazardous games of the men who lived by the gun.

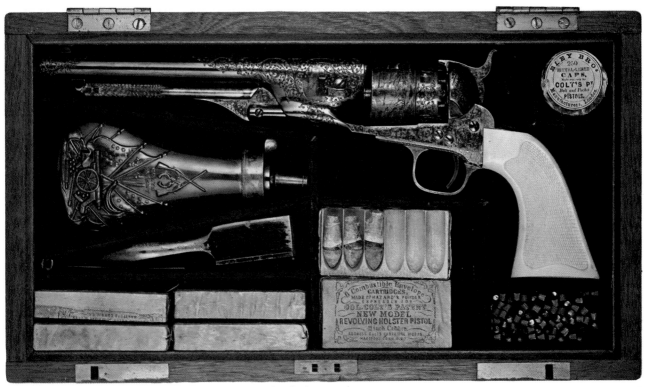

A deluxe kit for an 1860 Colt .44 includes an ornate powder flask, a bullet mold (the chisel-shaped object) and percussion caps (bottom right and in the container at top right). Also included were five boxes of prefabricated paper cartridges, one opened.

Cut down in a gunfight, two cavalrymen lie sprawled outside a Kansas dance hall while local matrons register disdain. Army paydays often brought bloodshed as soldiers blew their wages at bars and bordellos.

was not going to kill me in the presence of his wife and children."

Evidently to allay Ford's alarm, Jesse unbuckled his gun belt and threw it on the bed. Then he appeared to busy himself by climbing up on a chair and dusting a picture that hung on the wall. Ford saw his chance. "Without further thought or a moment's delay I pulled my revolver and leveled it as I sat. He heard the hammer click as I cocked it with my thumb and started to turn as I pulled the trigger. The ball struck him just behind the ear and he fell like a log, dead."

Bob Ford pleaded guilty to the murder of Jesse James and was sentenced to death. Governor Crittenden then kept his part of the bargain and pardoned him.

Six months after his brother's death, Frank James, fearing that he too would be assassinated, surrendered upon the governor's assurance of a fair trial. Crowds of Missourians cheered Frank as he was taken to jail.

In Gallatin, scene of the James boys' close call 14 years earlier, a jury acquitted him on a single count of murder. Frank was 40 at the time and lived peaceably for 32 more years, long enough to see a slew of imitators such as Butch Cassidy's Wild Bunch try to emulate the exploits of the old James gang.

Although they began their career by rustling and robbing banks, the Wild Bunch achieved real notoriety when they turned their attention to trains. Living up to their name, the gang pulled off one of their more spectacular heists near Wilcox, Wyoming, on June 2, 1899. After halting the Union Pacific's Overland Limited, Cassidy and his men detached the express car and set a stick of dynamite underneath—enough to open it like an egg crate. More dynamite blew the safe apart, sending currency wafting through the night air. The outlaws scooped up $30,000 and rode off.

The Wild Bunch followed up their first thunderous

train job with three more. Pinkerton's men were soon on their trail, along with a posse of gunfighters organized by the railroad itself. Realizing that such determined pursuers would eventually catch up with him, Cassidy decided to transfer his operations down to South America. He journeyed to New York sometime in late 1901, accompanied by a trusted confederate, Harry "Sundance Kid" Longbaugh of Sundance, Wyoming, and also by Longbaugh's lady love, Etta Place. After taking in the city sights, they sailed to Buenos Aires and new opportunities.

During the next decade, Cassidy, the Sundance Kid and Etta robbed banks and trains all across South America. The ultimate fate of the trio remains a mystery. Stories circulated that they were killed in a battle with troops in Bolivia or Uruguay, but more reliable reports indicated that they returned to the U.S. and lived to a ripe old age.

While gangs such as the James boys and the Wild Bunch wielded their guns for personal gain, another breed of killers worked alone and largely without material profit. To these loners, many of them Southerners embittered by the Civil War, the West offered an area where their private furies could be acted out with little restraint. Emotionally maimed and socially alienated, these desperadoes frequently murdered in a blaze of temper or simply out of sudden impulse—and none more profligately than John Wesley Hardin.

Born in Bonham, Texas, in 1853 and the son of a Methodist minister, Hardin was a good-looking boy, slight of build and handsome in a square-jawed way. Like most solitary killers, he embarked upon his homicidal career before emerging from adolescence. He was about 14 when he stabbed and wounded a bigger boy who taunted him about some graffiti he had written on the schoolhouse wall, a puppy-love paean to a girl in the class. By age 15, he had shot and killed four men: an ex-slave who challenged him to a fight and three Yankee soldiers, two whites and a black, who pursued him afterward.

A half dozen or so killings later, in Abilene, Kansas, young Hardin came under the wing of that cattle town's legendary marshal, Wild Bill Hickok. The old gunfighter-turned-lawman drank and whored with the young killer and gave him paternal advice. But their relationship was cut short when Hardin committed one of his most callous crimes. One night at the American House Hotel, where he was staying, Hardin became irritated at the snoring of a stranger in the next room. To put a stop to it, he began firing bullets through the wall. The first bullet merely woke the man; the second killed him.

Aware that the marshal would not take kindly to this, Hardin quickly fled in his undershirt. He exited through a window and ran onto the roof of the hotel portico—just in time to see Hickok arriving with four policemen. Hardin leaped from the roof, hid in a haystack for the rest of the night and then left Abilene

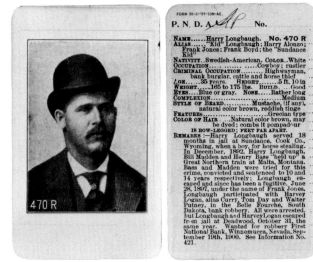

Mug shots and lengthy descriptions of Butch Cassidy *(left)* and the Sundance Kid were distributed by Pinkerton's Detective Agency.

Wild Bill Hickok: the saga of a dubious Galahad

When the glorifiers of the West began casting about for a single figure who could symbolize the lawman as hero, the most conspicuous—and eager—volunteer for that honor was James Butler Hickok. He had all the right attributes: courage, good looks, a sharpshooter's eye and a peerless appreciation of his own ferocity.

Born in 1837 in Illinois, Hickok emigrated to Monticello, Kansas, as a young man. There the ready belligerence that earned him the nickname Wild Bill also won him a brief job as a constable. Later, after serving as a Union scout in the Civil War, Hickok became a professional gambler and, in his best-known confrontation, outshot a fellow cardsharp in the public square of Springfield, Missouri. Eastern journalists began to seek him out after this classic duel, and Hickok obliged them with some out-and-out whoppers: he claimed that, among other feats, he had once picked off 50 Confederates with 50 bullets and a wonder-working rifle.

Still, some of Hickok's deeds were real and heroic. As an Army scout in 1868, he rescued 34 men from an Indian siege in Colorado by galloping through the attackers to summon help. He subsequently kept the peace in Hays City and Abilene, Kansas, killing four men in the line of duty. He cut an awesome figure in these towns; one visiting cowboy remembered him standing "with his back to the wall, looking at everything and everybody from under his eyebrows—just like a mad old bull."

But Wild Bill's glory was short-lived. In 1871 in Abilene, he loosed

Wild Bill sports a mass of long hair as a contemptuous challenge to scalp-seeking Indians.

a fusillade at a group of quarrelsome drunks, killing one troublemaker—and one policeman. The city council fired him, and his career slid downhill to a squalid chaos of booze, gambling and arrests for vagrancy. By 1876, plagued by eye trouble and the threatened loss of his marksman's gifts, he had wandered to Deadwood in Dakota Territory. One afternoon a sad-

dle tramp named Jack McCall, convinced that Hickok had killed his brother in Kansas, sneaked up behind him at a poker table and shot him in the head. The very cowardice of the act testified to Wild Bill's potent reputation. Before he was hanged, McCall reportedly said he had not dared to meet Hickok face to face because "I didn't want to commit suicide."

on a stolen horse. "They tell lots of lies about me," Hardin complained years later. "They say I killed six or seven men for snoring. Well, it ain't true. I only killed one man for snoring."

Whatever the provocation, his toll mounted. Hardin was not quite 25 when he claimed his final victims. Discovered living in Florida by Pinkerton detectives, he fled, gunning down two men in a shoot-out with the authorities near the state line. He then took up residence in Alabama. One night in Mobile, he killed two men after a poker game in which he had won $3,500. By Hardin's own count, and his reckoning was probably not far off, these were his 43rd and 44th victims.

He remained at large in Alabama for 10 more months, until the Texas Rangers learned of his whereabouts. On July 23, 1877, he was cornered in the smoking car of a train at Pensacola Junction, Florida, on the way back from a gambling foray. As lawmen rushed him from both ends of the car, Hardin reached for his pistol but it caught in his suspenders. After he had been subdued and bound to a chair, one of the officers told him, "John Wesley Hardin, you are the worst man in the country"—then tempered his critique by handing him a cigar.

Shipped back to his native Texas, Hardin was tried in Austin for just one of his 44 self-acknowledged killings—the slaying three years before of a deputy sheriff. That one, ironically, could almost have been justified as self-defense, and the jury recognized it by finding him guilty only of second-degree murder. The sentence was a mere 25 years, and between abortive attempts to escape from prison, he studied algebra, theology and the law behind bars. In 1894, after he had served 15 years of his term, the governor pardoned him.

Hardin then opened—of all things—a law office in El Paso. But he spent more time arguing in saloons than in court. When his girlfriend was arrested for carrying a pistol, Hardin was overheard making threats against the arresting officer, a policeman named John Selman. Some days later, on August 19, 1895, Selman stepped into the Acme saloon, spotted Hardin at the bar shaking dice with a friend, walked up behind him and shot him dead. A jury acquitted Selman, apparently in gratitude for his having rid Texas of a major menace.

The perverse, gun-toting heroes of Hardin's stripe possessed an aura of tragedy, a sense of lives gone ter-ribly wrong. Among those recorded in the Old West's annals of infamy, the most unlikely was the downy-cheeked, blue-eyed orphan lad they called Billy the Kid. Perhaps because he looked so harmless and acted that way most of the time, Billy exerted a special appeal despite a comparatively modest record of homicides. In contrast to the 44 deaths notched by John Wesley Hardin, for example, the Kid reportedly once claimed a toll of no more than 21—"one for every year of my life"—and may have dispatched only nine victims. Nonetheless, newspapers the country over headlined his exploits while he lived, and within 10 months of his death, no fewer than eight novels were published romanticizing his career.

Billy, who had been baptized Henry, took his stepfather's first name and may not even have known his surname. He was born around 1860, probably in New York City. His father evidently died early, and when Billy was 14, his mother died of tuberculosis in Silver City, New Mexico, where she had supported the family by taking in boarders. Billy stayed out of trouble until age 15, when a lawman put him in jail for his role in a trivial practical joke. After two days behind bars, Billy wormed his way up the chimney and fled into Arizona. There, at 17, while working as a teamster hauling logs, he shot down his first victim, a blacksmith who had made fun of the rootless youngster and knocked him down.

The Kid's next killings grew out of his penchant for forming strong emotional attachments to people who helped him. He went back to New Mexico, hired on as a cattle guard and quickly was swept up in a violent economic power struggle in Lincoln County. Witnessing the murder of his boss by the opposing faction in this feud seems to have tripped the trigger on some fatal quirk in Billy the Kid. After a posse formed by his faction captured the killer and a deputy sheriff in cahoots with the enemy, Billy and another hired hand coldbloodedly gunned them down, along with one of their own who evidently had tried to protect the prisoners. Three weeks later, when lawmen sought to arrest him, Billy and other members of the faction holed up in a store in Lincoln and killed the sheriff and mortally wounded a deputy. In a final shoot-out between the Lincoln County factions in July 1878, Billy's bullets claimed yet another life.

At 18, the Kid was now a fugitive from enough mur-

In a rare photograph of a frontier showdown, a gunman stalks a foe *(at fence)*. The anonymous duel took place in Quartzite, Arizona, after a saloon argument. The prey fired once before running away.

der warrants to ensure a trip to the gallows the moment he was caught. But he remained in Lincoln County, rustling cattle, and in March 1879 the new territorial governor, Lew Wallace, arranged a secret meeting with the young outlaw. Wallace, a retired Union general who was then writing the final chapters of his classic novel *Ben Hur,* hoped to make a deal with Billy—a pardon for his crimes in exchange for the Kid's testimony on other killers in the county. The cautious Kid showed up at the house where the governor was waiting one night, carrying a Winchester rifle in one hand and a revolver in the other. The two men negotiated terms, but the district attorney refused to honor the deal and defied Wallace's orders. Remanded to jail, the Kid simply slipped off his handcuffs—his hands were small and his wrists large—and took his leave.

Billy began to hang around nearby Fort Sumner on the Pecos River, where he developed a fateful friendship with Pat Garrett, the bartender in Beaver Smith's saloon. Six feet four inches tall and fast on the trigger, Garrett was elected sheriff of Lincoln County in the fall of 1880. One of the first tasks handed Garrett was the apprehension of his erstwhile customer and friend.

After weeks of trailing the Kid, Garrett finally trapped Billy and some of his friends in an abandoned stone building in a place called Stinking Springs. They surrendered later that day because, as Billy explained to Garrett, the outlaws were famished and could smell the posse cooking dinner.

A jury took just one day to convict the Kid of murdering the former county sheriff. Billy was sentenced to hang, but the jail could not hold him long enough.

He played his old trick of slipping out of his handcuffs, slugged the guard with the released shackles and then shot him dead. He seized a double-barreled shotgun from the sheriff's office and waited in a window on the balcony of the jail until the other guard, Robert Olinger, came running across the street.

"Hello, Bob," Billy called with a grin. When Olinger looked up, Billy fired and then smashed the shotgun and threw the pieces down at the corpse. "Take it, damn you," he told the dead deputy. "You won't follow me any more with that gun." He seemed reluctant to leave the building. Brandishing a pair of revolvers from Garrett's office, he remained at the jail for nearly an hour. According to a report later submitted to the sheriff, "He danced about the balcony, laughed and shouted as though he had not a care on earth."

Billy's time was running out. Sheriff Garrett caught up with him three months later, on July 13, 1881, at a ranch at Fort Sumner, the town where they had first met. That night, through happenstance, the two men found themselves at the ranch of Pete Maxwell, an old friend of Garrett's. As each stalked an unknown man in a darkened room of a cabin, they came so close that they were practically touching. "Quickly as possible," recalled Garrett, "I drew my revolver and fired, threw my body aside and fired again. The second shot was useless; the Kid fell dead. He never spoke." He was with his many victims.

At 21, the late Billy the Kid entered into legend. One of the chief promoters of his glorification was none other than the man who did him in, Sheriff Pat Garrett. Teaming up with an itinerant journalist, he produced an error-riddled account of his onetime friend's brief and brutal life. Famous now in his own right, Garrett went on to serve as a captain in the Texas Rangers and win an appointment from President Teddy Roosevelt as a customs collector. He bought a ranch in New Mexico but eventually proved to be too slow on the draw. One day in 1908, a neighbor with whom he had long feuded gunned down the killer of Billy the Kid.

The line between guardians of the peace and gunslingers, between good men and bad, was frequently blurred in the Old West. Gunfighters and gamblers often won election or appointment to the variety of peace offices on the frontier—town or federal marshal, county sheriff, state ranger. Not infrequently, they carried on their old pursuits in the new job.

One of the most warlike of the peace officers was the notorious Texan Ben Thompson. In 1880, he was operating the lucrative faro concession upstairs at the Iron Front saloon when the citizens of Austin elected him marshal. A jovial, well-mannered man who wore a silk stovepipe hat, dapper suits and carefully waxed mustache, Thompson was one of the most ruthless gunmen in Western history: He later admitted to 32 killings as a private citizen. Thompson lasted only a little over a year as a lawman; the townspeople reluctantly accepted his resignation after he killed an old enemy in a San Antonio shoot-out. "Others missed at times," wrote Bat Masterson, "but Ben Thompson was as delicate and certain in action as a Swiss watch."

The colorful Masterson himself was a much-feared gunslinger and lawman. He was reputed to have dispatched a dozen men while sheriff of Ford County in and around Dodge City, where he and his brothers Ed and Jim all served as lawmen during the 1870s. Such was Bat's reputation that lesser men gave way without forcing him even to draw his guns.

The ultimate responsibility for maintaining order in the Old West—for keeping the lawmen as well as the gunmen in check—belonged to the men armed not with guns but with gavels. Many of the early judges were untrained, typically tradesmen doubling in brass, and the brand of justice they dispensed frequently was as makeshift as the frontier towns they tried to police. They often had to set up court in a store or saloon and face disdain and disrespect, even danger, from their constituents.

Magistrates required the firmness and iron nerve demonstrated by Robert M. Williamson, an early district judge in Texas. Williamson was widely known as "Three-Legged Willie" because he walked on a peg leg attached at one knee, with his own extremity, withered by a childhood illness, bent behind him. But there was nothing wrong with Willie's backbone. Sent to Shelbyville to establish a court, he had no sooner improvised a courtroom in the general store than the local spokesman informed him that no such court was needed in those parts. By way of emphasis, the man tossed his bowie knife on the bench and announced, "This, sir, is the law in Shelby County." Whereupon Three-Legged Willie whipped out his pistol, whacked it down beside

the knife and roared, "This is the constitution that overrules your law!"

It was almost always the federal judges, the magistrates of the U.S. district court, who brought the cutting edge of law and justice to the frontier. These judges usually had legal training, and they had to pass the muster of the President who appointed them and of the Congress that confirmed them. One of the most difficult of the new federal benches in the Western territories was the U.S. Court for the Western District of Arkansas, based in Fort Smith. This district exercised jurisdiction over white-connected crime in 70,000 square miles of the infamous Indian Territory. During the early 1870s, it was one of the most lawless areas of the West, a haven for gunslingers and outlaws and the site during a period scarcely longer than a year of no fewer than 100 murders.

To this bench in 1875 came the remarkable man who soon would win fame as the "Hanging Judge" of Fort Smith. Judge Isaac Charles Parker was only 36 years old, but he had already served as city attorney in his hometown of St. Joseph, Missouri, as a backwoods local judge and as a two-term Representative to the U.S. Congress. He brought to the federal bench a special concern for the plight of the Indians, an imposing personal presence and a rigid Methodist upbringing that had taught him the punishment of evildoers was an imperative of divine justice.

Parker promptly set his stern stamp upon the court. During the first session, which lasted eight weeks, his court convicted 15 of 18 defendants accused of murder. Parker sentenced six of them to death. These defendants were not big-time gunfighters but anonymous men moved by small, sordid motives. One had murdered a young cowboy to get his fancy boots and saddle; another had borrowed a Winchester from a friend, then used it to kill him on a whim. Their simultaneous execution on an immense gallows built to Parker's orders brought a crowd of 5,000 spectators and newspaper attention nationwide.

This was only the beginning. Parker had been invested by the President and Congress with unusual powers to cope with the unique problems of Indian Territory. He and his marshal were authorized to hire a small army of 200 deputy marshals to fan out and bring back lawbreakers. And Parker was given final authority over all

A disbeliever in tempering justice with mercy, "Hanging Judge" Isaac Charles Parker sentenced a total of 160 men to the gallows during two controversy-ridden decades of keeping rein on Indian Territory.

crimes committed in the Territory, which meant that his decisions could not be appealed to any higher court. The only hope for a man he condemned to death was a pardon or commutation of sentence by the President.

To keep up with the procession of prisoners brought in by his legions of deputies, Parker maintained court from 8:30 a.m. to nightfall six days a week. He sometimes held night sessions as well, walking the mile home afterward in the dark, alone and unarmed, with utter disregard for his personal safety. He conducted the trials with dispatch—too swiftly, some grumbled, for a defense attorney to prepare his case properly. During his first 14 years on the Fort Smith bench, Parker sent 46 men to the gallows for murder or rape.

Parker did not revel in this record. On one occasion, he wept from the bench after pronouncing the death sentence. "I even favor abolition of the death penalty," he said, "provided that there is a certainty of punishment, whatever that punishment may be, for in the uncertainty of punishment following crime lies the weakness of our halting justice."

None of his capital cases caused Parker as much exasperation as the recurrent appearances before him of a leather-faced female miscreant named Belle Starr. Starr's criminal career grew out of her consuming passion for gunslingers and bandits. She had been the mistress of Cole Younger, member of the James gang and the wife successively of a horse thief and of the Cherokee outlaw Sam Starr. "I am a friend to any brave and gallant outlaw," she boasted to a reporter, and the press played her up romantically as everybody's favorite criminal.

Though Belle acted as an organizer, planner and fence for rustlers, horse thieves and bootleggers who distilled and sold whiskey to the Indians, Judge Parker had a hard time nailing her. To stay out of court, she bribed and sometimes seduced his deputies. Even after the judge managed to put her behind bars for nine months for stealing a neighbor's horses, she still managed to frustrate the judge. Her lawyers went over Parker's head to the White House to win a Presidential pardon for her horse-thief son and a commutation of sentence for her murdering lover, a desperado who called himself Blue Duck. To the judge's relief, Belle Starr was shot and killed from ambush in 1889, probably by her newest husband.

Parker suffered more important frustrations. To ease the court's heavy case-load, and to reprove what many considered his high-handed trial tactics, Congress kept chipping away at his authority. Beginning in 1883, large sections of his jurisdiction were removed and given to other federal district courts. Then, in 1889, Congress extended to Parker's capital-case defendants the same right of appeal to the Supreme Court that existed in other federal courts. Defense attorneys, seizing upon what Parker called the "flimsiest technicalities," flocked to the high court. During a seven-year period, 50 of Parker's 78 death sentences were appealed, and the Supreme Court reversed and remanded 37 of those cases.

Continuing to wage what he called the contest "between civilization and savagery," Judge Parker persevered until July 1896. Then, suffering from diabetes and exhaustion, he took to his sickbed and died four months later at age 57. In 21 years, he had tried an astonishing total of 13,490 cases, and 9,454 had resulted in guilty pleas or convictions. Tributes poured in calling him the greatest judge in the history of the West. In any event, as one citizen solemnly remarked, he had been "good enough for any law-abiding people, and too good for some."

Leadville's Ice Palace, with a 19-foot statue of Lady Leadville gracing its entrance, stands as a celebration of the town's silver wealth in 1896. Assembled at a cost of some $20,000, it required 5,000 tons of ice, covered five acres and remained open from New Year's until midspring, when warm weather made most of it too dangerous for occupancy.

VII. THE FINAL FLOURISHES

Clouds of steam from power saws rise in the late 1860s over the Albion lumber mill, located 115 miles north of the San Francisco area.

A treasure richer than gold

Awhirl with the racketing activities of its booming new industry, the Albion lumber mill, on California's Mendocino County coast, typified the logging outposts that were bringing to a still-incredulous world the prodigious treasure of the Far Western forests. It had all the requisites: a dry, flat point of land near a river and close enough to deep water to load schooners; hillsides sloping steeply to the river, the better to slide logs to the water—and, of course, unparalleled stands of conifers.

Here the great evergreens were principally coast redwoods. Inland and to the north, the rugged land was covered with Douglas fir, Sitka spruce, sugar pine and western redcedar. Against their colossal boles, loggers from the depleted forests back east leveled axes and saws that seemed ludicrously inadequate to the task. But with courage, tireless strength and a wide range of inventive techniques, these men, antlike in their Bunyanesque surroundings, prevailed to harvest a resource far greater than the West's fabled gold and silver.

Undaunted by the immense girth of a Sitka spruce, two turn-of-the-century "fallers" prepare to have at the giant. Their double-bitted axes were a Western-forest innovation, as was the elevated perch of planks driven into slits cut in the trunk, made necessary by the huge swelling at the base.

Redwood loggers in California's Humboldt County show off a good day's work in the 1890s. This whopper measured more than 12 feet across at its base. Crews found specimens up to 18 feet thick, which could take two men a week to fell, trim and cut into manageable lengths.

15. Kingdom of the loggers

When Sam Wilkeson, an agent for the Northern Pacific Railroad, first saw the Western forests in the summer of 1869, he was thunderstruck. "Oh! What timber," he wrote. "These trees—these forests of trees—so enchain the sense of the grand and so enchant the sense of the beautiful that I linger on the theme and am loth to depart. Forests in which you cannot see and which are almost dark under a bright midday sun—such forests, containing firs, cedars, pine, spruce and hemlock, envelop Puget Sound and surpass the woods of all the rest of the globe in size, quantity and quality of the timber."

Wilkeson was able to support his rhapsodic assessment with cold facts. The great trees—he called them "monarchs to whom all worshipful men inevitably lift their hats"—yielded an incredible five times more timber than the trees of the Eastern woodlands. In 1869 alone, he noted, the Puget Sound area had disgorged "over 170 million board feet" (a board foot measured one foot by one foot by one inch). Furthermore, after decades of commercial logging, the Northwestern forests, "covering hundreds and hundreds of square miles," were "as yet scarcely scarred."

Even then, Wilkeson vastly underestimated the woodlands. They covered not hundreds and hundreds of square miles but hundreds of thousands—the greatest concentration of the greatest trees known to man.

The exploitation of those colossal forests began in the 1820s, and lasted for about nine decades, gaining strength and momentum year after year. During this pioneer period of logging, tens of thousands of men headed west. Leaving behind the depleted forests of the East they ventured forth for profit—and for something much more. The timberlands of the West offered a challenge, an adventure, an unencumbered way of life, a chance to be part of a new and exciting endeavor.

All were dumbfounded by their first sight of the Northwest's tremendous trees. Principal among them was the Douglas fir, named after a young Scottish botanist, David Douglas, who studied the towering behemoths on an expedition to the Puget Sound area in 1823. Ranging southward from British Columbia into western Oregon, and benefiting from the heavy rains that fell there annually, Douglas firs commonly reached a height of 250 feet, a diameter of 10 feet and an age of 700 years. Growing freely under favorable conditions, they were so plentiful that they became the primary source of the world's lumber. Their wood, a lumberman's dream, was straight-grained and tough, ideal for heavy-duty construction.

Another of David Douglas' finds was the western yellow pine, or ponderosa, a handsome tree that often exceeded 165 feet in height and four feet in diameter. The strong and rough-textured wood was good for almost every use; many a settler in the Northwest built his house entirely of ponderosa pine.

Other Western species proved to be particularly well suited to specific uses. The Sitka spruce, ounce for ounce the strongest wood in the world, made the best ladders. The elegant, ginger-scented wood of the Port Orford cedar took a fine finish and was in demand for coffins, and the western hemlock turned out to be excellent for flooring, paneling and furniture. It also became the chief source of wood pulp for the paper industry.

And then there were the redwoods—also known as sequoias in honor of the Cherokee chief Sequoyah— two species of them, one more unbelievable than the other. The taller of the two species, the coast redwood, flourished in a 500-mile-long section of the fog-shrouded coastline from the Oregon border south to Monterey Bay; a good-sized specimen could tower 350 feet from a base that was 15 feet in diameter.

A stand of California redwoods looms over a clearing in this 1890s photograph by A.W. Ericson, who stood his child beside one of the giants to dramatize its size.

The coast redwood's inland cousin, the Sierra redwood, was slightly shorter but its girth was even more massive; many specimens measured more than 20 feet in diameter, and some patriarchs were 40 feet wide. These monsters thrived on the Sierra's dry summers and heavy winter snowfalls. The largest known specimen, the 3,000-year-old General Sherman tree, was calculated to weigh 1,400 tons and contain enough wood to build 40 five-room houses. For commercial loggers, both species were a king-sized bonanza; their wood, amazingly resistant to weathering and rot, made unsurpassed shingles, house siding and railroad ties.

The first commercial logging venture in the Northwest was launched in 1827 on the Columbia River by Dr. John McLoughlin, a Hudson's Bay Company regional factor, who needed wooden boxes to ship furs. He set up a little sawmill with a rude mechanical saw, driven by water power, that could cut 3,000 board feet of lumber per day.

But West Coast logging would remain a minor industry until a substantial local market for lumber developed. Under normal circumstances that might have taken half a century or more; but the course of history was suddenly changed in 1848. The discovery of gold at Sutter's Mill signaled the start of the wild stampede known as the California Gold Rush. The subsequent mass migration of gold-crazed argonauts to the Far West populated the empty land, thereby opening an ever-growing market for the vast timber resources at hand. In a decade, from 1850 to 1860, California's population soared from 93,000 to 379,000.

The demand for lumber—for houses, for stores and for industries—grew insatiably. San Francisco was at the

A GUIDE TO THE WESTERN WOODLANDS

Of all plant life, trees need the most water; and since much of the American West was arid or semiarid, the great Western forests were found either hard by the Pacific or in the mountains, where air and soil were moist much of the time. Within those areas, distribution of species varied according to such traits as tolerance of shade and resistance to wind and cold. Some, such as the ponderosa pine and Douglas fir, could withstand a wide range of conditions and so spread over great areas. Among the most restricted were the sequoias, a family that before the great weather and soil changes of the glacial period had covered most of the hemisphere.

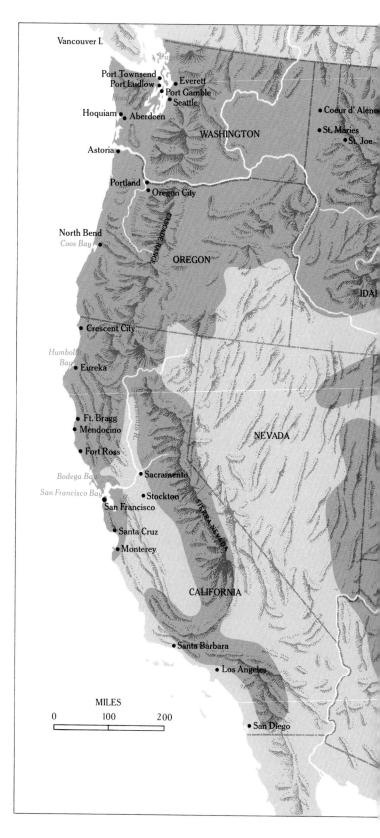

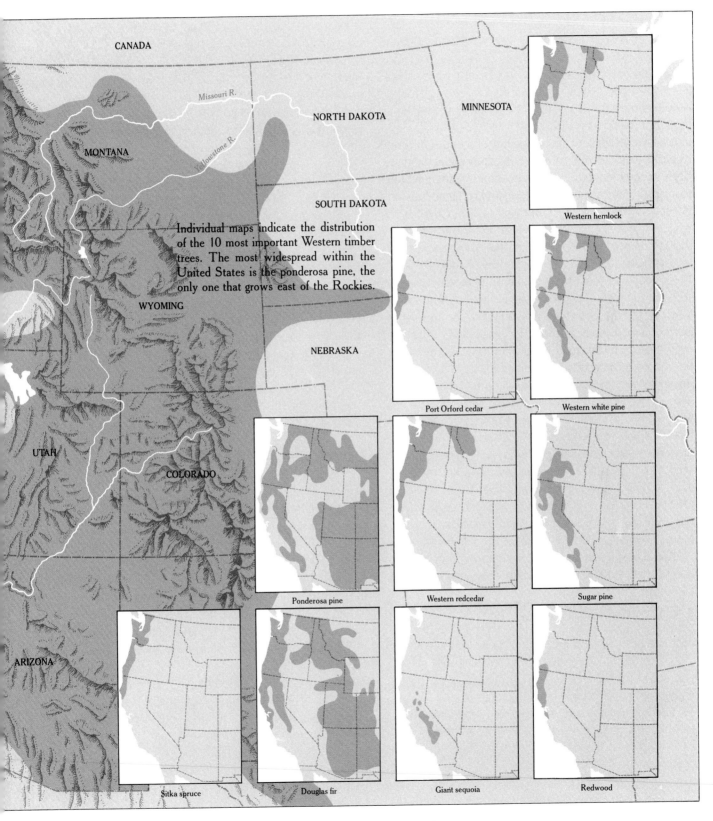

CANADA

Missouri R.

NORTH DAKOTA

MINNESOTA

MONTANA

Yellowstone R.

SOUTH DAKOTA

Individual maps indicate the distribution
of the 10 most important Western timber
trees. The most widespread within the
United States is the ponderosa pine, the
only one that grows east of the Rockies.

WYOMING

NEBRASKA

UTAH

COLORADO

Western hemlock

Port Orford cedar

Western white pine

ARIZONA

Ponderosa pine

Western redcedar

Sugar pine

Sitka spruce

Douglas fir

Giant sequoia

Redwood

hub of it all, with a population that rocketed from 2,000 at the beginning of 1849 to 55,000 by 1855. Six times, in the space of 18 months between December 1849 and June 1851, the ramshackle, jerry-built boomtown burned to the ground; each time it was frantically rebuilt, in the process consuming millions upon millions of board feet.

In 1849, the 10 sawmills operating in California could scarcely make a dent in the sudden demand for lumber. Canny ship captains bringing in gold-seekers filled their holds and piled their decks with lumber from everywhere—from the East, from Norway, Chile, even Australia. But anyone with half an eye could see how ridiculous that was, considering the timber carpeting the hills up and down the entire West Coast.

Heretofore, Western logging had been a hit or miss seasonal business. The mill-owners bought most of their timber from pioneers clearing land for farms; the sawmills operated only during the warm, dry summers, and shut down in the rainy winters. But now, mill operators everywhere sought to build up large stockpiles to keep the saws buzzing 12 hours a day six days a week the whole year round. Teams of professional woodsmen invaded the forests, and sharp-eyed "timber cruisers" prowled the Pacific Coast, seeking out the most desirable stands to cut. Some companies bought land outright; others thriftily paid only for "stumpage"—the right to clear timber. A few unscrupulous lumbermen simply marched in and committed trespass, logging private and government land without so much as a by-your-leave. By 1859, the Pacific Coast as a whole could boast a production of more than 300 million board feet of lumber annually, compared to a mere 25 million a decade earlier.

It took the talents of a fascinating crew of entrepreneurs to forge this great new industry. One of the earliest and most resourceful was William Talbot, a ship's captain and lumber trader from East Machias, Maine, who sailed around Cape Horn in September 1849. Together with his brother's friends, Andrew Pope and Captain J.P. Keller, who were already in San Francisco, Talbot established a sawmill in Gamble Bay on Puget Sound.

Equipped with a steam-driven saw, their Puget Mill Company started by cutting a modest 2,000 feet of wood a day from logs felled on the spot or bought from settlers. Within a few months, production doubled and then redoubled, and a second mill was put into operation. By 1857, the mill was cutting eight million feet a year—enough to fill a ship each week. As production increased and more or less caught up with local demand, Pope and Talbot aggressively sought out foreign markets; soon, ships and crews from the company were equally at home in Valparaiso, Honolulu, Manila, Hong Kong, Shanghai and Sydney.

By now the company owned close to 35,000 acres of timberland and had bought stumpage rights to thousands more. But the heart of the business was still the milling complex at Port Gamble on Puget Sound, which was becoming a veritable replica of a New England coastal village. Raised under the tenacious and conservative direction of Pope and Talbot, the company prospered well even after the death of its founders.

There were other such stories throughout the Northwest—some ending in failure, some in multimillion-dollar success. Though the heroes of those stories were a varied lot, they had in common a bold, powerful will and rugged individualism. None ever gained dominion over the others; the raw material that they dealt with and the markets that they supplied were too gigantic and widespread to be graspable by any monopoly.

For the loggers who were assigned the tasks of felling the trees and getting them to market, the forests of the Northwest posed a whole new set of problems. Indeed, nothing in their experience had prepared them for the monsters they now confronted.

Clem Bradbury, a sturdy, self-reliant lumberjack from York County, Maine, got a rough indoctrination. At 28, he had spent most of his life hewing white pine in the woods of his native state. In January 1847, he was in Oregon country, within sight of the lower Columbia River, about to lay his ax against a tree that soared straight up, nearly 300 feet into the sky. At the base, the bole swelled outward until it was eight feet thick. The tree, an immense Douglas fir, had been standing there for centuries, perhaps 1,000 years.

Bradbury fell to. But sinking his cut barely 16 inches, he halted in astonishment. From the wound rushed a fountain of pitch—barrel upon barrel of crude turpentine. To continue was impossible; Bradbury put down his ax and that night in the bunkhouse he said very little. By morning, however, the heavy flow of pitch had ceased, and

In a contemporary sketch, loggers in 1853 set about felling a 302-foot sequoia by drilling holes through its 28-foot diameter with a huge auger. Wedges were driven into the holes and the wind did the rest.

he resumed chopping at the same tree. At last, after six hours of backbreaking labor, the fir groaned and thundered to the ground. Back home, Bradbury could have felled half a dozen white pines in the time it had taken him to conquer this one Western giant.

Grand schemes and Herculean machines were needed to cope with these behemoths. In the East, one man equaled one tree. Out West, the choppers or fallers (never called fellers, although their job was to fell trees) almost always worked in pairs and seldom attacked a big tree at ground level. They cut high for several reasons. A tree standing on a hill offered unsafe footing for a faller, so a platform of sorts had to be employed. A tree growing out of thick underbrush was hard to reach with fast-swinging axes. A swollen base was too time-consuming to chop through; pitch collected there and the bole was often riddled with less than perfect wood, the fibers having been stretched and loosened over the years by the swaying of the trunk.

Some lumbermen built elaborate platforms to stand on, 12 to 20 feet up the trunk, while others preferred springboards, or platforms, inserted right in the trunks of the trees. Facing each other on their perches, one man swinging his ax right-handed and the other left-handed, the fallers fashioned a single undercut with a sculptor's care, then moved to the opposite side of the tree and made a flat, horizontal cut only deep enough to rob the tree of support. This had to be done so skillfully that when the fallers hollered "Timber!", tossed their axes into the brush and hurtled down from their springboards, the tree would fall in a true direction. Sometimes to impress someone or win a bet, a faller would plant a stake in the forest 200 feet from the tree, and if all went well, the falling trunk would drive the stake straight into the ground.

An alternative method was to bore holes with an auger all around the trunk of a tree, then insert large steel wedges in the holes and drive them deep into the tree with battering ram logs. That done, a stiff gust of wind finally toppled the monster. The procedure, however, could take several weeks, and in later years, redwood loggers tried stuffing the holes with sticks of dynamite. The charges would then be set off simultaneously. The method was spectacular but uncertain. A redwood was brittle and could shatter into useless fragments on impact with the ground, so loggers took pains to lay out a long, soft bed of boughs to cushion the fall. But with dynamite, the direction of fall could not be precisely controlled, and quite a few valuable trees were lost that way.

An even greater challenge than taking down the giant trees was the prodigious task of hauling them to the mills. Trees that grew at the water's edge were no problem; they could simply be floated away. But the forests extended many leagues inland from the nearest shore, into vast stretches of wild mountain country.

Skidroads—broad pathways leading generally downhill and laid with thick timbers—made their appearance in the Puget Sound area in the 1850s. Teams of oxen, yoked in pairs, grunted and strained over these routes, sliding and yawing, as they pulled a chained-together string of a dozen enormous logs. But the skidroad had its limitations: It could not be used on a hill whose gradient was too steep for the oxen and could not be more than a couple of miles long, because not even the doughtiest of the animals were strong enough to pull the logs much farther.

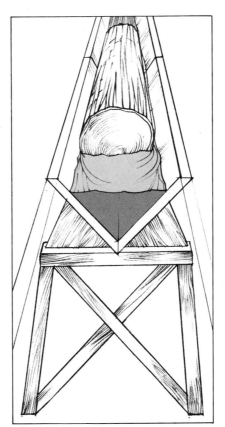

The log chute, a spectacular device, was the first that did not rely primarily on the muscle power of men or beasts. The course was downhill and gravity did most or all of the work. In essence, the chutes were long troughs, usually made of peeled tree trunks that served as conduits for the logs. One of the most famous chutes was built high above the Klamath River just north of the Oregon-California border by John Cook, a logger from Michigan. Cook boasted that logs sent down his 2,650-foot chute made the trip in 22.5 seconds, which came out to 90 miles an hour. The logs arrived smoking from the friction and hit the river with a tremendous sizzling splash.

Chutes were a wonderful rapid transit device as far as they went, but they could cover only one or two slopes. The answer for greater distances was the flume, a man-made river built of boards and fed from a reservoir high in the hills. A device that ran up to 20, 40 or even 50 miles, the flume carried not only logs but lumber, shingle bolts, cordwood, posts and railroad ties at speeds up to a mile a minute.

A river was the ideal flume, capable of floating logs and timbers of all sizes. And so the loggers of the Far West mounted great drives, with huge log rafts, down the major rivers flowing to the Pacific Ocean. But this too required ingenuity. Rapids in the higher reaches of some of the rivers were treacherous, and narrow stretches were prone to monumental jams. In places, loggers built a splash dam of timbers where the river squeezed between high banks, and stored their harvest of felled trees in the pond behind the dam. When the pond was swollen to capacity, the spill gate in the splash dam was pulled away, releasing a flood that the loggers called the

Workers lay a cradle of cross ties for a skidroad in California about 1880. Once the ties were in place, the cradle was partially filled with earth, and logs could then be yanked down the road by cables from the steam donkey engine in the background.

splash. The rush of water sluiced the stored logs down the stream toward sawmills.

In the 1880s a series of inventions transformed logging—dramatically and forever. A family of strong, steam-driven machines began an era that lumbermen called highballing—and with it came a breath-taking acceleration in the movement of logs and lumber.

For years, bearded Ephraim Shay of Haring, Michigan, had been seeking new ways to speed up the movement of logs from the forest and his mill. He had seen some fellow lumbermen use railroad locomotives on iron-faced tracks to pull trains of logs, but the engines' effectiveness was sorely limited in the mountainous timber country. They were often too heavy for the loggers' wooden trestles and poorly ballasted roadbeds. Furthermore, the powerful thrusting rods that ran from the pistons to the driving wheels provided uneven traction.

Shay's solution centered on transmitting power using gears rather than rods. A geared shaft ran from the engine to each wheel, meshing with a ring of gears on the wheel. Locked in its gears, the wheel could not spin. The Shay locomotive was an all-weather, all-terrain log mover.

Shay's invention was widely admired. Loggers swore that a Shay could hunker down and climb a tree if it had a mind to, and that was only a slight exaggeration. Its smoothly meshing gears enabled it to haul cars full of logs up grades as steep as 3 per cent. The engine's relatively light weight in proportion to its power was a crucial factor on flimsy logging roadbeds, and the universal joints enabled it to hold to the rails on a bend so extreme that, according to loggers, the headlight would shine back over the engineer's shoulder into the firebox behind him.

Ephraim Shay never got rich from his invention. The first engine he sold brought him $1,070. When he turned

his design over to other manufacturers, he accepted $10,000 in royalties and then refused further payments. He was evidently content to know that, from 1880 on, the fame of his name spread with every geared locomotive that chuffed into the deepest forests.

Two months after Shay received the patent on his machine, a mechanical monster smaller than any locomotive but bulkier than a yoke of oxen appeared in the redwoods of Eureka, California. It sat on heavy wooden skids and consisted of an upright wood-burning boiler with a stovepipe on top, and a one-cylinder engine that drove a revolving horizontal drive-shaft with a capstanlike spool at each end for winding rope. It was the Dolbeer Steam Logging Machine, and it would be recorded as the greatest labor saver in the industry's history.

Invented by John Dolbeer, a New Hampshireman who went west to join the gold rush, the machine was dubbed a "donkey engine" by loggers who felt it looked too puny to be dignified with a rating in horsepower. But Dolbeer visualized the engine as an infinitely more efficient way than ox-power to snatch logs out of ravines and haul them to a skidroad or stream.

On Dolbeer's maiden model, patented in April 1882, a manila rope 150 feet long and four and a half inches in diameter was wrapped several times around a gypsy head—a revolving metal spool mounted on a horizontal shaft. The loose end was carried out to a log and attached to it. Then, with a head of steam built up in the high-pressure boiler, the spool revolved and the incoming rope hauled the log toward the donkey. In later years, strong steel cable, winding and unwinding on rapidly turning drums, gave the donkey engine a pulling range of 1,500 feet, allowing loggers to drag fulllength logs over the ground, bumping and battering everything in its path.

The "donkey show," as the logging operation came to be called, was a hair-raising spectacle. Guy ropes moored the "donkey" to nearby trees, and a wire cable trailed off into the forest and vanished. The engine's whistle screamed a series of blasts. What happened next was vividly described by Ralph Paine, a turn-of-the-century author: "There was a startling uproar in the forest. It sounded as if trees were being pulled up by the roots. In a moment a log came hurtling out of the underbrush nearly 1,000 feet away. It burst into sight as if it had wings, smashing and tearing its own pathway—bounding toward you as if the devil were in it, breaking off some trees as if they were twigs, leaping over obstacles, gouging a way for itself."

The donkey engine made possible an even more awesome and exciting kind of logging. It was called high-lead logging and it required the services of a daredevil known as a high climber. His job was to prepare a "spar tree." He began by scaling a tree to a point 150 to 200 feet in the air, lopping off limbs on his way up. Hanging precariously, he topped the tree, chopping or sawing off its crown or perhaps setting dynamite charges to blast off the topmost 25 feet or so. A heavy pulley block was attached to the top of the decapitated tree and guy lines were affixed to the spar to hold it steady. The completely rigged tree supported a main line or lead block weighing a ton or more and through the block ran the cable that would be connected to the enormous logs lying on the forest floor.

A boy called a "whistle punk" gave the go-ahead signal; the engineer opened the donkey's throttle, and the line sped through the block on top of the spar. Out in the forest the incoming log reared up like some berserk prehistoric monster and went charging, one end high in the air, through the brush until the donkey dropped it with a resounding crash in the yard.

Everything was out of scale in the forests of the Northwest—the colossal woodlands and the massive trees that grew there, the tools and techniques that were invented for felling the trees and getting the timber out of the woods, the brawling, muscular loggers and the tall tales they spun at night by the flickering light of bunkhouse lanterns. Their hero was the legendary Paul Bunyan, the essence of the mighty logger—bigger than Goliath, stronger than Hercules, more fearless than Spartacus.

To hear the lumberjacks tell it, their Paul never did anything halfway. As a young man he lived in a great cave, and one winter night he was awakened by a loud crash outside. A falling body had shattered the ice on a nearby frozen lake. Bunyan spied a pair of ears protruding from the water. He waded a mile out—up to his chest—grabbed the ears of a baby calf and dragged it ashore. It was blue all over, either from the cold water or because that was The Winter of Blue Snow, which turned everything blue. The calf stayed blue even after

Bunyan nursed it to health, named it Babe and made it his boon companion. Loggers never did agree on the exact size of the fully grown blue ox, but Babe was big enough to pull anything with two ends to it and thus help Paul Bunyan and his crew log the country from one end to the other.

Nobody ever took Bunyan's measure either, but it was said that whenever he ordered a new pair of boots they were delivered lashed down on two railroad flatcars. The giant lumberman liked to put his mark on the tree trunks by pinching pieces out of them with his fingers. With his four-bladed ax he chopped down four trees at a time, and on days when he really felt ambitious, he would haul out his great timber scythe and mow down whole sections of forest at a single sweep.

The reality of the loggers' daily lives, however, was far removed from legends of Paul Bunyan. The only thing they could count on with certainty was that they would engage in backbreaking, life-threatening labor from dawn to dusk. Even for the most experienced and careful individuals, accidents lurked at every stage of the logging, milling and shipping process. Before his blade or saw bit into bark, the logger walking from camp to tree was in danger. Weighed down by heavy wedges, balancing an ax on one shoulder and a limber saw twice as long as his own height on the other, he could fall and be cruelly slashed if he so much as tripped over a root.

While making his cuts in a huge tree trunk, he could lose his balance and tumble off his springboard eight or more feet to the ground. If a crashing tree should happen to knock loose a branch high aboveground, the severed limb—often as thick as a man's body—could plummet downward and explode like a mortar shell.

Few jobs were as dangerous as that of the windfall bucker, whose task it was to saw apart wind-felled trees in order to clear the way for good timber that was purposely being felled. The bucker had to look out for more than the huge logs he was sawing through. He might suddenly hear the cry of "timber" and the familiar swish of a falling tree and look up to see a giant Douglas fir coming straight for him at lightning speed.

The high climbers, the spar men and pulley riggers, on their lofty perches 200 to 300 feet above the forest floor also risked a grim variety of accidents. Such a climber could sever his safety rope with a misdirected

Tools and trappings of the timberman's trade

The woodsmen who arrived in the West from the Eastern and Midwestern forests brought their axes, saws and peavies with them. But challenging terrains and trees of unprecedented proportions taxed some of the old tools. New techniques had to be invented, and with them new implements.

East of the Cascades or the Sierra, few trees required a falling saw more than six or seven feet long (the girth of the trunk plus two or three feet of travel for saw strokes). But western red-cedars and Douglas firs often required 10-foot saws, and the redwoods and giant sequoias took blades up to 18 feet long. Loggers never before had to make undercuts eight to 10 feet above the ground to get above a tree's base flare. The invention of the springboard solved that problem; the springboard, in turn, required a new kind of ax. To cut a notch in a trunk that was deep and narrow enough to hold the springboard's pointed tip firmly, an axhead was needed narrower and longer than the old 4½-by-9-inch blade. And so the Western falling ax was born, with a double-bitted head more than a foot long and 3½ inches wide.

The sawyer's second most important tool was the container for his saw lubricant, which thinned the pitch that spilled on the blades; it was always called oil, although it usually was kerosene. Oilcans were available, but most loggers preferred a quart whiskey bottle; they could then claim that they needed a new one for each quart of oil.

LUBRICANTS
Lubricants were carried in cans or bottles fitted with hooks that could be hung on branches or jabbed into the tree bark. Thin spouts or notched corks emitted the lubricant in drops.

FALLING SAW
The faller's crosscut was long (like this 10 footer) and narrow, so it would sink quickly into the tree and let anti-binding wedges be driven into the cut.

FALLING AX
The Western ax, with a longer, narrower blade than Eastern axes, had a longer haft—up to four feet—to reach into the heart of trees eight feet in diameter.

BROADAX
Most useful in the field, where there were no mills, the broadax had a chisel-like blade to square logs in trestles and flumes.

SPRINGBOARD
The tip of this faller's perch had a metal V-lip that dug into the upper wood of a notch in the tree trunk and thus wedged the springboard firmly in place.

BUCKING SAW
The bucker's crosscut was used for cutting up felled trees. This model was designed for use by either one or two men.

ax blow. A gust of wind could catch the falling top of a tree a man was topping and swing it around to brush him from his perch. Or the swaying trunk could split and spread apart, giving the high climber only a moment to drop far enough down the tree to avoid being pinched to death between his rope and the tree trunk.

One peril that struck terror into the heart of every woodsman was fire. Once started, a forest fire was unstoppable except by an act of God. The worst fires ever known theretofore in the West occurred in 1902. Following a sweltering, dry summer throughout the Pacific Coast region, a searing, merciless wind from the deserts east of the Cascades and the Sierra swept over the mountains toward the Pacific on September 11. Everyone knew how the fires started: cinders from donkey engines and locomotives, sparks from stovepipes, spontaneous combustion. Dozens started at once, from Canada down to California. One hundred and ten separate conflagrations were counted. Forests exploded like guncotton, the fires driven by winds from behind and pulling in great upward drafts of air from ahead. Many fires "crowned"—speeding through the treetops like waves of breaking surf.

Eventually, following seven days of inferno, the wind shifted around to the west; clouds rolled in from the Pacific Ocean and, mercifully, it began to rain. By September 17 the last of the fires had finally died out.

Something like three quarters of a million acres—an area as big as Yellowstone National Park—had been consumed by the flames. The official estimate was 12 billion board feet of timber lost. The human toll was put at 35 deaths—astonishingly few considering the number of lives that had been threatened. But bad record keeping and undiscovered bodies made it impossible to tally the casualties in the forest. No one ever really knew how many men, women and children died, their ashes mingling with those of the trees.

Whether by fire or other peril, an average of one logger died every day from 1870 to 1910—a total of 7,500 according to one educated guess. It was said that a man's life expectancy as a logger was seven years—no more.

The dangerous nature of the job and the boredom of the camps generated a mighty pressure for the loggers to get into town every so often and blow off steam. In any logging town there were brightly lit blocks, lined with saloons and honky-tonks, cheap restaurants and lodging houses. Skid Road, as these "entertainment centers" were known, provided a most sumptuous array of pleasure palaces designed to pop the logger's eyes, make him feel as powerful as Paul Bunyan, relieve him of his tensions and cash, and bring him back again and again for more.

Lumberjacks all over the West agreed that of the thousands of saloons in their ken, one stood out as absolutely the grandest of all—Erickson's, on Burnside Street in the rough, tough North End of Portland, Oregon. Running in a huge rectangle around an immense room was a bar that had to be the biggest monument to alcohol in the entire world—684 feet of mirror-polished mahogany, and every foot of it jammed with happily imbibing loggers. With a gargantuan free lunch available day and night and whiskey poured at two shots for a quarter, the customers could want for nothing. There were dozens of gaming tables where a customer could squander his stake. Around the mezzanine level ran a row of cozy, curtained booths where he could do his drinking, dining and love-making in private.

As the booze flowed tempers occasionally flared and gave way to fighting marked by a savage fury. When loggers fought, they eschewed knives or pistols; their weapons were bludgeon-like fists for smashing, thumbs for gouging and calked boots for stomping the will out of an opponent. A man who came out second-best in such a fight often bore the visible marks of defeat for a long time, and loggers said he had a case of "lumberjack smallpox."

While the Northwest's Skid Roads never lacked liquor and excitement and danger, until the 1860s they were conspicuously short of women. Many settlements near the sawmills had a ratio of only one woman to every ten men, and that one was usually a pioneer wife who had crossed the plains with her husband and family.

But time rectified that deficiency; most every logging town had its bawdy house eventually, and they positively proliferated in Portland and Seattle, twin meccas of every West Coast logger. The greatest of all probably was Duke Evans' Paris House in Portland, which stretched the length of a city block. Evans claimed it housed one hundred girls, although police never netted more than 83 in one raid.

A more glamorous establishment was perfected in Seattle by an entertainment genius named John Considine. It combined a saloon, theater and house of ill fame all in one attractive package. Considine imported the celebrated nude dancer Little Egypt from New York for the opening of his People's Theater, and charged only a dime admission. Considine became so successful that he went legitimate, took the theater part of his idea and parlayed it into the nation's first vaudeville circuit.

More than one member of the fair sex had by now concluded that the money to be made on Skid Road could just as well flow into a lady's handbag as a gent's wallet. The madams who provided female companionship to the loggers, sailors and mill hands of Portland and Seattle were a colorful group, and like John Considine they put on a good show. Mary Cook, a 285-pound valkyrie who ran the Ivy Green in Portland, acted as her own greeter, standing at the entrance to the bar amiably waving a large cigar. If a man extended a finger, she would blow three perfect smoke rings around it and wish him luck. Big Mary was also her own bouncer. If need be, without for a moment losing her sunny disposition, she could pick up a troublemaker and throw him bodily out the door.

Perhaps most significant in the growth of the Western lumber business was the coming of the industrial age, launched in the West by the railroads. In the 1850s and 1860s, thousands upon thousands of miles of new track had been laid. Each mile required 2,600 heavy wooden ties, supplied by the big Eastern lumber companies.

But this enormous business was only a suggestion of what was to come. In 1869, the Union Pacific Railroad and the Central Pacific met at Promontory, Utah, thus linking Sacramento with Omaha, Nebraska, and the East. In 1883, track-laying crews for the Northern Pacific Railroad closed the last gap in the 1,700-mile route between Duluth, Minnesota, and Portland. A decade later, James H. Hill's Great Northern Railroad hooked up Minneapolis with Seattle. Now lumber from the world's richest forests took only a few days to reach the vast Eastern market.

Between 1880 and 1910, the new corporate day of logging arrived. The timber barons of the Great Lakes States had long been interested in the forests of the Far West and the Rockies. The railroads finally made it feasible for them to buy land there. And in scarcely 30 years, production in the Western forests soared from 660 million board feet a year to more than eight million.

No one was quicker to seize the opportunities than Frederick Weyerhaeuser. A quiet and cautious man who went to bed early, to church regularly and to the kitchen often for buttermilk, Weyerhaeuser bore little resemblance to the stereotype of the domineering, ostentatious tycoon. But he was a quintessential lumberman, who had run dozens of companies in eight states and had dominated the lumber trade east of the Rocky Mountains for many years.

Weyerhaeuser started moving west around 1890. He visited the California redwood lands, traveled to Alaska, and made several trips to inspect the immense Douglas fir forests of Washington and Oregon. On January 3, 1900, he bought 900,000 acres of timberland, mostly Douglas fir, in Washington for $5.4 million. A lanky, Lincolnesque Hoosier named George Smith Long was hired to superintend the new firm, which was known as The Weyerhaeuser Timber Company.

A top judge of lumber and an authority on marketing, Long went to work with consummate skill and tact. He built a new mill at Grays Harbor in Washington and another near Portland, and expanded Weyerhaeuser Timber's holdings to 1.5 million acres by 1903. The company also established the subsidiary Potlatch Lumber Company with $3 million in capital and thousands of acres of white pine forest in northern Idaho and began sawing 135 million board feet a year for a lumberyard that covered 65 acres.

Weyerhaeuser flourished from the moment he moved west, but he and his colleagues encountered a number of acute problems. The catastrophic fires of September 1902 burned more than 20,000 acres of the company's best timber. And as the decade wore on, a new and extremely serious problem arose in the woods: wide-scale labor unrest among the loggers and mill hands. In the age of big business, these men sel-

Before he became the colossus of timber barons in the West, Frederick Weyerhaeuser had built up profitable mills in Wisconsin, creating one of the Lake States' largest complexes of companies.

dom dealt directly with their top bosses, and they found it increasingly hard to win raises, promotions or redress for grievances. Wages were low, risks high, hours and working conditions poor. The workers began listening to labor organizers, and started banding together for protest demonstrations and even strikes. The year 1905 saw the formation of a new all-encompassing labor union whose trumpet blast to action—"Workers of the World, unite!"—would soon win many followers among loggers and mill hands of the Northwest. The union was the Industrial Workers of the World, known as the I.W.W.; its members referred to it by the name Wobblies.

In 1907, the Wobblies tested their strength in a Portland sawmill strike, demanding an eight-hour day (down from 11 hours) and wage increases based on a $3 daily minimum (up from about $1.50). Although the strike failed, two years later the Wobblies mounted an organizing drive in and around Spokane.

It was a spectacular show and virtually tied up the area for weeks. Union speakers poured into town, and the authorities passed an ordinance making street oratory a jail-worthy misdemeanor. The Wobblies were delighted to have been handed a dramatic cause—free speech. One by one, 600 Wobblies mounted a soapbox,

got arrested and proceeded to eat up the town's prison funds. When the town fathers realized that it was costing them thousands each week to feed their prisoners, they restored free speech and released the Wobblies.

Some companies gave workers a 10-hour day, small pay raises and insurance against on-the-job accidents. But most shared the view of Weyerhaeuser's son, Frederick, Jr., who said, "I hope that we shall not have to concede an eight-hour day, and I particularly hope we shall not have to recognize the unions." In time, the lumbermen had to do both.

Meanwhile, the ruthless exploitation of the forests continued. Land laws enacted by Congress favored the lumber interests. The well-intentioned "land-lieu" clause of an 1897 act provided that anyone who wished to donate his woodland acreage to a protected forest area could claim an equal amount of land elsewhere. It proved to be a windfall for lumbermen, who traded overcut timber for virgin acreage. It was an even equal bonanza for the railroads. The Northern Pacific cheerfully relinquished the least desirable 540,000 acres of its millions of acres in return for 320,000 acres of splendid ponderosa pine in Oregon, 120,000 acres of white and ponderosa pine in Idaho, and 100,000 acres in Washington, most of it Douglas fir.

A few people were beginning to realize that there was something rotten in the woodlands. But the public notion of conservation was limited. Most citizens thought it consisted mainly of stopping lumbermen from stealing public land. The real trouble was waste—profligate waste by careless or uncaring loggers, by unthrifty sawmill techniques, by preventable forest fires.

It took years for those who understood the problem—mainly scientists and professional forest managers known as foresters—to convey their conservation message. The best-known member of the group was John Muir, the lyrical naturalist who tramped about the wilderness extolling its spiritual values and damning the "laborious vandals" who cut down California's invaluable sequoias. It was Muir who told the world that lumbermen were continuing to fell trees in two Sierra groves even after the area was protected by law.

The conservationists were poorly organized, but as time passed and the ravage of the forests became increasingly apparent, people began to take them more seriously. The Sierra Club, which Muir founded in 1892

to fight forest mismanagement, began to win converts; by the turn of the century it counted 700 select members, whose influence far outweighed their numbers. But truly effective conservation had to wait until the right man came along. That man was a well-connected young zealot named Gifford Pinchot.

Pinchot had studied at the National School of Forestry in France and learned the techniques of forest management in Europe, where woodlands once "logged out" had been restored and kept productive for centuries. He returned home in 1891 and wangled a job running an experimental forest at Biltmore, the Asheville, North Carolina, estate of railroad magnate George W. Vanderbilt. Pinchot carefully put into effect what he had learned in Europe. His staff kept the forest floor free of debris to reduce the risk of fire. Instead of "clear-cutting," or felling every tree in a tract, he took mature trees only. The remaining trees reseeded themselves, so that the forest was in a constant state of rejuvenation. Under controlled conditions, trees grew larger and faster than they did in the natural state.

At the age of 31, Pinchot won an appointment to a seven-man national forestry committee, newly established under the Department of the Interior. In February 1897, just before leaving office, President Grover Cleveland, in response to a recommendation by the committee, transferred 21 million acres of timberland from the public domain into 13 protected forest reserves.

Lumbermen protested, and Pinchot supported them. He lobbied to temper the restrictions on the forest reserves with the magic word "use." By the end of the year, Congress decreed that lumbermen should be permitted to use the reserves, but under strictly controlled conditions, designed to "improve and protect the forest within the reservations and to furnish a continuous supply of timber for the use and necessities of the citizens of the United States."

Pinchot was appointed Chief of the Agriculture Department's Division of Forestry under President McKinley. Thus installed, Pinchot launched a campaign to improve efficiency by transferring all government forest work to that division. He gained a natural and powerful ally when Theodore Roosevelt became President. The two men had known each other for years; they saw eye to eye on the need to husband the nation's timber. Roosevelt's first message to Congress stressed

Pinchot's theme of controlled and enlightened use: "The fundamental idea of forestry is the perpetuation of the forests by use. Forest protection is not an end in itself; it is a means to increase and sustain the resources of the country."

The battle was won. Pinchot's division, renamed the United States Forest Service, was charged with protecting and maintaining the reserves. As time went on, Frederick Weyerhaeuser and other lumbermen came over to Pinchot's way of thinking. Soon Pinchot-trained foresters were working in the woodlands on logging companies' payrolls, and young lumbermen of the big-business generation were discussing conservation measures at social functions that Pinchot held at his Washington, D.C., home.

By 1910, conservation was a working reality. California millmen were producing lumber from second-growth redwood forests with trees 100 to 150 feet tall that had sprung up since their grandfathers clear-cut the area 60 years earlier. Those first loggers had left standing a few worthless redwoods, trees too old or flawed to yield salable lumber. And the seeds from those lonely survivors had sired the new generation. With just a little intelligence and care, the treasure would last forever.

What was once a fine stand of sugar pine lies in a jumble of logs and splinters after a "clear-cutting" operation whereby loggers simply felled every tree in a tract. Spurred by scenes like this, the United States expanded nearby Yosemite National Park in order to protect adjoining sugar pine forests.

Naturalist John Muir, standing by a redwood in 1902, led the new forest conservation movement. Trees, he once wrote, were "the very gods of the plant kingdom, living their sublime century lives in sight of Heaven, watched and loved and admired from generation to generation!"

407

16. The last great frontier

By the early 1890s, the Old West was becoming the new. It had not happened swiftly. The mountain men who roamed the Rockies in the early 19th Century had been outmoded by a falling demand for beaver and by depletion of the animals themselves. The Pony Express riders who thundered into legend were rendered obsolete by the humming wires of the telegraph. Buffalo hunters put themselves out of business—and sealed the fate of the Plains Indians—by killing off all but a few of the great beasts that had once numbered 13 million. Cattle barons wrote the end to their own era by reckless overgrazing—although ranching survived as a prudent business, conducted behind barbed wire. And, not least, the prairie schooner had given way to the railroads that now crisscrossed the continent.

The chugging locomotives and their commodious cars brought with them new techniques and new equipment—irrigation, modern plows, steam-powered harvesters and threshers—that made farming possible on the semiarid plains. New towns sprang up to serve the farmers as marketing centers, and a witness described the surge of settlement: "A train will glide over the waste and stop at some point where the railroad has decided to build a town. Men, women and children will jump out, and their chattels will tumble out after them. From that moment the building begins."

Thus, as early as 1890, a compendium to the national census stated that "there can hardly be said to be a frontier line." But, in fact, there was. It lay far to the north in an enormous landmass that had been purchased from Russia for a song and was thereafter woefully neglected by the United States. The territory was called Alaska—an Aleut word meaning continent or mainland.

First pioneered in the name of Russia by the 1741 expedition of explorer Vitus Bering, Alaska quickly became a source of thick and lucrative sea otter pelts for ruthless Russian hunters. By 1799 the fur trade was thriving and a long-sought fur monopoly was established. But by 1856 Alaska was for sale: The Russians needed money to pay their Crimean War debts.

The Russians were well aware of the American passion for expansion, and St. Petersburg instructed its urbane minister to Washington, Edouard de Stoeckl, to try to peddle Alaska to the United States. But Stoeckl's efforts were interrupted in 1860 by the overtures to another conflict—the American Civil War.

Seven years later, with that war over, Russia remained desirous of selling Alaska. Stoeckl reopened negotiations, this time with William H. Seward—a shrewd, sometimes devious man who had been Abraham Lincoln's Secretary of State and was now serving in that same capacity under President Andrew Johnson. As it happened, Seward was an ardent expansionist who was even more eager to buy Alaska than Stoeckl was to sell it.

Stoeckl was astonished when Seward offered five million dollars—the very price for which the Russian had been ordered to hold out—and he was even more amazed when Seward, without waiting for a response, allowed that he might up the ante to $5,500,000. There was a reason for Seward's nervous rush: He wanted to have the Alaska deal ready to present to Congress for ratification before that rebellious body adjourned at the end of March. Delighted by Seward's seeming naïveté, Stoeckl eventually managed to nudge the American up to seven million dollars.

On the evening of March 29, Stoeckl visited Seward's home to impart the good news that Czar Alexander II had approved the deal. Finding Seward playing cards with his family, Stoeckl offered to go the State Department the next day to complete work on the treaty that would consummate the transaction.

"Why wait until tomorrow, Mr. Stoeckl?" asked Seward. "Let us make the treaty tonight."

With a diplomat's instinctive reaction to unseemly

An 1867 cartoon portrays Alaska as a block of ice bought by President Andrew Johnson and Secretary of State William Seward. Dissidents throughout the United States dismissed the country's newest acquisition as unusable, uninhabitable and unworthy of purchase.

PREPARING FOR THE HEATED TERM.

King Andy and his man Billy lay in a great stock of Russian ice in order to cool down the Congressional majority.

haste, Stoeckl offered a mild protest. "But your Department is closed," he said. "You have no clerks, and my secretaries are scattered about the town."

"Never mind that," replied Seward, "if you can muster your legation together before midnight, you will find me awaiting you at the Department, which will be open and ready for business."

Seward was as good as his word, and at 4 a.m. on March 30, 1867, the American Secretary of State and the Russian plenipotentiary appended their signatures to a 27-page document that consigned Alaska to the United States. In those final hours, Stoeckl had managed to squeeze another $200,000 out of Seward; the final price was $7.2 million.

In return, the U.S. took title to an area of 586,000 square miles—twice the size of Texas—for a little less than two cents an acre. As time would eventually prove, it also received a land beyond price for its fur-bearing animals, timber, coal, copper, gold, oil and salmon fisheries.

Unfortunately, those treasures were jealously guarded by a cruel climate and some of the world's most savage terrain. Just to get into the Alaskan landmass, pioneers had to struggle through dense forests and across glacier-ridden mountain ranges, mighty rivers and boundless tundra. The relatively mild Panhandle region in the south was drenched by rain or cloaked in

fog at least 200 days a year. Along the Yukon and Kuskokwim rivers, winter held sway for eight months a year, with temperatures bottoming out at -70 degrees F. In the summer, mosquitoes and black flies were so numerous that they killed pack animals on the hoof and drove strong men to the brink of insanity. Moreover, to develop the sprawling wilderness in the face of those hostile elements there was a human nucleus of only about 30,000 indigenous peoples, mostly of Eskimo, Aleut or Indian blood, and some 900 Americans.

At the time, critics saw only those disadvantages. Outraged by the treaty-signing they called a "dark deed done in the night," they derided Alaska itself with such epithets as Walrus-sia, Seward's Icebox and, of course, Seward's Folly. The U.S. Congress, embroiled in a feud-to-the-death with Andrew Johnson and his Administration, did not rush to carry out the provisions of the treaty. And even after it finally authorized the money for Alaska's purchase, it placed the immense territory under the jurisdiction of a single customs officer with four deputies and an Army officer who commanded no more than 250 soldiers.

But William Seward never lost faith. In 1870, at the height of the hubbub, a friend asked him what he considered the most significant act of his long and illustrious career. Without hesitation, Seward declared: "The purchase of Alaska! But it will take the people a generation to find that out."

The realization of Alaska's worth came to at least one American much sooner than that. He was Hayward M. Hutchinson, who had been in the flourishing Alaskan port of Sitka when Seward made his deal. With some San Francisco partners, Hutchinson paid $350,000 to buy all the assets of a Russian company that had held the Czar's charter to hunt fur-bearing seals on the Pribilof Islands, two tiny specks in the Bering Sea off the Alaskan coast.

Then, acting in the name of conservation while actually seeking exclusive hunting rights, Hutchinson and his associates in 1870 persuaded Congress to pass an act making the Pribilofs a protected federal preserve and limiting the annual seal harvest to 100,000 skins. Sealing rights were leased to the highest bidder—none other than Hutchinson's Alaska Commercial Company, which agreed to pay an annual rent of $55,000 plus a royalty of $2.625 on every sealskin taken.

The fur-seal breeding grounds on the Pribilof Islands drew not only people who slaughtered the seal but at least one conservationist as well. Henry W. Elliott made several trips to the area and campaigned for 40 years to curtail the killing.

The hunters were attuned to the 30-million-year-old rhythms of the yearly seal migration. After feeding and sleeping in the open Pacific for seven or eight months during winter and spring, the seals returned to the Pribilofs each summer in astronomical numbers. At dawn each day, a dozen hunters would dodge among the rocks and grassy hummocks, trying to get between the sea and the place where thousands of young males and old bull bachelors were sleeping together far from the breeding grounds (by law, cows and calves were spared). Rising to full height, the hunters would shout, "Hai! Hai!" In moments a few startled seals would head inland toward the tundra plateau. That was all it usually took to set off a fin-slapping stampede.

The seals were herded toward the killing ground a mile or two away, in effect carrying their own skins to the salthouses. There, at the signal "Strike!" from a foreman, the hunters would crush the skulls of 100 to 150 full-furred seals with five-foot-long hickory bludgeons. Most of the best pelts were later sent to London, where furriers had perfected the arts of curing and dyeing.

The seal harvest continued, paying into the U.S. Treasury an annual average of $317,000—by itself a fair rate of interest on the original Alaskan investment. Yet despite the success of the sealers, Alaska attracted little attention from its proprietors—until a couple of drifters awakened everyone with a start.

Late in 1879, when Richard Harris and Joseph Juneau stepped unsteadily off a ship at Sitka, their prospects could hardly have been less promising. Harris, according to a man who knew him, was "an inveterate drunkard." As for Juneau, "between hooch and squaws he never had a cent to get away on." Now, they still owed the fare for their passage and they had to find work.

At the time a mining engineer by the name of George Pilz was grubstaking prospectors and paying them four dollars a day to fan out over Alaska's Panhandle region. Pilz's return, should there be any, was his choice of two claims from every three his men might stake. With that understanding, Harris and Juneau set forth in July 1880 with a boat, three months' provisions and a couple of Indian guides.

Less than two weeks later, the sorry pair stopped at an Auk village, where they bought hooch (short for hoochinoo, a skull-splitting distillate of bark, berries, molasses and yeast) and the close companionship of Indian women, paying for their pleasures with the food and equipment Pilz had given them. Before they could offer their boat for trade it floated away with the tide. Only seven weeks after they had left, Harris and Juneau returned to Sitka, boatless, foodless, penniless and hung over. Following them, however, was the principal Auk chief named Cowee, to whom they had promised a handsome reward if he led them to a productive gold field. Cowee had taken them to the mouth of a small stream on the Gastineau Channel, but after some desultory panning, Harris and Juneau had shrugged the place off. Now, while they were engaged in explaining, with great prevarication, their recent misfortunes to Pilz, Cowee showed up and displayed some rich gold quartz he had found at the shunned site.

That placed Pilz in a dilemma. The season was running short, and the only men Pilz could find available for hire were Harris and Juneau. Left without options, Pilz gave the dissolute pair fresh supplies and sent them off in a canoe. This time, after arriving at the headwaters of the stream and climbing a mountain, they came upon a gulch where thousands of years of erosion had deposited gravel veined with gold. Harris and Juneau staked claims not only for mining rights but for a 160-acre townsite. Later, other miners would name the town after Juneau—and it would eventually become Alaska's capital.

The Silver Bow, as Harris called it after a mining district in Montana, was a fabulous strike. One claim, owned by a Californian, yielded more than $66 million in the 35 years that it was worked. Less fortunate was Dick Harris, who with various partners took out gold worth $75,000, squandered it, and died broke in 1907. Juneau, who made about $18,000, had nothing left after two years. He died in 1899 and was buried in the town that bore his name.

With prospectors, always an unruly lot, pouring into the region around the Silver Bow, Alaska was clearly reaching the stage when it required a healthy dose of law and order. But although Washington was perfectly willing to rake in whatever profits Alaska could offer, Congress refused to provide anything in return, and the territory remained largely ungoverned. Cried a Presbyterian missionary named Dr. Sheldon Jackson: "In all that country there is no law—there can be no restraint—and the lowest animal passions of the rough miners, trappers, hunters, soldiers and sailors rage unchecked."

As matters turned out, it was Jackson himself who brought government of a sort to Alaska. Although he was a bare five feet tall, every inch of him burned to serve the Lord and the people of Alaska. During a brief 1877 visit to the territory he had been shocked by its plight. Returning south, he spent the next several years touring the country from Denver to Boston—with frequent lobbying stops in Washington—delivering an impassioned plea on behalf of Alaska. He also had more than 100,000 circulars printed, urging voters "to rally and flood their congressmen with petitions asking special attention to the claims of Alaska."

Jackson's efforts paid off in the spring of 1884 when Congress, awash with petitions from 25 states, passed the Organic Act of Alaska, which placed the territory under the civil and criminal law of Oregon. It also created a governor and a district court with a judge and a district attorney, a marshal, four deputies and a clerk.

Those provisions were sorely tested during the 1890s when Alaska's population figures nearly doubled. According to the census of 1900, the natives and 4,300 sourdoughs, as white Alaskans called themselves in honor of their dietary staple, had been joined by 26,000 cheechako (the Chinook word for newcomers). Most of the surge stemmed from the discovery of gold on the Yukon and Klondike rivers, and especially at a bleak place on the northwest coast called Cape Nome.

The rush to Nome began late in 1898 after three prospectors panned about $1,800 worth of gold out of a gulch on Anvil Creek, three miles from the coast. By winter, cheechakos and sourdoughs alike had streamed to the scene from the States, from the Canadian side of the Klondike, from every corner of Alaska.

Then, one day in the summer of 1899, an old man named John Hummell, too feeble to give much thought to going to the inland creeks and toiling in the permafrost, took a walk on Nome's black sand beach. Gold is where you find it, the old prospectors said, and Hummell found it at the water's edge.

The gold lay right underfoot, practically in the way. Within hours a throng of men—and a few women—were on the beach, spading up the sands. They were working history's richest "poor man's diggings," so called because the sand was laced with gold that required no heavy investment or effort to harvest. All that a miner needed was a shovel, a bucket and a gold pan or, preferably, a rocker. The latter was a device resembling a baby's cradle, and it functioned on the same principle:

To reach the lucrative gold fields in Canada's Klondike from the Alaskan Panhandle, aspiring argonauts first had to scale the mighty Chilkoot Pass. Of those who completed the trek only one out of 10 discovered any gold at all.

pour in a shovelful of sand and a pailful of water; then swing the rocker gently back and forth. This lullaby motion did for gold what it does for a baby—caused it to settle down.

Using that technique, some 2,000 miners took out two million dollars along a 42-mile stretch of beach before the summer came to a close, By the end of the year, the newborn town of Nome sported four hotels, six restaurants, 12 general merchandise stores, a bank, a bookstore—and, predictably, 20 saloons.

But it was even more notable for its condition of legal chaos. Because no one was experienced in mining a beach, no one knew quite how to go about allocating claims made on sand. After much dispute, the diggers settled on a space measured on each side by the length of a long-handled miner's shovel, which worked out to about 20 square feet. But the system broke down each day when the tide rushed in, driving the miners back to high ground and smoothing over all traces of their labor before the water receded.

Inevitably, quarrels over claims led to a blizzard of lawsuits, clogging the docket of Alaska's single federal judge. Finally, even an obtuse Congress got the message and passed legislation providing Alaska with three U.S. district judges. That was followed in 1906—the same year that the gold petered out on Nome's beach—by an act that granted Alaska limited representation in the person of a nonvoting delegate in the U.S. House of Representatives. And in 1912, four and a half decades after William Seward had made his purchase, Alaska was at last given full status as a Territory of the United States with an elected legislature of its own.

During those 45 years in limbo, a tough breed of Americans had mapped the Alaskan interior, stringing telegraph wires along it. They had challenged the Yukon River, running its rapids in rugged scows and using it for a frozen dog-sled highway in winter. In the Panhandle, they had built a stub railway over lofty White Pass on the way to the Klondike. To reach central Alaska from the port of Valdez they had hacked out a wagon road leading 376 miles over mountain barricades to a broad valley. There they flung up a town called Fairbanks, where law and order abided almost from the beginning.

They had also wrested many fortunes from their intransigent surroundings. Aside from the gold, they found massive green cliffs of copper, with ore up to 70 per cent pure, upstream on the glacier-fed Chitina River. They harvested furs and created the salmon industry with true Yankee ingenuity. They had tamed the land, but they had not yet conquered it. For generations to come, Alaska would remain the last great American frontier.

Farther south, the earlier frontiers that had loomed large in American history were passing into a new era. They were perhaps best illustrated in the states of Texas and California, where pioneer determination was still very much alive.

In Texas, the transformation spun out of the obsession of a one-armed (due to a logging accident) and extraordinarily bull-headed man, Pattillo Higgins, who was convinced that a fortune in petroleum lay beneath a low hill called Spindletop in the rice country four miles south of the town of Beaumont. Gas and foul-smelling sulfur fumes rose from fissures in the hill's surface, and Higgins was certain that they denoted the presence of oil.

In 1892, Higgins and several partners formed a company and bought 2,700 acres on and around the hill. But after seven years they had nothing to show save three dry holes. Finally, in desperation, Higgins ran an ad in a trade journal offering to share in "a great, oil-bearing concession." He got only a single reply, and when the interested party—one Anthony Lucas—showed up in Beaumont, Higgins had nothing to offer but a long tale of frustration.

Lucas, however, was immediately entranced by Higgins' dream. An unusual fellow, Lucas was Austrian born, had studied engineering at the Polytechnic Institute in

Graz and had served in the Austrian Navy before crossing the Atlantic to seek his fortune in the United States. Since then, he had designed a gang-saw for Michigan lumber mills, mined gold and copper in the West, and drilled for salt in Louisiana.

Lucas had accumulated some money, and now he handed Higgins $11,000, gave him a note for another $20,000, and guaranteed him 10 per cent of any profits from the enterprise. The new partner agreed to pay for the drilling while taking a 90 per cent interest in the venture.

Lucas erected a rig that featured a relatively newfangled rotary drill, which cut through the earth with a bit spinning at the end of a column of pipe, and went to work on a fourth hole at Spindletop. After six months of trying to penetrate the hundreds of feet of loose sand that lay under the hill, Lucas was stony broke. But undeterred, he exchanged seven eighths of his interest for funding from a pair of Pittsburgh speculators, and started drilling a fifth hole.

On the morning of January 10, 1901, three drillers began to lower 1,020 feet of drill pipe that they had pulled out to replace a worn bit. And then it came.

Without warning, the well roared. It spewed mud. It hurled four tons of drilling pipe skyward. As the lengths of broken, flying metal came clanging down, the hole emitted gas and showers of rock. Finally, with a bang like the very crack of doom, it sent up a towering black geyser such as the continent had never seen before.

Thus began—at a time when the Old West was being consigned to the history books—the biggest, wildest boom the region had ever known. Forty thousand people descended on Beaumont in the next few hectic months. They came looking for a new kind of job, a new adventure. On the outskirts of the once-sleepy town on the Neches River arose a forest of wooden derricks. Five hundred fly-by-night oil companies suddenly materialized, many of them with no more excuse for existing than a lease on a few square feet of ground. Land prices exploded: from $200,000 to nearly one million dollars an acre within the "proved area," tapering down to $1,000 for outlying acres up to 150 miles away.

But the boom set off by Higgins' obsession and Lucas' determination reached far beyond the environs of Beaumont. From the very moment it blew in, Spindletop's gusher started to change the oil industry of the United States. Although salt domes similar to Spindletop were common along the Gulf Coast, they had previously been ignored by oil seekers: They bore no relation to the familiar geology of earlier fields in Pennsylvania—areas where petroleum was mostly contained in shallow sands or porous limestone.

Stumbling onto a treasure fit for King Solomon

Though oil was the West's great 20th Century bonanza, gold continued to dazzle men's eyes and stop their hearts. One of the most sensational finds occurred in 1914 at the Cresson mine in Cripple Creek, Colorado.

A crew under Dick Roelofs, an engineer whom the absentee owners had left in charge of the mine, was working in a tunnel 1,200 feet underground. They were cutting their way along a good lode when they suddenly holed through hard rock into a cavity, technically known as a geode.

One look was enough for Roelofs. He ordered a vault door installed at the opening, posted armed guards and summoned two witnesses of sound character to accompany him. Only then did he actually step through the new steel door into a wonderland of solid gold.

The underground room was 20 feet long, 15 feet wide and 40 feet high. Its walls blazed with millions of gold crystals and 24-carat flakes as big as a thumbnail. Pure gold boulders littered the floor amid piles of white quartz-like spun glass. It was the wealth of every miner's dreams.

Roelofs' most trusted miners set to work and stripped the geode in four weeks, thereby enriching the mine owners by the huge sum of $1,200,000. Dick Roelofs, too, profited no little from the Cresson geode. He soon became known from coast to coast as the "miracle miner," and was made a major stockholder in the mine. Fame and fortune enabled him to put first things first: He removed east to New York to enjoy women and wine.

The Old West eyes the new in this 1911 ad for a Pierce-Arrow car. The painting was made by a Californian named Edward Borein, a onetime itinerant ranch hand who called himself the "Cowpuncher Artist."

Spindletop not only demonstrated that gas and oil were frequently trapped on the tops or flanks of salt-dome formations, but also proved that the Southwest harbored subterranean reservoirs of petroleum that were far greater than any tapped in 40 years of drilling in the Northern states. The first six wells at Spindletop produced, among them, more petroleum per day than all the other oil wells then known in the world. Best of all, the great Western oil rush came at a time when the rapidly proliferating automobile (178 factories were producing cars by 1904) provided a soaring new demand for petroleum.

The era of exploration inspired by Spindletop's black geyser was marked by strikes whose names still echo in the history of the West: Glenn Pool, Indian Territory, 1905; Cushing Field, Oklahoma—with its satellite towns of Drumright, Dropright, Alright and Damnright—1912; El Dorado, Kansas, 1915; Ranger, Texas, 1917; Desdemona (formerly Hogtown) and Burkburnett, Texas, 1918; Ponca City, Oklahoma, 1918; Signal Hill at Long Beach, California, 1921; and the East Texas Field, 1930.

In California, the revolution was less dramatic but no less complete. To meet the critical food shortage that occurred after the discovery of gold, California ranchers had built their herds to the point of overproducing. But after a few years cattle raising was overshadowed by a much more profitable enterprise—wheat growing. In rich new soils, with normal rainfall, an acre would yield 30 or 40 bushels of wheat worth $1.50 or more per bushel.

Wheat output skyrocketed. In 1873 California became the United States' biggest wheat-producing state. "Wheat, wheat, wheat," exclaimed a journalist traveling between Stockton and Merced, "nothing but wheat as far as the eye can reach over the plain in every direction. Here is a man who 'has in' 20,000 acres; here one with 40,000 acres, and another with some still more preposterous amount—all in wheat."

The wheat craze was soon replaced by an even headier boom in other crops. As irrigated acres expanded and new feeder lines provided direct connections to the transcontinental railroads, many ranchers turned to raising perishable fruits and vegetables for lucrative Eastern markets. California by 1899 was the nation's biggest producer of grapes and several orchard fruits. Enormous train loads of oranges, lemons and limes were shipped out and distributed throughout the land. On dinner tables in New York, Boston, Philadelphia and Chicago, more and more glasses were filled with California wines.

Everything about California, its fruits and vegetables, its clear air and the sunlight on its tawny hills, seemed made of purest gold. These assets, talked up by casual visitors as well as by professional publicists, attracted the very rich and the very poor, the robust and the wheezy asthmatic. People from everywhere dreamed of settling in California with their own "rancho," albeit only a few acres and a cash crop of chickens—or avocados.

It was also in California where the Old West gave way to its myth. Hardly had the film industry settled in Hollywood in 1910 than a new panorama of the West appeared on the screen. From William S. Hart and Tom Mix to Gary Cooper, Gene Autry, Roy Rogers and John Wayne, the straight-shooting heroes had clean fingernails and usually wore white hats; villains were unshaven and clad in black; horses frequently received billing over the damsels who had grown all too accustomed to being rescued. And justice always prevailed.

These idealized visions of the Old West bore little relation to the real lives of the cowboys, ranchers, soldiers, miners and settlers who had populated the region; but seldom did the myths violate the hopes of those who had crossed the plains—or of the people who have since been affected in myriad ways by remembering them. Nations, too, must dream.

The most American part of America

As America entered the 20th Century, the heady, pioneering days of the Old West were mostly ended. The Indians had long since been removed to reservations—even Geronimo had been pacified and died of old age in 1909. The Army abandoned many of the forts that once dotted the West, and the rude territories became solidly thriving states, Arizona and New Mexico joining in 1912 as the last of the contiguous 48.

Five great railroads now traversed the land, carrying one million passengers a year, and thrust their avenues of steel into the farthest reaches of the cattle and sheep country. Settlers of every description thronged Westward, bringing with them new techniques and machinery—irrigation, steam-powered harvesters and threshers—that made the plains the granary of the world.

Texas became a colossus of cotton as well as cattle and oil, producing 3.4 million bales yearly on seven million fertile acres. A vast and sophisticated mining industry turned its energies to copper with 100 million pounds a year—while extracting one million dollars a day from played out gold and silver mines.

Telephones and automobiles were knitting the West together, as was Wells, Fargo with its 37,766 miles of express routes and 2,829 offices. The day of the

war-painted Sioux and Indian-fighting soldier, of the beaver-trapping mountain man and trailblazing explorer, of the Oklahoma Sooner and Nebraska sod-buster, the hardscrabble rancher and lonely sheepherder, the cowboy and Pony Express rider was finally over. But not really. For it was they who had eternally shaped the character of the nation. "The West," a chronicler once wrote, "is the most American part of America."

Coloradans bring their traditional animal-drawn work vehicles together with a new steam tractor and power thresher for a photograph during a turn-of-the-century harvest. By 1890, new farm technology had reduced to three man-hours the labor necessary to produce an acre of wheat—down from 61 hours only a quarter of a century before.

417

The 1901 discovery of "black gold" at Spindletop in Beaumont, Texas, triggered an oil boom reminiscent of the goldrush times. This forest of derricks sprang up alongside Spindletop's Boiler Avenue when speculators divided tracts into pieces as small as one thirty-second of an acre and sold them to drillers.

A lone Wyoming cowboy looks over his shoulder at an airplane scouting for strays—in a scene symbolizing the turning of the Old West into the New.

INDEX

Numerals in *italics* indicate an illustration of the subject mentioned.

A

Abilene, Kansas: as cattle town, 278; lawlessness in, 375–377; saloons in, 334
Adair, John, brand of, 314
Alamo, the, 74, *diagram* 82–83; Davy Crockett at, 84–88, *86–87;* Jim Bowie at, 78, 84–88; Martín de Cós at, 81
Alaska frontier, 408–412
Alcohol: corn whiskey distilling, *29;* during gold strikes, 136–*137,* 143; hooch, 410; and loggers, 402–403; at rendezvous, 67; in saloons, 344; and trade with Indians, *60–61*
Alder Creek, 114–118
Algonquin Indians, 21, 25; at Fallen Timbers battle, *26–27,* 28–30; raids, 18, 23
Allen, Eliza (Sam Houston's wife), 77
Allison, Clay, 346
American Revolution, 21–28
American River, 128, 130, 140, 195
Ames, Oakes, 194, 198
Apache Indians, *map* 215, 229–234, 254; gambling by, 356; religious rituals of, 222; as scouts, 260–261, *263;* at Skeleton Cave battle, 261–262; women, *209*
Appalachian Mountains, 18, *map* 19; Daniel Boone at, 22; migration over, 28
Applegate, Jesse, "A Day with the Cow Column in 1843," 112–113
Arapaho Indians: at Beecher's Island battle, 248–249, *250–251;* at peace council of 1840, 212; and Sand Creek massacre, 234–235; and treaties with U.S. government, 235–237
Argonauts. *See* Forty-niners; Sourdoughs
Arikara Indians, *map* 215; and mountain men, 65–67; as scouts, 260
Arkansas River, 43, 320, 358
Ashley, William, 64–67
Assiniboin Indians, 61
Atchison, Topeka and Santa Fe Railroad, 199, *map* 200; and cattle ranches, 278, 295; and towns, 330, 337
Athabasca, Lake, *map* 34, 58, 60
Aull, James, 336
Aull, Robert, 336
Austin, Stephen F.: death of, 95; and first American colony in Texas, 74–76, *75;* in Texas Revolution, 79–81
Authentic Life of Billy the Kid, An, 379
Axes, for loggers, *400–401*

B

Badlands, South Dakota, 241
Baldwin, Joseph Glover, 143
Bandits. *See* Outlaws

Bannock Indians, 37–42
Barnum, P.T., 345
Barwise, J.H., brand of, 314
Bascom, George, 229
Bastrop, Baron de, *75*
Bat (Cheyenne). *See* Roman Nose
Bear Flag revolt, 48
Bear River City, Wyoming, *326–327*
Bears: as danger to trappers, *16–17, 54–55;* and Davy Crockett's pet, *85;* in games, 73, 136, 358
Beaumont, Texas, 413–415, *418-419*
Beckwourth, Jim, *38*
Beecher, Henry Ward, 345
Beecher's Island battle, 248–249, *250–251,* 258
Behan, John, 365–366
Bella Coola Indians, 34
Belt, Francis, 183–184
Benteen, Frederick W., at Little Bighorn battle, 267
Benton, Jessie (John Frémont's wife), 44–49
Benton, Thomas Hart, 44–45, 189
Bering Sea, 409
Bering, Vitus, 408
Berninghaus, Oscar, *Through Hostile Country,* 156–157
Best Friend of Charleston (locomotive), *192*
Bierstadt, Albert, landscape painting by, *12–13*
Big Foot (Miniconjou chief), 241
Big Four, 189–191, 194. *See also individual men*
Bighorn River: Custer battle at, 264; Manuel Lisa at, 64; steamboats on, 188; trapper's fort on, 36
Billy the Kid, 377–*379*
Birch, James, 165
Bismarck, North Dakota, steamboats at, *178–179*
Black Bart (Charles Boles), 173
Blackfish (Shawnee chief), 22–23
Blackfoot Indians, 214, *map* 215; Colter's escape from, 36; and horses, 216; and mountain men, 65–67
Black Hills: gold at, 125, 151, 235–236, 264; Indians in, 214
Black Kettle (Cheyenne chief), 216, 234–235
Blacks: as cowboys, 302; as roustabouts, 184
Blaine, James G., 194
Bligh, D.G., 368, 371
Bloody Knife (Arikara scout), 265
Bloomer, Amelia, 345
Blue Licks battle, 22
Bodmer, Karl, paintings by, *14–15, 50–55, 225*

Boone, Daniel, 21–23, *22*
Boonesborough, Kentucky, 22–23
Borein, Edward (cowpuncher artist), painting by, *415*
Boughton, George H., *Too Near the Warpath, 20*
Bouyer, Mitch, at Little Bighorn battle, 265–266
Bow and Arrow Ranch, 313–317
Bowie, Jim, *78;* at the Alamo, 78, 84–88; knife, *78;* in Texas Revolution, 79, 81, 84–88
Braddock, Edward, 21
Bridger, Jim, *39;* as scout, 257; and survival of mountain men, 38; as trapper, 64–65
Brown, James J., *148–149*
Brown, Molly (Unsinkable Molly Brown), *148–149*
Brown, William, 261–262
Bruff, Joseph Goldsborough, sketches by, *132–133*
Bryan, Rebecca (Daniel Boone's wife), 22–23
Buchanan, James, 155
Buffalo, 32; herd, *10–11;* history robe made from, *213;* and Indians, 214, 216, 222, *223;* tipis made from, *217*
Buffalo Bill. *See* Cody, William Frederick (Buffalo Bill)
Bull Head, Henry (Sioux policeman), 240–241
Burnett, William, 198
Bustamante, Anastacio, 79
Butterfield, John, 165–166
Butterfield Overland Mail Company, 165, 173
Butterfield Overland Mail Route (Oxbow Route), *map* 164

C

Cabeza de Vaca, Alvar Nuñez, 69
Cabins, pioneer, 118–121, *120–121*
Cadillac, Antoine de la Mothe, 23
Cahokia, Illinois, 23–25
California Trail, *map* 106–107
Cameahwait (Shoshoni chief), 35
Cape Horn, route to West, 111–114, 130, 134
Carson, Christopher (Kit), *38;* as guide for Frémont, 45, 48–49; as scout, 257; and sheep drive, 283
Cartier, Jacques, 56
Cartwright, Charlotte, 118–120
Cascade Mountains, 118, *map* 142, 145
Casement, John Stephen, 195–198
Cassidy, Butch, 370, 374–*375*
Catawba Indians, 18
Cathedral Rock (Citadel Rock), *14–15*
Catlin, George, 218; book by, 46; painting

by, *77;* sketches by, *46–47*

Cattle: brands for, *281, 314;* care of, by cowboys, *307–312,* 320; as industry, 274–283, *295,* 313; longhorns, *272–273, 278, 279,* 337; and range wars, 291–295, *294;* roundups, 313–317; rustlers, 279–282, 317; Santa Gertrudis, 274, 278; towns, 337–338; trail drives, 281, 297, *300–301,* 317–*321;* on Westward trails, *110,* 112–113

Cattle trails, *map* 319

Cayuga Indians, 21

Cayuse Indians, 110

Cedar trees, *map* 392–393; Port Orford, 390; tools for felling, 400; western, 385

Central Overland, California and Pikes Peak Express, *map* 164

Central Pacific Railroad, 189–201; and gold spike, *199,* 403; governmental support for, 189–191; rivalry with Union Pacific, *194,* 195–199; scandals, 194, 201

Chamberlain, Henrietta (Richard King's wife), 278, 279

Champlain, Samuel de, 56

Chasm of the Colorado, The (Moran), *8–9*

Cherokee Indians: outlaw, 381; as Sam Houston's friend, 77, 79

Cheyenne Indians, 214–216, *map* 215; at Beecher's Island battle, 248–249, *250–251;* birth-to-death passage of, 218–222; at Little Bighorn battle, 237–238; at peace council of 1840, 212; raids, 198–199, 260; at Sand Creek massacre, 234–235; scalping by, *235;* and treaties with U.S. government, 235–237; at Washita Massacre, 262–263

Cheyenne, Wyoming: as cattle town, 317; as railroad town, 198, 346; women in juries in, 340

Chicago & Rock Island Railroad, 191, 201

Chilkoot Pass, *412–413*

Chinese laborers, on railroads, *194,* 195–198

Chiricahua Apache Indians, 229–234

Chisholm Trail, 318, *map* 319

Church of Jesus Christ of Latter-day Saints. *See* Mormons

Cimarron River, 37, 320

Circle Dot Ranch, 313–317

Cities. *See* Towns and cities

Civil War: and Alaska purchase, 408; Frémont in, 48; James brothers in, 367; and railroad construction, 191; and Texas cattle, 278; and westward movement, 330–332

Clanton, Billy, 365–367

Clanton, Ike, 366–367

Clark, George Rogers, 23–28

Clark, William, 32–36, *33,* 50

Clay, Henry, 78

Cleveland, Grover, 405

Clyman, James, 64–65

Cochise (Chiricahua chief), 229–232

Cody, William Frederick (Buffalo Bill), 238, *257–260,* 346

Coeur d'Alene Indians, *109*

Colfax, Schuyler, 194

Colter, John, 36–37

Colter's Hell, 36, *map* 66

Colton, Walter, *Three Years in California,* 135

Colt revolver. *See* Pistols

Columbia River, 118, 392, 394

Comanche Indians, *205, map* 215; and counting coup, 230; and horses, 216–218, *218–219;* Jed Smith's death by, 37; and Laramie treaty, 226–228; at peace council of 1840, 212; raids, 76, 94, 260; religious rituals of, 222–224

Comstock, Henry, 147–150

Comstock Lode (gold and silver mines), *map* 142, *diagram* 146–147, 147–151

Conservation, forest, 404–407

Contract & Finance Company, 194

Cook, Mary, 403

Copper Mining, 416

Corpus Christi, Texas, 274, 278, 317

Cortés, Hernando, 314

Cós, Martín de, 80–81, 90

Cotton, in Texas, 416

Coulson, Sanford B., 188

Cowboys, *296–301;* bunks of, *306–307;* and cattle drives, *300–301,* 317–*321,* 334; code of behavior, 305–306; and gambling, *354–355;* pay for, 278, 309; and range wars, 291–*294;* and round-ups, 313–317; and rustlers, 317; in saloons, 334; sky as clock for, *317;* tools and clothes of, 302–305, *303, 308–309;* vaqueros, *272–273, 304–305,* 314; work of, 307–313, *312. See also* Ranchers

Cowee (Auk chief), 411

Crawford, William, *24*

Crazy Horse (Oglala Sioux), 216; at Fetterman Massacre, 256; at Little Bighorn battle, 237–238, 271

Credit Mobilier, 194

Creek Indians, 30, 77

Cripple Creek, Colorado, gold at, 126, 145, 150, 348, 414

Crittenden, Thomas, 371–374

Crocker, Charles, 190, 194–198

Crockett, Davy, 84–88, *86–87*

Crook, George: and Apaches as scouts, 260–261; and Geronimo, 232–234; and Little Bighorn battle, 264–266; on Sioux Indians as horsemen, 218

Crow Indians, 191, 214, *map* 215; as scouts, 260, 265

Cumberland Gap, *map* 19, 22

Curren, James, *334–335*

Custer Battlefield, *diagram* 267. *See also* Little Bighorn battle

Custer, George Armstrong, 252, 260, *270;* at Little Bighorn battle, 188, 237–238, *263–271, 268–269;* as showman, *202–203;* at Washita Massacre, 235, 262–263

Custer's Demand (Schreyvogel), *202–203*

D

Dakota Sioux Indians, 356; buffalo robe, *213*

Davis, Jefferson, 189, 254

Davy Crockett's Almanack, *85*

Day with the Cow Column in 1843, A (Applegate), 112–113

Deadwood, South Dakota, *124–125,* 151, 376

Death of a Gambler (Russell), *354–355*

Delano, Alonzo, *Pen Knife Sketch, 161*

Delaware Indians, *24,* 228

Denver & Rio Grande Railroad, *152–153*

Denver, Colorado: as boomtown, 144, 145, 148; as Queen City of the Plains, 346–348, *348–349;* women as settlers of, 342–343

Detectives, 368; Pinkerton, 370–371, 375, 377

Dickerson, Susannah, 86, 88

Digger Indians, 42

Doctors, 334–335, *342*

Dodge City, Kansas: Bat Masterson at, 380; as cattle town, 278, 320–321; entertainment at, 344; gambling in, 364; as king of cattle towns, 337–338

Dodge, Grenville M., *190–191,* 195, 201, 346

Dolbeer, John, 398

Dolbeer Steam Logging Machine (donkey engine), *396,* 398–399, 402

Dolly Varden (silver mine), *122–123*

Donner, George, 114, 118

Donner, Jacob, 114, 118

Donner Party, 114–118, *115*

Douglas, David, 390

Douglas fir trees, 385, 390, *map* 392–393, 394–395; exploitation of, 404; high climber on, *398;* tools for felling, 400; and Weyerhaeuser Timber Company, 403

Downieville, California, 134–137

Downie, William, 134–136

Draper, Bettie, 18–20

Draper, John, 18–20

Durant, Thomas C. (The Doctor), 189, 191, 199, 346

E

Earp, James, 364

Earp, Morgan, 364–367, *365*

Earp, Virgil, 364–367, *365*
Earp, Wyatt, 364–367, *365;* and Eddie Foy, 344
Eddy, William, 114–118
El Paso (gold mine), 145
Emigrant Trail, 191
Engine 30 (locomotive), *193*
Entertainers, 339–*345*
Erickson's bar, token for, *402*
Ericson, A.W., photograph by, *391*
Eskimos, 409
Expressmen: as freighters, *154–155,* 161–163, *162–163;* as mail carriers to miners, 160–*161;* as Pony Express riders, *158–159,* 166–167, 170; and stage lines, *156–157,* 163–*173, 171*

F

Fall of the Alamo (Onderdonk), *86–87*
Fallen Timbers battle, *26–27, 28–30*
Fargo, William, 172–*173*
Farmers: and barbed wire, *292–293;* in produce industry, 415; and rivalry with towns, 338–339; sodbusters, *284–287;* and new technology, 417. *See also* Pioneers
Far West (steamboat), 188–189, 266
Fetterman Massacre, 237, 256
Fetterman, William, 237, 256
Fillmore, Millard, 189
Fir trees, *map 392*–393, 400. *See also* Douglas fir trees
Fitzpatrick, Tom (Broken Hand), 65, 108, 110
Flags, *94–95, 166*
Fletcher, Baylis John, 317–321
Fletcher's Route, *map 319*
Flora (keelboat), *50–51*
Ford, Bob, 371–374
Foreigners: and railroad construction, *194,* 195–198; as steamboat roustabouts, 184
Forest fires, 403–404
Forsyth, George A., 255; at Beecher's Island battle, 248–249, *250–251,* 258
Fort Abraham Lincoln, 188–189, 264
Fort Barrancas, 31
Fort Bend, 89, 94
Fort Benton: freight wagons at, *154–155;* steamboating to, 175–176, 180, 187
Fort Berthold, 186
Fort Boise, 109
Fort Bridger, 114
Fort Buford, 238
Fort Cheyenne, 241
Fort Chipewyan, 58
Fort Churchill, 167
Fort Clark, *52–53*
Fort Dodge, 260
Fort Ellis, 264
Fort Fetterman, 264

Fort Fork, *map 34*
Fort Hays, 260
Fort Kearney, 167
Fort Keogh, 313
Fort Laramie: trading post, 104, 108; and treaty with Indians, 226–228
Fort Larned, 260
Fort Phil Kearny, 256
Fort Pitt, 22
Fort Randall, 252
Fort Rankin, 234–235
Fort Riley, 260, 262
Fort Robinson, 238
Fort St. Michael, 31
Fort St. Rose, 31
Fort Sill, 212
Fort Smith, 165, 380–381
Fort Sumner, 378–379
Fort Wallace, 248
Fort Walla Walla, 109
Fort Wayne, 30
Forty-niners, *132–133, 135;* and alcohol, 136–*137;* costs for, 125, 134, 136, 140–143; entertainment for, 136–*137,* 143; and foreigners, 137–140, 143; gold fever, 128–130, *129,* 131–135; lawlessness of, 137, 140, 143; methods for mining gold, 134, *138–139;* and women, 136–137. *See also* Miners
Fort Yuma, 165
Foster, William, 118
Foy, Eddie, 344–*345*
Franciscan friars: as missionaries, *68–69;* as ranchers, 305
Fraser River (Bad River), *map 34*
Frémont, John Charles (Pathfinder), *44;* at Bear Flag revolt, 48; court martial of, 48; death of, 48–49; expeditions of, 45–48; as governor, 365; Kit Carson as guide for, 38
French Gulch (gold mine), 134
French and Indian Wars, 56–58
Frontiersmen, *235;* dangers for, 20–21; and Indians, 220; tools of, 20. *See also* Mountain Men
Fur trade, *50–55;* in Alaska, 408, 409–*410;* Hudson's Bay Company, 56–60, *57;* Missouri Fur Company, 64; North West Company, 34, 58–60; rendezvous, 37, *40–41,* 66, 67; and value of furs, 50, 67; *voyageurs, 56–61, 57. See also* Trappers
Fur traders: English, 56–60; French, 56–58; Scottish, 34, 58–60

G

Gallatin, E.L., 309
Gallatin, Missouri, 368, 374
Gall (Hunkpapa Sioux), 237, 271
Gamblers: in boomtowns, 359–364, *360;*

cheating by, 359–364, *361, 362–363;* Indians as, 356–358; on steamboats, 358–359, 364; tools of, *357, 358*
Games: bears in, 73, 136; horses in, *72–73,* 218
Garfield, James A., 194
Garrett, Pat, 378–*379*
Gatewood, Charles, 234
General Sherman tree, 392
Geronimo (Mimbres Apache), 216, 232–234, *233;* death of, 416
Ghost Dance, 238–239
Gibbon, John, in offensive attack against Sioux Indians, 264–266
Gidden, Joseph F., *292–293*
Giddings, George, 165
Gila River Trail, *map 106–107,* 161
Gillespie, Charles B., 136
Gluck, Adolph, badge of, *338*
Gold, *map 142,* 226; methods of separating, 134, *138–139,* 411–412; settlements, 136–143; types of, *139*
Gold strikes, Alaska, *map 142,* 410–412
Gold strikes, California, 122, 128–144, *map 142;* ads for, *130, 131;* effect of, on logging, 392; foreigners at, 137–140; and gold fever, *129;* sheep drives to, 283
Gold strikes, Colorado, 122, 126, *map 142,* 144–148, 150, 348
Gold strikes, Montana, 122, *map 142,* 280
Gold strikes, Nevada, *map 142,* 147–151
Gold strikes, South Dakota, 125, 235–236. *See also* Black Hills
Gold strikes, Utah, *map 142*
Gold strikes, Washington, *map 142*
Gold strikes, Wyoming, *map 142*
Goldwater, Michel (Big Mike), 336–337
Goodnight, Charles, brand of, 314
Goodnight-Loving Trail, *map 319*
Gould, Jay, 201
Grand Canyon, *8–9*
Grant, Ulysses S., 187; in Mexican War, 254; and peace with Apaches, 232; and railroad scandal, 194
Grattan, John L., 228
Graves, Uncle Billy, 114–118
Great Basin, 37, 48, 189, 191
Great Die-Up, The, 282
Great Lakes, 56, 58, 214–215
Great Northern Railroad, 199, *map 200,* 403
Great Salt Lake, 48, 114
Great Slave Lake, *map 34*
Green River rendezvous, 37, *40–41*
Greenville, Treaty of, 30
Gros Ventre Indians, *50–51*
Guillaume, L.M.D., painting by, *90–91*
Gunfighters, *350–355, 378;* Billy the Kid, 377–379; Butch Cassidy's Wild Bunch,

374–*375;* James brothers, 367–374; John Wesley Hardin, 375–377; and notorious lawmen, 379–381; at O.K. Corral, 364–367; soldiers as, *374;* tools of, *372–373;* Wild Bill Hickok, 257–260, 375, *376*

Guns, of cowboys, 304–305, 307. *See also* Pistols; Rifles

H

Haines, J.W., flume designed by, *397*
Half-breeds, 61
Hamilton, Henry (Hair Buyer), 22, 25–28
Hangtown. *See* Placerville (Hangtown), California
Hardin, John Wesley, 375–377
Harriman, Edward, 201
Harris, Richard, 410–411
Harrison, Benjamin, 330
Haslam, Bob (Pony Bob), 166–167
Hayden, Ferdinand Vandiveer, 49
Hearst, George, 150–*151*
Hearst, William Randolph, *151*
Heath, Lillian, *342*
Hebard, Grace, *342*
Hemlock trees (western), 390, *map* 392–393
Hensley, Josephine (Chicago Joe), *347*
Hickok, James Butler (Wild Bill): as marshal and gunfighter, 375, *376;* as scout, 257–260
Higgins, Pattillo, 413–414
Hill, James Jerome (One-eyed Old Sonofabitch), 201
Holladay, Ben, 167–*171,* 173
Holliday, John (Doc), *366;* and Eddie Foy, 344; at O.K. Corral, 364–367
Hollister, S.E., *16–17*
Homestake (gold mine), 151
Hopkins, Mark, 190
Horses: and cowboys, *298–299, 310;* in games, *72–73,* 218, 358; and Plains Indians, 216–218, *218–219;* for Pony Express, *158–159;* for roundups, 315, 316; thieves, *352–353*
Hotelkeepers, 332–334
Houston, Sam, *77;* drinking of, 76, 77–79; in politics, 77–79; as Republic of Texas president, 94–95; in Texas Revolution, 81–84, 89–94, *90–91, 92–93*
Howard, Oliver O., 232
Howden, James, 195
Huddle, William, painting by, *92–93*
Hudson, Henry, 56
Hudson's Bay Company, 105; and control of trade, 56–60; in logging industry, 392; trading posts, 109; *voyageurs, 57*
Humboldt River, 42, 114
Hunkpapa Sioux, 224–226

Huntington, Collis P., 189–191
Hutchinson, Hayward M., 409

I

Ida Stockdale (steamboat), 187
Illustrations of the Manners, Customs, and Condition of the North American Indians (Catlin), 46–47
Independence, Missouri, *map* 106–107, 108
Independence (steamboat), 180
Indiana Girl, The, 136–137
Indians, *205–211;* agents for, 236; in American Revolution, 22–28; buffalo hunting by, 222, *223;* and cattle drives, 318–320; counting coup by, 222, 230; coupsticks of, *230, 238–239;* as cowboys, 302, 305; culture of, 204, 254–255; and expressmen, 156, 166–167; gambling by, 224, 356–358; and miners, 140; and missionaries, 305; and pioneers, 104, *105,* 111, 112; population of, 21, 204, 214, 255; and railroads, 198–199; on reservations, *236;* scalping by, *47,* 222, *235;* and steamboats, 185–188; supernatural aids used by, *226–227, 230, 231;* torture by, 23, *24;* and trade goods, 60–61; and trappers, *40–41, 64,* 65–67; and treaties with U.S. government, 226–228, 232, 235–237, 330; wars, *242–247, 248–271. See also* Plains Indians
Indian Territory, 318, 330; lawlessness in, 380–381
Indian wars, *242–247, 248–271;* Beecher's Island battle, 248–249, *250–251,* 258; Fetterman Massacre, 237, 256; Little Bighorn battle, 237–238, 263–271, *268–269;* Skeleton Cave battle, 261–262, *263;* Washita Massacre, 235, 262–263
Industrial Workers of the World (I.W.W.), 404
Industry: cattle, 274–283, *295;* logging, 392–394, 403–407, *406–407;* mining, 150–151; produce, 415; salmon, 412; sheep, 283–295
Ingerton, Harry, 306
Ingles, John, 18–20
Ingles, Mary, 18–20
Ingles, William, 18–20
Iowa Indians, *map* 215
Irish laborers, on railroads, *194,* 195–198
Iroquois Indians, 21
Isham, James, sketches by, *58–59*
Ivers, Alice (Poker Alice), 359

J

Jackass Mail Route, *map* 164
Jackson, Andrew (Old Hickory): expansionist politics of, 18; and Sam Houston, 76, 77; as soldier and gentleman, 30–*31*
Jackson, Sheldon, 411
James, Frank, *369;* bank robberies, 367–368; train robberies, 368–371; trial of, 374
James, Jesse, *369;* bank robberies, 367–368; death of, 371–374; train robberies, 368–371
Jameson, Green, Alamo fortifications by, *82–83*
Jefferson, Thomas: and Lewis and Clark expedition, 32, 34, 36; and Louisiana Purchase, 8
Jesuit priests, *109,* 110–111
J Lazy J Ranch, 313–317
John J. Roe (steamboat), 187
John Robinson's Great World Exposition, 339
Johnson, Andrew, 262, 408–*409*
Jones, Canada Bill, 358–359
Jones, Thomas ap Catesby, 135
Josephine (steamboat), 188
Judah, Theodore Dehone, 189–190
Julesburg, Colorado, 198, 235
Juneau, Joseph, 410–411

K

Kansas City, Missouri, stockyards, *295*
Kaskaskia, Illinois, 23–25
Kearny, Stephen, 48, 254
Keller, J.P., 394
Kenedy, Mifflin, 274–278, *275*
Kepplinger, P.J., 361–364
Key West (steamboat), 188
Kicking Bear (Sioux mystic), 238–239
King, Clarence, 49
King, Richard, 274–280, *275*
King's Mountain battle, 21
Kingston, New Mexico, newspaper, *334–335*
Kiowa Indians, *207;* children, *220;* and Custer, *202–203;* and Laramie treaty, 226–228; native lands of, 214–215; at peace council of 1840, 212; pride of, 204; raids, 260
Klondike River, 411–412
Knight, John, *24*
Kohrs, Conrad, 280–283
Kountz, William J., 188

L

La Barge, Joseph Marie, 185–187
Labor unions, 404
Lakota Indians, 33, 216
Lamar, Mirabeau, 90–91
Lapwai mission, 109
Laramie, Wyoming, 198, 340, 343
Lathrop, Mary, *342*
Lawlessness: in Alaska, 412; cheating by

gamblers, 359–364; of cowboys, 304–305; in mining towns and boomtowns, 137, 140, 143; vigilantes, 143, 280–282, 338. *See also* Gunfighters; Outlaws
Lawmen, 282; notorious, 378–381
Lawyers, *342–343*
Leadville, Colorado, 148, 345, *382–383*
Lease, Mary, *343*
Leavenworth, Henry, 65
Leavenworth and Pikes Peak Express, *map* 164
Lee, Robert E., 187, 254, 274
Legion of the United States, 28–30
Leonard, Zenas, 42, 44
Leroux, Antoine, 65
Leutze, Emanuel, *Westward the Course of Empire Takes Its Way, 96–97*
Lewis and Clark expedition, 32–36
Lewis, Meriwether, 32–36, *33*, 50
Liberty, Missouri, 367–368
Likens, Sadie, *343*
Lincoln, Abraham, 408; and Frémont, 48; and Pinkerton, 370; as railroad supporter, 190, 191–194
Lincoln County War, 377
Lindneux, Robert, painting by, *250–251*
Lisa, Manuel, *61–64*
Little Bighorn battle, 237–238, 263–271, *map* 266, *diagram* 267, *268–269*
Little Bighorn River, *map* 266, *diagram* 267; Custer at, 264–271; steamboats on, 188
Little Eagle No. 2 (steamboat), 188
Little Egypt, 403
Little Turtle (Miami chief), 26
Loggers, *386–389;* dangers for, 399–402; felling trees by, 394–*395;* and flumes, *397;* inventions for, *384–387*, 397–399, 414; and skidroads, 395–397, *396;* tools of, *400–401;* and women, 402–403
Lone Dog (Dakota Sioux), buffalo robe painted by, *213*
Longbaugh, Harry (Sundance Kid), 370, 374–*375*
Los Angeles, California, *map* 200
Louisiana Purchase, 8, 32, *map 35*, 35
Louisiana Territory, 19, 43
Lowman, Mary, *342*
L S Ranch, 315–316
L U Bar Ranch, 313–317
Lubricants, for saws, *400*
Lucas, Anthony, 413–414
Luella (steamboat), 187
Lumbermen: forest exploitation by, 404–405, *406–407;* and labor unions, 403–404; and loggers' work, 394–402, *395, 396, 398;* and logging industry, 392–394, 403–407; and Western trees, *384–385*, 390–393

M

McCall, Jack, 376
McClellan, George, 254, 370
Mackenzie, Alexander, *34; Voyages from Montreal,* 34
Mackenzie River, *map* 34
McKinley, William, 405
McLaury, Frank, 366–367
McLaury, Tom, 366–367
McLoughlin, John, 392
Mah-to-toh-pa (Plains Indian), *46*
Mail service, *map* 164; costs, 160–161, 165; Pony Express, 155, *158–159*, 166–167, 170; routes, 164; and stage lines, *156–157*, 163–166, 167–173, *168–169;* to miners, 160–*161*
Majors, Alexander, 162–163, 166, 170
Mandan Indians, *186, map* 215; and Lewis and Clark expedition, 33; and Manuel Lisa, 61; religious rituals of, *225;* self-torture of, 46; trade with, *52–53;* value of women to, 65
Manifest Destiny, 44; in churches, 108–111, 119; paintings about, *49, 96–97*
Marquette, Jacques, 182
Marshall, James Wilson, 128, 144
Marsh, Grant, 187–189, *188*
Martha (steamboat), 185–187
Maskelyne, John Nevil, 361–364
Mason, R.B., 128, 135
Masterson, Bat: and Eddie Foy, 344; as lawman, 351, 380
Matchless Silver Mine, 345
Maxwell Cattle Company, Ltd., 295
Medicine Tail Coulee, *diagram* 267, 270
Meek, Joe, *39*
Merchants, *331, 335–338, 337*
Métis, 61
Mexican War, 254–*255;* effect of gold discovery on, 128, 135
Milam, Benjamin, *81*
Miles, Nelson, 234
Miller, Alfred Jacob, paintings by, *40–41, 64*
Miller, Joaquin, 45
Millet Ranch, 311
Mimbres Apache Indians, 232–234
Miners, *122–127, 144–145;* dangers for, 150; lawlessness of, 137, 140, 143; mail for, 160–*161;* methods of mining gold, 134, *138–139. See also* Forty-niners; Sourdoughs
Miniconjou Sioux Indians, 241
Mining: Alaska, 411–412; camps, 136–140; cyanidation in, 151; as industry, 150–151; tools, *126–127, 138–139, 146–147,* 151
Minnesota Massacre, 228–*229*

Minnetaree Indians, 35
Missionaries, pioneers as, 108–111, *109,* 119. *See also* Franciscan friars
Mississippi River, 214–215, 358
Missouri Fur Company, 64
Missouri Indians, *map* 215
Missouri River, 104, 313–316; as railroad terminus, 189, 198; steamboats on, *174–179, 183, 186,* 358; trade on, *50–53;* trapping on, 61–64; as waterway west, 180–189
Mixed-bloods, 61
Mohawk Indians, 21
Mojave Desert, 37
Montana Brand Book, 281
Montana (steamboat), 180
Montana Stockgrowers Association, 313–315
Moran, Thomas, *The Chasm of the Colorado, 8–9*
Mormons, 48, 106–107, *119*
Morris, Esther, *340*
Morris, Nelson, 295
Mountain men, *38–39, 99;* and Indians, *64,* 65–67, 214. *See also* Trappers
Mount Davidson, 147–150
Mount, William, painting by, *129*
Muir, John, 404–*407*

N

Nalin (Apache girl), *209*
Nantaje (Apache scout), 261
Navajo (Navaho) Indians, *206,* 254; decimation of, 257; dry painting of, 226–*227*
Newhouse, Sewell, *The Trapper's Guide,* 62–63
New Orleans battle, 31
New Orleans, Louisiana, *map* 200, 357–358
Nez Percé Indians, 109, *map* 215
Nicollet, Joseph, 44
Nome, Alaska, 411–412
Northern Cheyenne Indians, 187, 265
Northern Pacific Railroad, 199, *map* 200; and lumber industry, 403, 404
Northfield, Minnesota, 371
North West Company, 34, 58–60
Northwest Passage, 34

O

Oglala Sioux Indians, *238–239;* at Little Bighorn battle, 237–238; and pioneers, 104
Oil rush, 413–415
O.K. Corral shoot-out, 364–367, *diagram* 367
Old Dry Diggings. *See* Placerville (Hangtown), California
Old Spanish Trail, *map* 106–107, 161

Old Walton Road, *map* 19
Omaha, Nebraska, 198, 339, 403
Onderdonk, Robert, *Fall of the Alamo*, *86–87*
Oneida Indians, 21
Onondaga Indians, 21
Oregon & California Railroad, 171
Oregon Territory, 45–48
Oregon Trail, *map* 106–107, *map* 164; day on, *112–113;* as East-West link, 161; Frémont's survey of, 45; mail service on, 163–164; pioneers on, 99, 104–108, 108–111
Osage Indians, 235
Oto Indians, 33
Otter Belt (Comanche Indian), *205*
Outlaws: cattle rustlers, 279–282, 317; horse thieves, *352–353;* in Indian Territory, 380–381; stagecoach robbers, 119, 173; women as, 375, 377, 381. *See also* Gunfighters
Oxbow Route, *map* 164

P

Pacific Railroad Act, 190
Pacific Union Express Company, 173
Paiute Indians, 167
Palmer, Joel, 104–108
Panama, Isthmus of, as route to West, 114, 130, 134
Paris, Treaty of, 56–58
Parker, Isaac Charles (Hanging Judge), 380–*381*
Particular Time of Day (Pawnee Indian), *208*
Patent-medicine show, 339–344
Paul Bunyan tall tales, 399
Pawnee Indians, *208, map* 215; as scouts, 260; warrior, *231*
Pawnee, Kansas, ad, *333*
Paxson, Edgar, painting by, *268–269*
Peace River, *map* 34
Pen Knife Sketches (Delano), *161*
Philadelphia (locomotive), *193*
Pierce, Franklin, 254
Pikes Peak, *43*, 144–145
Pike, Zebulon M., *43*
Pilz, George, 410–411
Pinal Apache Indians, 229
Pinchot, Gifford, *405*
Pine trees, *map* 392–393; exploitation of, 404, *406–407;* ponderosa (western yellow), 390, 392; sugar, 385
Pinkerton, Allan (The Eye), *370*
Pinkerton's National Detective Agency, 370, 371, 375, 377
Pioneers, *96–103*, 104–121; cabins of, 118–121, *120–121;* dangers for, *110, 115;* and Indians, 104–*105*, 111, 112; sodbusters, *284–287;* timber sale by,

394; trails taken by, 106–107
Pistols: army issue, *259;* Colt, *259*, 304–305, *372–373;* Smith and Wesson, *346*
Place, Etta, 375
Placerville (Hangtown), California, 134, 140
Plains Indians, 204–241, *map* 215; adolescents, 220–221; birth-to-death passage of, 218–222; buffalo hunting by, 214, 216, 222, *223;* children, 218–*220*, 221; in games, 221–222; men, 221–222; and polygyny, 216; religious rituals of, 222–227, *225*, 238–239; as scouts, 260–262; supernatural aids of, 226–*227, 230, 231;* tipis of, *217;* and treaties with U.S. government, 226–228, 232, 235–237; wars, *231, 242–247,* 248–271; women, 220–222, *229. See also individual Indians and tribes*
Platte River, 191, 198, 216, 321
Poinsett, Joel, 44
Point, Nicolas, *109*
Point Pleasant battle, 21
Polk, James Knox, 48, 128, 254
Pony Express, 155, 166–167; debts, 170; horses of, *158–159*
Pony Express and Central Overland Route, *map* 164, 170
Pope, Andrew, 394
Portland, Oregon, 403, 404
Potlatch Lumber Company, 403
Powder River, 188, *map* 266
Powell, John Wesley, 49
Prentiss, Narcissa (Marcus Whitman's wife), 108–110
Pribilof Islands, 409–*410*
Promontory Summit, Utah, 199, 403
Pueblo Indians, *map* 215
Puget Mill Company, 394
Puget Sound, 390, 394–397
Pullman, George Mortimer, 201
Puyallup Indians, 356

R

Railroads, *152–153, 201;* and cattle industry, 278; engines, *192–193;* foreign laborers on, *194,* 195–198; forest exploitation by, 404; laying track for, 198, 199; and lumber industry, 397–398, 403; and Pony Express trail, 167; as replacement for steamboats, 175, 180; trestle, *196–197. See also individual railroad lines*
Ranchers, *277;* and barbed wire, *292–293*, 310–311; cattle, 274–283, 295; in Mexico, 305; produce, 415; and range wars, 291–295, *294;* and rustlers, 279–282; sheep, 283–295. *See also* Cattle; Cowboys
Rattlesnake Dick, 173

Rattlesnake Mountains, *133*
Redwood trees, 385, *388–389, map* 392–393; coast, 390–392; conservation of, 405; felling tools for, 400; and John Muir, *407;* Sierra, *391*, 392; and Weyerhaeuser Timber Company, 403
Reed, Estelle, *343*
Reed, James, 114, *118*
Reed, Margaret, *118*
Reed, Virginia, 118
Remington, Frederic, 243; paintings by, *158–159, 296–297, 300–301*
Rendezvous, *map* 66, 67; at Green River, 37, *40–41*
Reno, Marcus A., at Little Bighorn battle, 264–271
Reservations, Indian, *236*
Returns-Again (Hunkpapa Sioux), 224–226
Richardson, Albert, 175, 332
Rich Bar (gold mine), 134, 136–137
Rifles: by Meriwether Clark, 32; flintlock, 20; Hawken, 38; muzzleloader, *88–89;* repeating, 223; Spencer, 195, 199, 248, 258; Springfield, *258–259*
Rio Grande River, 254, 274, 279
Rivermen, 180–189; and Indians, 185–188; pilots, 181, 183–187; roustabouts, 184, *185*
Robert Campbell (steamboat), 187
Rockefeller, William, 295
Rocky Mountains, *map* 34, *122–123, map* 142, *map* 392–393; beaver in, 50; Cathedral Rock, *14–15;* exploration of, 45; gold in, 145, 175; Indian tribes at, 214–215; and Lewis and Clark expedition, 33; pine trees in, 393; pioneers in, *102–103*, 110–111; railroads in, *152–153*, 189, 191; travel in, 170; Wind River region, *12–13*
Roelofs, Dick (Miracle Miner), 414
Roman Nose (Cheyenne warrior), 248, 250
Roosevelt, Theodore: in cattle industry, 295; and conservation, 405; and Geronimo, 234; and Pat Garrett, 379; and railroad scandals, 201
Rosebud Creek, 237, 263–265, *map* 266
Rose, Edward, 64–65
Ross, William J., 261–262
Roundups, 313–317, *diagram* 316; sky as clock for, *317*
Russell, Charles: *Death of a Gambler, 354–355;* paintings by, *154–155, 298–299; When Guns Speak, Death Settles Disputes, 350–351; When Horseflesh Comes High, 352–353*
Russell, Majors & Waddell, 162–163, 166, 170
Russell, William Hepburn: and Ben Holladay, 170; in freighting business,

162–163, 166; and monopoly on mail service, 173
Russians, sale of Alaska by, 408–409

S

Sacajawea (Shoshoni princess), *33, 35*
Sacramento, California, 140, 195, 403
Saddles, *308–309, diagram 309*
St. Louis, Missouri: railroad terminus at, 189; steamboats at, *174–175, 183,* 184, 187
Saloonkeepers, *322–323,* 334
Saloons, *322–323,* 330; entertainers in, 339–344, *345;* and loggers, 402–403; women in, 344
Salter, Susanna, *343*
Salt Lake River Valley, 37–42, *map 106–107*
Salt River Canyon, 261–262
Saluda (steamboat), *183–184*
San Antonio and San Diego Mail Route (Jackass Mail), *map 164*
San Antonio's Market Plaza, *70–71*
San Carlos Borromeo mission, *68–69*
Sand Creek massacre, 234
San Francisco, California: as boomtown, 140–143, *141;* demand for lumber by, 394; freight business in, *172–173;* gambling in, 359, 361; and mail service to miners, 160
San Jacinto battle, 89–94, *90–91*
Santa Anna, Antonio López de: at the Alamo, 84–88; surrender of, *92–93,* 94; in Texas Revolution, 79–94
Santa Fe Trail, 43, *map 106–107,* 161, *map 164*
Santa Gertrudis Creek, 274–278, 280
Santee Indians, *228–229*
Sarsis Indians, 216
Saucy Jack (Catawba Indian), 21
Sauk and Fox Indians, *210*
Saws, for loggers, *400–401*
Scalping, *47, 222, 235*
Schoolteachers, 335, *343*
Schreyvogel, Charles: *Custer's Demand, 202–203;* painting by, *242–247*
Scouts, 256–262; Indians as, 260–262
Selman, John, 377
Seneca Indians, 21
Sequoia trees. *See* Redwood trees
Sequoyah (Cherokee chief), 390
Settlers. *See* Pioneers
Seward, William H., 408–409
Shawnee Indians, 18–23
Shawnee Trail, *map 319*
Shay, Ephraim, 397–398
Shay locomotive, 397–398, 402
Sheep: dogs, *288–289;* herders, 283–288, *289–291;* and range wars, 291–295, *294;* shearing, 288–291, *290–291*
Sheridan, Philip, 248, *256;* and Buffalo Bill Cody, 260; and Custer, *202–203,*

262–264, 266; and Indians as fighters, 252–254; subjugation of Indians by, 248, 256
Sherman, William Tecumseh: on Army deserters, 135; and Custer, 263; as lawyer, 335; quoted, 232, 252, 260
Shoshoni Indians, 35, *map 215*
Sierra Madre, 233–234
Sierra Nevada, *map 106–107, map 142;* Donner Party in, *115;* exploration of, 42, 48; freight wagons in, *162–163;* gold in, 130, 141, 145; pioneers in, 111; railroads in, 189, 191, 195–198; redwoods in, 392
Silver, *map 142,* 147
Silver Bow (Gold mine), 411
Silver strikes, Arizona, *map 142,* 365
Silver strikes, Colorado, *map 142,* 346–348
Sioux Indians, 65, *211, map 215,* 260; at Beecher's Island battle, 248–249, *250–251;* encampment of, *218–219;* and Fetterman Massacre, 237, 256; and horses, 216, 218; at Little Bighorn battle, 188–189, 237–238, 264–271; and Minnesota Massacre, *228–229;* on promises of the white man, 236; raids, 112, 185–188, 198; and Sand Creek massacre, 234–235. *See also individual tribes*
Sitka, Alaska, 409, 410
Sitting Bear (Kiowa chief), 212–214
Sitting Bull (Hunkpapa Sioux chief), 216, *228;* death of, 238–241; name of, 224–226; quoted, 235–237, 238, 271; vision of, 265
Skeleton Cave battle, 261–262, *263*
Smith, Deaf, *92–93*
Smith, Jedediah, 37, 64
Smith, Joseph (Mormon), 119
Smith, Julia, *229*
Smoky Hill Trail (Butterfield Overland Despatch), *map 164*
Snake River, 36, 109
Sod houses, *284–287*
Soldiers, *242–247,* 248–272, *map 252–253;* clothing of, *264;* as deserters, *135;* mutilation of, *261;* scouts for, 256–262, *257;* weapons of, *258–259*
Sourdoughs, *411–412*
Southern Pacific Railroad, 199, *map 200*
South Platte River, 346, 348
Spalding, Eliza, 108–109
Spalding, Henry, 108–109
Spence, Pete, 366
Spindletop, oil discovery at, *418-419*
Sports. *See* Games
Spotted Eagle (Sioux Indian), *211*
Springboard, for loggers, *400–401*
Spruce trees, *map 392–393;* Sitka, 385, *386–387,* 390

Stagecoaches, *156–157,* 167–173, *168–169;* for mail delivery, 163–165; routes for, 164; travel by, 165–166, 170–171
Stanford, Leland, *190–191,* 199
Stanton, Charles, 114
Starr, Belle, 381
Steamboats, *174–179;* dangers for, 180–181, *183–184;* gambling on, 358–359, 364; and Indians, 185–189, *186;* kinds of, *182;* pilots on, *181,* 183–187; roustabouts on, 184, *185*
Stevens, John, paintings by, *229*
Stilwell, Frank, 366
Stoeckl, Edouard de, 408–409
Story, Nelson, 281
Strobridge, James Harvey (One Eye Bossy Man), 195
Stuart, Granville, *281–282*
STV Ranch, 315
Sublette, Milton, 64–65
Sublette, William, 64–65, 67
Suffrage for women, *340–341*
Surveyors, 49
Sutter, John, 128, 140, 144
Sutter's Mill, gold discovery at, 128, 144, 392
Swan Brothers Cattle Company, 321
Sweetman, Luke, 313–317

T

Talbot, William, 394
Tall Bull (Cheyenne chief), 260
T-Anchor Ranch, 306
Taylor, Zachary, *254–255*
Terry, Alfred, in offensive attack against Sioux, 263–266
Teton Lakota Indians, 33, 216
Tevis, Lloyd, 173
Texas Land and Cattle Company, 295
Texas Rangers, 279, 377, 379
Texas revolution, 79–94, *90–91;* the Alamo, 78, 81–88, *86–87;* and surrender of Santa Anna, *92–93,* 94
Thompson, Ben, 380
Thompson, William, 281–282
Three Years in California (Colton), 135
Through Hostile Country (Berninghaus), *156–157*
Tipis, *diagram 217*
Titanic (ocean liner), 148
Todd, Alexander, 160–161
Tombstone, Arizona, 364–367
Tongue River, 257, 264
Too Near the Warpath (Boughton), *20*
Topographical Engineers, Corps of, 44
Towns and cities, *324–329;* entertainers of, 339–345; and farmers, 338–339; king of the cattle towns, 337–338; land rush for, 330–332; Queen City of the Plains, 346–348, *348–349;* townspeople in, 332–345. *See also specific towns and cities*

Townsmen, *324–329;* entertainment for, 339–*345;* and growth of cities, 345–349; and land rush, 330–332; types of, *331, 332–338, 334–335, 337;* and women as settlers, *340–343, 347*

Trade: goods, *60–61;* with Indians, *50–51, 52–53,* 60–61; in Southwest, *70–71;* and steamboats, *186*

Trail drives. *See* Cattle

Trails to the West, *map* 106–107

Trappers, 105; dangers for, *50–51, 54–55,* 67; equipment of, *62–63;* and Indians, *40–41, 64,* 65–67; of Manuel Lisa, 61–64; at rendezvous, 37, *40–41,* 66, 67. *See also* Fur trade; *Voyageurs*

Trapper's Guide, The (Newhouse), 62–63

Travis, William Barret, 80, 84–88

Trees. *See individual kinds*

Truckee Lake, 114–118

Tuolumne River, 42, 130

Turkey Leg (Cheyenne chief), 199

Turner, Frederick Jackson, frontier hypothesis of, 6-7

Turtle Creek battle, 21

Tuscarora Indians, 21

Twain, Mark, 168

Two Hatchet (Kiowa Indian), *207*

U

Union Pacific Overland Limited, 374

Union Pacific Railroad, *map* 200, 327, 346; and gold spike, *199,* 403; governmental support for, 189–191; rivalry with Central Pacific, *194,* 195–199; scandals, 191–194, 201

United States Army, 219, *235, map* 252–253; and Cochise, 229–232; and Geronimo, 232–234; in Mexican War, 254–*255;* posts, 226–228, 249–253; and Sand Creek massacre, 234–235; scouts for, 256–262, *257;* sidearm, *372–373;* 6th Infantry (Missouri Legion), 65; small numbers in, 255; and steamboats, 187–189; supplies for, 161; Topographical Engineers, Corps of, 44; Union Army, 190, 191. *See also* Soldiers

United States Cavalry, *156–157,* 330; 5th Regiment (Crook), 260, 261, *263;* 7th Regiment (Custer), 188, 235, 237–238, *240–241,* 260, 262–271. *See also* Soldiers

United States government: and Alaska, 408–*409,* 411, 412; and Army posts, 226–228; and forests, 404, 406; and judges, 380–381; and soldiers' pay, 249; and treaties with Indians, 226–228, 232, 235–237, 330

Ute Indians, *map* 215, 254

Utley, Robert M., 6-7

V

Van Buren, Martin, 44

Vanderbilt, George W., 405

Vanderbilt, William K., 295

Varnum, Charles, 265–266

Vincennes, Indiana, 23–28

Voyages from Montreal (Alexander Mackenzie), 34

Voyageurs, 56–61, *57. See also* Trappers

W

Waddell, William Bradford, 162–163, 166, 170

Wagons, *diagram* 117; features of, *116–117;* first used by pioneers, 108–109; freight, *154–155,* 161–164, *162–163*

Wagon trains, *96–103;* dangers for, *110;* day on Oregon Trail, *112–113;* first used by pioneers, 110–111

Waiilatpu mission, 109–110

Walker, Joseph Reddeford, *37–44,* 48

Walker, T. J., brand of, 314

Wallace, Lew, 378

Walla Walla River, 109–110

Walsh, Thomas Francis, *150*

Walworth, James, 278

War of 1812, 30–31

Warrior's Path, *map* 19

Wasatch Mountains, 37, 114

Washington City and California Mining Association, 132

Washita Massacre, 235, 262–263

Watchful Fox (Sauk and Fox), *210*

Wayne, Anthony (Mad Anthony), 23, *26–27,* 28–30

Weapons: at the Alamo, *82–83;* Bowie knife, *78;* of Indian-fighters, *258–259;* of Plains Indians, 222. *See also* Guns; Pistols; Rifles

Webster, Daniel, 189

Wells, Fargo & Company, 171–173, 416; stagecoach, *168–169;* strongbox, *172*

Wells, Henry, 172–*173*

Western Trail, *map* 319

Westward the Course of Empire Takes Its Way (Leutze), *96–97*

Weyerhaeuser, Frederick, 403–*404*

Weyerhaeuser, Frederick, Jr., 404, 405

Weyerhaeuser Timber Company, The, 403

Wheeler, George Montague, 49

When Guns Speak, Death Settles Disputes (Russell), *350–351*

When Horseflesh Comes High (Russell), *352–353*

White Bear (Kiowa chief), 204

White Cloud (Sioux chief), 223

White Cloud (steamboat), *183*

White Contrary (Plains Indian), 248

White-Geese-Sounding-on-Waters (Poker Jim), 358

Whitman, Marcus, 108–110

Wild Bunch, 370, 374–375

Wilde, Oscar, 344–346

Wilderness Road, *map* 19

Willamette River, 111, 118

Williams, Bill (Old Bill), 65–67

Williamson, Robert M. (Three-Legged Willie), 380

Wimar, Charles, painting by, *10–11*

Wind River, *12–13,* 36, 45

Wobblies (I.W.W.), 404

Womack, Bob (Crazy Bob), 145

Women: and cowboys, 306, 313; as gamblers, 359; in juries, *340;* and loggers, 402–403; in mining towns and boomtowns, 136–137, 143, *148–149;* as missionaries, 108–110; as outlaws, 375, 377, 381; as pioneers, 108–118, 120–121; in saloons, 344; scarcity of, in West, 120–121; as settlers of towns, *340–343, 347;* on steamboats, 185; suffrage, 340–*341*

Women, Indian, *209, 229;* chastity of, 220–221; and death, 222; doeskin painting of, *221;* gambling by, 224; work of, 216, 221–222

Woodhull, Victoria, 345

Woodson, Samuel H., 163–165

Wounded Knee battle, *240–241*

Wright, Robert M., *337–338,* 344

Wymore, George, 368

X

XIT Ranch, 295, 307, 318

Y

Yellowstone National Park, 36

Yellowstone River, 64; and Custer, 263–264; Indians at, 214, 216, 237; roundup on, 313–316; steamboats on, 188

York (George Rogers Clark's servant), 32, *33*

Yosemite National Park, 406

Young, Brigham, 48, 119, 165

Younger, Bob, 371

Younger, Cole, 371, 381

Younger, Jim, 371

Younger, John, 371

Yuba River, 130, 134–136

Yukon River, 411–412

Z

Zane's Trace, *map* 19

PICTURE CREDITS

Congress; 164, Map by Rafael D. Palacios; 166, Courtesy the Huntington Library, San Marino; 167, Courtesy The Oregonian; 168, Gjon Mili, Courtesy Wells, Fargo Bank History Room, San Francisco; 171, Courtesy The Oregonian; 172, Benschneider, Courtesy Wells Fargo Bank History Room; 173, Courtesy Wells, Fargo Bank History Room; 174-175, Courtesy Kansas State Historical Society, Topeka; 176-177, H.G. Klenze, Courtesy Montana Historical Society; 178-179, Courtesy State Historical Society of North Dakota, Bismarck, N.D.; 181, E.E. Henry, from the Collection of David R. Phillips; 182, Drawing by Rafael D. Palacios; 183, Courtesy Missouri Historical Society; 185, *Missouri Deck Hands on the Fontanelle*, William Cary, copied by Oliver Willcox, Courtesy The Thomas Gilcrease Institute of American History and Art, Tulsa, Oklahoma; 186, The Fire Canoe, William Cary; 188, Courtesy Dorothy Blunt Hagen and Dr. James K. Blunt; Courtesy The State Historical Society of North Dakota, Bismarck, N.D.; 190, Courtesy Union Pacific Railroad Museum Collection; 192-193, Courtesy Culver Pictures; Paulus Leeser, Courtesy Collection of URS/Coverdale and Collpitts Inc.; Frank Lerner, Courtesy of URS/Coverdale and Collpitts Inc.; 194, Courtesy Bettmann Archive; 196-197 Courtesy The Seattle Historical Society; 198, Courtesy Southern Pacific Transportation Co.; 199, Courtesy Stanford University Museum of Art, Stanford Collection; 200, Map by Rafael D. Palacios based on maps in *Travelers Official Guide of the Railway and Steam Navigation Lines in the United States and Canada*, June 1893, and the assistance of Barry Combs, Union Pacific Railroad; Timothy L. Johnson, Southern Pacific Transportation Co.; Jack W. Kelly, Santa Fe Railway; and Albert M. Rung and Frank Perrin, Burlington Northern, Inc.; 201, Courtesy Library of Congress; 202-203, *The Life and Art of Charles Schreyvogel, Painter-Historian of the Indian-Fighting Army of the American West* by James D. Horan, original painting in The Thomas Gilcrease Institute of American History and Art, Tulsa; 205, Courtesy History Division, Natural History Museum of Los Angeles County; 206, Edward S. Curtis copied by Frank Lerner, Courtesy Rare Book Division, The New York Public Library, Astor, Lenox and Tilden Foundations; 207, Courtesy Smithsonian Institution National Anthropological Archives; 208, Courtesy Smithsonian Institution National Anthropological Archives; 209, Edward S. Curtis copied by Frank Lerner, Courtesy Rare Book Division, The New York Public Library, Astor, Lenox and Tilden Foundations; 210, Courtesy Smithsonian Institution National Anthropological Archives; 211, L.A. Huffman, Courtesy David R. Phillips; 213, Benschneider, Courtesy South Dakota State Historical Society; 215, Map by Rafael D. Palacios; 217, Drawings by Nicholas Fasciano, adapted from drawing of Arapaho tipi cover in the Vincent Colyer Collection, Smithsonian Institution, and drawings in *The Indian Tipi; Its History, Construction and Use* by Reginald and Gladys Laubin, copyright 1957 by the University of Oklahoma Press; 218-219, Courtesy Library of Congress; 220, Courtesy Smithsonian Institution National Anthropological Archives; 221, Paulus Leeser, Courtesy Oklahoma Historical Society; 223, Frank Lerner, Courtesy National Collection of Fine Arts, Smithsonian Institution; 225, Courtesy Thomas Gilcrease Institute of American History and Art; 227, Courtesy Fifth Annual Report of the Bureau of Ethnology, 1883-1884 Smithsonian Institution; 228, Courtesy Denver Public Library, Western History Department; 229, Herb Orth for LIFE, Courtesy Minnesota Historical Society; 230, Benschneider, Courtesy National Park Services, Department of the Interior; 231, Courtesy National Collection of Fine Arts, Smithsonian Institution; 233, Courtesy Bettmann Archive; 235, Courtesy History Division, Natural History Museum of Los Angeles County; 236, Courtesy of Smithsonian Institution, NAA; 238-239, Edward S. Curtis copied by Richard Henry, Courtesy Rare Book Division, The New York Public Library, Astor, Lenox and Tilden Foundations; 240-241, Courtesy The Huntington Library; 242-243, *On the Skirmish Line*, from *The Life and Art of Charles Schreyvogel: Painter-Historian of the Indian-Fighting Army of the American West* by James D. Horan, original painting in the collection of Mr. and Mrs. Sandford S. Brown; 244-245, *Surprise Attack,* from *The Life and Art of Charles Schreyvogel: Painter-Historian of the Indian-Fighting Army of the American West* by James D. Horan, original painting in The Thomas Gilcrease Institute of American History and Art, Tulsa; 246-247, *Defending the Stockade*, from *The Life and Art of Charles Schreyvogel: Painter-Historian of the Indian-Fighting Army of the American West* by James D. Horan, original painting in the collection of Mr. and Mrs. Bronson Trevor; 249, Paulus Leeser, Courtesy West Point Museum Collections, United States Military Academy; 250-251, *The Battle of Beecher's Island* by Robert Lindneux, copied by Benschneider, Courtesy The State Historical Society of Colorado; 252-253, Map by Rafael D. Palacios; 255, *The Storming of Monterey,* lithograph by Kelloggs & Thayer, copied by Paulus Leeser, Courtesy Connecticut Historical Society; 256, Courtesy The New York Public Library, Astor, Lenox and Tilden Foundations; 257, Benschneider, Courtesy The Buffalo Bill Historical Center, Cody, Wyoming; 258-259, Ken Kay, Courtesy West Point Museum Collections, United States Military Academy; 261, Courtesy United States Army Field Artillery Center and Fort Sill Museum; 263, *Lieutenant Ross's Attack* by Frederic Remington, Courtesy the New York Historical Society; 264, From *Army and Navy Journal*, Washington, D.C., March 5, 1870, p. 458, Courtesy General Research and Humanities Division, The New York Public Library, Astor, Lenox and Tilden Foundations; 266, Map by Rafael D. Palacios; 268-269, *Custer's Last Stand* by Edgar S. Paxson, Courtesy Whitney Gallery of Western Art, Cody, Wyoming; 270, Courtesy National Park Service Department of the Interior; 272-273 Courtesy California Historical Society; 275, Paulus Leeser, Courtesy the King Ranch, Inc.; 276-277, Courtesy David R. Phillips Collection; 279, Paulus Leeser, Courtesy The King Ranch, Inc.; 281, Courtesy Western History Research Center, University of Wyoming; 282, Courtesy Montana Historical Society, Helena; 284-285, Courtesy A.A. Forbes Collection Western History Collection University of Oklahoma Library; 286-287, Courtesy Solomon D. Butcher Collection,

Nebraska State Historical Society; 289, Courtesy Moorhouse Collection, University of Oregon Library; 290-291, Courtesy Oregon Historical Society; 292-293, Jim Olive, Courtesy The Museum of Texas Tech University-Ranching Heritage Center; 293, Courtesy Northern Illinois University Archives; Charles Phillips, Courtesy Ellwood House Museum; 294, Courtesy Denver Public Library, Western History Department; 295, Brown Brothers; 296-297, *The Longhorn Cattle Sign,* Frederic Remington, Courtesy Amon Carter Museum, Fort Worth, Texas; 298-299, *Wild Horse Hunters,* Charles M. Russell; 300-301, *Stampeded by Lightning,* Frederic Remington, Courtesy Thomas Gilcrease Institute, Tulsa, Oklahoma; 303, Courtesy Montana Historical Society, Helena; 304, Dean Austin, Charros at the Roundup, James Walker, Courtesy Carl Dentzel Collection; 307, W.G. Walker, Courtesy Western History Research Center, University of Wyoming; 308, Benschneider, Courtesy Colorado State Museum; 309, Robert Royal, Courtesy Royal Armour Museum, Madrid, photograph authorized by the Patrimonio National; 310, L.A. Huffman, Courtesy Coffrin's Old West Gallery, Miles City, Montana; 312, Charles J. Belden, Courtesy Whitney Gallery of Western Art, Cody, Wyoming; 314, Courtesy Montana Historical Society, Helena; 316, Drawings by Nicholas Fasciano; 317, Drawing by Walter Johnson; 319, Map by Nicholas Fasciano; 321, Trail Herd to Montana, W.H.D. Koerner, Courtesy Whitney Gallery of Arts, Cody, Wyoming; 322-323, Courtesy Collection of Fred and Jo Mazzulla, Denver, Colorado; 324-325, Courtesy Kansas Historical Society, Topeka; 326-327, Courtesy The Oakland Museum, Andrew J. Russell Collection; 328-329, Courtesy Barker Texas History Center; 331, Courtesy Western History Collections, University of Oklahoma Library; 333, Courtesy Kansas State Historical Society; 334-335, Courtesy Museum of New Mexico; 336, Henry Groskinsky, Courtesy Boot Hill Museum, Inc.; 337, Courtesy Kansas State Historical Society; 338, Henry Groskinsky, Courtesy Boot Hill Museum, Inc.; 340, Courtesy Denver Public Library Western History Department; Henry Beville, Courtesy Library of Congress; 341, Courtesy Wyoming State Archives and Historical Department; 342, Courtesy Wyoming State Archives and Historical Department, Western History Research Center, University of Wyoming; Denver Public Library, Western History Department; Kansas State Historical Society; 343, Courtesy Kansas State Historical Society; Wyoming State Archives and Historical Department; Denver Public Library; Western History Department, Kansas State Historical Society; 345, Courtesy Burton Devere Collection; 347, Courtesy Montana Historical Society; 348-349, Courtesy Denver Public Library, Western History Department; 350-351, Copied by Oliver Willcox, Courtesy Thomas Gilcrease Institute of American History, Tulsa; 352-353, Copied by Linda Lorenz, Courtesy Amon Carter Museum, Fort Worth, Texas; 354-355, Copied by Benschneider Courtesy J. Laurence Sheerin; 357, John Zimmerman, Harrah's Automobile Collection, Reno, Nevada; 358, Benschneider, Courtesy Tombstone Courthouse State Historic Park, Arizona State Parks; Benschneider, Courtesy Arizona Historical Society (2); 360, John Zimmerman Collection of Frank Roza Jr.; 361, John Zimmerman, Collection of Robert C. Pollock, John Zimmerman, Collection of William R. Williamson; 362, John Zimmerman, Collection of William R. Williamson; John Zimmerman, Collection of Ronald Brooks; 363, John Zimmerman, Collection of Willima R. Williamson (2); Tom Tracy, Collection of Greg Martin; 364, Ken Kay, Courtesy H. Mason Collection; 365, Courtesy Arizona Historical Society, Tucson; 366, Courtesy Library of Congress; 367, Drawing by Nicholas Fasciano; 369, Courtesy Denver Public Library, Western History Department; 370, Courtesy Pinkerton's Inc., New York; 372, Ken Kay, Courtesy Private Collection, except bottom, Charles Phillips, Courtesy The Wallace Beinfeld Collection, Studio City, California; 373, Ken Kay, Courtesy Private Collection; 374, Courtesy Charles W. Carter Collection, Archives Historical Department, The Church of Latter-day Saints, Salt Lake City, Utah; 375, Courtesy Pinkerton's Inc.; 376, Copied by Oliver Willcox, Courtesy Thomas Gilcrease Institute of American History and Art, Tulsa; 378, Roscoe G. Willson Collection, Courtesy American Heritage Publishing Co., Inc., New York; 379, Courtesy Western American Collection, Beinecke Library, Yale University, New Haven, Connecticut; 381, Courtesy Signal Corps, No.1110B/3202, Brady Collection in National Archives; 382-383, Courtesy Library State Historical Society of Colorado; 384-385, Carleton E. Watkins, Courtesy The Bancroft Library; 386-387, Benjamin Gifford, Courtesy University of Oregon Library; 388-389, A.W. Ericson, Courtesy Humboldt State University Library; 391, A.W. Ericson, Courtesy Humboldt State University Library; 392-393, Map by Rafael D. Palacios; 395, Courtesy Hank Johnston Collection; 396, Courtesy Collection of Robert J. Lee; 397, Drawing by Don Bolognese; 398, Courtesy University of Oregon Library; 400, Floyd Lee, Courtesy Seattle Historical Society; 400-401, John Zimmerman, Courtesy Fort Humboldt State Historic Park California, Department of Parks and Recreation, Eureka, Calif.; 402, Mike Dunn, Courtesy Georgia-Pacific Historical Museum Portland, Oregon; 404, Courtesy Weyerhaeuser Company Historical Archives; 405, Courtesy Library of Congress; 406-407, H.C. Tibbits from the TIME-LIFE Picture Agency; 407, Hugh J. Gib; 409, From *Frank Leslie's Illustrated Newspaper,* April 20, 1867, Courtesy Library of Congress; 410, Barry McWayne, Courtesy University of Alaska Museum; 412-413, E.A. Hegg, Courtesy Photography Collection Suzallo Library, University of Washington; 415, Courtesy Library of Congress; 416-417, Courtesy Colorado Historical Society; 418-419, Courtesy Fred A. Schell and American Petroleum Institute Historical Photographs; 420-421, Courtesy Buffalo Bill Historical Center.

Acknowledgments. The editors wish to thank the following:

Graphor Consultation; Maurice Gagnon; Robert Galarneau; Greg Labute; McGill University, McLennan Library; Jennifer Meltzer; Shirley Sylvain; Jocelyn Wakefield.